Constructing Identity in Contemporary Spain

Constructing Identity in Contemporary Spain

Theoretical Debates and Cultural Practice

EDITED BY

JO LABANYI

OXFORD
UNIVERSITY PRESS

OXFORD
UNIVERSITY PRESS

Great Clarendon Street, Oxford OX2 6DP

Oxford University Press is a department of the University of Oxford.
It furthers the University's objective of excellence in research, scholarship,
and education by publishing worldwide in

Oxford New York

Auckland Bangkok Buenos Aires Cape Town Chennai
Dar es Salaam Delhi Hong Kong Istanbul Karachi Kolkata
Kuala Lumpur Madrid Melbourne Mexico City Mumbai Nairobi
São Paulo Shanghai Singapore Taipei Tokyo Toronto
and an associated company in Berlin

Oxford is a registered trade mark of Oxford University Press
in the UK and in certain other countries

Published in the United States
By Oxford University Press Inc., New York

British Library Cataloguing in Publication Data
Data available

Library of Congress Cataloging in Publication Data
Data available

ISBN 0-19-815993-5
ISBN 0-19-815994-3 (Pbk.)

1 3 5 7 9 10 8 6 4 2

Typeset in 10/12pt Sabon by Graphicraft Limited, Hong Kong
Printed in Great Britain
on acid-free paper by
Biddles Ltd, Guildford and King's Lynn

Acknowledgements

The editor wishes to thank the following for their permission to reproduce the material listed below: El Imán, SA (still from *Río abajo* reproduced as Fig. 4); Museo Municipal, Madrid (Madrid fiesta posters reproduced as Figs. 5, 6, 7); El Deseo, SA (still from *Pepi, Luci, Bom y otras chicas del montón* reproduced as Fig. 8); Antonio Sánchez (photographs of Barcelona reproduced as Figs. 11, 12, 13). My thanks also to Jon Wilson of the Photographic Unit, Birkbeck College, for photographing the details from Carmen de Burgos's novellas in the editor's collection, reproduced as Figs. 1, 2, 3. The essays included in this volume by Cristina Mateo and Josep-Anton Fernàndez, and an earlier version of that by Jo Labanyi, appeared previously in the *Journal of the Institute of Romance Studies*, 6 (1998), whose permission to reprint is gratefully acknowledged. The essay by Paul Julian Smith previously appeared in the *Journal of Spanish Cultural Studies*, 1.2 (2000); we thank Taylor & Francis Ltd. for granting permission to reprint.

Contents

List of Illustrations

Notes on Contributors

MARK ALLINSON is Senior Lecturer in Hispanic Studies, Royal Holloway London. He works on modern and contemporary Spanish literature and culture, with a particular interest in subcultures. He has published articles on Spanish theatre and cinema, and is author of *A Spanish Labyrinth: The Films of Pedro Almodóvar* (I. B. Tauris and St Martin's Press, 2001).

LOU CHARNON-DEUTSCH is Professor of Hispanic Languages and Literature at the State University of New York at Stony Brook. Her books include *The Spanish Short Story: Textual Strategies of a Genre in Evolution* (Támesis, 1985), *Gender and Representation: Women in Nineteenth-Century Spanish Fiction* (John Benjamins, 1990), *Narratives of Desire: Nineteenth-Century Spanish Fiction by Women* (Pennsylvania State University Press, 1994), and *Fictions of the Feminine in the Nineteenth-Century Spanish Press* (Pennsylvania State University Press, 2000). Her edited volumes include *Estudios sobre escritoras hispánicas en honor de Georgina Sabat-Rivers* (Castalia, 1992), and (with Jo Labanyi) *Culture and Gender in Nineteenth-Century Spain* (Oxford University Press, 1995). She has served as President of Feministas Unidas, and is a member of the Editorial Advisory Board of the *Journal of Spanish Cultural Studies*.

PETER WILLIAM EVANS is Professor of Hispanic Studies at Queen Mary London. He is the author of *The Films of Luis Buñuel: Subjectivity and Desire* (Oxford University Press, 1995) and *Women on the Verge of a Nervous Breakdown* (British Film Institute, 1996), and the editor of *Spanish Cinema: The Auteurist Tradition* (Oxford University Press, 1999). He has also published various books on Hollywood cinema. He is a member of the Editorial Advisory Board of the *Journal of Spanish Cultural Studies*.

JOSEP-ANTON FERNÀNDEZ is Lecturer in Catalan at Queen Mary London. His research interests include issues of gender, sexuality, and national identity in modern Catalan fiction, poetry, film, and television, and he is currently writing a book on questions of legitimization and identity in contemporary Catalan culture. He has published articles on Josep Carner, Mercè Rodoreda, Quim Monzó, and Terenci Moix, and the books *Another Country: Sexuality and National Identity in Catalan Gay Fiction* (Modern Humanities Research Association, 2000) and *El gai saber: una introducció als estudis gais i lèsbics* (Llibres de l'Index, 2000).

JOSEBA GABILONDO is Associate Professor at the Basque Studies Program, University of Nevada, Reno. His first degree in Basque philology at the University of the Basque Country was followed by a Ph.D. in comparative literature at the University of California-San Diego. He has published various articles on Basque culture, and his forthcoming book *Archaeology of Global Desire: New Hollywood, Spectacle Hegemony, and the Commodification of Otherness* will be published by Duke University Press. He is currently working on a second book *After Spain: Postnationalism and Subject Formation in Basque and Spanish Cultures*.

JESSAMY HARVEY is currently completing a Ph.D. at Birkbeck London on 'The Feminizing Process: Constructing Girlhood in "La Nueva España" '. Her published and forthcoming articles focus on the construction of girlhood in twentieth-century Spain. She contributed a number of entries to the *Encyclopedia of Contemporary Spanish Culture*, ed. Eamonn Rodgers (Routledge, 1999).

JO LABANYI is Professor of Spanish and Cultural Studies at the University of Southampton and Director of the Institute of Romance Studies, School of Advanced Study, University of London. Her edited volumes include (with Lou Charnon-Deutsch) *Culture and Gender in Nineteenth-Century Spain* (Oxford University Press, 1995), and (with Helen Graham) *Spanish Cultural Studies* (Oxford University Press, 1995). Her most recent book is *Gender and Modernization in the Spanish Realist Novel* (Oxford University Press, 2000). She is currently preparing a book on early Francoist cinema, and is the co-ordinator of a five-year research project *An Oral History of Cinema-Going in 1940s and 1950s Spain*, funded by the Arts and Humanities Research Board, with colleagues in Spain and the United States. She is founding editor of the *Journal of Spanish Cultural Studies*, co-editor of the *Journal of the Institute of Romance Studies* (from 2001 *Journal of Romance Studies*), and general editor of the book series *Re-Mapping Cultural History* (Berghahn Books).

ANJA LOUIS recently completed a Ph.D. thesis in the interdisciplinary area of law and literature at Birkbeck London, focusing on the Spanish writer Carmen de Burgos in the light of feminist legal theory. She has published an article on Carmen de Burgos and the question of divorce. Her research interests include melodrama and the visual arts.

CRISTINA MATEO recently completed her Ph.D. in sociology at Goldsmiths London, on the ethnic identity of second-generation Spanish migrants in London.

PARVATI NAIR is Lecturer in Spanish at Queen Mary London, and recently completed a doctorate on community identities in contemporary Spain at Birkbeck London. She organizes the seminar series in 'Ethnicity and Migration' at the Institute of Romance Studies, School of Advanced Study, University of London. Her published and forthcoming articles focus largely on issues of ethnicity and migration in a range of cultural texts, in particular photography and music; she is currently preparing a book on cultural aspects of ethnicity and migration in Spain.

DEBORAH PARSONS is Lecturer in English at the University of Birmingham, and teaches on the literature of the late nineteenth and twentieth centuries. She has interests in European modernism and contemporary culture, early film, and connections between literature and the visual arts. Her research focuses on modernism, space, and the city; and she is the author of *Women, Cities, and Modernity: Streetwalking the Metropolis* (Oxford University Press, 2000). She is currently working on a study of the urban fairground and carnival as a landscape of modernity, and on a book on Madrid in the 1920s.

CHRIS PERRIAM is Professor of Hispanic Studies at the University of Newcastle, where he is a member of the Centre for Gender and Women's Studies. His main research interests are in contemporary Spanish cinema and literature in the contexts of cultural and gay/queer studies. His publications include *The Late Poetry of Pablo Neruda* (Dolphin Book Company, 1989) and *Desire and Dissent: An Introduction to Luis Antonio Villena* (Berg, 1995). He is currently writing on issues of masculinity and its representation in Spanish cinema of the 1990s; and has co-authored *A New History of Spanish Writing from 1939 to the 1990s* (Oxford University Press, 2000). He is a member of the Editorial Advisory Board of the *Journal of Spanish Cultural Studies*.

XON DE ROS is Lecturer in Modern Spanish Studies at King's College London. She has published articles on film and literature in a number of collective volumes and journals, and is a member of the Editorial Advisory Board of the *Journal of Spanish Cultural Studies*.

ANTONIO SÁNCHEZ is Lecturer in Spanish at Birkbeck London, and has recently completed a Ph.D. on postmodernist culture in contemporary Spain, which is being revised for book publication. His research and teaching interests focus on cultural theory and contemporary Spanish fiction, film, urban studies, and photography. He has published articles on contemporary Spanish fiction, film, and culture, and is currently researching a book on twentieth-century Spanish photography in relation to modernization, migration, memory, and cultural identities.

ISABEL SANTAOLALLA is Reader in Spanish at Roehampton University of Surrey, London. She has published on postcolonial literature, cultural studies, and film, with emphasis on the representation of ethnicity and gender in anglophone and Hispanic cultures. Her most recent publication is the edited volume 'New' Exoticisms: Changing Patterns in the Construction of Otherness (Rodopi, 2000).

PAUL JULIAN SMITH is Professor and Head of Department of Spanish and Portuguese in the University of Cambridge. He has written ten books and co-edited three on Spanish and Latin American literature, cinema, and culture. His most recent books are The Theatre of García Lorca: Text, Performance, Culture (Cambridge University Press, 1998) and The Moderns: Time, Space, and Subjectivity in Contemporary Spanish Culture (Oxford University Press, 2000). He is an editor of the Journal of Spanish Cultural Studies.

XELÍS DE TORO is a novelist and cultural practitioner, and has taught at the Universities of Birmingham and Oxford as Xunta de Galicia Leitor in Galician. His publications include the multi-media work Terminal (1994); the novels Seis cordas e un corazón (1989), Non hai misericordia (1990, Premio de Narrativa Cidade de Lugo), and Os saltimbanquis no paraíso (1999); and children's literature.

Introduction:
Engaging with Ghosts; or,
Theorizing Culture in Modern Spain

JO LABANYI

IT is often said that, with the exception of its Galician 'Celtic fringe', Spain has no tradition of ghost stories. Such a view depends, of course, on what one means by 'ghosts'. I should like here to draw on Derrida's historical-materialist reading of ghosts in *Specters of Marx* (1994) in order to argue that the whole of modern Spanish culture— its study and its practice—can be read as one big ghost story. By 'modern' I mean here the period corresponding to bourgeois modernity and its corollary, the modern nation-state, whose ideological beginnings, in Spain as elsewhere, date back to the mid-eighteenth century but which, in the case of Spain, becomes firmly implanted as a hegemonic model—not always realized in practice—from the mid-nineteenth century. The complex relationship of Francoist Spain to modernity and of post-dictatorship Spain to postmodernity (in many respects an intensification of modernity rather than a break with it—except in the important respect of postmodernity's evaluation of mass culture) are issues that will be discussed later in this Introduction and in several of the essays in this book. In claiming that the whole of modern Spanish culture can be read as one big ghost story, I mean two things. First, that critical writing on modern Spanish culture, by largely limiting itself to the study of 'high culture' (even when the texts studied are non-canonical), has systematically made invisible—ghostly—whole areas of culture which are seen as non-legitimate objects of study because they are consumed by subaltern groups. As Derrida notes, ghosts are the traces of those who were not allowed to leave a trace; that is, the victims of history and in particular subaltern groups, whose stories—those of the losers—are excluded from the dominant narratives of the victors: particularly under capitalist modernity with its competitive, market-led equation of value with success. It is not for nothing that the official discourses of the modern nation-state—in their imposition of a uniform model of bourgeois culture and consequent categorization of popular and mass culture as 'uncultured'—have dismissed ghost stories as popular superstition, nor that they remain endemic in the popular imaginary, including that of Spain if one defines ghosts in Derrida's terms. I have subtitled this introductory essay 'theorizing culture in modern Spain' since the process of rendering ghostly those areas of culture consumed by 'history's losers' is a process specific to the construction of the modern nation-state. As I hope to show, there are two fundamental ways in which modernity has rendered popular and mass culture ghostly: by marginalizing it and, in a more complex strategy akin to the psychoanalytic mechanism of disavowal (simultaneous affirmation/denial), by cannibalizing it. It can in some respects be argued that postmodernism, as the cultural expression of postmodernity, is characterized by the recognition—in the spectral form of the simulacrum—of modernity's ghosts: a point I shall develop later in this essay.

It is crucial here to take account of Bourdieu's perception, in his classic analysis of the ways in which 'taste' constructs class distinctions (1986), that cultural objects are classified as 'high' or 'low' not on account of their intrinsic qualities or even the status or intentions of their producers, but according to who consumes them and their modes of consumption. That is, 'high culture' is that which is appreciated in a detached, disinterested manner for its 'purely' aesthetic (formal) qualities, while 'low culture' is that which is enjoyed for its functional qualities (hence the attention to meaning rather than form) in a participatory festive manner seen as 'vulgar' by the 'refined'. (I leave aside here the often forgotten issue of the 'middlebrow', on which Bourdieu is so acute, which negotiates an upwardly or downwardly mobile course through its awkward relation to both extremes; given the huge social changes that have taken place in twentieth-century Spain, there is important work to be done on the ways in which upwardly and downwardly mobile groups have charted their social realignment through their modes of cultural consumption.) Thus in Spain certain areas of popular culture—rarely mass culture, with the exception in certain periods of cinema—have been included in the canon because they have been taken up by intellectuals who have consumed them in a non-popular (that is: detached, aesthetic) manner: for example, the *romance* (ballad) and flamenco, both of which have been converted into a kind of spurious 'popular sublime' privileging their tragic variants and sidelining their much more frequent festive, if not carnivalesque, aspects. One may note that, in the case of flamenco at least, this has involved a parallel masculinization of the medium, supporting Huyssen's perception (1988) that popular and mass culture are often feared as a contamination of the feminine. The case of flamenco is particularly indicative since—as Mitchell (1994) has shown—it has been aestheticized ('redeemed') by being posited as the product of mythical 'primitive' origins, eliding the more vulgar reality of its late nineteenth-century development as part of an urban drinking subculture linked with prostitution and its early twentieth-century assimilation, in various hybrid forms, into the mass-cultural, largely bawdy music-hall repertoire.

Histories of modern Spanish culture, and the individual critical studies that support them, tend to construct a seamless narrative which tells the story of the evolution of high-cultural tastes, given an appearance of continuity through the emphasis on influences. But this is a kind of trick continuity editing, like that used in classic Hollywood cinema, which edits out the much more messy heterogeneity and discontinuity of cultural processes, such as the cultural historian Walter Benjamin—self-designated ragpicker rummaging among ruins—delights in excavating through his investigations of a miscellany of cultural products and practices that give the 'structure of feeling' (Raymond Williams's later term) of the culture of a specific period (Benjamin 1983; Frisby 1988: 187–265). Here 'culture' is understood in its broad anthropological sense of an all-embracing symbolic system constituted by the life practices of a given society. While anthropology—as witnessed by several of the contributions to this volume—has been hugely influential on contemporary cultural studies, there is also here a need to beware the temptations of simplifying the messy heterogeneity of lived cultural experience. Bourdieu, who came to the sociology of culture from a grounding in anthropological research, is sceptical about the possibility of the most sympathetic anthropological 'participant observer' avoiding the ethnocentric imposition onto 'other people's culture' of tidy classification schemes which say more about the observer's methodology than about the cultural practice of the observed (Bourdieu 1997). For

Bourdieu, the only (partial) solution is to subject one's objectifying methodology to a similar objectifying critique. 'Non-legitimate' forms of culture can be rendered 'ghostly' not just by being ignored, but also by being represented through ideological schemes that are those of 'legitimate' culture, the supreme legitimizing body being, of course, the academy. The consolidation of the modern nation-state —which for the first time in history introduces the idea that the nation is based on 'one race, one language, one culture' (that of the bourgeoisie) rather than being a heterogeneous mix (Hobsbawm 1990)—took place in Spain in the mid- to late nineteenth century when there was a concerted attempt, through the writing of histories of 'national literature' and (under the Restoration) the promotion of the realist novel 'mapping' the entirety of the nation, to develop the concept of a 'Spanish national culture' (Labanyi 2000a). In practice this is the culture of Castilian as the language of the state administration. Thus Spanish America is included for imperialistic reasons, while Catalan, Galician, and Basque are not, except in the subordinate category of 'dialects' (Basque remains beyond the pale since it obviously could not be fitted in under this label); some late nineteenth-century histories of 'Spanish literature' even include Portuguese as a subset of the 'national'. The institutional organization of the study of culture on national lines—constituting the separate disciplines of 'English literature', 'French literature', 'Spanish literature'—by definition limits the study of culture to that of 'high culture' (loosely referred to as 'literature') because the whole notion of a 'national culture' goes hand in hand with the relegation to oblivion of popular and mass culture.

Indeed, Gramsci (1991: 342–85) noted the remarkable cosmopolitanism of popular literature, observing that, if Italian popular audiences preferred foreign authors, this implied that those authors enshrined in the national canon did not 'speak' to the bulk of the national populace. The same was true in Spain from the start of the commercialization of print in the mid-nineteenth century until the 1980s, when Spanish authors for the first time started to top bestseller charts (Montero in Graham and Labanyi 1995: 317). It was precisely to counter the increasing flood of imported mass-produced commercial literature that the late nineteenth-century canon of 'Spanish literature' was constructed, as the same national bourgeoisies that identified with capitalist modernization found themselves culturally threatened by the globalizing effects of the capitalist market economy (for it can be, and has been, argued that globalization goes back to the beginnings of modernity, predicated on empire). In particular, the capitalist subordination of culture to the laws of the market, via the newly developing culture industries, took the control of taste—and hence over the policing of the class system—away from the bourgeois cultural elite which, in order to maintain its guardianship of 'national culture', was forced to identify this as elite minority culture. The notion that 'national culture' is constituted by 'great works' also necessarily limits the study of culture to that of individual artists, rather than seeing culture as an overall network of life practices. By concentrating on individual artists and ignoring modes of consumption, it is also possible to present this selective view of 'national culture' as 'objective' since the processes whereby taste is constructed are elided.

Paradoxically, the development of the concept of 'national culture', beginning in the Romantic period, is also accompanied by the mythification of folk culture as an expression of the national 'soul'. For this mythification of the popular represents its selective co-option by intellectuals for 'high' culture, parallelling the nation-formation process which aimed to incorporate the lower orders (previously left to their own devices provided they paid taxes and provided conscripts for the army) into 'the nation', replacing cultural heterogeneity with uniformity. The early twentieth-century avant-garde intellectuals who rebelled against the bourgeoisie by co-opting (cannibalizing) elements of popular and mass culture—a process that was particularly marked in the case of the Spanish avant-garde—can in practice be seen as consolidating this process of the 'nationalization' of culture through the incorporation into bourgeois culture, through their subjection to high-cultural modes of consumption of non-bourgeois cultural forms.

Or perhaps it would be possible to make an alternative reading of the Romantic and avant-garde co-option of popular culture—and, in the latter case, of mass-cultural forms such as cinema and the fairground—by recognizing the presence of these subaltern cultural forms as ghostly presences which destabilize the bourgeois cultural project. This would depart from conventional readings because it would not see this destabilization as the result of anti-bourgeois rebellion on the part of Romantic or avant-garde artists, for, although most of them—on the political right as well as the political left—certainly had such anti-bourgeois intentions, their aesthetic mode of consumption of popular or mass culture was irremediably bourgeois. Rather, this destabilization would be seen as stemming from the ghostly traces within Romantic and avant-garde high-cultural products of popular or mass-cultural forms, demanding reparation for their appropriation by forcing the bourgeois consumer to recognize—fleetingly, as with all ghostly apparitions—the alien cultural habits which insist on adhering to them, despite the aestheticization process. Derrida's reading of ghosts is a historical-materialist one because he insists that they are not a psychological projection but that they are 'really there', summoning us with their look (1994: 7). Indeed, he argues that, just as there is a mode of production of the commodity, so there is a 'mode of production of the phantom' (1994: 97), for ghosts are the return of the repressed of history—that is, the mark of an all-too-real historical trauma which has been erased from conscious memory but which makes its presence felt through its ghostly traces.

It is in this second, and perhaps more important, sense that I propose that modern Spanish culture can be read as a ghost story. A key difference, frequently commented on, between Anglo-Saxon cultures (which generally have been the winners in modernity) and Latin cultures (which generally have been modernity's losers) is that the latter tend to choose as their national heroes and heroines not those who triumphed but those who lost spectacularly because of their refusal to compromise: that is, using the modern language of the market, those who refused to 'sell out' to history's (foreign, capitalist) winners. This glorification of heroic losers can be read not just as a 'making a virtue of necessity' in the absence of a gallery of victors, but, more positively, as a strategy for ensuring the ghostly return in the future of history's victims; that is, ensuring that those who were not allowed to leave a trace on the historical stage do leave their trace in the cultural arena. I have myself in the past (Labanyi 1989) criticized the writers of 1898 and later writers such as Américo Castro, Camilo José Cela, and Juan Goytisolo for constructing a mythical view of history as 'what might have been'. I would now want to reread this repeated manœuvre as a strategy for rehabilitating the ghosts of history: that is, recreating in spectral form that which the history of modernity has consigned to oblivion. For histories of the nation and of national literatures—and here again we must remember that the writing of national history is a specifically modern project—are written by the winners of history, for whom the losers are at best an embarrassment, at worst (as under early Francoism) the enemy. While history has, of course, always been written (and rewritten) by the winners, modernity has specifically meant the implantation—even in countries where Catholicism has remained dominant—of a Protestant-based work ethic whereby success is equated with moral strength and failure with moral weakness: an ethic whose psychological and material consequences for those social groups and countries which have been modernity's losers has been immense.

In this sense Francoism, which historians are now starting to rethink not as a rejection of modernity but rather as a form of conservative modernity (Richards 1998), subscribed just as much as its liberal and socialist antagonists to the modern capitalist ethos of progress—that is, put crudely, a view of history based on the notion that those who triumph are by definition the best. Indeed, the defeat of democratic forces by fascism in the Spanish Civil War can be seen as a major contributing factor to the late twentieth-century Western loss of belief in the political master narratives of liberalism and socialism, for how could their defeat by fascism in Spain be reconciled with a view of history as progress? The relation of Francoism to popular and mass culture is a complex one. Francoist cultural repression relegated those suspected of opposition to the ghostly status of 'the disappeared'—consigned to physical or cultural death—but its repression of popular and mass culture was selective. Indeed, while the regime's anti-intellectualism had devastating effects on high-cultural production, it exalted certain resemanticized versions of popular and mass culture—notably, folklore, cinema, and sport. The result, by way of reaction, was the emergence of an intellectual opposition for whom popular and mass culture were irremediably ideologically tainted, and who therefore set about the task of ideological subversion by high-cultural means, through the creation of a neorealist art cinema, an intellectualized 'social-realist' novel, and above all 'social poetry'—the inevitable result being failure to reach the masses. No doubt the Francoist co-option of popular and mass culture is a major factor in the continued lack of critical attention paid by Spanish scholars to anything other than high-cultural forms—though the recycling of Francoist kitsch (that is, of Francoism's popular and mass-cultural products) by postmodern film directors such as Almodóvar and by gay cultural critics such as Terenci Moix has started to lay the basis for a reassessment of Spain's popular and mass-cultural past. Nonetheless it remains noticeable that the postmodern pastiche of mass (but no longer popular) cultural forms found in much Spanish fiction and film since the 1970s draws largely on American rather than indigenous models.

I have elsewhere (Labanyi 2000b) attempted a spectral reading of Spanish literature and film of the transition and post-transition period, suggesting that what passes for postmodern pastiche and play can in many cases be read as the return of the past in spectral form —what Derrida (1994: 11) calls the 'virtual space of spectrality'. It seems significant that the shadowy figures of history's losers and *desaparecidos* which insist on returning in so much Spanish fiction and film of the transition and since—for example, the novels of Marsé, Muñoz Molina, Llamazares; the films of Erice, Patino, even Saura—do so via reference to a variety of popular or mass-cultural forms: cinema, the thriller, family photographs. For the return to demand reparation of the victims of modern Spanish history is also a demand for recognition of the popular and mass-cultural forms whose modes of consumption constitute the lifestyle of the 'ghosts of history'; that is, modernity's losers. Given that, as noted before, the mass public has often preferred foreign cultural products—especially in the case of cinema and popular fiction, and now television (though Smith's essay in this volume challenges this received idea)—even the pastiche of Hollywood and of the English-language thriller genre can be seen as an act of reparation to Spanish popular tastes that have been despised. It is noticeable that the postmodern pastiche of popular and mass-cultural forms goes together with a vogue for historical pastiche: the spectral embodiment of those forms of cultural experience designated 'illegitimate' by modern bourgeois culture is thus allied to the 'virtual resurrection' of the past. This is indeed a postmodern 'end to history' in the sense of an end to the seamless, homogeneous histories of national culture which, since the inception of the modern nation-state, have edited out those cultural practices which did not conform to bourgeois high-cultural taste.

The global neo-liberal order which has now triumphed in Spain can be seen as having contrary effects. On the one hand it threatens to impose an ethos of the market in which only the winners count. If Spain's accelerated modernization, especially intense in the 1970s and early 1980s, and its successful integration into the 'New Europe' have transformed it from one of modernity's losers into one of postmodernity's winners, then there is a risk that the 'ghosts of history' will remain relegated to the margins and, indeed, that new ghosts will be created. Many would argue that the former was the case with the refusal of the 1992 quincentennial celebrations to confront the ethical implications of Spain's colonial past, and that the latter is the case with the current reluctance to admit the existence of rascist practices in the media and in society. But, on the other hand, the new postnational order means the definitive end of monolithic versions of national culture, dominated by the bourgeois canon of 'good taste'. We can no longer talk of 'Spanish culture' but must use formulations such as 'the cultures of Spain' or, perhaps better since it replaces national proprietorship with geographical coexistence, 'culture(s) in Spain'—hence this book is not titled *Constructing Spanish Identity* but *Constructing Identity in Twentieth-Century Spain*. This effectively means that bourgeois culture no longer holds a monopoly: the end of the nation-state based on 'one race, one language, one culture' means a plural society not only because different ethnicities and languages are recognized as legitimate on an equal basis with Castilian (in theory), but also because modes of cultural consumption other than those governing bourgeois taste are also given official recognition, and often financial support. Here it is important not to lose sight of the fact that postmodern cultural hybridity is not, as neo-liberal market theory often claims, a giant shopping mall offering freedom of choice to all, but is governed by the increasingly multinational culture industries who have broadened and diversified modes of cultural consumption precisely in order to construct audiences as 'popular' and thus inferior. If Spain's access to—or rather, domination by—the multinational media makes Spaniards fully integrated citizens of the neo-liberal world order, this means that, while they are no longer constructed as second-class citizens with regard to northern Europe and the United States, they have entered a world order in which almost everyone is, through the mass media, constructed as 'second class'.

   If Spain has been seen as, and has seen itself as, one of modernity's losers, this is not only because it did not fully fit the capitalist model of modernization based on urbanization and industrialization: in practice, as Shubert (1990) and others have argued, this did not prevent it from assimilating the ideology of capitalist modernization. It is also because, when measured against bourgeois norms of taste, Spain's cultural production has often seemed wanting—in quantitative, if not qualitative, terms. Indeed, few Spanish writers of the modern period have achieved international recognition—not even

Galdós; Lorca is an exception because his status as a victim of history marks him out as 'typically Spanish'. Those modern artists or filmmakers who did achieve international recognition (Picasso, Gris, Dalí, Buñuel) had to move abroad or (in Dalí's case) be adopted by a foreign artistic movement (surrealism). It is only with the move to postmodernity, with its celebration of the global and of popular and mass culture, that at least a few Spanish cultural practitioners—Almodóvar, Pérez-Reverte, Joaquín Cortés—have made their international mark in terms of popular as well as critical acclaim. However, if we look at Spanish culture of the modern period through non-bourgeois lenses—that is, paying attention to non-bourgeois cultural forms—we get a very different picture.

The fact that the wealth of Spanish popular cultural practices has attracted the attention of foreign tourists, from the time of Mérimée through to today's package-tourist industry, has made Spaniards sensitive to the patronizing implications of such celebrations of 'the traditional'. Indeed, this foreign exoticization of Spanish popular culture has tended to make Spaniards internalize the equation of popular culture with the pre-modern and archaic, with the result that intellectuals keen to stress Spain's modernity have ignored or dismissed it, forgetting that popular culture is something that evolves and continues through modernity—and postmodernity—in new hybrid cross-overs with mass-cultural forms. The more Spaniards have felt that they are seen as cultural inferiors, the more they have stressed the importance of high culture (Ortega y Gasset's 1926 essay *La deshumanización del arte* is a classic example), or else have tried to dignify popular and occasionally mass-cultural forms with high-art status. This has led not only to an undervaluing of the inventiveness of popular and mass culture, but to a blindness to the creative possibilities of cultural hybridization, seen as threatening both high and popular culture with contamination by a supposedly degraded (that is, commercial) mass culture. In fact, Spanish culture presents an especially rich panorama of hybrid cultural practices, given the large-scale human traffic between rural and urban areas throughout the modern period and still today: it has been noted that Spain's particularly brilliant early twentieth-century avant-garde was the product of precisely such a traffic. Additionally, in an interesting case of cultural hybridization, the rapidity of change in the last three decades has taken many Spaniards from predominantly oral cultural habits to a postmodern secondary orality based on the audio-visual media, bypassing the whole high-cultural edifice on which modernity is erected. Of course much popular culture, being based on live 'performance', is not recorded for the scholar's benefit (and the recording process itself changes the product). But mass culture is by definition mechanically reproduced and, while much is lost (for example, in the area of early Spanish silent film), even minimal exploration shows that there is a wealth of material in libraries and archives whose study reveals a much more complex and dynamic view of Spanish culture than does that of high culture alone.

For popular and mass culture by definition cannot be studied as individual texts: first, because they are so obviously part of a commercial culture industry that requires sociological analysis of modes of production and distribution, and of habits of audience consumption; second, because their consumption is normally communal rather than individual; and third, because in a majority of cases they do not exist as texts (though video recording does now enable audiences to reproduce live events and media output, allowing them to be replayed much as one rereads a text).

Another obstacle to the study of popular and mass culture in Spain is the largely Marxist inheritance of the anti-Francoist opposition, whose members played a major role in shaping cultural policy and habits, as well as in revitalizing the university system, after the end of the dictatorship, particularly under the Socialist government of 1982–95 when many of them held political positions. The British school of cultural studies, originating in the 1950s with the work of Raymond Williams and Richard Hoggart, and most influentially with the Birmingham Centre for Contemporary Cultural Studies first under Hoggart and later Stuart Hall, was a response to the more orthodox Marxist suspicion of mass culture (and relegation of popular culture to the archaic) evidenced by the Frankfurt School theorists Adorno and Horkheimer (but not Benjamin), who saw the culture industry as an ideological apparatus (not necessarily owned by the state but manipulated by it) for the indoctrination of the masses under late capitalism. Williams and the Birmingham Centre turned instead to the heterodox Marxist cultural theorist Gramsci, whose view of culture as an interactive process whereby audiences can co-opt the cultural products they consume for their own purposes allowed a more complex reading of popular or mass culture (the two terms tending to be collapsed in English, unlike Spanish), which allowed it to be viewed as having—at least in part—a positive political function. Many would say that this tendency went too far, producing a kind of left-wing populism that all too readily supposed that popular or mass culture is, by definition, subversive; indeed, the tendency in English to use the term 'popular culture' for what, strictly speaking, is mass culture is a sign of this idealizing tendency. Nevertheless, Spanish studies of popular and mass culture—the latter in particular are now increasing significantly—have until recently tended to equate the former with the marginal if not the archaic, stressing its 'difference' and underestimating the effects of hybridization (as, for example, in San Román's recent book on gypsy culture, *La diferencia inquietante* (1997), though she does stress the cultural agency of her gypsy subjects and show them operating in a contemporary urban environment); or to study the latter in terms of data relating to profits and corporate ownership—that is, as one more area of the late capitalist economy, without considering modes of consumption or subjecting its contents to cultural analysis (there are signs that this is now changing, particularly in analysis of popular music; see, for example, Méndez-Rubio 2001). The essays in this volume are intended to go beyond traditional anthropological concepts of cultural Otherness, and beyond the traditional Marxist view of culture as the superstructural by-product of an all-determining economic infrastructure. In this way it is hoped to comply with Derrida's ethical imperative of giving ghosts (in this case, the subaltern cultural forms that have been edited out of modernity's cultural narrative) 'a hospitable memory [. . .] out of a concern for justice' (1994: 175).

In particular, this volume aims to represent culture as a 'recycling' process in which nothing is lost but returns in new hybridized forms, adapting to changed circumstances. This recycling process responds to a view of history as discontinuous but at the same time marked by doublings-up and superimpositions: in short, a view of history that is dynamic but which—unlike that constructed by the master narratives of progress—is moving in many directions simultaneously. The methodologies of cultural analysis used in the various essays are themselves witness to a process of intellectual 'recycling' or hybridization, which we hope will give readers a sense of possibilities for cultural analysis that they may themselves want to take further. For, given that culture is by definition a process of hybridization, the study of culture has to be interdisciplinary. The volume bears the subtitle *Theoretical Debates and Cultural Practice* because its aim is both to explore a range of areas of twentieth-century Spanish culture that fall outside the canon of individual 'great works', and—most importantly—to introduce readers to a range of cultural debates across disciplines. In keeping with the stress on history's discontinuities, the selection of essays does not claim to offer a panoramic view of twentieth-century Spanish culture; they stand as examples of different approaches to different cultural issues. The various sections group the essays thematically in order to highlight a variety of ways in which culture can be used for the purposes of identity formation. Each section is introduced by a brief introduction highlighting and contextualizing key debates. It will be obvious that there is considerable overlap between the sections, and that many articles could have been included in more than one section: this overlap should be taken as an indication of the complexity of cultural processes which play multiple functions and cannot be separated into tidy categories. In particular, it was decided not to have a separate section for peripheral nationalisms, so as to avoid marginalizing these as the 'Other' to a supposedly 'mainstream' Spanishness. As should be evident, questions of non-state national identities (Catalan, Galician, Basque) cross all sections of the volume. As should also be clear, all identities —Catalan, Galician, Basque, *madrileño*, gypsy, immigrant, emigrant, female, gay—are inextricably entwined with each other; with 'unmarked' identities—male, white, bourgeois, Spanish—whose unmarked nature makes them so elusive despite their normative nature; and with notions of the European, the American, and the global. This does not mean that everything is interchangeable with everything else in a postmodern pick-and-mix, but rather that modernity is the period when the capitalist exchange economy brought everything into relationship with everything else, a phenomenon that postmodernity has merely taken further.

WORKS CITED

Benjamin, W. (1983). *Charles Baudelaire: A Lyric Poet in the Era of High Capitalism*. London: Verso.
Bourdieu, P. (1986) [1979]. *Distinction: A Social Critique of the Judgement of Taste*. London: Routledge.
—— (1997) [1980]. *The Logic of Practice*. Stanford, Calif.: Stanford University Press.
Derrida, J. (1994). *Specters of Marx: The State of the Debt, the Work of Mourning, and the New International*. New York: Routledge.

Foster, H. (1996). *The Return of the Real: The Avant-Garde at the End of the Century*. Cambridge, Mass.: MIT Press.

Frisby, D. (1988). *Fragments of Modernity: Theories of Modernity in the Work of Simmel, Kracauer and Benjamin*. Cambridge: Polity Press.

Graham, H., and Labanyi, J. (eds.) (1995). *Spanish Cultural Studies: An Introduction*. Oxford: Oxford University Press.

Gramsci, A. (1991). *Selections from Cultural Writings*, ed. D. Forgacs and G. Nowell-Smith. Cambridge, Mass.: Harvard University Press.

Hobsbawm, E. J. (1990). *Nations and Nationalism since 1780: Programme, Myth, Reality*. Cambridge: Cambridge University Press.

Huyssen, A. (1988). *After the Great Divide: Modernism, Mass Culture, Postmodernism*. Basingstoke: Macmillan.

Labanyi, J. (1989). *Myth and History in the Contemporary Spanish Novel*. Cambridge: Cambridge University Press.

—— (2000a). *Gender and Modernization in the Spanish Realist Novel*. Oxford: Oxford University Press.

—— (2000b). 'History and Hauntology; or, What Does One Do with the Ghosts of the Past? Reflections on Spanish Film and Fiction of the Post-Franco Period', in Joan Ramon Resina (ed.), *Disremembering the Dictatorship: The Politics of Memory since the Spanish Transition to Democracy*. Amsterdam: Rodopi, 65–82.

Méndez-Rubio, A. (2001). 'Popular Music as Cultural Criticism', *Journal of Spanish Cultural Studies*, 2: 119–26.

Mitchell, T. (1994). *Flamenco Deep Song*. New Haven: Yale University Press.

Richards, M. (1998). *A Time of Silence: Civil War and the Culture of Repression in Franco's Spain 1936–1945*. Cambridge: Cambridge University Press.

San Román, T. de (1997). *La diferencia inquietante: viejas y nuevas estrategias culturales de los gitanos*. Madrid: Siglo XXI.

Shubert, A. (1990). *A Social History of Spain*. London: Unwin Hyman.

Part I

Ethnicity and Migration

Editor's Introduction

THE four essays included in this section trace the complex cultural processes by which 'old' and 'new' ethnicities have been, and are, constructed in Spain as well as in Spanish diasporic communities abroad—this last, an important topic which is often overlooked. (An obvious subject still largely awaiting cultural analysis—though briefly touched on in de Toro's essay in Part IV of this volume—is that of the Spanish—particularly Galician—diasporic communities in Latin America; Leo Spitzer's autobiographical study of the role of cultural memory in the life practices of the Austrian Jewish exile community in Bolivia (1998) provides a suggestive model for such work.) In all of these essays, the question is raised of who stands to benefit from such cultural representations of ethnicity, and how such benefit is inextricably mixed with a libidinal investment: pleasure and consumption are thus crucial factors. While the essays by Charnon-Deutsch (on the construction in the modern period of the 'imaginary gypsy') and by Santaolalla (on contemporary representations in Spain of negatively marked ethnic 'Others') stress the libidinal investments of those who have been responsible for such representations of ethnicity, and of those who have consumed or do consume them, the essays by Nair and Mateo concentrate rather on the ways in which cultural stereotypes can be appropriated and used to their own advantage by the subaltern group concerned (gypsy convicts in Córdoba, second-generation Spanish migrants in London). These last two essays also base themselves on ethnographic fieldwork in a specific location, whereas the first two offer an overview: diachronic in the essay by Charnon-Deutsch, synchronic in that by Santaolalla. What emerges in all these essays is that ethnicity cannot be studied in terms of a neat binary opposition between 'self' and 'Other', for various reasons. First, because the construction of the dominant national order—'naturalized' by the supposition that it is ethnically unmarked; that is, 'the norm'—depends for its existence on the categorization of subaltern groups as 'Other'. As a supposedly visible and biological marker of difference, 'race' fits this purpose particularly well; hence the 'trouble' caused by those whose physical appearance or temperament does not fit their supposed ethnicity, as illustrated by the perennial fascination with the gypsy baby-snatching myth discussed by Charnon-Deutsch, in which a child is brought up by the 'wrong' ethnic group. Second, because such ethnic constructions are based on complex patterns of identification crossing the ethnic boundaries which at the same time they are responsible for creating—indeed, it is in such 'border crossing' that the libidinal investment lies. And third, because constructions of ethnicity are the result of complex, ongoing negotiation processes between dominant and subaltern groups, which cannot eliminate the uneven power relations that by definition are the context for constructions of ethnicity, but which require the subaltern to be an active partner in the process, whether through collusion or contestation (or both at the same time). Thus Charnon-Deutsch, while dealing mainly with those responsible for constructing the 'imaginary gypsy', notes that gypsies have from the start been extremely successful in manipulating for commercial purposes the cultural stereotype of 'gypsyness' projected onto them by others: a classic case of the inextricable merging of collusion and contestation.

The essays in this section also stress the role of institutionalized discourses—from those of the nineteenth-century nation-formation process to those of the penal system and the contemporary media and advertising—and the complex cultural alignments produced by their co-option of subaltern cultural forms and representations. A related major issue here is the importance—increasing progressively through the passage from capitalist modernity to late capitalist postmodernity—of commercialization which turns ethnicity into a marketable product; this commodification sometimes produces financial gain for those who are the objects of representation, but most often it benefits those who find gratification through the consumption of—and thus identification with—the exotic. The ambivalence of this relationship to ethnically marked 'Others' is discussed by Santaolalla who suggests that, despite the strong and often unacknowledged racism in contemporary Spain (as in the violent race riots against Moroccan migrant workers in El Ejido, Almería, in February 2000), Spaniards derive a certain gratification from the fact that the new phenomenon of large-scale immigration (mostly from North Africa) constructs their country as a desirable, economically advanced nation.

All four essays also stress the notion of identity as performance: not in the sense that it is 'staged' (though it may be, especially when financial gain—or, in the case of the gypsies in Córdoba prison, remission of their sentences—is likely to be the result), but in the sense that it is always strategic, or, in the case of the subaltern, tactical: I refer here to de Certeau's distinction (1988: pp. xix, 34–9) between 'strategy' as goal-oriented behaviour by those operating from within an institutionally sanctioned zone of power, and 'tactics' as an 'art of the weak' who are forced to improvise since they operate from without the power system. Hence identity is something that is 'managed' and 'patrolled' (Mateo's terms), and always 'identity for someone': that is, aimed at an audience (which, as Mateo shows, constantly mutates in the course of the 'performance of everyday life'). Indeed, the visibility of markers of ethnic difference requires ethnicity to manifest itself through techniques of exhibition and spectacle, both of which are fundamental to the everyday life of urban modernity and to the postmodern media. Mateo's essay—the one most explicitly concerned with how subaltern groups 'fashion' their identity—shows the importance here of cultural memory, which may take the form of unconscious habits transmitted through repetition, in creating a sense of a legitimized past, as well as that of fashion in permitting multiple allegiances to second-generation migrants who are moving between a range of possible identifications. Mateo's essay also—importantly—points to the importance of irony in allowing subaltern groups a degree of mastery over the repertoire of cultural stereotypes within which they operate.

These four essays also show the need for scholars coming out of a background in (literary or cinematic) textual analysis—the case with the majority of contributors to this volume—to have a knowledge of other disciplines when analysing life practices and the cultural representations that underscore them. Charnon-Deutsch thus draws on cultural anthropology, making particular use of Bourdieu's notion of 'symbolic [or cultural] capital': a concept that is also central to the essays by Nair and Mateo. Nair draws on the revisionist anthropology of Clifford, and on de Certeau's notion (1988: 117) of space as 'a practiced place' which largely coincides with the ethnographic notion—elaborated by Bourdieu and Clifford—of 'the field' as a space that is 'discursively mapped and corporeally practised' (de Certeau glossed by Clifford 1997: 53–4). These ethnographic concepts are supplemented by the insights into colonial ambivalence of Bhabha's postcolonial (and poststructuralist) cultural criticism, which shows 'race' to be a discursive formation that furthers power relations precisely through ambivalence, in such a way that concepts of 'difference' by definition depend on their negation. Postcolonial theory also provides the main framework for Santaolalla's essay, in particular Bhabha's work on the ambivalent fetishization of the ethnically marked body. As she notes, the lack of attention by most Spanish scholars to the insights of postcolonial theory suggests a desire to disown the cultural legacy of Spain's colonial past; or, alternatively, the lack in contemporary Spain of any 'market value' for Spain's imperial past. This postcolonial framework is, in her essay, put together with theoretical work on the globalization of the media, showing how the specificity of contemporary Spain's repertoire of ethnic representations intersects with global phenomena such as the fashion for Latino culture; here her essay picks up points that will be developed in Smith's study of TV drama in Part IV. Mateo's essay merges ethnographic fieldwork, informed to a large extent by Bourdieu's notion of cultural capital and de Certeau's notion of the 'tactics of the everyday', with sociological work on the processes of identity formation in social groups, together with cultural studies research into youth subcultures—this last will be picked up in Allinson's essay in Part III of this volume.

All of these essays show that identity is a discursive formation that relies on the creation and manipulation of stereotypes, and that, while stereotypes are a necessary simplification of a complex reality, the manner of their functioning is never simple—an issue that is central to this volume. Indeed, the particularly evident stereotyping to which Spain has been subject under modernity, when it became the 'Other' for those nations wishing to construct themseves as 'modern', allows the study of modern Spanish culture to make a particularly important contribution to cultural theory on identity formation—provided one does not forget to include in this study the stereotypes of other ethnicities (internal and external) that Spain has created for domestic consumption.

WORKS CITED

Certeau, M. de (1988). *The Practice of Everyday Life*. Berkeley and Los Angeles: University of California Press.
Clifford, J. (1997). *Routes*. Cambridge, Mass.: Harvard University Press.
Spitzer, L. (1998). *Hotel Bolivia: The Culture of Memory in a Refuge from Nazism*. New York: Hill & Wang.

Travels of the Imaginary Spanish Gypsy

LOU CHARNON-DEUTSCH

THE portrayal of the Spanish gypsy provides a useful grounding for the study of discursive formations implicated in the evolution of European nationalisms. Spanish culture has had a dual relation with the master narrative of orientalism, both as a culture that has repressed a constitutive element of its historical identity, projecting it onto the figure of the exoticized gypsy (Colmeiro 1998), and one that has represented, from the 1700s onward, an exoticized Other to its northern European counterparts. To understand fully the role that the internal colonization of the Spanish Romany played in the construction of Spanish nationalism, cultural critics need to analyse the economic and productive forces that impinge on the discursive practices that participated in the construction of that identity. My objective is to refocus the field of gypsy studies by recognizing the interdeterminacy of fields of representation—visual, literary, historical, and anthropological—that, seen together, expose the constructedness of the imaginary Spanish gypsy. In order to see this symbolic interface in its proper light, as a form of cultural capital with determined exchange values, I will begin by briefly surveying the historical contexts for the definitions of constituent ethnicities and the collapse of gypsy identities into Andalusian identity, which by the twentieth century came to stand for Spanishness both outside and, to an extent, inside Spain's cultural arena.

As Edward Said has argued, colonialism and imperialism are facilitated by emphasizing difference and stratification. In the case of the Romany, who in early chronicles are described not as conquered peoples but as invaders, we can still speak of an internal colonization that parallels (inter)cultural colonization in specific ways. Nation-building and nationalism have a direct impact on the way ethnic groups are constructed simultaneously as diseased members of a body that should be, if not amputated, at least quarantined, and as exotic assets to some imaginary pluralist society. When nationalism is on the rise, issues of difference generally gain prominence and ethnic myths proliferate; the disenfranchised of a nation are measured against the progress and patriotism of dominant groups and usually found wanting. The Otherness of the disenfranchised group is often then maximized (as was the case in seventeenth-century Spain), or in some instances sanitized and provisionally subsumed into the national identity when there is an economic incentive to do so for reasons of exchange of cultural capital.[1]

COMING TO TERMS

Where we find this Otherness first manifested is in the discursive practices of emerging capitalist states where gypsies were always imagined in permanent exile from some 'other' place beyond national borders. In order to trace the evolution of the concept of gypsyness from earliest times, it is valuable first to distinguish three discursive categories which, causally related and often coexistent, have achieved great symbolic prominence in Europe. The first, 'gypsies' with a lower-case 'g', is what Benedict Anderson would call an unbound seriality, by which he means a broad or 'open-to-the-world' group originating in print culture. Anyone exhibiting nomadic or rebellious tendencies can be classified as a gypsy; gypsies can be from anywhere and nowhere; there are gypsy scholars, bohemian artists, and gypsy 'kings' all with no ethnic affinity with the Romany. The imaginary Bohemia that these 'gypsies' inhabit, as Evlyn Gould points out,

[1] The term cultural capital derives from Pierre Bourdieu's work where it implies that cultural or symbolic goods are exchanged according to patterns of class. Here I use the term in a more global sense to mean that cultural goods are exchanged among hierarchized nations (hence my term cultural colonization) as well as among dominant and marginal groups within a nation. Thus the exchange, production, and distribution of a symbolic product like the passionate Carmen or flamenco music are tied both to a nation's cultural credentials as well as to its exclusionary practices that materially affect Romany populations. For example, the cultural status of Spain among its neighbours was enhanced once northern Europeans began to idealize the gypsy and to equate Andalusian with gypsy identity. It was in Spain's interest to capitalize on this ethnic association by buying into the romanticization of the gypsy, but this romanticization and gypsification of the Andalusian clashed with the enlightenment goal of the ethnic assimilation of Gypsies. How the exchange value of this cultural good determined the conditions of the Romany has yet to be understood.

persists: 'Bohemia continues to be conceived still today as the social performance that both dramatizes ambivalence about cultural identity and legitimates ambivalent cultural response' (1996: 32). In other words, it is still desirable to identify with the freedom-loving, restless vagabond as gypsies are so often imagined.

The second category, designated here as 'Gypsies' with an upper-case 'G', is a racialized designation that nevertheless is heavily indebted to the previous category. Already in the seventeenth century Spain's political advisers or *arbitristas*, such as Sancho de Moncada and Padre Huélamo, were concerned with questions of blood and legitimacy, and debating whether Gypsies were a race or a self-selected confederation of thieves, tinkers, musicians, and fortune-tellers. Moncada is ambiguous about Gypsy racial status: on the one hand he classifies Gypsies as ruffians who band together as thieves and ought to be exterminated. On the other, he sprinkles his text with citations from the Bible implying that Gypsies descended from Egyptians who were cast out of Egypt to atone for their sins. With the discovery of the Sanskrit origin of Romany in 1777, it was no longer fashionable to speak of Gypsies as Egyptians and to refer to their dialect as a rogue's tongue or *jerigonza*, and historians and philologists rallied to construct a more modern (non-biblical, scientifically based) myth of origin that still holds among many scholars: Gypsies are descendants of Pariah classes who left northern India sometime between the fifth and tenth centuries. Their diaspora continues today because of strict endogamous practices and taboos against interrelations with *payos* (non-Gypsies). Coupled with centuries of negative stereotyping, the imagined 'purity' of the Gypsy race encouraged societies to isolate and often stigmatize their Roma communities, reinforcing negative conclusions regarding their religious practices and ability to be good citizens. Gypsies as a racialized category came into clearest focus in the nineteenth century with the rise of physical anthropology, which distinguished groups according to the 'hard' aspects of ethnicity such as skin pigmentation and cranium size. In his 'objective' classification of degenerate types in *L'uomo delinquente* (1876), Cesare Lombroso relied on such racialized categorizations, claiming that criminality was a consequence of atavistic biological stigmata and that certain races, like Gypsies, were more predisposed to crime than others. Spanish social anthropologist Rafael Salillas, in *El delincuente español: el lenguaje* (1896: 208–9), concurred: 'Los gitanos, por su natural y por su modo de vivir, son más afines á la

sociedad delincuente que á la sociedad común' [Gypsies by nature
and occupation are more akin to the delinquent than the normal
element of society].[2] The nefarious consequences of this racial-
ization occurred during the Second World War when uncounted
numbers of Romany perished, many exterminated in the Nazi death
camps.[3]

The third category are most commonly referred to in English as
Roma, Romani/y, or Travellers. Subsets of this category are the
subjects modern anthropologists and sociologists endeavour to study
independently of the fictions and stereotypes that have accrued to
the other two categories. Today's social scientists reject received
stereotypes and avoid references to ancient cultures, blood-lines,
racial purity, and other pseudo-scientific designations, and examine
instead the actual conditions and relations of specific ethnic groups
such as the Romanichals, Kalderash, or Calés. For cultural anthropologists, ethnic identities are more usefully thought of as instru-
mentalist rather than primordial since race has been shown to be a
very inadequate marker of ethnicity. Although Romany groups
inhabit every European country, they have not been studied until
recently by social anthropologists because, 'too close to home for
comfort' (Okely 1983: 56), they were not considered a separate
culture. But in recent decades dozens of anthropological studies
have begun to appear, such as Isabel Fonseca's controversial *Bury
Me Standing* (1995) or, in Spain, Teresa de San Román's *Gitanos
de Madrid y Barcelona* (1984) and *La diferencia inquietante* (1997;
Catalan original 1994). Anthropologists may argue certain univer-
sals, for instance that the Romany are an ethnic identity bound by
an often strict, self-imposed exclusivity and centuries of repression,
persecution, and ghettoization, but they also recognize that each
Roma group has a geography of limited expanse, a national identity,
and a history bound up with the histories of European nation-
states that too often diminish or overlook altogether their participation. Racialized thinking and nuances of the gypsy stereotype
creep into the work of modern anthropologists and ethnologists,
nonetheless.

Recent controversies concerning the unexamined theoretical under-
pinnings of ethnology highlight the need to broaden interdisciplinary

---

[2] All translations into English are mine.
[3] For an overview of the Nazi persecution and genocide, see Hancock (1992).

approaches to the study of ethnicity.[4] The interdependency of the three categories described above is so complex and resilient that it would be a mistake to study any one of them in isolation from the other two. The cultural critic, poised at the intersection of cultural anthropology and cultural criticism, can perhaps best gauge the co-determinancy of nationalism and symbolic practices. It is in the lateral shifts in European consciousness back and forth from one to the other that we start to see the political stakes at work in all three: how the unbound category of the gypsy, a romantic fantasy based in and disseminated by the world of print culture, music, and graphic representation, inflects the more bounded categories of Roma that are the subject of modern anthropology and history; how the passionate, freedom-loving gypsy gets superimposed onto the diasporic Gypsy communities mistakenly imagined as culturally and racially isolated from the Gorgios (*payos* in Spain); and how the latter impact on the subclassifications used by cultural anthropologists who measure Romany participation in urban and industrial economies and their complex cultural and social interrelation with the Gorgios.

BORDER CROSSINGS

Although above I referred to it as a romantic construct, the Spanish gypsy is not in any simple way the creation of the French Romantics. The evolution of this icon evolved from the travel of print, visual, and musical culture back and forth across the Pyrenees, beginning even before Cervantes's *La gitanilla* (1613). It fed off of historical documents as remote as Sebastian Munster's *Cosmographia* (1544) or Heinrich Grellmann's *Die Ziegeuner* (1783), and as local as the acrimonious treatises of the *arbitristas* like Moncada and Huélamo who struggled to define the Gypsy 'problem' for a nation seeking scape-

---

[4] These debates within anthropology centre primarily on the ambivalent status of ethnography and its latent positivism, the location of ethnic and cultural identity, and the questionable objectivity and role of ethnologists and ethnographers in interpreting culture. For a discussion of the debates regarding the relevance and methodology of ethnographic research, see Hammersley (1992) and Clifford and Marcus (1986). For a summary of issues relating to the conceptualization of ethnicity, see Banks (1996) and especially Jones (1997).

goats. Both categories, gypsies and Gypsies, are fused in the fabulous accounts of the nineteenth-century Bible salesman George Borrow, who borrowed heavily from Spanish Golden Age sources as well as living informants and philologists to create a veritable encyclopedia of known gypsiology. In turn, Borrow bequeathed many, if not all, of the loathsome or fabulous stereotypes that quickly got grafted onto Preciosa's romantic progeny: Azucena, Carmen, Mignon, Fedalma, Moréna, and Esmeralda all owe something to the picaresque imagination of 'Don Jorge', as Borrow is referred to in Spain. Spanish philologists and folklorists also perpetuated Borrow's concept of the fictitious gypsy even when their stated intention was to correct his vision with that of their 'truer' Gypsy based on more historically accurate texts and scientific observation. The anonymous J.M.'s *Historia de los gitanos* (1832), the first modern history of Spanish Romany, would not have been possible without the fertile exchange between Spanish and other European cultures.

As part of this exchange, ancient myths were recycled, imported, and exported to and from Spain with amazing tenacity. The baby-snatching myth is exemplary: first appearing in Italian Luigi Giancarli's comedy *La zingana* in 1545, it was incorporated into Lope de Rueda's 1567 *Comedia llamada Medora*, and from there recycled in Cervantes's *La gitanilla* (1613) and its many adaptations in Holland, France, and England. It reappeared in Spain in García Gutiérrez's *El trovador* in 1836, possibly borrowed from Victor Hugo's *Notre Dame* (1831) which, in turn, may have been inspired by Antonio de Solís y Rivadeneira's *La gitanilla de Madrid* (1681, written and/or produced in the 1630s), an adaptation of Cervantes's novella. Through García Gutiérrez's *El trovador*, it was then exported to Italy to serve Verdi for his version in *Il trovatore*. The horror of the stolen baby raised by the 'wrong' ethnic group (but unfailingly exhibiting traces of the 'right' identity) seems never to lose its appeal for European bourgeois cultures. Long after revisionist writings debunked the historical accuracy of the myth, foundlings, adoptions, and baby theft continued to be popular plot devices, sometimes reversing the ethnicity of the stolen child. George Eliot's Fedalma (*The Spanish Gypsy*, 1853) was raised by a Spanish nobleman, and George Sand's Moréna (*La Filleule*, 1869) by an aristocratic French family, but the message of the incommensurability of races carries through these reversals. With such an enduring fictional presence, it is logical that even today travellers, ethnographers, and historians should feel the need to validate or refute the myth.[5]

Once railways and modern shipping lanes made travel less onerous, Spain became one of the key places to visit and report on the nature, customs, and dialects of the Gypsies, possibly because the origin of Spanish Gypsies was regarded as even more racially obscure than that of 'oriental' (Eastern European) Gypsies, and because their habitats, in Cadiz, Granada, and Seville, were more easily accessible. In a Europe obsessed with race, national origins, and bohemian nonconformity, Spain was a powerful magnet. The Romantic traveller was in flight from a world in which mercantilism and a regulated, domesticated, bourgeois existence were thought to be crushing the Romantic spirit. What he pursued were 'los contrastes culturales, lo agreste, lo insólito, la diversidad de paisajes, el mestizaje, el medievalismo, el orientalismo' [cultural contrasts, the agrarian, the unusual, more varied landscapes, *mestizaje*, medievalism, orientalism] (González Troyano 1987: 15). For Europe's idle classes this meant varying the 'grand tour' itinerary to venture into Hungary in pursuit of Pushkin's *Tzigany*, or southern Spain whose roads and inns made travelling difficult but whose ruins, antiquities, and racial diversity appealed to the Romantic imagination. Andalusia seemed to fulfil every Romantic's notion of an exotic locale. At roughly the same time that the Orient was 'invented', Andalusia was constructed as a dream world where the course of time could be slowed, life savoured to its fullest, and the disturbances and hypocrisy of the modern, 'civilized' world of large European capitals avoided.

As a result of fertile interchanges among musicians, performers, writers, artists, and curiosity seekers, dance spectacles began to occupy a larger share of the foreigner's entertainment, and picturesque descriptions of the Triana district in Seville and the Albaicín district and Sacromonte caves of Granada became requisite colourful asides in the European travelogue previously dominated by descriptions of monuments and cathedrals. Many travellers echoed eighteenth-century attitudes, such as Jean François de Peyron's opinion (1783) that Gypsies were a pack of thieves who 'only seek to rob and injure you' (García Mercadal 1962: 765), but few shared

---

[5] Its pull continues into the present era. For example, see the account of Polhemus (1968) who spent a summer in the 1960s with a Romany family in Guadix, and tells the story of 'granny' who claimed to be the English-born daughter of a schoolteacher and a soldier who died in the First World War.

Jean-François Bourgoing's conclusion that Gypsies 'should have been purged from society a long time ago' (García Mercadal 1962: 366): the gypsy was becoming a popular symbolic good, which meant that its iconographic and ethnographic status had to be constantly refined and interrogated. Rebelling against the previous generation of Enlightenment explorers, French travellers especially produced a radical change in the European attitude towards Spanish local colour (Herr 1973: 13). Following the Napoleonic Wars, the list of tourists to Spain reads like a Who's Who of French culture: between 1806 and 1870 Alexander Laborde, René Chateaubriand, Prosper Mérimée, Louis Viardot, Edgar Quinet, Henri Beyle (Stendhal), Théophile Gautier, Victor Hugo, Alexandre Dumas *père* (travelling with artists Charles Giraud and Louis Boulanger), Antoine de Latour, Gustave Flaubert, Auguste-Émile Bégin, and George Sand all made pilgrimages to Spain and embellished their travel acounts, letters, or stories with romanticized adventures. The Romantics were later followed by artists such as Alfred Dehodencq, Gustave Doré, Édouard Manet, and Henri Regnault, who filled their sketchbooks with images of gypsies that appealed to the new French taste for 'realistic' renditions of exotic locales and peoples.

Many of these tourists were blind to the performative aspects of gypsy spectacle, imagining, or at least allowing their readers to imagine, that the passion exhibited by dancers and musicians extended beyond a staged production into their private lives. This satisfied their desire to witness something spontaneous, the natural expression of gypsy passion, when in fact, long before the mid-nineteenth century, dance performances had already evolved into a routine that included the preliminary ritual of locating a guide (or more likely the guide spotting the foreigner), the guide offering to arrange a spectacle usually performed only for the initiated, and the payment of a determined fee ritualistically delayed but always exacted—what Dumas aptly termed the 'adieux métalliques' (213).[6] If there ever was a spontaneous form of gitanesque dance, it vanished during the nineteenth century with the 'transformation of its performers into authentic professionals and, at the same time, of flamenco song and dance into a commodity on sale to *señoritos* and tourists' (Bernal Rodríguez in González Troyano 1987: 121–2). It was perhaps because they

---

[6] The earliest mention of a paid dance recital that I have found is in Gil Vicente's 1521 *Farça de las çinganas.*

recognized their own bourgeois bohemia for the mirage performance community that it was that the French were eager to convince them-selves of the spontaneity and authenticity of the performances they witnessed in Seville or Granada, when in fact the Spanish Romany, wise to what the market would bear for a colourful gypsy perform-ance, were in full control of the illusion.

At the same time that northern Europeans were placing gypsy fan-tasies like von Weber's Preziosa, Bizet's Carmen, or Verdi's Azucena in Spanish settings with music adapted to European tastes, Spanish composers were beginning to export compositions heavily inflected by a suddenly popular gypsy music. Sarasate's *Spanish Dances* incor-porated gypsy melancholic rhapsodies with rhythmic figures, ori-ental arabesques, and the clapping that characterized the *cante jondo* (Baumann 1996: 124). Later Albéniz, Granados, Falla, and finally Rodrigo, the last of the Spanish neo-Romanticists, would follow with their vast repertoire of Andalusian cantos, preludes, rhapsodies, serenatas, and *seguidillas*. Roma musicians for their part adapted 'gypsy' music in their own repertoires, preparing the stage for what could be called the twentieth-century 'flamenco wars' when debates such as those waged in Hungary about folk versus gypsy sources of national music were played out in Andalusia. The Romany particip-ated in the gypsy craze in a variety of ways. A great deal of imagina-tion had to be put to work to convert the subjects foreign tourists saw and sketched in Andalusia into the wonderful Carmens that so mesmerized armchair voyagers. By the same token, a great deal of effort was put into the performance on behalf of the Romany to ensure that the illusion succeeded. That these entertainers under-stood the performative aspect of gypsyness and its role in enticing foreign visitors to Spain is clear from the many confabulations, tricks, and jokes at the tourist's expense.

NEW INVESTMENTS

Gitanesque music was also fostered in Spain by an elite class of *señoritos* (landowners' sons) whose elaborate *juergas* combined heavy drinking, commercial sex, and cathartic music (Mitchell 1994: 47). With the agrarian oligarchy's migration to the cities, however, gitanesque music and dance gained wider appeal and with this expansion, evidenced by the growing popularity of the *café cantante*, flamenco underwent what many purists deplored as a period of decadence. The rhetoric of decadence and salvation peculiar to the flamenco complex that we associate with the first decades of the present century is a reminder that its history is a contested terrain where various classes and groups still fight over questions of quality, authenticity, and definitions. When confronted by the plethora of books on this subject one is immediately struck not only by the vast discrepancies, for example in the *cante jondo* genealogical tree, but also by the passion of those who claim authority to speak accurately on the subject of flamenco's ethnic origins. One reason for the glaring lack of consensus is that modern discussions of flamenco origins are tied up with unresolvable issues relating to Romany ethnic identity, and to understand the true import of the flamenco wars, one has to study what is to be gained or lost by Spaniards who make certain claims regarding this identity. It is also important to recognize that the various French and British versions of this rhetoric of loss, a reaction to localized economic and social realities, may have inflected Spanish debates about flamenco's ethnic origins. The same degeneration panic that contaminated the Falla group of intellectuals who 'rescued' flamenco from vulgarization in the 1920s by devising a gypsy pedigree (Mitchell 1994: 160–77) also permeated the discourses of ethnologists and folklorists who already by the mid-nineteenth century were lamenting the disappearance of the 'pure' British Gypsy.

The modern idealization of the Spanish gypsy cannot be studied without reference to Spanish flamencology but foreigners also played an important, understudied role in the exportation of Spain's cultural icon. For visitors to the 1889 Exposition Universelle in Paris like Catulle Mendès, the dancing *gitana* had become the emblem of Andalusia, and Andalusia a trope for Spain itself: 'L'Espagne amoureuse et violente, l'Espagne qui joue de la guitare et du couteau, l'Espagne des grandes routes où sonnent les grelots des mules et les fusillades des bandits, l'Espagne des corridas sanglantes, qui allume aux chamarrures des spadas et aux rouges blessures des taureaux les yeux et les cœurs de ses belles filles' [the violent, passionate Spain, the Spain of the guitar and the knife, the Spain of vast routes where are heard the sounds of mule hoofs and bandits' gunshots, the Spain of bloody *corridas* that illuminates with sword flashes and with the red of wounded bulls the eyes and hearts of its beautiful daughters] (1889: 9). This long-brewing fusion of Roma, Andalusian, and

Spanish identity had serious consequences for Europe's vision of Spain as a whole, as well as for the Spanish Calés. If the Spanish gypsy was collectively imagined as passionate, mysterious, physically attractive, bizarre, primitive, tragic, musical, demoniacal, anarchic, lazy, deadly, a symbol for freedom and poetic liberty (to name the most common stereotypes), Romany groups were bound to be patronized or infantilized, or, when they did not match the ideal, misunderstood, despised, and neglected.

For travellers who invested heavily in the gypsy ideal, the confrontation with Calés was apt to prove a great disappointment (a feeling often expressed by the more gullible tourists), but for others the gypsy romance was stubbornly prolonged into the present century. For example, the interests of British folklorists and Spanish 'art-religionists' coincide in the fabulous works of Walter Starkie: *Raggle Taggle* (1934), *Don Gypsy* (1936), and *In Sara's Tents* (1953). In addition to the preservationist's obsession with disappearing music, Starkie combined the male tourist's penchant for late-night carousing, post-Romantic European idealizations of Spain's 'difference', and an overwrought imagination, all of which brought him into prolonged contact with Andalusian Romany entertainers and mark his popular travelogues as an important stage in the evolution of Spanish gypsophilia. The stated goal of his travels may have been to collect Spanish tunes and lyrics, but Starkie imagined himself a modern-day *pícaro* pursuing the 'adventure' of poverty and passing as a Romany. While he seems to have had little difficulty living this dream in a very material sense, what he passed along to Hispanists regarding Romany character and traditions was primarily gleaned from histories and travelogues he consulted in his study at Trinity College Dublin, George Borrow chief among them. His books also reflect a broad range of literary readings: the *Celestina*; *Alonzo, mozo de muchos amos*; the *Lazarillo*; Cervantes's *Novelas ejemplares*; *Don Juan Tenorio*; virtually every story about scoundrels, *pícaros*, brigands, and men like himself with an abiding wanderlust. From these readings and his own personal observations, Starkie sketched for the English-speaking world a composite image that replaced Borrow's more sombre picture: gypsy men were wonderfully illogical, crafty, and generous with the wine-skin, while the women were exotic and sensual Egyptian goddesses.

To conjure images of 'gypsy Spain', Starkie also rehearsed all the more unusual traditions and myths mentioned by previous chroniclers even if he did not himself witness them: the *diclé* (virgin cloth), the *hokano baro* or 'great trick' that Borrow had copied from Alcalá's seventeenth-century picaresque novel, elaborate wedding feasts and birthing celebrations, snippets of Romany philosophy, the practice of eating *mulo mas* (carrion), tales of baby-snatching, and other legends borrowed from the pages of the *Journal of the Gypsy Lore Society*. One of the more enduring myths that Starkie recirculated was that of the African origin of Spanish Calés proposed by Francisco de Sales Mayo (Quindalé) in *El gitanismo: historia, costumbres y dialecto* (1870) and later imported into the flamencologist's spurious repertoire of *gitano* origins. Starkie embellishes his descriptions of women with references to Egypt and the Pharaohs. With echoes of Isaac Muñoz's sultry novels, he constantly remarks on women's animal and queenly attributes as well as his privileged position as exotic specimen hunter: 'As I gazed at her sitting there, combing her hair, entirely unconscious of my presence, I felt like a hunter in the forest stalking a gorgeous bird of Paradise. I was afraid to move lest she should awake from her daydreaming, spread out her wings and fly away. Her haughty indifference thrilled me more than any restless familiarity of manner, for I felt that she was Pharaoh's daughter—the chosen bride of the Gypsy chief, bringing with her the magic of the East' (1937: 95). Borrowing a line from Spanish playwright Jacinto Benavente, he describes the desired sublime effect of the dancing gypsy: 'her flesh burns with the consuming heat of all eternity, but her body is like the very pillar of the sanctuary, palpitating as it is kindled in the glow of sacred fires [. . .]. The loves and hates of other worlds pass before our eyes and we feel ourselves heroes, bandits, hermits assailed by temptation, shameless bullies of the tavern—whatever is highest and lowest in one' (1937: 329).

While every step carried travellers like Starkie towards a new place and adventure, it also required a journey back in time, to 'compare these wanderers of today with the description written by chroniclers who witnessed the arrival of the Original Band in 1417' (1953: 12). This journey back served to substantiate that, although Gypsies were succumbing to the attractions and obligations of modern life, they had been successful at fusing together the 'new mechanical civilization with the ancient patriarch way of living' (1953: 14). Even the 'miraculous developments' in science and technology could not alter an immutable way of life: 'while the great mass of mankind is being regimented into fixed types, the Gypsy is becoming more Gypsyish than ever before. He has gone back spiritually to the outlook of his grandfather, and he possesses the almost fantastic quality of the Gypsies of a hundred years ago. He sees the modern inventions, the motor, electricity, telephone, but he makes use of them in accordance with his Gypsy temperament' (1953: 14).

By the end of the Civil War, however, and more so by the end of the Second World War, it became increasingly difficult for Europeans to imagine Spain as the 'eternal vacation' spot where sleepy towns were immune to the outside world. Reminiscing in *Farewell Spain* (1937) about her pre-war travels, Irish novelist Kate O'Brien lamented: '[t]here will be no more sentimental travellers—anywhere. Their excuse and occasion will have been removed in that day of uniformity which we are agreed is the distracted world's only hope' (1985: 3). Most post-Second World War writers interject pessimistic notes about Spain as a state of mind it is time to lay to rest. Gerald Brenan's *The Face of Spain* (1956) paints a dreary picture of poverty and bitterness against a backdrop of more pleasant memories of pre-Civil War travels. After such bloody conflicts, it would take a heroic measure of nearsightedness to pursue the Spanish dream of the 'eternal vacation', and with this diminishment of the magical Spanish travel-scape came various shifts in Spanish racialized thinking about Gypsies.

For the most part, the crudest myths and anecdotes—recycled unremittingly during the hundred years from J.M.'s influential *Historia de los gitanos* (1832) until F. M. Pabanó's 1915 *Historia y costumbres de los gitanos*—were refuted in the 1950s onward as the study of documents yielded to modern fieldwork techniques, but there are myriad exceptions. José Carlos de Luna introduces *Gitanos de la Bética* (1951: 7) by complaining that 'Don Jorgito' may have dealt with Gypsies in jails, inns, and on the road but he had penetrated their customs very little. Yet Luna and his contemporaries filled their texts with uncredited paraphrases and quotes from Borrow, as well as from other historians and philologists who followed in his footsteps such as Pabanó, and they continued to essentialize Gypsies by repeating long lists of stereotypical traits and behaviour that are discouragingly familiar to readers of nineteenth- and early twentieth-century tracts. Under the collective influence of nineteenth-century ethnographers and travellers with their taste for the exotic, together with the rehabilitated, poeticized (Lorquian) version of the 1920s

plus its 1930s re-romanticization by Starkie and its 1940s politicization with the early Francoist *españolada* or folkloric film musical, it is
perhaps inevitable that a 1950s poet like Luna should wax poetical
about Gypsy atavism:

El cerebro de los gitanos es [. . .] resbaladizo y tortuoso como esas veredillas
que caprichosamente se enroscan entre chumberas y pitacos empinándose
hasta la cueva negra de hollín de las malas intenciones en las que bullen los
alacranes del rencor. Otras, se ofrece liso, reseco por la extraña lumbre que
también lo ciega; ancho para que los atavismos rueden con fragor de truenos,
o hirviendo como un mar de lava que la fantasía y la quimera surcan sin
timón ni rosa de los vientos. (1951: 11–12)

[The Gypsy brain is [. . .] as slippery and tortuous as the paths that capri-
ciously wind between the prickly pear trees and magueys upwards to the
dark soot-covered cave of bad intentions in which the scorpions of animosity
boil over. Other times it is smooth, dried by the strange light that also blinds
it; wide enough for the atavisms that rumble around inside it, or boiling like
a sea of lava through which fantasy and illusion travel without helm or
compass.]

Taking his cue from Sales Mayo, Luna uses elaborate images to dif-
ferentiate between what he calls Betic Gypsies on the one hand, and
Hindu or 'zincali' Gypsies on the other, typifying the Egyptianization
of Spanish Calés during the Franco era. The superior Betics, according to Luna, were of Sumerian origin who migrated to Spain from
Northern Africa before and during the Moorish invasions and thus
have no racial affinity with 'Hindu' or 'Hungarian' groups.[7] These
Gypsies who preceded the Moorish invasion became talented interpreters and disseminators of the ancient dances of the Romans (1951:
173) and subsequently branded the Moorish music with their distinct
personality to such a degree that this music resembles very little the
Arab music of Northern Africa (1951: 142). Luna's fantastic Gypsy
genealogy partakes of many of the fallacies of Nazi-era anthropologists who, prior to the Second World War, endeavoured to separate
strains of pure and mixed Zigeuner. What connects them is the com-
pulsion to represent the Gypsy race as slightly outside the range of

---

[7] Luna claimed that the Andalusian Gypsies were descendants of tribes of people
whom Ramses III had conquered and expelled from Egypt (1951: 15). The issue of a
North African descent of southern Spanish Gypsies has not been settled definitively.
François de Vaux de Foletier argued (1974: 53) that there was no linguistic evidence
that Gypsies had migrated north from Africa and that, on the contrary, the Caló of
southern Spain contained Greek words.

human norm. A true Gypsy dance is by 'instinct' disconcerting, unpredictable, undefinable, rebellious, and scandalous:

Los bailes gitanos pican, arañan y aturden porque ellos aportan a su simplismo un caudal de gracia y ñáñaros de despabilidísima intención, servidos por cuerpos que ondulan como grímpolas, saltan y crepitan como piñas de rescoldo, y se retuercen, alumbran y queman como llamas de carrasca encrespadas por mengues retozones y rijosos. (1951: 190)

[Gypsy dances sting, scratch, and bewilder because they bring to their simplicity a wealth of grace and sexual bravado intended to arouse, executed by bodies that sway like pennants, leap and crackle like pine cones in hot embers, and twist, give off sparks, and burn like the flames of pin oaks stirred up by frolicking, lewd devils.]

However proud of the accomplishment of 'nuestros gitanos' [our Gypsies], most descriptions of Gypsy customs written during the Franco regime articulate the vast difference between Gypsies and more civilized, non-Gypsy populations. 'Our Gypsies' are cleaner, more affluent, and better dressed, and they have progressed further than 'less civilized' Hindu Gypsies, but they still neglect the comforts and aesthetics of those higher up on the scale of human progress.

A host of books published around the same time as *Gitanos de la Bética* focus on Gypsy origins primarily in order to establish an authoritative genealogy of *cante jondo*: Cándido Ortiz de Villajos's *Gitanos de Granada* (1949), Anselmo González Climent's *Flamencología* (1955), J. Caballero's *El baile andaluz* (1957), Domingo Manfredi Cano's *Los gitanos* (1959), J. Amaya's *Gitanos y cante jondo* (n.d.), Antonio Mairena and Ricardo Molina's *Mundo y formas del cante flamenco* (1963), and Máximo Andaluz's *Gitanerías* (1964). Nearly all discussions of Gypsy origins celebrated Andalusian Gypsies as the 'aristocrats' of the various groups because they had assimilated the artistic and spiritual qualities of the 'original' inhabitants of Andalusia. Some of these authors, however, diminished the *gitano* contribution to the flamenco complex in order to elevate Andalusia to the status of the true mother of flamenco and *cante jondo*. For example, portraying flamenco as a musical gumbo, Caballero exalted all of its individual ingredients: the Andalusian latent predisposition for flamenco music, the happy admixture of Arab and Gypsy spice, a dash of Jewish and Christian flavour. Yet even in texts in which the anthropomorphized Andalusia—passionate, musical, changeable, and anarchical—was recognized as the progenitor of flamenco music, discussions of the 'mysterious' Gypsy race continued to obscure discussions of Calé ethnicity.

In Spain the backlash against the neo-Romantic ethnicizing of flamenco in the 1930s, and more recently by 1950–1960s gitanophiles, began almost immediately and continues today.[8] Whatever position researchers take on flamenco's origins, they feel equally qualified to speak on issues relating to Roma ethnicity. Timothy Mitchell's work is just the last in a very long line of dissertations on the origins of flamenco that challenge or confirm common perceptions and misconceptions of Romany identity. Determined to debunk the ethnic revivalism of the 1950s, *Flamenco Deep Song* goes to exaggerated lengths not merely to impugn gitanocentric theories of the origins of the flamenco complex, but to deracialize Spanish *gitanos*, even though he claims that his intention is not to minimize their role in the creation of flamenco (1994: 95). He disputes the racial core of gitano identity by challenging the 'legendary gitano endogomy' and even the Romani source of Caló, arguing that gypsiologists have 'always' been aware of the difference of Spanish *gitanos*, a non-racial confluence of groups including exiled Moors in the seventeenth century, whose core ethnic identity is defined by their mode of life. Mitchell's privileging of habitus and class over ethnicity in the flamenco complex, and his thesis regarding flamenco as a 'psychodrama' originating in the 'traumatized classes', are necessary correctives; but in his drive to debunk the *gitano* pedigree, he leaves readers with an inadequate, under-theorized picture of Romany ethnicity and with the debatable idea that those best qualified to define this ethnicity are non-*gitanos*: 'A gypsy is not the most reliable guide as to who is a gypsy and who is not' (1994: 60). Racial purity is indeed a social construct just as flamenco purity is a mirage, and

---

[8] By neo-Romantic ethnicizing of flamenco I refer primarily to travellers like Walter Starkie who, up until the Civil War, fed their readers idealized tableaux of Spanish Gypsy life. However, those like Falla, Lorca, and their contemporaries, who earlier claimed that the most authentic flamenco musicians and dancers were Gypsies or that the Spanish *gitano* was superior to other European Roma groups, contributed to this trend. I am grateful to Eva Woods for pointing out that, even during the Republic, films such as *El rey de los gitanos* (1933), *Los claveles* (1935), *El gato montés* (1935), *María de la O* (1936), and the immensely popular *Morena Clara* (1936), which was the biggest box-office draw of the Republican era before its director Florian Rey came out in support of Franco (Gubern 1986: 36), propagated neo-Romantic stereotypes.

Spain is an 'ethnic chaos' as Mitchell argues, but his notion of *gitano* identity fails to discriminate adequately between unreliable sources like Cervantes, Borrow, or Mérimée, and the more credible reports of gypsiologists like Bertha Quintana, Merrill McLane, or Jean-Paul Clébert. By using the term *gitano* (with lower-case 'g'), Mitchell ensures that readers understand that the category he is discussing is sentimental rather than primordial, but this also implies that some ethnic identities are less 'proper' than others. He does not, for instance, write *andalusians* or *spaniards* even though these groups share the same 'ethnic chaos' as the Romany and have a sentimental content just as unbound as the *gitanos*. In the end Mitchell's *gitano* might serve to characterize the mixed ethnic element involved in the flamenco entertainment complex but it leaves us with an inadequate idea of Romany ethnicity. What is lacking still is a proper study of Calé identity informed by recent theoretical debates about race and ethnicity.

Such a study will involve confronting a series of methodological and ethical questions that cut across disciplinary boundaries. Is it possible to characterize an ethnic identity without dwelling on disparaging categorizations that have accrued to it in the past? In other words, in what sense do characterizations of ethnicity prolong negative stereotyping? Is it better to validate and celebrate differences in a tactical move to promote ethnic pride, or to obscure and elide them to promote acceptance, assimilation, and homogenization; and in whose interest is it to adopt either strategy? Would emphasis on Roma ethnicity obscure problems of other non-ethnic-based minorities, thus prolonging exclusion and inequality? How can the contradictory formations within ethnic cultures be recognized in a neutral way? How can the discussion of ethnic identity promote a critique of the political economy without adversely affecting the material conditions of the Roma? How are cultural practices related to economic and political practices? Is celebrating the 'gypsyness' of flamenco dance and music a disservice or a strategic move that can have social and cultural benefits for an oppressed minority? Is it elitist to pit definitions of ethnicity based on modern sociological theory that speak 'for' the Roma against self-definitions by the subjects who are the interested parties but who do not have access to elite Western methodologies? Only by addressing such issues will cultural critics be able to achieve a critical re-evaluation of Spanish culture.

WORKS CITED

Anderson, B. (1998). *The Spectre of Comparisons: Nationalism, Southeast Asia and the World*. London: Verso.

Banks, M. (1996). *Ethnicity: Anthropological Constructions*. London: Routledge.

Baumann, M. P. (1996). 'The Reflection of the Roma in European Art Music', *Journal of the International Institute for Traditional Music*, 38.1: 95–138.

Borrow, G. (1923) [1841]. *The Zincali: An Account of the Gypsies in Spain*. New York: G. Wells.

Bourdieu, P. (1994). *The Field of Cultural Production: Essays on Art and Literature*, ed. and trans. Randal Johnson. Cambridge: Polity Press.

Brenan, G. (1956). *The Face of Spain*. New York: Grove Press.

Caballero, J. (1957). *El baile andaluz*. Barcelona: Noguer.

Clifford, J., and Marcus, G. E. (eds.) (1986). *Writing Culture: The Poetics and Politics of Ethnography*. Berkeley and Los Angeles: University of California Press.

Colmeiro, J. (1998). 'Exorcising Exoticism: Rehispanizing Carmen', unpublished talk presented at State University of New York at Stony Brook.

Dumas, A. (1989) [1885]. *De Paris à Cadix: impressions de voyage*. Paris: Éditions François Bourin.

Fonseca, I. (1995). *Bury Me Standing: The Gypsies and their Journey*. New York: Random House.

García Mercadal, J. (ed.) (1962). *Viajes de extranjeros por España y Portugal*, iii: *Siglo XVIIII*. Madrid: Aguilar.

González Troyano, A. (ed.) (1987). *La imagen de Andalucía en los viajeros románticos y Homenaje a Gerald Brenan*. Málaga: Diputación Provincial de Málaga.

Gould, E. (1996). *The Fate of Carmen*. Baltimore: Johns Hopkins University Press.

Grellmann, H. (1783). *Die Zigeuner*. Dessau: Verlags-Kasse.

Gubern, R. (1986). *La guerra de España en la pantalla*. Madrid: Filmoteca Española.

Hammersley, M. (1992, repr. 1998), *What's Wrong with Ethnography*. New York: Routledge.

Hancock, I. (1992). 'Gypsy History in Germany and Neighboring Lands: A Chronology Leading to the Holocaust and Beyond', in D. Crowe and J. Kolsti (eds.), *The Gypsies of Eastern Europe*. Armonk, NY: M E. Sharpe, 11–30.

Herr, E. F. (1973). *Les Origines de l'Espagne romantique: les récits de voyage 1755–1823*. Paris: Didier.

J. M. (1832). *Historia de los gitanos*. Madrid: Librería Europea.

Jones, S. (1997). *The Archaeology of Ethnicity: Constructing Identities in the Past and Present*. London: Routledge.

Lombroso, C. (1876). *L'uomo delinquente*. Milan: Hoepli.

Luna, J. C. de (1951). *Gitanos de la Bética*. Madrid: EPESA.

Mendès, C., and Darzens, R. (1889). *Les Belles du monde*. Paris: E. Plon, Nourrit.

Mitchell, T. (1994). *Flamenco Deep Song*. New Haven: Yale University Press.

Moncada, S. de (1974). *Restauración política de España*, ed. J. Vilar. Madrid: Instituto de Estudios Fiscales, Ministerio de Hacienda.

O'Brien, K. (1985) [1937]. *Farewell Spain*. Boston: Beacon.

Okely, J. (1983). *Changing Cultures: The Traveller-Gypsies*. Cambridge: Cambridge University Press.

Pabanó, F. M. (1915). *Historia y costumbres de los gitanos*. Madrid: Giner.

Polhemus, L. B. (1968). *Good-bye Gypsy: Living with the Gypsies of Spain*. Glendale, Calif.: A. H. Clark.

Said, E. (1978). *Orientalism*. New York: Pantheon Books.

Sales Mayo, F. de (Quindalé) (1870). *El gitanismo: historia, costumbres y dialecto de los gitanos*. Madrid: Victoriano Suárez.

Salillas, R. (1896). *El delincuente español: el lenguaje*. Madrid: Victoriano Suárez.

San Román, T. de (1984). *Gitanos de Madrid y Barcelona*. Bellaterra: Universidad Autónoma de Barcelona.

—— (1997) [1994]. *La diferencia inquietante: viejas y nuevas estrategias culturales de los gitanos*. Madrid: Siglo XXI.

Starkie, W. (1937). *Don Gypsy: Adventures with a Fiddle in Southern Spain and Barbary*. New York: E. P. Dutton.

—— (1953). *In Sara's Tents*. London: Murray.

—— (1961) [1934]. *Spanish Raggle Taggle: Adventure with a Fiddle in North Spain*. London: Penguin.

Vaux de Foletier, F. de (1974). *Mil años de historia de los gitanos*. Barcelona: Plaza & Janés.

3

Elusive Song: Flamenco as Field and Passage for the *Gitanos* in Córdoba Prison

PARVATI NAIR

FLAMENCO has long provided the Western imaginary with a location for passion. Popular definitions of the word 'flamenco' blur the music with the dance style and the Andalusian with the gypsy, yet intimate that these are separate and interdependent components of a single regional and cultural expression.[1] It would appear that the *gitano*, with his supposed darkness of skin, eyes, and temperament, exemplifies in extreme the southern Spaniard when viewed as exotic or passionate Other. Consider the following description by William Washabaugh in his *Flamenco: Passion, Politics and Popular Culture* of the singer El Agujetas, father of one of the protagonists of my project: 'He was dressed all in black. His billows of curly black hair framed a scarred face that Clint Eastwood would covet [. . .] And then Agujetas began to sing, though at the time I would have said that his voice was not singing, so much as ripping and tearing at his soul. Standing about two feet from my face singing fire [. . .], Agujetas had *me* transfixed and my *wife* stunned' (1996: pp. x–xi). The singer mesmerizes his audience, stuns them, with this unbridled onslaught of embodied emotive Otherness. What is more, entire theatres in Paris and the United States have been known to have sold out to those wishing to witness the force of his cry.[2]

Washabaugh's initiation to flamenco is by no means unique. Throughout its history, flamenco has propelled itself on guarantees of emotive heights—or 'catharsis', to use Mitchell's term (1994)—

---

[1] Leblon (1995: 95) states that, following the Spanish Constitution of 1978, Andalusia expressed its cultural difference from the rest of Spain through the symbol of flamenco.

[2] See the entries on Agujetas in Álvarez Caballero (1994) and Pohren (1988) for more details of Agujetas's life and career.

which have allowed its practitioners the means to a living. If today it offers visions of impassioned alterity to non-Spanish audiences, it evolved by doing much the same for those wealthy enough to afford such frenzied visions within Andalusia.[3] Its early development as the musical expression of an urban underclass sustained by the sponsorship of wealthy patrons has left it a legacy of association with the socially marginal.[4] Nowhere does flamenco seem so 'authentic' as when articulated by those whose nameless and insignificant lives form the very dregs of society; namely, those members of an underclass further marginalized by incarceration. Thus, of the *cante jondo* or deep song repertoire, the *saeta carcelera*, sung originally by convicts behind bars, has traditionally been considered the most 'authentic', and hence moving, of songs of repentance sung during the Holy Week period (Mitchell 1994: 99–103). That prison populations in Andalusia have long been largely comprised of a motley underclass which falls under the loose ethnic label *gitano* leads to a triangle of cultural associations built on the multiple connotations surrounding the words '*gitano*', 'prison', and 'flamenco'.

It therefore seemed somewhat incongruous to read in the British newspaper the *Independent on Sunday* (Hayward 1996) that flamenco is currently practised in the penitentiary of Córdoba as a form of rehabilitation for long-term prisoners. Roles appear to have switched and what emerged as the expression of trauma among social outcasts has become the means of reinserting them, or perhaps inserting them, into mainstream society. Córdoba prison's flamenco workshop was set up nearly ten years ago in order to draw *gitano* prisoners, the majority of whom are there on drugs-related charges, into participating in educational activities. Such workshops aim largely to divert prisoners from established drug dependencies and to prepare them for reincorporation into society. The *gitanos*, who are largely illiterate or partially literate, have consistently been resistant to other forms of rehabilitation and yet willingly opt for this project. A professional guitarist, Rafael Trenas, trains them in lyrics and techniques under the close supervision of the *educador* [rehabilitation officer] in charge of the prisoners, Antonio Estévez, who qualified in

---

[3] See Grenier and Guibalt (1990) for more general discussion of the 'Other' in relation to anthropological perspectives on music.

[4] Steingress (1991: 16–32) relates the 'afición' for flamenco to the transmission of extremes of emotion to the audience through the song, connecting this to the growing social 'alienation' experienced under modernity.

criminology at the Sorbonne University, Paris. The choice of music ranges from the long-standing prison flamenco tradition to other conventional forms of *cante*, such as *bulerías*, *tarantos*, and *siguiriyas*. Estévez's close personal friendship with José Arrebola, President of the Confederación Andaluza de Peñas Flamencas, has led to the National Penitentiary Flamenco Song Contest in which convicts from all over Spain are invited to take part. Held biennially in the Córdoba prison, it is sponsored by the Confederación, itself dependent on funding from the Consejería de Cultura of the Junta de Andalucía. Winners of this contest earn remission on their sentences, and prizewinners from prisons elsewhere in the country can apply for transfer to Córdoba in order to continue their flamenco training. Of the three penitentiary contests held so far, Antonio de los Santos El Agujetas, son of the Agujetas mentioned above, was the winner on one occasion, and another *gitano*, José Serrano Campos, won the other two. In recent years, these singers have been allowed to perform at public *peña* gatherings of flamenco *aficionados*, accompanied by the rehabilitation officer. In 1997, Agujetas and Serrano were taken to studios in Granada under the auspices of the Confederación de Peñas to record the compact disc 2 *gritos de libertad*. In late 1997, both Agujetas and Serrano were released from prison, the former having completed his foreshortened term and the latter on bail, whereby he has to report back from time to time.

This essay will examine the effort to rehabilitate the *gitano* prison population through flamenco. Use of the creative arts as a form of rehabilitation in prisons is widespread in Spain as elsewhere, a case in point being the flourishing theatre group run by Elena Cánovas Vacas in Yeserías women's prison in Madrid (Cánovas Vacas in Peaker 1996). The Unit for the Arts and Offenders report on 'Music in criminal justice settings' observes that the arts can offer prisoners a way to refashion perceptions of themselves and hence to revise their social attitudes (Unit for the Arts and Offenders 1996). Additionally it provides them with an interest that may continue after release and may even provide them with a livelihood, as with some of the actresses from Yeserías who have gone on to act for television, as Elena Cánovas Vacas informed me in a telephone conversation in 1998. What is different about the Córdoba project is that the flamenco workshop calls upon the perceived ethnic identity of the prisoners, thus requiring them to draw forth aspects of their socio-cultural experiences and identifications prior to entering prison. It further depends upon perceptions of 'essential' identity, innate talents or propensities guaranteed by ethnicity, since all the prisoners taking part are *gitanos*. (They are also all male: although flamenco dance classes started in the women's wing in 1997, by June 1998, when I visited the prison, the women's workshop had shut down due to lack of funding—the male workshop had clearly been given priority.) The entire scenario is set up according to a series of preconceived essentialist contrasts based on difference and hierarchy. First, the workshop places *gitanos* under the tutelage of *payos* (non-gypsies), subordinating one ethnicity to the other in keeping with social norms. Second, the personal and communal criminal histories of the *gitanos*, their liminal status as convicts, segregates them from those who permit them the practice of the *cante*. The policed space of prison means that the rehabilitation officer and the guitarist represent authority inasmuch as the *gitanos* must acquiesce to the requirements placed upon them in order to earn further favours. The impotence of the *gitanos* contrasts with the rights exercised by the authorities to 'visit' flamenco upon them or not. Such disciplinary boundaries turn the workshop into a bounded zone of confrontation with difference, conceived in binary terms, within which the 'unruly Other' (represented by the *gitano* convicts) is fashioned in the shape of the 'disciplined self' (prescribed and represented by the *payo* authorities).

The framework for my analysis aligns James Clifford's redefinition of the ethnographic field in terms of routes of travel rather than as enclosed space (hence my description of flamenco as 'field and passage') with Homi Bhabha's postcolonial focus on the subaltern articulation of cultural differences, which allows a degree of resistance to dominant cultural norms (hence my use of the term 'elusive song'). My claim is that, in the case of the prison workshop, flamenco becomes a hegemonic tool of negotiation whereby the cultural ideal of rehabilitation is superseded by a social reality of complex negotiations and engagements. Flamenco thus becomes the vehicle whereby aesthetic endeavour refigures social relations, in such a way that prisoners and prison authorities alike occupy interstitial spaces that generate cultural change and movement. Although Foucault's discussion of the 'technologies of the self' involved in the disciplinary process (1977) obviously underlies this discussion, I have preferred to draw on Clifford and Bhabha because of their insistence on the complex two-way nature of power relations.

Clifford writes against the grain of established traditions of anthropological practice, whereby Western ethnographers remove themselves from 'home' and for an extended period of time 'visit' the foreign Other, whose ways they observe and record for posterior analysis once back 'home'. Clifford contests the validity in postmodern, postcolonial times of the spatial and hierarchical distinctions implicit in conceptions of ethnography as a practice of displacement from one fixed location to another and as attention by the intellectual to what is distinct and different from the self. He bases his argument on Michel de Certeau's definition of 'space' as 'discursively mapped and corporeally practised' (Clifford 1997: 53–4), constituted by people's movements in, around, and through it. Thus he states that the 'field' should be viewed as a 'cluster of embodied dispositions and practices' (1997: 71) rather than as a location, so that ethnography takes place as engagement *en route*. The borders which demarcate the field thereby reveal themselves as unstable and renegotiable, so that distinctions of inside and outside, home and abroad, centre and periphery display their ambivalence. Thus today's world of blurred cultural and political borderlands forces ethnography to question its own practices in order to 'reinvent its traditions in new circumstances' (1997: 61). Ethnography's long-standing reliance on travel must therefore be seen not as a 'getting to' but as a 'going through', as ethnographic subjects are constituted through complex processes of relationship.

Clifford's problematization of the ethnographic field extends to a questioning of the epistemic authority of ethnographic texts. For, as he notes, the textual nature of the discipline renders lived experience into translation as cross-cultural hegemonic encounters are inscribed into authoritative texts. This point is of obvious relevance to the writing of this chapter. Much of it is based on two interviews conducted by me in Córdoba in 1998, one with four *gitanos* (Antonio de los Santos El Agujetas, José Serrano Campos, and two others who gave their names as just Justo and Manuel) in the prison in the presence of the rehabilitation officer, Antonio Estévez, and the President of the Confederación Andaluza de Peñas Flamencas, José Arrebola; and the other with the last two on their own. The meeting with the prisoners took place, interestingly, in the prison chapel. Earlier on, I had been requested not to ask awkward questions and to approach the *gitanos* as 'artistas', not convicts. During our meeting, the prisoners stressed more than once that 'el flamenco nos ha salvado, gracias a estos dos hombres' [flamenco has saved us, thanks to these two men], referring to the rehabilitation officer and the President of the Confederación. This may well be true, but no doubt it was also in their interest to repeat this. Clearly the encounter, which after all was arranged through official channels, was somewhat forced and the only discourse readily available was institutionally sanctioned. Given the predominant orality of the prisoners' backgrounds, it is hard to imagine the circuitous routes through which the prisoners navigate their way through institutional life and after it. Much of this chapter is therefore reconstructed, tenuous. Behind the reiterated socio-cultural 'ideals' of the workshop organizers, only the song is discernible. The efforts at music-making must therefore be considered for their performative potential.

Clifford's plotting of the ethnographic course has been compared to the image of an airport where multiple encounters take place within contexts of travel and translation. Nothing could be further away from the enclosed and ordered space of prison. Yet, like the ethnographic 'field', the flamenco workshop presents rehabilitation as a contestable site, epitomizing the contradictions of the ethnomusical negotiations outside of its walls. Thus the myth of the *gitano* as 'flamenco auténtico' differentiates *gitanos* from the other convicts in the prison, who are by default *payos*, but only to create a majority of the former since 80 per cent of the inmates are said to be *gitanos*. This supposedly innate propensity allows them to take part in this rehabilitation activity whilst purportedly believing that they are only expressing what is 'natural' to them. Thus what appears to the authorities as obedience can also be interpreted as an act of self-assertion that is potentially threatening since, if the *gitano* is seen as 'authentically flamenco', he is also seen as 'authentically truant'. If an ethnic propensity to flamenco and to criminality is seen as intrinsic to *gitano* identity, and yet rehabilitation (whose goal is to achieve a distancing from the latter) is attempted through the former, then a bizarre paradox emerges in which music produces an overlap between the concepts of rehabilitation and truancy. At the same time, the flamenco workshop allows the authorities to draw boundaries around the prisoners through techniques of reward and punishment. These include increasing or decreasing the number of cigarettes allowed per day for singing well or badly respectively; allowing or withholding weekend home visits; and denying the prisoner the privilege of taking part in the workshop if he does not 'deserve' it, reinstating him once he has earned this privilege through good behaviour in other areas of prison life. Thus the authorities know that they can touch the perceived core of *gitano* identity whilst offering the workshop as a kind of seduction for the furthering of it. In this way the authorities affirm their own rights and highlight their own boundaries.

The rehabilitation officer clearly plays a key role in determining the forms that rehabilitation will take. In general, rehabilitation is considered a vital aspect of the penal process, whereby the denial of personal freedom serves in theory to reshape or reform the individual. The professed goal is the successful reinsertion of the invididual into society by providing him, where possible, with the means to make a living without resorting to crime. In my interview with him, Estévez said that his job was to 'hacer cosas' [do things] with the prisoners, to be an 'animador' [facilitator] providing them with occupational therapy that would allow the time to pass. In his view, their low literacy levels made them take 'naturally' to music, which temporarily took their minds away from a drug habit that only a few ever really overcome. Estévez described *gitanos* generally as a marginal people, given to apathy, disorganized, and living only for the present. The flamenco workshop and contest, he said, offered a few of them the chance of acquiring a measure of social status.

However, the distinction between authorities and prisoners is perhaps not as stark as it may seem at first sight. The rehabilitation officer Antonio Estévez, the former director of the prison Francisco Velasco, and the guitarist Rafael Trenas are all three *payos* who grew up in *gitano* neighbourhoods. Their personal associations go back a long way and they perceive flamenco to be a core part of their lives and formative to their sense of identity. Estévez and Velasco are close friends of José Arrebola, President of the Confederación Andaluza de Peñas Flamencas. Funded by the Junta de Andalucía through the Confederación, one or more *peñas* exists in most Andalusian cities. Their purpose is decidedly 'purist': to keep alive the traditions of flamenco by maintaining it as an 'art' free from contamination by commercialization. The *peñas* regularly stage shows by young performers with commentary and informal professional guidance provided by more established artists, many of whom are *gitanos* (though some only for professional purposes) and who are viewed as the bedrock of tradition. An unspoken ethnic and gender distinction nevertheless exists when it comes to running the *peñas* and holding the purse strings. Whilst performers tend to be from both communities and sexes, the presidents and managing committees of the bigger *peñas* are *payos* and male, as are most of the members of the adjudicating panels at the many competitions organized on a regular basis. The most obvious binding factor among those who run these clubs is their common vision of flamenco as a 'treasure'. *Peña* organizers come from a variety of walks of life, generally middle-class: Antonio Núñez, Presidente de las Peñas de Cádiz, works for Radio Cádiz; José (Pepe) Arrebola, the overall head of the Confederación, is a regional sales manager for Sureña beer. For these men, flamenco is an 'afición' and almost a 'family matter'. At the same time, they consider themselves to be custodians of the art, although in practice, in order to convince themselves and others that they are maintaining its purity, they must engage in continuous negotiations, taking the art with them as they follow the cross-currents of such arrangements. Funds from the Junta de Andalucía have not risen in over eight years and so must be sought from members' pockets or through their links with companies which can be persuaded to sponsor events. The sociability of the Andalusian lifestyle opens the way for complex networks of personal and professional relations which often result in the indefinite deferral of the scheduled. What is more, the professional becomes visibly embroiled with the socio-cultural. Thus Arrebola is able to justify taking time off from his demanding job to attend to *peña* matters, by promoting his brand of beer at these gatherings. It does not seem too far-fetched to propose that, for Velasco and Estévez, the professed aim of rehabilitation serves as something of an excuse for drawing flamenco into their professional lives, allowing them to integrate aspects of their own socio-cultural experiences.

In this sense, the prison authorities reveal themselves as more committedly 'flamenco' than many of the prisoners who are supposedly genetically so. Their determination to carry on with the prison *peña* despite a lack of proper funding, since no provision is made for it in the rehabilitation procedures prescribed by the Ministry of Justice, the Ministry of the Interior, or the Dirección General de Instituciones Penitenciarias, is evident from the fact that they have on occasion had to dip into their own pockets to keep the workshop running. The prison workshop's greatest impact is not within the penitentiary institutions but rather within *peña* circles: 'Están en la calle o están en la cárcel, pero *son* flamencos' [They're in prison or outside, but they're fundamentally *flamencos*], said Estévez of the *gitanos*. The roots of this flamenco essentiality are perceived as embedded in their *gitano* ethnicity. In his introductory comments to the compact disc *2 gritos de libertad,* Arrebola describes the workshop as a 'Peña de altas paredes, muros de granito, puertas grandes de hierro que impiden la libertad de lo humano y cerrojos de sonidos negros escalofriantes, que en ningún momento podrán impedir la libertad del conocimiento, de la expresión, de los sentimientos y del grito sagrado del cante' [A *peña* with high granite walls, large iron doors that curtail human freedom, and locks that close with a terrifying sinister clang, but which cannot curtail freedom of knowledge, expression, or emotion nor that of the *cante*'s sacred cry]. Flamenco is seen as a 'divine' vocation, a birthright which cannot be contained by restrictions to personal freedom; indeed, it is implied that it is perhaps heightened by such constraints, as if prison were some dark night of the soul. Thus, again on the leaflet to the compact disc, Arrebola describes the winners of the Penitentiary Contests as 'dos magníficos cantores dignos de figurar en los carteles más importantes de *nuestro* flamenco' [two magnificent singers worthy of figuring among the major attractions of *our* flamenco]. The imagery is quasi-religious; the disc itself proof that flamenco officialdom can nurture the art.[5] The prison matter of *gitano* rehabilitation clearly overlaps with the attempted preservation of musical traditions in an overall cultural context of slippage, experimentation, and change. Woven into this preoccupation, nevertheless, are the constrictions and pressures of the moment with their many social implications. Thus, at the time of my fieldwork in 1998, the fourth Penitentiary Song Contest, planned for October 1997, still had not taken place owing to financial constraints and the rehabilitation officer's prolonged ill health. A change in prison director, with the new incumbent having no personal involvement or investment in flamenco, had cast further doubt on the contest's viability. The workshop has been suspended on occasions when the organizers have had to attend to other professional duties. With regard to the choice of *cante* used in the workshops, in practice the organizers' insistence on maintaining the purity of the art bows to the

---

[5] Steingress (1991) and Mitchell (1994) explore the popular religiosity that accompanies Andalusian attitudes to flamenco, Steingress calling it 'una sustitución artístico-secular' [a secular artistic substitute] (1991: 85). In my conversation with the prisoners, conducted in the prison chapel, it was evident that the discourse of religion (in terms of sin, punishment, pardon, salvation) sat easily alongside the parallel discourse of rehabilitation from crime.

prisoners' musical experience: the range practised is mostly in the style of Camarón de la Isla, whose music is well known to them, rather than the older and more traditional *cante* from the 1920s of Manuel Torre, for example.

The *gitanos* in the prison manifest a variety of attitudes to flamenco. Some had no awareness of the music prior to their incarceration. Others had varying repertoires learnt from their sociocultural milieux. One claimed that he was a distant cousin of Joaquín Cortés. Of the two winners of the penitentiary contests, José Serrano had occasionally sung in *salas de fiestas* [night clubs]. Married, with five children, three of whom were conceived while he was in prison, and a grandchild in Seville, Serrano was sentenced to a twenty-year term for aiding and abetting homicide. His repertoire of songs is limited and, when asked what he would do when released, he said 'cantar si me sale algo y volver a lo mío, que es vender lotería' [sing if something turns up and go back to what I did before, selling lottery tickets]. Illiterate still and uncertain of his age, Serrano's priority has consistently been to be reunited with his wife and family. Indeed, his prison sentence was extended beyond its original term, despite the remissions earned for winning the contest twice, on account of his having 'forgotten' to return after weekends spent at home. In spite of such 'bad behaviour' which would normally warrant being grounded, Serrano was permitted to appear from time to time at public *peña* events. The other prizewinner, Antonio Agujetas, carries with him the legacy of his name. His father El Agujetas rose to international success but was ostracized by the *gitano* community of his native Jerez de la Frontera when he abandoned his deaf-mute wife and eleven children, four of whom are also deaf-mute; he now lives with a Japanese woman (Pohren 1988: 351–2; Pasqualino 1995: 94–8).[6] The aura surrounding the Agujetas name is one of predestined tragedy, a 'natural' disposition to *cante grande* or the deepest of deep song. For the flamenco purists, the father's alienation from his community meant that the spotlight shifted to his son Antonio Agujetas. Nevertheless, in 1981 the latter was sentenced to twenty-two years in

---

[6] Pasqualino writes: 'The rumours about Agujetas are so extravagant that they border on myth. His absence from the local scene perhaps fuels the legend [. . .] Part true and part fable, it should be taken into account, not only because it is regarded as the explanation of the power of his song, but also because it is a model that provides a point of reference for the community of San Miguel' (1995: 95, my translation of the French original). There are a large number of Japanese studying flamenco at dance schools in Jerez de la Frontera, some of them extremely talented.

prison for repeated drug-related assaults. His attendance at the workshop was part of the usual prison life of headcounts, shared cells, and timetabled duties. He has a considerable repertoire of *cante* and his singing style bears a recognizable likeness to that of his father. Interestingly, despite his closeness to the older forms of *cante grande* and despite their keenness on tradition, the panel at the Penitentiary Song Contest awarded the first prize twice to Serrano, whose style is more akin to that of contemporary singers such as Camarón or Pansequito. Professed cultural ideas of preserving traditions are thus dislodged by the social reality of changing undercurrents in musical tastes.

As for the matter of flamenco's effectiveness as rehabilitation, this remains painfully questionable. Since his release in October 1998, a few months after my interview with him, Agujetas has performed at *peñas* and has found occasional employment at *tablaos*, where he has inevitably had to comply with contemporary musical tastes which require *cante* to harmonize with the guitar and to give precedence to the dance.[7] Thus the unharnessed *cante grande* of his paternal line has to reinvent itself as it accommodates shifts in the surrounding socio-cultural contexts. According to the Presidente de las Peñas de Cádiz, with whom he is in touch, much of the rest of his time is spent in bars. The compact disc recorded by him and Serrano in March 1997 was still on sale in only one flamenco shop in Madrid at the time of my research in 1998, though it has subsequently become more widely available. Its official media launch by the Confederación de Peñas—supposedly tangible evidence of rehabilitation, convincing in its social visibility—had still not materialized in 1998 nor, to my knowledge, since.

Clifford's questioning of the 'field' of ethnography and its related academic practices includes discussion of its overlap with cultural studies. He cites various examples where the distinction between ethnographic work and cultural studies becomes blurred, proving the invalidity of research practised on the premiss of spatialized difference, whether real or metaphorical. His vision of ethnography as mobile and flexible facilitates a dialogue with Homi Bhabha's probing of the temporal and spatial boundaries around complex cultural conjunctures (Bhabha 1994: 40–6). Bhabha's postcolonial perspective revises modern conceptions of cultural difference and authority in

---

[7] See Manuel (1989) for a discussion of social shifts in flamenco styles.

order to reveal the ambivalence within such rationalized views of Otherness. He insists that cultural meaning is historically contingent and 'multi-accentual' (1994: 177), so that cultural differences are without common measure. The emphasis falls instead on the discursive articulation and rearticulation of culture 'as an uneven, incomplete production of meaning and value [. . .] produced in the act of social survival' (1994: 172). This view of culture as a strategy of survival forces a rethinking of conceptions of social identity and social affiliation, highlighting the historical contingency and displacement of the subaltern who move through the borderlands where the terrains of difference overlap. Bhabha's postcolonial focus homes in on the edges of the ethnocentricities of modernity so as to tease out 'a range of other dissonant, even dissident, histories and voices' (1994: 5). With their temporal attention focused on the present as a moment of displacement or crossing, the social reality of the subaltern is transitional.

This view of culture as a process of negotiation, displacement, and tradition, rather than a fixed structure of binary oppositions, reveals the prison workshop as a site for a politics of everyday life. Despite its social invisibility, being inside the prison's walls, it is not on the periphery of society but is an interstitial space where tradition is reinscribed through the contingencies and complexities of subaltern lives. As such, it is necessarily performative. Clifford's plotting of the field as an embodied route opens the way for Bhabha's focus on the ongoing negotiations that take place at interstitial zones. If the *gitanos* are obviously subaltern when viewed through the prism of institutional categories, then the *peña* organizers are also subaltern in their manœuvrings to gain recognition and funds, knowing that their movements only brush the edges of larger sanctioning bodies. The workshop thus becomes a site as much for their rehabilitation as for that of the prisoners. In either case, rehabilitation ceases to denote a kind of preparation for the future, a suspension of the present in anticipation of something better. Nor can it be seen simply as a means of anointing the tablet of tradition, for this too can be recreated only in the present. The time of flamenco as rehabilitation is clearly in the here and now, an engagement with the complexities of the present as a way of getting on. Flamenco as a cultural process exceeds the normalizing grip of prison rehabilitation just as it defies the efforts of *peña* enthusiasts to freeze it into a 'treasure'. The song thus eludes containment. In its ongoing struggle for social survival, it mirrors the subaltern crossings of cultural terrains. Agujetas's trajectory through prison and beyond most clearly shows the rehabilitation process embodied in the workshop to be a plural, ongoing process. The inherited identity of his musical traditions, his liminal status as a newly released convict, and the social expectations of acclaim raised by his prize and the compact disc reveal his *cante* as a means of engaging with the present and at the same time of overcoming it. The projections of ethnic alterity commonly assigned to flamenco are thus utilized to invent and reinvent the cultural self. Flamenco becomes doubly performative: a musical performance that shows cultural identity, like ethnicity, to be an experiential—that is, performative— process. Despite its objective of fixing identity through 'normalization', the prison workshop must be remembered as an intermediary space of cultural renewal, politically and socially charged by the passage of the *cante*.

WORKS CITED

Álvarez Caballero, A. (1994). *El cante flamenco*. Madrid: Alianza Editorial.
Bhabha, H. K. (1994). *The Location of Culture*. London: Routledge.
Clifford, J. (1997). *Routes*. Cambridge, Mass.: Harvard University Press.
Foucault, M. (1977). *Discipline and Punish*. London: Allen Lane.
Grenier, L., and Guibalt, J. (1990). ' "Authority" Revisited: The "Other" in Anthropology and Popular Music Studies', *Ethnomusicology*, 34.3: 381– 97.
Hayward, V. (1996). 'The Ballads of Cordoba Gaol', *Independent on Sunday* (6 Oct.): 40–1.
Leblon, B. (1995). *Gypsies and Flamenco*. Hatfield: University of Hertfordshire Press.
Manuel, P. (1989). 'Andalusian, Gypsy and Class Identity in the Contemporary Flamenco Complex', *Ethnomusicology*, 33.1: 47–65.
Mitchell, T. (1994). *Flamenco Deep Song*. New Haven: Yale University Press.
Pasqualino, C. (1995). 'Dire le chant: anthropologie sociale des gitans de Jerez de la Frontera', doctoral thesis. Paris: École des Hautes Études en Sciences Sociales.
Peaker, A. (ed.) (1996). 'Creative Time: The Second European Conference on Theatre and Prison, 10–13 April 1996', conference proceedings, University of Manchester.
Pohren, D. (1988). *Lives and Legends of Flamenco*. Madrid: Gráficas Flavián.

54   Parvati Nair

Steingress, G. (1991). *Sociología del cante jondo*. Jerez de la Frontera: Centro Andaluz de Flamenco.
Unit for the Arts and Offenders (1996). 'Music in Criminal Justice Settings', report, University of Loughborough.
Washabaugh, W. (1996). *Flamenco: Passion, Politics and Popular Culture*. Oxford: Berg.

4

Ethnic and Racial Configurations in Contemporary Spanish Culture

ISABEL SANTAOLALLA

IN modern times Spain has seen itself, with due acknowledgement of an endogamous gypsy community, as an ethnically homogeneous country. Even though under Franco lip-service was paid to the idea of cultural heterogeneity, the real force of the regime's propaganda lay in its emphasis on a unifying concept of nationalism, to some degree acknowledging regional difference, but stressing shared historical and cultural legacies, and glossing over the country's non-European ethnic and racial traditions. Yet the denial of that heritage in the self-perception of the majority of the population is coming under increasing pressure at a time of changing cultural and social patterns. The Spain of the last decade or so has seen increased immigration— Portuguese, North African, Sub-Saharan, South American, Filipino —while the growing conspicuousness of ethnic and racial minorities beyond traditional metropolitan settings is forcing Spaniards to contend with new socio-economic circumstances. Although a number of studies attest to a greater awareness of the sociological, economic, legal, or humanitarian issues involved, there is a surprising lack of work willing to engage with the more cultural or ideological dimensions of the phenomenon (analyses, say, of the type carried out in Britain by Stuart Hall or Paul Gilroy, to mention just two).[1] This study will examine the extent to which some instances of the media

---

[1] Recent studies are Calvo Buezas (1995), Ramírez (1996), Izquierdo (1996), Tello (1997), San Román (1997), Gregorio (1998), Manzanos (1999), or the SOS Racismo *Informe anual sobre el racismo en el estado español* (1999). Television programmes and documentaries on the topic include *Catarsis* (1997), *Ponte en su piel* (1993), *Inmigrantes: la vida por un papel* (1997), *Emigrante, negro, busca* (1997), *Inmigrantes: en manos de las mafias* (1997), to mention a few.

—film, TV sitcoms, and advertising—can be used to track changing patterns in formulations of ethnic and cultural identity in contemporary Spain.

Over the last few years, Spanish culture—particularly popular culture—has seen an escalation in the propagation of 'ethnically loaded' images, rhythms, and stories. These images do more than simply reflect the changing reality of an increasingly multi-ethnic society. Ideological and rhetorical mechanisms turn representation into a process of production, rather than one of simple replication: inherent in representation are a series of manipulative processes—which Becker identifies as 'selection', 'translation', 'arrangement', and 'interpretation' (1986: 121–35)—that can, and often do, place the subject and object of enunciation in an unbalanced power relation. The fact that these workings are camouflaged or even erased from the final product turns representation into a productive instrument of hegemonic discourse. As Hall insists (1990: 222), identity is a 'production', which is 'never complete, always in process, and always constituted within, not outside, representation'.

All this acquires special relevance in discussion of issues related to minority groups, because the consequences of the manipulative powers of representation have been felt with special intensity by those lacking access to the channels of representation, who have been 'defined' by dominant groups on their own terms. We are all 'ethnically located', but the hegemony traditionally exercised by white ethnicities has resulted in whiteness being naturalized as the norm, as a non-marked ethnic identity. Opposed to the 'invisibility' of whiteness, 'coloured' identities become subject to processes of categorization and stereotyping, with the subsequent propagation of interested definitions of ethnic identity. The need to respond to the dominant ethnic image-making has led to radical re-examinations of these processes, and it can be argued that the most interesting insights on the question have been predicated by and in relation to individuals connected with the postcolonial experience.

Although in the strictest sense postcolonial theory and criticism concern themselves with the effects of (European) colonization on societies and cultures, in a wider sense they bear witness, to cite Homi Bhabha, to 'the unequal and uneven forces of cultural representation involved in the contest for political and social authority within the modern world order' (1994: 171). Bhabha's reflections—an eclectic combination of original thought and reformulation of concepts such as Said's 'orientalism', Foucault's 'discursive formations', Freud's 'fetishism', and Bakhtin's 'hybridization'—acquire special relevance here, as they offer a key perspective for examining not only the poetics but also the politics governing the representation of ethnic minorities in contemporary Spain, whether or not their presence bears any relation to the country's remote colonial history.

Much recent thinking and writing on the representation of racial and ethnic Otherness is indebted to Said's concept of 'orientalism', a term through which he refers to the network of discourses which the West, using the stereotype as its main strategy, has relied on for the creation and projection of an image of the Orient that serves its own interests (Said 1987). Bhabha reformulates Said's notion of the stereotype by emphasizing its essentially ambivalent nature, which he relates to Freud's theory of sexual fetishism, inasmuch as the stereotype allows the individual to perceive the object of his or her anxieties as, citing Bhabha again, 'at once an "other" and yet entirely knowable and visible' (1983: 23), thus depriving it of much of its threatening potential. But when Bhabha refuses to accept fixity as an essential constituent of the stereotype and replaces it with his concept of ambivalence, he is not only rejecting deterministic and dogmatic modes of analysis, but also empowering the Other—that subject which is 'at once an object of desire and derision' (1983: 19)—with destabilizing potential. Because the stereotype is 'as anxious as it is assertive', the discourse which strategically uses it inevitably exposes its slipperiness and ambivalence in the very process of proclaiming its authority.

This chapter will analyse the images of 'racialized' or 'ethnicized' identities in some instances of present-day Spanish culture in a way that moves beyond the mere 'positive/negative image' taxonomy, in order, as Bhabha suggests, to interrogate 'the discursive and disciplinary place from which questions [about such identities] are strategically and institutionally posed' (1987: 5). The wider aim of this approach is to explore the ways in which cultural narratives are modifying or reformulating collective Spanish identity. This is what Bhabha—in line with arguments advanced by political analysts such as Gellner (1964), Seton-Watson (1977), Anderson (1987), and Hobsbawm (1991)—calls the 'cultural construction of nationness' in his essay 'DissemiNation', where he draws attention to 'the complex strategies of cultural identification and discursive address that function in the name of "the people" or "the nation" and make them the immanent subjects of a range of social and literary narratives' (1994: 140).

The mass media are generally recognized as privileged sources for the construction of collective identity, since they are the site where the dynamics between globalization and localism, as well as between modernization and tradition, are more dramatically staged. The recent new display of ethnic identities in the Spanish mass media demands analysis of the narratives in which they are inscribed. Although images of ethnicity share a common trait—namely that they are often constructed as a 'they' different from the normative 'we'—it would be simplistic to assume that all 'non-whites' are assigned a single role in Spanish culture: each ethnic identity has specific associated meanings, and the differences as well as the similarities in the treatment of the various groups demand attention, as do the contexts in which they appear. Consequently, in the section that follows, representations of gypsies and of immigrants are discussed under separate headings.

'OTHER' BODIES

Gypsies: Insider Others

Gypsies have lived uninterruptedly in Spain for almost four centuries, yet they are still regarded as an Other, distinct from normative Spanishness, and continue to suffer virulent social and representational discrimination. Until very recently, representations of gypsyness have almost exclusively carried either the mark of criminality and marginalization or the double trace of 'exoticism' and 'authenticity' as strategies to promote the image of a genuine 'España de charanga y pandereta' [folkloric and festive Spain], both for domestic consumption and for touristic purposes. Even the language, to this day, clings to old habits as gypsyness is habitually identified with negative connotations—as in Jordi Pujol's recommendation to the citizens of Barcelona not to behave 'como gitanos' [like gypsies] towards visitors at the 1992 Olympic Games (Dolç i Gastaldo 1996: 173).

Nevertheless, against this rather bleak background a breakthrough would seem to have taken place: gypsyness is becoming more 'respectable' and even fashionable both in Spain and abroad. The present situation, however, clearly differs from earlier periods when the projection of gypsyness became fashionable, as for instance in the cinema of the Second Republic and early Francoism, where—as Labanyi has argued—gypsyness helped construct the folkloric as 'the basis of a national popular cinema' in the former case, and 'as an instrument of nation formation' in the latter (1997: 221). Now flamenco music has migrated from a folkloric ghetto to international stages and screens: Joaquín Cortés's dance spectacle *Pasión gitana* triumphed at major venues world-wide and, dressed by fashion designers, Cortés himself was converted into a glamorous ethnic sex icon both in Spain and abroad (a profile heightened by press attention to his short-lived romance with black 'top model' Naomi Campbell). It could be argued that, in beginning to share international fascination with 'roots' and the 'exotic', Spain has sought to incorporate its own local ethnic subjects into the more global flux of images. Significantly, this is done in ways that emphasize those images that construct them as modern, eclectic, and hybridizing agents. This does not necessarily represent an unambiguously positive move for gypsies themselves. Although current images tend to compare favourably with earlier ones, their insistence on an essentialist notion of gypsyness may lead to a counter-productive fixity, as gypsies continue to be represented as 'ethnic', as opposed to 'normal', Spaniards.[2]

The cinema, too, has shown an interest in projecting a made-over image of gypsy culture. Carlos Saura's *Sevillanas* (1994) and *Flamenco* (1995) are good examples of a desire to project the potential for modernity of gypsy hybridity. In the latter, an emphatic avant-garde design manifest in the setting, and an insistence on the fusion of tradition and contemporaneity, govern the film from beginning to end. The aesthetics of this film clearly differ from the more patronizing, semi-ethnographic style of earlier instances of documentaries of this kind, such as Edgar Neville's *Duende y misterio del flamenco* [*Magic and Mystery of Flamenco*] (1952). In the Saura film, Manzanita and Ketama bring the film to a climactic ending located firmly in modernity, presented as an index of the evolution of the genre and, by extension, of the gypsy race. Elsewhere, Ketama's 'nuevo flamenco' [New Flamenco] rhythms were also interestingly used by Fernando Colomo as the score for his London-based comedy

---

[2] Perceval (1995) identifies a similar ambivalence in his discussion of the frequently harmful implications of xenophiliac as well as xenophobic discourses of identity.

El efecto mariposa [*The Butterfly Effect*] (1995). The film's closing sequence shows Ketama performing with Rosario Flores on a
London open-air stage at a utopian Millennium Eve Party, with
British and Spanish members of the audience dancing together to the
beat of their syncretic music.[3]

But although some ground has clearly been gained, old habits die
hard. Even well-intentioned films determined to avoid stereotypical
depictions of gypsyness sometimes fall victim to the related dangers
of fetishization and tokenism, as the 'ethnic' characters are often presented as metonymies of gypsyness, rather than as individual characters in their own right. *Alma gitana* [*Gypsy Soul*] (Chus Gutiérrez,
1995) and *Calé* [*Gypsy*] (Carlos Serrano, 1988) are two films that
exemplify this trend. For instance, *Calé* (a film marketed as a *risqué*
exercise in the exploration of interracial lesbianism) fails, despite its
title, to foreground the subjectivity of the gypsy woman (Rosario
Flores), concerned as it is with the personal and spiritual evolution of
the *paya* [non-gypsy woman] (Mónica Rándall). More positively,
however, the film appears to be aware of its own lapses, particularly
in the final scene, where the apparently 'utopian' triangular relationship formed by the two women and the white woman's boyfriend is
loaded with ambiguities inviting the spectator to read it as a sign that
relationships between *payos/as* and *gitanos/as* are inevitably characterized by unequal power structures. As the three drive away in a car,
the gypsy woman seems alienated not only from the world of the
payos, who sit at the front while she is relegated to the back seat, but
also from that of the gypsies who are performing in the streets, and
whom she can view only through the dividing car-window.

In the world of advertising, too, gypsyness has acquired greater visibility. Paralleling international fascination with 'roots' and racial
markers, gypsyness is used to conjure up, simultaneously, connotations of ancient 'authenticity' and modern 'youthfulness' and 'originality', all subject to the laws of the market for the promotion of,
say, cars (Joaquín Cortés's advertisement for Seat Ibiza), sunglasses
(Penélope Cruz in Andalusian outfit and designer glasses for General Ópticas), perfumes (María Pineda for 'Carmen' by Victorio &
Lucchino), crisps (as in the TV advert where a young German tourist bursts into flamenco song after eating an 'al estilo tradicional'

---

[3] Rosario Flores is one of the daughters of Lola Flores who, while not being herself
a gypsy, was one of the great icons of gypsyness in Spain from the 1940s onwards.

[traditional style] Matutano crisp), or designer clothes (as in the fashion feature for *El País Semanal* entitled 'Los Rodríguez, de pura casta' [The Rodriguez family, it runs in the blood], where an entire family of gypsies become models for a number of high-profile designers) (Vallés and López de Haro 1996). But the prevailing ambivalence that governs Spain's attitudes towards its gypsies is shockingly exposed in another fashion feature, also for *El País Semanal*, whose subtitle reads 'Inés Sastre, la modelo española más cotizada, [. . .] en un estilo que *resume con buen humor el tipismo andaluz*' [Inés Sastre, Spain's most highly valued model, in a style which *amusingly encapsulates typical Andalusian characteristics*' (López de Haro 1992: 78, my emphasis). Here, as in various of the previous examples, Andalusianness (evoked in the title) is in fact conflated with gypsyness (displayed through the images): the glamorous non-gypsy model appears centre-stage, in one picture shot against the blurred background image of a gypsy shanty town, in another holding hands with a gypsy street-child, and in yet another cross-dressing as a gypsy 'patriarch'. Thus the gypsy domain is invaded, and the markers of an essentialist, stereotyped version of it are appropriated as a mask, while the reality concealed by it is kept at a safe distance. Here, as in many other instances (Santaolalla 2000), the signs of ethnicity are lost in a vague and generic exoticism, at the limits of its own—to use Gallini's phrase, coined in another context (1998: 229)—'semantic dispersion'.

Immigrants: Outsider Others

Even when glamorized to such an extent as in this last example, gypsyness—the home-grown exotic—is not enough to satisfy the need for images of fetishized 'difference'. In glossy magazine adverts, a variety of more 'foreign' forms of exotica allows the Spanish consumer to fantasize over images that are constructed as clearly distant and yet easily accessible: a Playtex swimsuit turns women readers into the Maharani of the Moghul Indian palace seen in the background; the scent 'Jaipur' calls up the ambience of an eroticized Orient (synecdochically visualized as a naked female back); 'Cacharel pour L'Homme' takes men (so the advertisement reads) 'al encuentro del pueblo mauritano' [to an encounter with the Mauritanian people], allowing safe temporary identification with the manly nomad hovering behind the transparent bottle of perfume.

But these romanticized and eroticized images of Otherness belong almost exclusively to the world of press and magazine adverts or TV commercials. They tend to remain rather distinct from the treatment and meanings that members of those same ethnic communities acquire when they are inserted in the increasing number of fictional film texts that foreground the reality of immigration in present-day Spain, where they almost inevitably become pathologized characters in realistic problem-narratives, very often carrying a (sometimes only pseudo-) liberal message. These texts may be seen to work on two levels. First, as an exposure of the discrepancy between the expectations and realities of immigrant communities in Spain; and second, as a projection of the fantasy of Spain's further integration into that elite group of European countries whose economic status precisely attracts such immigration. In spite of all the problems and difficulties associated with immigration, it is perhaps reassuring for many to see Spain represented no longer as a country of emigrants but as somebody else's Utopia.[4]

Montxo Armendáriz's *Las cartas de Alou* [*Alou's Letters*] (1990), for instance, relies on 'road movie' conventions to narrate the odyssey of a young Senegalese man (Mulie Jarju) travelling from southern to northern Spain. The film maintains a difficult balance between empathy and distance, retaining the Otherness of the main character while also engaging the audience's emotional involvement—an identification to a large extent achieved by the device of conveying his words and thoughts in his native African language, the Spanish translation given only in subtitles.

For its part, Imanol Uribe's *Bwana* (1995) concentrates on the reaction of a conventional family who receive the shock of their lives when, during a Sunday picnic on the beach, they bump into a black African immigrant (Emilio Buale) who has just reached Spanish shores on a raft. The subjectivity of the black character is never explored (or even allowed expression, since his words are left purposely untranslated almost throughout), as the narrative's interest lies in the disruptive effects of the white madrileño family's encounter with the Other. The film has, however, a subversive potential that

---

[4] In this respect, Oliván's contention (1998) that contemporary European discourses of nationalism are to a large extent shaped by the role that minorities play as the 'functionally marginal' force sustaining an otherwise unsustainably competitive capitalist economy can usefully be applied to analysis of the role of ethnic minorities in Spanish culture. Oliván acknowledges his debt to Rubert de Ventós (1993).

stems from the ambivalence which Bhabha (1994) has shown to characterize the representation of the colonized. As I have argued elsewhere (Santaolalla 1999), regardless of the secondary position and fetishization ascribed to him by both story-line and camerawork, the black character emerges as the representative of a heroic, 'natural' masculinity, and as a positive antithesis to the *machista*, outwardly masterful but ultimately incompetent, Spanish male (Andrés Pajares).

Less ambiguous is *La fuente amarilla* [*The Yellow Fountain*] (Miguel Santesmanes, 1999), a film that resists political correctness and the opportunity to offer a positive version of immigrant life in Spain. The film's narrative reinforces every conceivable negative stereotype about the Chinese community, to the extent that the Chinese Embassy sought to prevent it from being shot and released. And yet, beyond its blatant representational abuse, the film does encourage audience identification with its sharp, energetic, sensitive mixed-race girl protagonist. One of Spanish cinema's few representations of second-generation immigrants, her role could be seen at least in part as an empowering portrait of Spain's emergent hybrid identities.

Changing social patterns in Spain are also providing material for both public and private television channels, where significant developments have taken place, especially in relation to the recent emergence and popularity of home-grown situation comedies, modelled on the successful American sitcom genre. A first phase, which saw the creation by TVE of a *taller de comedias* [sitcom workshop] towards the end of the 1980s, was soon followed by a second, as the private TV channels Antena 3 and Telecinco took up the genre, with national sitcom production rising dramatically (Maqua 1995: 140–1). As stated by Eduardo Esquide, executive producer of TVE, the main objective of these comedies is to produce 'un tipo de humor entendible para los espectadores españoles' [a kind of humour intelligible to Spanish viewers] (1993: 54), and their success, according to José Velasco, executive producer of Zeppelin TV, is attributable to the fact that people see 'cosas próximas, personajes cercanos, actores reconocidos y así se identifican más' [familiar characters, situations, and recognizable actors, all of which makes identification easier] (*Anuario* 1998: 206).

Given that television sitcoms are clearly intent on providing the spectator with familiar, recognizable images and stories, their content would appear to be key to the understanding of the audience's collective imaginary. But to concentrate exclusively on content would be to distort the impact of these programmes, since the symbolic procedures which construct collective identity (a sense of the self, strategies of inclusion and exclusion, a sense of historical memory) are different from—and sometimes even opposed to—the avowed intent of the mass media: access to a global market, interest in foreign affairs, the immediacy of an extended present (Wolf 1994: 196). Moreover, television products are not addressed to the whole of the viewing community but to a very specific segment of it, and thus its images and messages will only be relevant to a specific and variable social 'formation' (Fiske 1993: 121). Although more space would be needed for a full treatment of these issues, a few hypotheses can be provisionally advanced about the three main uses to which Spanish TV sitcoms put racial and ethnic characters.

There is, first, the inclusion, among the regular leads, of a 'token' ethnic character in what may look at least partly like an exercise in political correctness: the black female characters in *Canguros* [*Babysitters*] (Antena 3) and *Hermanas* [*Sisters*] (Telecinco)—their 'difference' clearly marked as unthreatening by the fact that they are a young babysitter and a nun respectively—come into this category.

Secondly, an ethnic character occasionally appears as the temporary protagonist of a story-line with a politically correct message: as in *Farmacia de guardia* [*24-Hour Chemist*] (Antena 3), one of whose episodes is devoted to the exposure of racist attitudes; or in *Médico de familia* [*Family Doctor*] (Telecinco), where ingrained prejudices about blackness are targeted as one of the characters at one point takes a black French doctor for a displaced African immigrant; or in *Ellas son así* [*Women are Like That*] (Telecinco) and *Periodistas* [*Journalists*] (Telecinco), where the hardships of immigrant life in 1990s Spain are highlighted through the plights of a Cuban lesbian in the former and an African male in the latter. When Vaca Berdayes praises *Farmacia de guardia* for its episode on racist attitudes and states that 'el medio televisivo puede ayudar a todos y servir de guía en comportamientos de solidaridad humanos' [TV can help everyone, and inspire public-spirited behaviour] (1997: 290), he is pointing to what seems to be a common didactic agenda behind recent expressions of Otherness in significant instances of Spanish mass culture.

Finally, a third category involves those instances where the inclusion of stereotypical ethnic(ized) characters serves comic purposes: examples include the Chinese and Argentine cooks in *Tío Willy* [*Uncle Willy*] (TV1), the black Cuban assistant in *La casa de los líos* [*Trouble in the House*] (Antena 3), or the 'moro' [Moor] in *Makinavaja* (TV2). Reliance on stereotypical characters is a recognized feature of TV sitcoms—together with the use of single locations (usually indoors), canned laughter, comic situations, and autonomous episodes. The problem here is that, because opportunities for the representation of ethnic minorities are still very limited, every ethnic character becomes a token for his or her community—a burden not shared by members of the dominant ethnic group (Mercer 1990).

In discussion of the foreign Other, Hispanic Americans deserve special mention, in the sense that, through historical, cultural, linguistic, and even literal family connections, their Otherness is of a relative rather than absolute nature. However, while historically Hispanic Americanness has hardly been alien to Spanish culture, its connotations in the 1990s have varied significantly. Like other 'exotic' material, Hispanic Americanness has also begun to acquire a higher profile in the Spanish media. This may be due partly to the increasing visibility of Latino culture internationally—above all, of course, in the United States. Salsa and carnival, for instance, inspire advertisements—in particular, for rum: Bacardi, Havana Club, Barceló—in ways that systematically identify Latin Americanness with 'sex and fun'. The almost total indifference to the rules of political correctness in Spain (despite the efforts of some TV sitcoms mentioned above) means that this stereotypical connection between the exotic, racialized body and the erotic—most noticeable in the Tía María and Ducados ads, both of which feature voluptuous dark-skinned females—circulates practically unexamined and uncriticized.[5] These stereotypes are especially productive in the dissemination of images that promote the Caribbean—Cuba, in particular—as a tourist destination, whether cultural, hedonistic, or sexual.

Hispanic Americans have also become protagonists in cinematic narratives of immigration of the type outlined above. Thus *La sal de la vida* [*The Spice of Life*] (Eugenio Martín, 1995), *Cosas que dejé en La Habana* [*Things I Left Behind in Havana*] (Manuel Gutiérrez

[5] An interesting exception is the monographic ¿*Racismo en las imágenes?* (Moreno 1990).

Aragón, 1997), *En la puta calle* [*Fuck All*] (Enrique Gabriel, 1998), and *Flores de otro mundo* [*Flowers from Another World*] (Icíar Bollaín, 1999) place Caribbean immigrants at the centre of their narratives. Significantly, although the films encourage the audience's emotional identification with the immigrant character(s), they miss the opportunity to invite reflection on the (post)colonial implications of their presence as Hispanic American ex-colonial subjects in the Spanish ex-metropolis.

'OTHER' TIMES/SPACES

This lack of analysis forms part of a larger pattern of historical neglect. Currently, Spanish mass culture in general shows a surprising reticence towards narratives that deal with the country's colonial past. One of the very few recent films that does anchor its narrative in that 'temporal space' is *Lejos de África* [*Out of Africa*] (Cecilia Bartolomé, 1995). However, even here, the historical events are relegated to the background, as the interracial friendship between a white girl and a black girl in colonial Guinea (Alicia Bogo and Yanelis Bonifacio respectively) is in practice used to 'explain' the physical and emotional development of the white girl, whose subjectivity is immediately foregrounded through a voice-over narration in which Susana—now an adult woman—recounts her own story. One can only speculate about the extent to which *Lejos de África* was inspired by the proximity of the 1998 centenary marking the end of the Spanish Empire overseas and the thirtieth anniversary of the Independence of Equatorial Guinea. However, the release in 1998 of *Mambí* (Teodoro and Santiago Ríos)—a direct attack on Spanish colonialism and military intervention set in the year of the loss of Cuba—and the sudden rash of material on the topic produced that year—at conferences and in summer schools, TV documentaries, newspaper articles, books—seemed to indicate a renewed desire (in practice rather short-lived) to recuperate from an at last partly critical perspective that forgotten part of Spanish history. The reasons for this ongoing historical neglect are implicit in a remark made by the directors of *Mambí*: 'A nosotros [los canarios] nos resulta más fácil abordar el tema. No tenemos sentimiento de culpa y eso ha evitado que nos enfrentemos al desastre de Cuba con temor' [It is easier for us, coming from the Canary Islands, to deal with the topic.

We don't have a guilt complex, so we haven't felt reticent about facing the Cuban 'disaster'] (Martín-Lunas 1998: 56). Regardless of the validity of their explanation of the contemporary failure to narrativize Spain's colonial past, it is nevertheless clear that present-day circumstances dictate the country's attitudes towards its own past. If Spanish mass culture shows a surprising indifference to the country's colonial history, this is surely partly due to the fact that—in contrast to, say, Britain—the idea of empire is almost totally absent from the collective imaginary of present-day Spaniards, of whatever social class or economic background. The length of time that has elapsed since Spain's status as an imperial nation, as well as its painful and progressive decline during the long decolonizing process, deprive that episode in its history of any market value in contemporary Spain. Although Franco's 'mission' had been to use Spain's colonial past as an ideological springboard for the promise of future national and international glory, the 'reality principle'—underdevelopment, isolation, repression—made the project sink into oblivion. With the advent of democracy, Spain seemed more concerned with the future and with its European dimension, and even the 500th anniversary of the Discovery of the Americas in 1992 did not manage to stir the Spanish colonial imagination into sustained creativity.

However, there is a sense in which that colonial past is being revisited in contemporary Spain, although perhaps not always consciously. In ways that recall Derrida's 'spectres' or Foucault's concept of a 'projective past'—whereby the past makes itself felt through a disguised presence which 'moves forward while continually encircling that moment of not-there' (Bhabha 1994: 254)—Spain's colonial legacy is making its presence felt through the regular appearance of Hispanic American characters, icons, locations, or stories (whether produced in Spain or co-produced with or purchased from a Latin American country) in mass culture. Besides the countless Latin American TV 'culebrones' [soap operas] or salsa music and dance performances, the cinema, too, is contributing to the abundance of images that are re-presenting Hispanic American-ness in the Spanish cultural market. Recent films like *Maité* (Eneko Olasagasti and Carlos Zabala, 1994), *Martín Hache* (Adolfo Aristaraín, 1997), *Sus ojos se cerraron* [*He Closed his Eyes*] (Jaime Chávarri, 1997), *Tango* (Carlos Saura, 1999), *El cuarteto de La Habana* [*The Havana Quartet*] (Fernando Colomo, 1999), to mention just a few, fit into a common symbolic space which reinscribes into Spain's present the collective Other which was—and at a deeper level perhaps still is—felt to be part of the country's collective identity.

CONCLUSION

Although most films, TV sitcoms, and adverts produced in Spain today may not be specifically concerned with questions of racial politics—the market is still predominantly mainstream and white—a growing number do now include 'ethnic' individuals or images of Otherness, whose mere presence counters their previous invisibility. According to Bhabha, the very act of representing Others creates a 'contact zone', a 'third space' of hybridity which, by virtue of its intrinsic ambivalence, allows other 'denied' knowledges to be heard (1986: 175). In this light, the new and increasingly varied spaces allocated to gypsies, immigrants, and ex-colonial subjects in Spanish culture could be seen to encourage—even if unintentionally in many cases—a re-examination of Spain's attitudes to its Others. However, the supposition that hybridity has a subversive power cannot be subscribed to unconditionally. As Spivak (1988), Ahmad (1992), Young (1995), and other cultural theorists have pointed out, Bhabha's notion of hybridity seems to ignore the negative semantic heritage of the term 'hybrid' as originally used in colonial discourse. Furthermore, because of its programmatic, conceptual nature, the notion of hybridity often fails to account for the specificities of local phenomena. This latter objection acquires special relevance in the Spanish instance. Contrary to the situation in other Western countries, the 'ethnic Other'—still lacking access to the channels of representation—has so far been the object, not the originator, of representation. Thus the visibility of hybridity in contemporary Spanish film, TV and advertising cannot be read as a subversive strategy used by the subaltern. Rather, it should largely be seen as a manifestation of Spain's eagerness to follow the global fashion for incorporating the hybrid into mainstream culture (Papastergiadis 1997: 257) or, to borrow the metaphor used by hooks (1992) and Root (1996), of 'devouring' or 'cannibalizing' the Other. Recent Spanish culture has discovered the value of Otherness—or, rather, of an edited version of Otherness which foregrounds a postmodern concern for ethnic authenticity and cultural hybridity while disavowing disturbing social realities—for reconciling the nation's desire for integration into the modernization and globalization process with a desire to retain the comforting feeling of continuity offered by local traditional culture.

WORKS CITED

Ahmad, A. (1992). *In Theory: Classes, Nations, Literatures.* London: Verso.

Anderson, B. (1983). *Imagined Communities: Reflections on the Origin and Spread of Nationalism.* London: Verso.

Anuario de la Televisión (1998). 'Las series nacionales protagonizan la temporada'. Madrid: GECA (Gabinete de Estudios de Comunicación Audiovisual), 206–10.

Appadurai, A. (1986). *The Social Life of Things.* Cambridge: Cambridge University Press.

Becker, H. S. (1986). 'Telling about Society', in *Doing Things Together.* Evanston, Ill.: Northwestern University Press, 121–35.

Bhabha, H. K. (1983). 'The Other Question...', *Screen*, 24.6: 18–36.

—— (1986). 'Signs Taken for Wonders: Questions of Ambivalence and Authority under a Tree outside Delhi, May 1817', in H. L. Gates, Jr. (ed.), *'Race', Writing and Difference.* Chicago: University of Chicago Press, 163–84.

—— (1987). 'Interrogating Identity', in *Identity. The Real Me: Postmodernism and the Question of Identity.* ICA Documents 6. London: ICA, 5–11.

—— (1994). *The Location of Culture.* London: Routledge.

Calvo Buezas, T. (1995). *Crece el racismo, también la solidaridad.* Madrid: Tecnos.

Dolç i Gastaldo, M. (1996). 'De la piràmide invertida al Políticament Correcte: del significat a la connotació', *Comunicació y Estudios Universitarios: Revista de Ciènces de la Informació*, 6: 169–75.

Esquide, E. (1993). 'Las cadenas preparan telecomedias para la próxima temporada', *El País* (24 May): 54.

Fiske, J. (1993). 'Audiencing: A Cultural Studies Approach to Watching Television', *Poetics*, 21.4: 345–59.

Gallini, C. (1998) [1996]. 'Mass Exoticisms', in I. Chambers and L. Curti (eds.), *The Postcolonial Question: Common Skies, Divided Horizons.* London: Routledge, 212–20.

Gellner, E. (1964). *Thought and Change.* London: Weidenfeld & Nicholson.

Gregorio Gil, C. (1998). *Migración femenina: su impacto en las relaciones de género.* Madrid: Narcea.

70 Isabel Santaolalla

Hall, S. (1990). 'Cultural Identity and Diaspora', in J. Rutherford (ed.), *Identity: Community, Culture, Difference*. London: Lawrence & Wishart, 222–37.

Hobsbawm, E. J. (1991) [1990]. *Nations and Nationalism since 1789: Programme, Myth, Reality*. Cambridge: Cambridge University Press.

hooks, b. (1992). 'Eating the Other. Desire and Resistance', in *Black Looks: Race and Representation*. Boston: South End Press, 21–39.

Izquierdo, A. (1996). *La inmigración inesperada: la población extranjera en España (1991–1995)*. Madrid: Trotta.

Labanyi, J. (1997). 'Race, Gender and Disavowal in Spanish Cinema of the Early Franco Period: The Missionary Film and the Folkloric Musical', *Screen*, 38.3: 215–31.

López de Haro, R. (1992). '¡Olé tu gracia!', *El País Semanal* (5 Apr.): 78–84.

Manzanos Bilbao, C. (1999). *El grito del otro: arqueología de la marginación racial*. Madrid: Tecnos.

Maqua, J. (1995). 'Sobre las risas enlatadas en las telecomedias españolas', *Archivos de la Filmoteca*, 19: 132–45.

Martín-Lunas, M. (1998). '*Mambí* no es oportunista', *El Mundo* (Madrid edn., 29 May): 56.

Mercer, K. (1990). 'Black Art and the Burden of Representation', *Third Text*, 10: 61–78.

Moreno Lorite, C. (1990). *¿Racismo en las imágenes? Un método para el análisis de imágenes fotográficas*. Madrid: SODEPAZ.

Oliván, F. (1998). *El extranjero y su sombra: crítica del nacionalismo desde el derecho de extranjería*. Madrid: San Pablo.

Papastergiadis, N. (1997). 'Tracing Hybridity in Theory', in P. Werbner and T. Modood (eds.), *Debating Cultural Hybridity: Multicultural Identities and the Politics of Anti-racism*. London: Zed Books, 257–79.

Perceval, J. M. (1995). *Nacionalismos, xenofobia y racismo en la comunicación: una perspectiva histórica*. Barcelona: Paidós.

Ramírez Goicoechea, E. (1996). *Inmigrantes en España: vidas y experiencias*. Madrid: Siglo XXI.

Root, D. (1996). *Cannibal Culture: Art, Appropriation, and the Commodification of Difference*. Boulder, Colo.: Westview Press.

Rubert de Ventós, X. (1993). *Los nacionalismos: el laberinto de la identidad*. Madrid: Espasa-Calpe.

Said, E. (1987) [1978]. *Orientalism*. London: Penguin.

San Román, T. (1997). *La diferencia inquietante: viejas y nuevas estrategias culturales de los gitanos*. Madrid: Siglo XX.

Santaolalla, I. (1999). 'Close Encounters: Racial Otherness in Imanol Uribe's *Bwana*', *Bulletin of Hispanic Studies*, 76: 111–22.

—— (2000). *'New' Exoticisms: Changing Patterns in the Construction of Otherness*. Amsterdam: Rodopi.

Seton-Watson, H. (1977). *Nations and States: An Enquiry into the Origins of Nations and the Politics of Nationalism*. Boulder, Colo.: Westview Press.

SOS Racismo (1999). *Informe anual sobre el racismo en el estado español*. Barcelona: Icaria Editorial.

Spivak, G. C. (1988). 'Can the Subaltern Speak?', in C. Nelson and L. Grossberg (eds.), *Marxism and the Interpretation of Culture*. Basingstoke: Macmillan, 271–313.

Tello, A. (1997). *Extraños en el paraíso: inmigrantes, desterrados y otras gentes de extranjera condición*. Barcelona: Flor del Viento.

Vaca Berdayes, R. (1997). *Quién manda en el mando: comportamiento de los españoles ante la televisión*. Madrid: Visor.

Vallés, A., and López de Haro, R. (1996). 'Los Rodríguez: de pura casta', *El País Semanal* (19 May): 86–93.

Wolf, M. (1994). 'Los medios de comunicación en la estructuración de la identidad colectiva: la coexistencia de lo contradictorio', in *Comunicación social: tendencias*. Informes Anuales de Fundesco. Madrid: Fundesco, 195–98.

Young, R. J. C. (1995). *Colonial Desire: Hybridity in Theory, Culture and Race*. London: Routledge.

5

Identities at a Distance: Markers of National Identity in the Video-Diaries of Second-Generation Spanish Migrants in London

CRISTINA MATEO

THIS chapter will discuss the markers of ethnic identity displayed by second-generation Spanish migrants in London (the sons and daughters of economic migrants who came to England in the early 1960s), illustrated by video-diaries made by them at my request. Volunteers were located by word of mouth through teachers and students at the Spanish School in Portobello, lecturers in Spanish departments at universities in London, and acquaintances who had contacts with second-generation members of the Spanish community. Once individuals expressed an interest, I arranged to meet them and explained that I would lend them my home video camera for a period of one month. The only instruction was to record a series of everyday scenes of their choice in order to illustrate their lives. I obtained a total of five video-diaries, three made by females and two by males. The video-diaries move between Spanish and English; I have quoted from them here in the original language used. It is important to clarify that, since these video-diaries form part of a wider ethnographic research project based on fieldwork validated by analysis of a variety of data, my discussion of the video-diaries is to a large extent based on information gathered from interviews with informants as well as on participant observation.

I hope to show how Spanish second-generation migrants construct a syncretic identity through use of a frontier language (Spanglish) together with a particular conception of a common past (characteristic of people with a diasporic experience) and the symbolic deployment of consumer practices. Such an identity is based on a refusal of essentialist labels that categorize them as a collective in binary terms as 'either Spanish or English', although, as we shall see, such essentialist labels are often deployed by them when referring to others. My use of the term 'syncretic' is intended as a critique of postmodern concepts of hybridity which often suppose a cultural amalgam free from conflict and unequal power relations. Here I follow the distinction made by Bécquer and Gatti (Werbner and Modood 1997: 447) for whom hybridity implies synthesis, whereas syncretism refuses synthesis and emphasizes contingency. Syncretic identity is, I contend, the more appropriate term for my research subjects because it assumes the precariousness of the identities (in this case Spanish and British) which, through their encounters, are modified and strategically reconstituted in an ongoing battle.

I shall focus on ethnicity as an aspect of identity since, in the diasporic situation experienced by second-generation migrants, identity is a means of patrolling ethno-cultural borders. Thus, for second-generation migrants living in the UK, 'identity at a distance' means watching British television, in many cases going to British schools, speaking English as well as or better than Spanish, yet constantly receiving information about Spain through periodic visits to the country, contact with relatives and friends, and exposure to the Spanish media. In addition, thanks to their parents' influence, second-generation migrants often go to Spanish social and religious events and may attend the Spanish School in Portobello or, in the case of those attending British schools, evening classes in Spanish language and culture. All these elements comprise their common past.

In trying to identify the strategies deployed by second-generation Spanish migrants in order to maintain a specific ethnicity, I have considered them as a youth subculture (Thornton 1995). My use of the term 'subculture' as an analytical tool does not suppose a group identity defined through resistance to a hierarchy of class or generation. Such a conception is problematic since it assumes that actors are fully aware of their cultural practices and that there is a coherent mainstream (Hall and Jefferson 1976; Hebdige 1979). I shall argue that there is a high degree of pre-reflectiveness and improvisation in the practices of these second-generation migrants, and that their notion of a mainstream is fluid and contingent.

All my research subjects—including the makers of the video-diaries as well as those filmed in them—are aged between 17 and 32. Although people in their thirties might not be considered part of youth culture, I argue in keeping with Thornton (1995: 102) that, since youth subcultures refuse to be fixed socially by investing in leisure, people older than 'traditional' youth may in certain circumstances—as with the second-generation migrants discussed here— find youth culture attractive as a way of postponing their social ageing. I hope to show that my research subjects operate as a subculture and at the same time are constructed in relation to, and form part of, a 'mythical mainstream' with three reference points. The first is Spain, understood as a place from their cultural past to which they might return but also as the now thoroughly European place which Spain has become since their parents—or they themselves if they have moved between countries—left. It is a mental space informed by images of Spaniards living in London, including members of the first generation, and of Spaniards in Spain, including relatives and friends. The second reference point is Britain, understood in the restricted sense of a place whose dominant cultural parameters are Anglo-Saxon. The third reference point is London as a site for syncretism and as a place where other displaced people (economic migrants, political refugees, etc.) originating from other parts of the world share a territory and make their lives. In this respect, the notion of a cosmopolitan London implies an entity that—however ambiguously —includes them, while Britain is an entity that excludes them.

As a youth subculture, second-generation migrants are immersed in what Bourdieu (1986) has called a 'stylization of life', as they loosen their ties with their families and at the same time postpone settling down with a partner or opting for a more fixed occupation. This period of experimentation with different roles and deferral of adult responsibilities has placed youth at the forefront of the search for and invention of new identities (Gilroy 1993). The video-diaries of my informants potentially reflect the symbolic structures used in this exploration process. However, on watching these video-diaries, one finds that they do not always convey a high degree of obviously significant data. Rather, they show people doing rather ordinary things which often seem to be of interest only to themselves. Sometimes what the participants say seems to be of no relevance whatsoever, as if the video were made purely to be kept on video cassette by them as a memory (I always give them a copy). At other times, they film things for an imagined public presumed to have a particular interest in what is being filmed: sometimes myself as someone from the Basque Country, sometimes a potential employer. For example, in one video, when some boys start to make jokes about ETA, another warns them, 'Cuidado, que la chica para la que estoy haciendo este vídeo es del País Vasco, y ¡a ver si se va a mosquear!' [Watch what you're saying because the woman I'm making this video for is from the Basque Country, and she may not like it!]. At another point in the same video-diary, the 30-year-old male making the film directed himself in Spanish to anyone 'out there' ('por ahí viendo el vídeo'), asking for a job as a graphic designer: 'Si necesitais un dibujo o un diseño, yo hago fotografía, diseño, dibujo, todo, ¡llamadme!, mi teléfono es...' [If you need something designed, a logo or something, I do photography, drawing, design, anything, call me, my number is...]. At certain points, the videos are addressed to an audience who has never been to England: one video-diary is introduced by a 17-year-old girl who addresses her remarks in Spanish to an imagined group of Spaniards who have just arrived in London, saying, 'Os enseñaré las mejores tiendas para comprar, los sitios más guay para pasarlo bien, discotecas, y así' [I'll show you the best shops to go shopping, the coolest places to go out and have a good time, clubs, etc.].

Apart from the shifting nature of the target audience, the subject position within each video-diary also changes. People are sometimes filmed talking and having a good time by one member of the group and then by another. Those being filmed may address themselves at certain points to the film-maker and at others to someone else. Sometimes a fixed camera is left to film everyday trivial events, such as washing up or people dancing at a party. It could be said that these video-diaries are not so much descriptive as performative. Here, I am referring to what Goffman (1959) terms the performative aspect of social identity, through which one is always attempting to influence other people's response to a specific identity. It could also be argued that the makers of these video-diaries are attempting to show the irrelevance of treating ethnicity as something different from the everyday. The everyday is important because it comprises pre-reflective habits (watching a particular soap or cooking food in a Spanish style) related to the concept of 'performative memory' developed by Connerton (1989), for whom some actions are passed on and reproduced by habit in an unconscious manner. Furthermore, many actions have an improvised quality. On one occasion, one of my informants stated that she was a Liverpool supporter because, when boarding the bus for her first day at school, she had to choose which side of the bus to sit on and, since her elder sister had chosen 'Chelsea', she chose the other option which was 'Liverpool'. The everyday also involves an intentionality which is often tactically deployed—as in de Certeau's concept of the tactics of the everyday (1988)—exemplified by their refusal to be classified as either English or Spanish, or even as second-generation Spanish migrants. To quote one example: 'Yo no soy como otros hijos de emigrantes que van todos los veranos a Galicia, yo prefiero irme a otros sitios, a Asia o Latinoamérica' [I'm not like those other members of the second generation who go back to Galicia every summer. I prefer travelling to other places like Asia or Latin America]. There are many statements of this kind, contrasting with their often stereotyped classification of Spanish or English people, and even of other members of the second generation; for example: 'La gente española suele salir mucho, en España la vida es más tranquila, es más fácil pasarlo bien' [Spaniards tend to go out a lot, in Spain life is more relaxed, it is easier to have fun] or: 'Aquí cuando la gente inglesa sale es para emborracharse. No se mezclan, creen que todo lo inglés es lo mejor' [When English people go out they get drunk and that's it, they don't mix, they think everything English is the best]; or: 'Hay gente aquí, hijos de emigrantes, que van casi todos lo veranos a Galicia de vacaciones, y eso es todo lo que saben de España' [People from the second generation often go to Galicia every summer and that's all they know about Spain]. This simplification, I would argue, is necessary to deal with the complex ethnic reality of their everyday lives.

These video-diaries must be viewed on two levels: as narrative accounts that provide access to cultural worlds, and as self-reflexive statements about the forms in which these cultural worlds manifest themselves. The narrative is shaped by the interaction between an implied spectator who changes in the course of the video-diary and the film-maker who may also change during the filming process. These shifts in the imagined audience determine the locations chosen and the narrative structure taken by the individual sequences: each video consists in several sequences, each filmed in a different location. This can be related to Goffman's idea of multiple 'stages' in the sense of specific social scenarios in which interaction is formally or informally organized. In the video-diaries, these scenarios may comprise the informant's bedroom; an interview with the informant's girlfriend/boyfriend or a member of the family; or everyday group or leisure activities. Narrative links are established through interviews or by the use of voice-over. For example, in one instance there is a voice-over presentation of the objects which the film-maker believes may be of interest to the researcher as imagined spectator. In another video, the girl filming the video-diary and her sister show all the objects in their rooms and the clothes in their wardrobes which they think the researcher might find relevant, such as a map of Spain or a flamenco costume. Each girl does this by pointing at the object with the camera while using voice-over to describe its significance. At other times, the film-maker simply provides a succession of random images amounting to a recollection of the moment, or indeed of a succession of unrelated moments. For instance, in one video-diary a fixed camera first films people dancing at an engagement party, then records the cooking of Christmas dinner. This can again be related to the nature of everyday actions which, as stated above, are a mix of the intentional (showing important ethnic markers such as a flamenco costume), the pre-reflective (showing a group of young men watching a Spanish football match on television as an illustration of something they frequently do), and the improvised (such as the aimless filming of cooking or dancing). The implication here is that identity is contingent and, as such, shifting. I am here combining Goffman's notion of the everyday as a site where certain repertoires of interaction are routinely enacted (Goffman 1959) with the poststructuralist refusal of essentialism characteristic of postcolonial discourse (I shall return to this). This combined methodology allows for a concept of ethnicity whereby one informant, as stated in an interview, can in one setting enjoy the rumba and the pasodoble, and in another appreciate the humour of Monty Python.

In these video-diaries one must bear in mind that the narrative structures used may be influenced by video-diaries recently shown on television (a frequent format in programmes aimed at young people or travel programmes), or by 'real-life advertising' such as the recent Superdrug campaign in the form of a home video depicting a series of young women using a particular Superdrug product as they normally would 'off-camera'. In fact, all the volunteers have a particular interest in film, journalism, or the social sciences (several are students of these disciplines). Such intertextual references additionally provide a comment on the participants' cultural identifications. Here it must be remembered that shifts in implied audience and subject position are intrinsic to all forms of ethnographic representation, particularly when the medium is visual. Video-diaries are thus particularly problematic sources of ethnographic information (Chaplin 1994: 186; Cubitt 1991: 59–61) for they involve the interpretation of everyday life not only through words but also through visual images whose interpretation is open.

It must also be remembered that the evidence provided by these video-diaries is necessarily partial and limited: only five have been made to date. Thus, although the video-diaries are useful sources if supplemented with other data (as they are here with interview data and participant observation), they have the value of forcing the researcher (myself) to question my own privileged interpretation. For there is space in the video data for other possible readings, since different viewers can select different images as the basis of their interpretation. I have deliberately left the videos in their original un-edited form so as not to curtail their openness. The shifts in imagined audience and subject position in these video-diaries highlight the inter-actional process at stake in the everyday. This is central to the theoretical premises of my research.

As stated above, my analysis of ethnic identity is based both on the concept of social interaction and on a poststructuralist position which sees ethnicity as a discursive construction (Derrida 1981), in which language and memory play an important role. My use of post-structuralism comes largely via postcolonial theory with its stress on cultural hybridity, despite my preference for the term 'syncretism' and my rejection of postcolonial theory's abstract analysis of ethnicity (Bhabha 1990; Chambers 1990) and my belief in the need for historical contextualization. Many poststructuralist studies of ethnicity leave out the dominant identities which by definition they should address, concentrating only on the dominant culture's 'Others'. In discussing the ethnic identity of second-generation Spanish migrants, I shall attempt to address both their identities as 'Others' and their relation to various dominant identities: Spanish visitors to London; Spaniards in Spain; the English; other British citizens. In this respect, my project follows certain aspects of Stuart Hall's analysis of identity as a process always in the making and never complete (Hall and De Gay 1996). According to Hall, identity is made up of sameness and difference: on the one hand, there is a common 'past' which may or may not be fictitious; on the other hand, we each reconstruct the past differently. Every position that marks boundaries of difference is established in relation to different points of reference; consequently every individual's identity is positioned in relation to several allegiances. In the case of the Spanish migrant community in London, I have argued that they are positioned in relation to at least three reference points: Spain, Britain, and London. These reference points constitute mental maps or landscapes through which they deal with ethnicity in everyday life. The relative importance of these reference points changes according to generation and life-stage. The video-diaries discussed here cannot be taken to represent the second generation as a whole since they capture only one life-stage: youth. They do, however, illustrate the impact of particular influences at a particular life-stage.

Belonging to a specific generation is significant because, unlike their parents for whom migration was temporary and economically motivated, most Spanish second-generation migrants are experienced settlers who have migrated and settled two if not three times. They have often gone back to live in Spain and then moved back to England with or without their parents. This equips them with considerable expertise in the management of their minority status, the reconstruction of identity, and the negotiation of cultural systems. For this reason, they may feel close to other people in similar biographical circumstances who are not of Spanish origin. Commonality of origin is not, therefore, necessarily defined by country of origin, but may be tied to a similar diasporic experience. Thus, biographical experiences shared by, say, Spanish and Italian second-generation migrants are crucial for the ever-unstable differentiation between 'them' and 'us'. This is illustrated in one of the video-diaries when a girl, speaking in Spanish, describes London as a very cosmopolitan place and then films the performance by a group of Chinese teenagers of a well-known American pop song as part of the Chinese New Year celebrations. The second generation's interest in other communities of similar diasporic origin is further demonstrated in another video-diary in which passers-by of Afro-Caribbean origin are asked to talk about the English, as well as in their use of linguistic borrowings from Afro-American and Afro-Caribbean culture when responding in English to questions on their ethnicity.

All this highlights the need to see syncretic identity as comprised of non-fixed boundary markers—a 'frontier language' or a shared past —which attempt to evade definition in terms of the binary opposition 'either Spanish or English'. 'Spanglish' operates as a perfect site of struggle against such binary constructions. In other words, syncretic identity means not being 'Spanish or English' but being something in-between. As a significant component of national identity, language can operate as a shifting marker of any diasporic group. The second-generation migrants studied in my research inhabit a position from which they think they know what being cool and trendy is in both Spain and Britain. They do this by using narratives of cosmopolitanism and irreverent irony when dealing with ethnicity. These narratives are located in interstitial positions between the three reference points listed above.

Thus the second generation use a narrative of cosmopolitanism based on the belief that they posses superior knowledge, similar to Bourdieu's analysis of the knowledge of the autodidact (Bourdieu 1977). In this case, this knowledge is not necessarily self-taught but derived from social origin, sometimes complemented by educational capital (as with those who go to the Spanish School in Portobello or to Spanish language and culture classes). In other words, their body of knowledge is rather like the cultural capital passed from generation to generation by members of the bourgeoisie, with the crucial difference that here this knowledge is undervalued by both the English and the Spanish because it is often not institutionally legitimized. In other words, they speak two languages and know about two cultures but do not always have the relevant diplomas. In fact, their knowledge is generally based on unconscious habit transmitted through repetition (Connerton 1989): for example, the memory of children's songs sung to them by their parents; or their media viewing, especially television. This lack of a legitimized past is compensated by a process of creative appropriation. This is seen in one sequence of a video-diary made by a Chelsea supporter who defines himself as a 'Spaniard' who lives in London and has supported Chelsea all his life. In this sequence, he tells the story of a well-known Spanish Chelsea supporter, nicknamed 'Vidi Vidi', known for being a hooligan. This story, emphasizing the supporter's nationality and the football team he supported, provides the maker of the video with the sense of a legitimized past.

It is also worth noting that the video-diaries' frequent ironic irreverence constitutes a dismissal of the high seriousness of the definitions of ethnicity in terms of language and common history found in much postcolonial theory. In one of the video-diaries, the film-maker—a 20-year-old female student—chose to interview her boyfriend who is half-Russian and half-Spanish. When asked by her in English whether having a Spanish mother had influenced him, he replied, 'In what way, how?', and when the question was clarified he ignored it and carried on talking about the programme he was watching on TV. After that, his girlfriend asked him to explain why he was wearing a T-shirt with a Spanish logo on it, and he said that it was an interesting story and that, if she wanted, he would tell her about it. He then recounted how his mother had been visiting the part of Spain her family came from. One of her brothers (his uncle), who worked for the local council, had been organizing an event promoted by, among other things, T-shirts, several of which he gave to the interviewee's mother who brought them back to London. The interviewee ended with the flippant comment 'so ends the story of the Spanish T-shirt', undermining the significance of what had been set up as an ethnic marker. In other instances, the aim is self-mockery. For example, in one of the video-diaries the male film-maker introduced in Spanish one of his friends in whose house they were filming as follows: 'César, gallego, hijo de emigrantes ¿qué tal?' [Hi César from Galicia, child of migrant parents!]. This comment shows a high degree of self-consciousness intended to inform the viewer (me) of their awareness of the topicality of the subject of ethnic identity, to the point either of not wanting to talk about it any more or of mocking the self-important tone of such debates. In another video-diary, a couple of young males watching *Eastenders* make jokes by moving between Spanish and English, with one of the characters Grant becoming 'la beca' [the grant] and another character Doctor Legg becoming 'Doctor Pierna' [Doctor Leg]. This brings an explicit ironic irreverence to the act of watching an English institution such as *Eastenders*, which they stereotypically categorize as a very English habit. In this way they comment ironically on their awareness of what being stereotypically English means. Indeed, when referring to their viewing of the soap they state that they do it 'como inglesitos' [like proper English folks]; the use of the diminutive in Spanish makes the irony obvious. These comments express a clear desire not to be classified from the outside as either English or Spanish. At the same time, it must be remembered that the video-diaries force people to talk about themselves and they may resort to the flippant remarks noted above as a tactic for dealing with their self-consciousness, rather than as a way of refusing ethnicity. This self-consciousness may itself be a response to feeling forced to talk about themselves as members of a group constituted from the outside, as in my categorization of them as 'second-generation Spanish migrants'. They may thus simply be refusing categorization by others, rather than ethnicity as such. This is suggested by the fact that, in group discussions, they tend to deploy a rather stereotyped categorization of others. For example, when commenting on advertising in Spain and Britain in a group discussion organized by a teacher, they made statements such as 'En España no hay censura en los medios de comunicación, y aquí sí' [In Spain there's no censorship of the media, unlike in Britain].

I have argued so far that the second generation attempt to refuse classification as members of a group through the use of narratives of cosmopolitanism and ironic irreverence. This coexists with their use of a common syncretic language (Spanglish) and their appeal to a common past (the sharing of key life-events such as going to Spanish language and culture classes, summer trips to Spain, or sharing habits inherited by parents such as knowing how to prepare Spanish food). Thus they also make the following kinds of statement: 'Claro que tenemos cosas en común, yo puedo entenderlos, las razones por las que han tomado ciertas decisiones, y las consecuencias de hacer eso' [Of course we have things in common, I can understand them and their reasons for taking certain decisions, and the consequences]. The apparent contradiction between their refusal to be classified as a group and their evident commonality shows that the second generation cannot be seen as a straightforward, uniform group. Here Hall's argument that identity is made up of sameness and difference is useful, since it reminds us that, in addition to the relationship of sameness and difference that exists between different cultures, any one group or community will contain significant differences within it. Such differences between members of the community manifest themselves symbolically through conflict. The ethnic identity of individual members of the community is never fixed because they are always attempting to cope with the ambivalence of the term 'community', which implies a common culture and identity at the same time as the existence of differences. This is illustrated clearly by the variety of responses found by the makers of one video-diary (a group of 17- and 18-year-olds) when interviewing passers-by, some of whom were other second-generation members from the Spanish School in Portobello, on the subject of 'the English'. For instance, responses such as 'No están mal' [They're all right] contrasted with 'Yo prefiero a la gente española' [I prefer Spanish people] or 'Los ingleses son racistas' [English people are racist]. These different responses paradoxically share a common element: the rather stereotyped nature not only of the answers but also of the question, which demonstrates a simplified view of ethnicity with regard to others, contrasting markedly with their own refusal of ethnic categorization. From these examples, we can conclude that the second generation combine a sense of self-perceived distinctiveness with a simplified view of those from whom they distinguish themselves: whether other Spanish people, other English people, or even other second-generation Spanish migrants. These simplifications are crucial for dealing with the complex ethnic reality they experience in everyday life.

The sharing of a common past displayed by the use of a frontier language (Spanglish) and by syncretic habits of media consumption is complemented by another form of consumption: their use of clothes. The final issue I wish to explore in the video-diaries is that of consumerism and lifestyle, since these are crucial means of displaying identity and particularly national affinities. Play and leisure are key scenarios for symbolic work and creativity which, as Willis (1990) has shown, take on a major importance when traditional value systems are eroded. Investing in leisure is therefore another way in which young people can reject rigid social classification under traditional categories of class or ethnicity. This is especially important for my research subjects since they are intent on defying categorization from the outside. By investing in leisure, second-generation Spanish migrants attempt to gain a space of 'invisibility' which leaves them scope for freedom of action. On the one hand, their reference points (the older generation, colleagues at work, friends from college, Spanish tourists in London, etc.) may pick up the messages conveyed by many of the symbolic markers they deploy. But, on the other hand, since their behaviour is not always intentional but often pre-reflective, their practices differ markedly from the deliberately visible use of style generally seen as characteristic of subcultural groups (mods, rockers, etc.). Thus they often express themselves by using clothes as markers that enable them to fit in and not be conspicuous, sometimes intentionally and sometimes unconsciously. Thus, when interviewed, they frequently claimed that they could not distinguish other members of the second generation from other Londoners by their physical appearance (style), even if this lack of visible difference was not a conscious goal. This claim not to look different from other young Londoners when in London is matched by the claim that when in Spain they do not pay attention to how they dress. The following statements demonstrate the mixture of intentional and pre-reflective elements in their daily practices: 'Yo nunca me he parado a pensar si tengo pinta española o no, por la ropa que llevo y eso' [I've never stopped to think whether or not I look Spanish in the clothes I wear]; 'En España me gusta adaptarme a la gente, y me visto más a la hora de salir que por ejemplo aquí' [In Spain I like to blend in with the crowd and dress up more than I would usually when in England]; or, as in the case of a group of Spanish Chelsea supporters who for the last nine years have gone to see Chelsea play wearing Chelsea football shirts: 'Somos todos españoles, hinchas del Chelsea' [We're all Spaniards who support Chelsea].

To conclude: the use by the second-generation migrants studied here of 'Spanglish', common key life-events, and common consumption and lifestyle practices demonstrates the existence of a specific ethnic identity which attempts to refuse the imposition of labels by others, while subscribing to a simplified way of categorizing others. This simplification, I contend, is necessary given their complex ethnic reality. I would also like to stress that their life-practices are not always marked by intentionality but in some cases are pre-reflective or improvised. As the following example from one of the video-diaries illustrates, there is a constant juxtaposition of signs illustrating their interstitial position in relation to three reference points: Spain, Britain, and London. This intersection forms the basis of the second generation's ethnicity. In this video-diary a young man is filming the entrance to his room (he still lives with his parents). He silently films his bedroom door which is covered by three objects: a Valencian flag, a Spanish coat of arms, and the logo (a bull) of the Peña Guiri. These three symbols attempt to state, as he then comments in Spanish, that he is someone from the Valencia region who is also Spanish though born in London—all of which makes him a member of the Peña Guiri: a club without a physical location or formal structure created by and for Spanish people born in the UK. It assumes affiliation to a notion of Spanishness based on the common diasporic existence of its members, who have known each other since childhood. The use of irony in the name ('guiri' is a derogatory Spanish term for 'foreigner') is a striking example of the ability to manipulate language for tactical purposes.

WORKS CITED

Anderson, B. (1983). *Imagined Communities: Reflections on the Origin and Spread of Nationalism*. London: Verso.

Bhabha, H. K. (ed.) (1990). *Nation and Narration*. London: Routledge.

Bourdieu, P. (1977). *Reproduction in Education, Society and Culture*. London: Sage.

—— (1986). *Distinction*. London: Routledge & Kegan Paul.

Certeau, M. de (1988). *The Practice of Everyday Life*. Berkeley and Los Angeles: University of California Press.

Chambers, I. (1990). *Border Dialogues*. London: Routledge.

Chaplin, E. (1994). *Sociology and Visual Representation*. London: Routledge.

Cohen, A. P. (1989). *The Symbolic Construction of Community*. London: Routledge.

Connerton, P. (1989). *How Societies Remember*. Cambridge: Cambridge University Press.

Cubitt, S. (1991). *Timeshift on Video Culture*. London: Routledge.

Derrida, J. (1981). *Positions*. Chicago: University of Chicago Press.

Douglas, M. (1979). *The World of Goods*. London: Penguin Books.

Gelder, K., and Thornton, S. (eds.) (1997). *The Subcultures Reader*. London: Routledge.

Gilroy, P. (1987). *There Ain't No Black in the Union Jack*. London: Hutchinson.

—— (1993). *The Black Atlantic: Modernity and Double Consciousness*. Cambridge, Mass.: Harvard University Press.

Goffman, E. (1959). *The Presentation of Self in Everyday Life*. Harmondsworth: Penguin.

Hall, S., and Du Gay, P. (eds.) (1996). *Questions of Cultural Identity*. London: Sage.

—— and Jefferson, T. (1976). *Resistance through Rituals: Youth Subcultures in Post-war Britain*. London: Routledge.

Hebdige, D. (1979). *Subculture: The Meaning of Style*. London: Methuen.

Hutchinson, J., and Smith, A. D. (eds.) (1996). *Ethnicity*. Oxford: Oxford University Press.

Renan, E. (1990) [1882]. 'What is a Nation?', in H. K. Bhabha (ed.), *Nation and Narration*. London: Routledge, 8–22.

Smith, A. D. (1986). *The Ethnic Origins of Nations*. Oxford: Blackwell.

Thornton, S. (1995). *Club Cultures*. Oxford: Polity Press.

Werbner, P., and Modood, T. (eds.) (1997). *Debating Cultural Hybridity: Multi-cultural Identities and the Politics of Anti-racism*. London: Zed Books .

Willis, Paul (1990). *Common Culture*. Milton Keynes: Open University Press.

Part II

Gender

Editor's Introduction

THE stereotypes mentioned in the introduction to Part I—and in particular their strategic recycling—form a major theme of this section, particularly in the essays by Louis, Harvey, Fernàndez, and Perriam. Louis and Perriam show how an early twentieth-century feminist campaigner and contemporary gay novelists rework the melodramatic conventions that are the stuff of popular fiction, in order to foreground and question accepted identity formations. In the latter case, Perriam notes that it is not always clear whether the use of clichés avoids perpetuating at least some of their negative connotations, transferring into the context of male–male relations the escapist, individualist fantasies that typify heterosexual romance produced for mass consumption; it might be fruitful here to apply to a gay context Radway's analysis of audience response in consumers of Harlequin romance (1984), which suggested that escapist fantasy played a positive role in the lives of the female readers. Louis's essay shows how the conventions of melodrama, with their simplification of reality into a binary opposition between good and evil, have been successively recycled since the French Revolution, frequently serving a radical political agenda but generally appealing to conservative gender stereotypes by perpetuating a negative model of woman as virtuous victim. Fernàndez examines the carnivalesque reworking of Catalan stereotypes of industrious bourgeois domesticity in the TV sitcom produced by the Catalan theatre group La Cubana, arguing that the self-reflexive, comic manipulation of stereotypes allows a reworking of gender relations—proposing a 'queer marriage' as a metaphor of social contract in contemporary Catalonia—while at the same time educating viewers in a repertoire of Catalan cultural traditions. Harvey's essay shows how Catholic stereotypes of the 'good girl' have influenced the identity formation of girls in certain social groups in Spain, showing how this process is actively engaged in by the girls concerned, and what is at stake in the process for them and their families. Additionally her essay shows how the stereotypes of popular Catholicism continue to shape the interpretation of daily life for some sectors of the population: here one might note de Certeau's observation that acceptance of 'miracles' is a popular cultural tactic for constructing an alternative model of history that allows the possibility of 'redemption' to those (especially women) excluded from the success stories narrated in dominant, causally structured historical narratives (de Certeau 1988: 16–18). This essay reminds us that we should not forget the importance of analysing conservative cultural formations.

The essays by Louis, Perriam, and Fernàndez also make important statements about the positive role that mass culture can play in the renegotiation of gender identities, given the stock association of mass culture with the feminine. For, as noted in Chapter 1, 'high' and 'low' culture are labelled such because of their respective modes of consumption, based in the former case on disinterested aesthetic detachment (supposedly male capacities) and in the latter case on participatory, bodily involvement (supposedly a female way of relating to the world). Mass culture thus invites consumers of whatever sex to respond in a 'feminine' fashion, encouraging the emotional and indeed bodily identification that is necessary for a cultural product to affect the identity formation of its consumer. As Louis asks in relation to Carmen de Burgos's use of melodrama to change public attitudes to the legal position of women, why should feminists denigrate mass-cultural forms that invite them to respond emotionally? Perriam, though more sceptical about the radical potential of the gay popular fiction that he analyses, implicitly asks the same question in relation to gay readers. In the case of Fernàndez's essay, the participatory, bodily response invited by the TV sitcom Teresina, SA is that of festive laughter, a traditional popular strategy for survival (see Parsons's essay in Part III) which allows carnivalesque reversal, sometimes shoring up hierarchy but permitting a certain renegotiation of positions while avoiding explicit confrontation: another 'tactic of the weak', to use de Certeau's term (1988: 34–9) referred to by Fernàndez. Fernàndez's demonstration of the subtlety of this TV sitcom, and of its attention to its local (Catalan) cultural context, should be read in tandem with Smith's essay on Spanish quality television in Part IV.

Louis, following the work on melodrama of Brooks and others, justifies melodrama for its insistence on speaking out and refusing to compromise: a reminder in our current age of postmodern relativism that there are some ethical imperatives which are not negotiable. De Burgos's use of melodramatic conventions for the purposes of feminist militancy is very different from the inward-looking emotional focus of the gay melodramas discussed by Perriam. Perriam's essay is important in warning us against the populist tendency in much cultural studies to regard popular culture (and non-male-heterosexual gender positions) as automatically contestatory, and in interrogating the whole notion of 'identity politics', particularly given the plurality of (often conflictive) homosexual culture(s) in contemporary Spain. At the same time, his essay stresses the importance of pleasure and identification in the reading process, asking what it might mean to say that a text is 'queerly readable'—a question implicitly asked also by Fernàndez's essay. Both Louis's and Perriam's essays comment on the importance of new commercial developments in the mass-marketing of popular fiction in allowing feminist and gay writers respectively to reach specific target audiences.

As Fernàndez notes, the TV sitcom is a particularly useful vehicle for renegotiating the relations between public and private. Harvey's essay shows how the private life of an exemplary Catholic little girl in 1930s Spain becomes the focus—through the attempt to secure her canonization—for a network of power relations grounded in the historical antagonisms of the Spanish Civil War but continuing today. This essay is concerned with the social and political investments in a 'sacrificial economy', based on the notion of substitution, which casts women in the role of sacrificial victims whose voluntary assumption of victimhood secures the redemption of men: while such a 'sacrificial economy' is predicated on the division between the public (male) and private (female) spheres, it nevertheless shows that the private always has a public dimension. It is also clear from Harvey's essay that this 'sacrificial economy' is not simply imposed by a patriarchal society but that it affords certain libidinal gratifications for girls and women, and that this is a process which continues today (as evidenced by the little girls and women who have written personal letters to the campaign to promote little Mari Carmen's canonization). The essay by Evans on the star persona of Victoria Abril explores the function of libidinal investment in regulating the relationship between public and private through its analysis of the ambivalent incorporation of women into the late capitalist economies of desire which the film industry—among other media—has played such a dominant role in promoting. Evans stresses the emancipatory potential of Abril's protean image, noting that her multifaceted persona warns us against simple categorizations of 'the feminine'. The conjunction of Harvey's and Evans's essays reminds us that female identity formations in contemporary Spain, while predominantly secularized and regulated by the globalized mass media, nevertheless still have available to them powerful 'scripts of femininity' (Harvey's term) deriving from earlier cultural scenarios. Indeed one may note the contrast between the Catholic 'sacrificial economy' which channels female desire for (extreme right) political ends, and the contemporary mass media's channelling of desire for the purposes of individual self-gratification, in a privatization of the political whose social and emotional consequences are problematic to say the least.

All of these essays show the importance of relating theoretical insights to historical specificity. Gender studies has developed as a discipline largely in the English-speaking world and in France—Italian feminist theory, largely ignored in Britain and the USA, is better known in Spain—and the application to Spain of theoretical insights derived from a northern European or North American context almost always requires some rethinking of paradigms. This places Spanish studies in the privileged position of being able to add something new to existing theoretical work. In particular, Evans notes that cinematic star theory, developed in the context of Hollywood, does not fit well with European cinema in general and with Spanish cinema in particular—a point that will be taken up by Allinson in Part III. Louis shows how, in early twentieth-century Spain, the 'woman's genre' of melodrama could be and was reinflected to serve the purposes of the feminist pro-divorce lobby. (The legal dimensions of de Burgos's work, incidentally, remind us that culture can have real effects on everyday life: de Burgos was cited as an influence in the official commentary on the 1932 divorce law of the Spanish Republic, as Louis notes.) Fernàndez draws on media theory to show how the popular American TV genre of the sitcom can be adapted for the purpose of redefining the 'family' in the context of the Catalan 'normalization' programme. Harvey's essay draws on a combination of theoretical writing on the construction of femininity and historical research into the practices of both official and popular Catholicism, in Spain and elsewhere: the result is a reading of the short life (9 years) of one little girl in 1930s Spain, and of the ways in which it has been constructed by posterity, from which broad cultural and political insights follow. The situation of this little girl's life within a network of concrete social and political connections shows the importance of archival research for the interpretation of one's material. In this case—as in the essay by Smith in Part IV—crucial parts of the 'archive' are found not in libraries but on the Internet. Indeed, Harvey's essay shows how the Internet has been taken up enthusiastically by conservative groupings to promote their cause: in this case, by a particular convent in Madrid which is campaigning for the canonization of a little girl who died in 1939 and abetting its cause through the marketing of associated merchandise advertised over the web. This example stands as a graphic illustration of the complex cultural alignments to be found in contemporary Spain. If the Franco regime has been seen as a form of 'conservative modernity', we have an example here of what one might call 'conservative postmodernity': a reminder that postmodernity is, indeed, a questioning of the notion of history as progress.

WORKS CITED

Certeau, M. de (1988). *The Practice of Everyday Life*. Berkeley and Los Angeles: University of California Press.
Radway, J. (1984). *Reading the Romance: Women, Patriarchy and Popular Literature*. Chapel Hill: University of North Carolina Press.

6

Melodramatic Feminism: The Popular Fiction of Carmen de Burgos

ANJA LOUIS

At first sight the phrase 'melodramatic feminism' might appear to be a contradiction in terms. While melodrama is associated with the feminine because of its concern with the display of emotion, its politics are often regarded as escapist and reactionary and thus likely to work against a feminist agenda. I hope in this essay to justify my use of the phrase 'melodramatic feminism' and its relevance to the popular novellas of the early twentieth-century feminist campaigner Carmen de Burgos. My discussion is divided into two parts. First, I discuss Peter Brooks's key concept of melodramatic excess. I shall take two features of melodrama that are usually seen as negative—its manichaean world view and its rhetorical excess—and show how they are used positively both in Brooks's theories and in de Burgos's 1921 novella *El artículo 438*. Since Brooks does not deal with gender issues, the second part of my discussion draws on Tania Modleski's feminist analysis of romance and the Gothic novel, and on the work of other feminist critics as appropriate. Their arguments will be used to justify the use of melodramatic devices in *El artículo 438* and in another popular novella by de Burgos, *El extranjero* (1923).

According to Brooks, melodrama originates in the French Revolution: 'the moment that symbolically, and really, marks [. . .] the dissolution of an organic and hierarchically cohesive society, and the invalidation of the literary forms—tragedy and comedy of manners—that depended on such a society' (1985: 14–15).[1] Gerould,

---

[1] See also Elsaesser (in Gledhill 1987: 44–5) who argues that one of the currents of the genealogy can be traced as far back as late medieval morality plays and other forms of oral narrative and drama.

while admitting that melodrama of revolution is a minor subgenre, argues that 'melodrama's central theme of oppressed innocence has regularly been perceived as an incitement to rebellion against tyranny by audiences suffering similar victimisation' (Bratton, Cook, and Gledhill 1994: 185). Indeed, its focus on the poor and downtrodden has frequently been used by the theatrical left to express revolutionary ideas to mass audiences. It is not surprising, then, that another peak period of melodrama came after the Russian Revolution. In the 1920s melodrama was politically promoted through funding by the Soviet state, while intellectually it was furthered by debate and theorizing by leading writers in the performing arts. In 1919 Anatolii Lunacharsky, playwright and drama critic, had written an influential article in which he argued that melodrama was a superior dramatic genre; following his lead other influential writers became interested in this genre which was supposedly best able to represent revolutionary ideology. Writers and theorists, like Viktor Shklovsky and Adrian Piotrovsky, experimented with its themes and techniques in the 1920s and modelled their popular propaganda theatre on the melodrama of the French revolutionary period, targeting a similarly radical new society and identifying many of the same opponents: the aristocracy, the clergy, and former rulers. In voicing the same need for heroes and villains conveying simplistic messages, this propaganda theatre replaced a Christian world view with dialectical materialism to ensure the ultimate triumph of the working class (Gerould in Bratton, Cook, and Gledhill 1994: 191–4).[2] Carmen de Burgos is, of course, writing at this time.

However, as is well known (see, for example, Gledhill 1987; Bratton, Cook, and Gledhill 1994), the history of melodrama also includes its use in popular fiction of the mid-nineteenth century, and its recycling in classic Hollywood cinema of the 1940s: in both cases, the reliance on melodramatic conventions is generally considered a means of instilling bourgeois values which reinforce stereotypical female roles. In both cases also, audiences were assumed to be largely female. Here it must be said that, in mid-nineteenth-century fiction at least, the dramatization of female virtue threatened but rewarded frequently articulated a class agenda aimed at empowering the middle classes or even the labour aristocracy by depicting the nobility as unscrupulous villains. The genre's denigration of the nobility

[2] For further details on melodrama in Soviet theatre, see Gerould (1980).

through the advocacy of superior middle-class virtues is empowering for the middle-class (or artisanal) male, but imposes on the heroine the role of angel of the hearth confined to the private sphere. Melodrama's historical association with the rise of the bourgeoisie can thus, at this particular historical juncture, make it progressive in class terms while simultaneously disempowering women—whose role is often relegated to that of virtuous victim. Melodrama could thus serve the purposes of the late nineteenth-century novel of domesticity and of 1940s Hollywood, articulating anxieties about male disempowerment—the threat no longer comes from the aristocracy but from women—by reinforcing bourgeois gender roles. The point that needs stressing here is that melodrama's radical potential in political terms has often been at odds with its representation of women. In adapting the radical potential of melodrama to a feminist agenda, de Burgos is acting in consonance with feminist demands of the time that the civil rights extended to male citizens by political liberalism should also be extended to women.

Carmen de Burgos's writing career coincided with a time of unprecedented social change in Spain. As Catherine Davies notes, '[her] life spanned the nineteenth and twentieth centuries and her work marks the dramatic transition from an unchanging Spain to one which was radically up-to-date. The modernizing process of the first three decades of the twentieth century repositioned women in society' (1998: 117). For the first time in Spanish history, women organized themselves in a variety of organizations with varying feminist objectives. Amongst the most important were ANME (Asociación Nacional de Mujeres Españolas [National Association of Spanish Women]) and the Cruzada de Mujeres Españolas [Spanish Women's Crusade], established in 1918 and 1921 respectively (Scanlon 1986: 195–212; González Calbet 1988: 51–6). Both mobilized in favour of women's rights; the latter, founded by de Burgos herself, campaigned, amongst other things, for a modernization of the divorce law. De Burgos's own efforts in this lengthy process were recognized by the divorce law expert Francisco Delgado Iribarren (1932: 75), who commended her work in his official commentary on the law of 2 March 1932 when Spain finally received one of the most liberal divorce laws of the time. He particularly highlighted the opinion poll she had conducted in the *Diario Universal* as early as 1903, published in book form as *Divorcio en España* (1904), citing some of the opinions expressed.

According to Davies, the first three decades of the twentieth century also initiated a boom period in Spanish literature which redefined the relationship between writers and their reading public: 'With increasing literacy rates a potential readership expanded rapidly across class and gender divides. [. . .] Production increased and [. . .] their work reached the masses as never before and helped redefine the relations between class, community and nation while actively contributing to the changes in social relations' (1998: 117–18). Carmen de Burgos took advantage of one of the biggest publishing events of her time, namely the conversion of fiction into an article of mass consumption on an unprecedented scale, which set out to satisfy the demands of, and to educate, a growing reading public. She was one of the original contributors first to El Cuento Semanal (1907), a new publishing phenomenon which issued mass-produced popular novellas in pamphlet form on a weekly basis, and, more importantly, to its followers, La Novela Corta and La Novela Semanal (the two novellas under discussion were published in the latter; see Fig. 1). While it is extremely difficult to form a clear picture of the readership, some points can be established. Given the print-runs of anything from 75,000 to 400,000 (Sainz de Robles 1966: 111–12), we can conclude that this is indeed mass-produced fiction. The format, with illustrations, assumes a less educated readership: one can in practice follow the plot by looking only at the pictures. Advertisements for shaving foam and other male utensils suggest that the gender of the readership may not have been entirely female; indeed, in a nice irony, de Burgos's novella *El artículo 438* contains an advertisement for a remedy for male impotence, facing its last page which is a swingeing indictment of male injustice against women (Fig. 2). Most importantly, since these novellas were sold mainly by subscription (see Fig. 3), we can conclude that people would read the novellas week after week rather than choosing just their 'favourite authors'. By using not only the genre of melodrama but also this particular series with its subscription format, de Burgos ensured that she would reach readers who had had little if any contact with feminist issues, thus obliging readers of all kinds to confront such matters.

Looking at the generic features of melodrama, we find that all forms share a few fundamental characteristics: the indulgence of strong emotionalism, extreme states of being, and the desire to express all. These characteristics have by and large encouraged

Fig. 1. Front cover of Carmen de Burgos's novella
El extranjero, published by La Novela Semanal

critics to treat melodrama as vulgar and degraded near-tragedy. Peter
Brooks, however, argues that this attitude blocks an understanding of the genre's premisses. 'What we most retain from any consideration of melodramatic structures', he maintains, 'is the sense
of fundamental bipolar contrast and clash. The world according to
melodrama is built on an irreducible manichaeism, the conflict of
good and evil as opposites not subject to compromise' (Brooks 1985:
36). Despite the simplicity of this manichaeism, in a melodrama of
political protest these binary oppositions become a useful means of
easy recognition: the reader can take a side and accept its credo. The
refusal to compromise is, of course, politcally crucial.

Un hombre débil
es un hombre incompleto

La energía, el poder y la actividad son
los atributos del sexo fuerte, y éstos son
los que logrará usted combatiendo
desde hoy mismo su inapetencia y su
debilidad con el poderoso reconstitu-
yente y conocido **Jarabe de**

HIPOFOSFITOS SALUD

32 años de éxitos crecientes
Unico aprobado por la Real Academia de Medicina

AVISO: Rechace usted todo frasco donde no se lea **HIPOFOSFITOS**
SALUD, impreso en tinta roja.
En la Argentina pídase **HIPOFOSALUD.**

Fig. 2.   Advertisement printed at the end of Carmen
de Burgos's novella *El artículo 438*

In *El artículo 438*, for example, both protagonists are introduced
to us almost instantaneously through description of their physical
features. While the preceding marital fight sets the tone, the description of their physical appearance confirms readers in their belief
and ensures that they identify the heroine as the character of
oppressed innocence. First the male protagonist Alfredo is introduced as follows:

Era un hombre muy alto, regular de carnes, de color moreno, con el cabello
negro alisado en torno de la frente ancha; la nariz prominente, los labios
groseros, un bigote poblado, con largas guías hacia arriba, y unos ojos grises,
indecisos, rodeados de un halo morado, donde se marcaban esas hincha-
zones y esas arrugas que graban las orgías y el cansancio de los placeres. Era

Fig. 3. Subscription rates for La Novela Semanal,
advertised in Carmen de Burgos's *El artículo 438*

un tipo de hombre guapo y buen mozo, capaz de inspirar ardientes pasiones
á las mujeres vulgares, pero antipático, repulsivo, con su aire de petulancia y
degeneración, para un espíritu un poco delicado. (de Burgos 1921: 6)

[He was a very tall, dark man, of average build, whose black hair was
smoothed down around his broad forehead, he had a prominent nose, thick
lips, a densely populated moustache the ends of which were turned upwards,
and grey, vacillating eyes, ringed with purple, and with swellings and wrinkles
recalling orgies and satiation with pleasure. He was the type of strapping,
good-looking man able to inspire ardent passion in vulgar women, but with
a petulant, degenerate air unpleasant to those of a more delicate spirit.]

Immediately after this portrait, the reader is given an account of the
heroine, aptly named María de las Angustias [Mary of the Sorrows]:

Ella era una mujercita de estatura regular, de formas finas, redondeadas y graciosas, con esa gracia un poco felina de las mujeres de Granada, todas ritmo y ondulación. La línea de los hombros era perfecta y unía, por medio de una garganta firme y torneada, el busto á la cabeza de cabellos castaños y ondeados. La tez tenía ese tono pálido y ardiente de las morenas-blancas; el rostro, de la misma suavidad de líneas, ofrecía un aspecto de la cándida pureza humana de las vírgenes de los primitivos italianos. (1921: 6)

[She was a small woman of average height, with fine, rounded, graceful features, and that slightly feline grace of the women of Granada, all rhythm and undulation. The line of her shoulders was perfect, and connected her bust to a head of wavy, chestnut hair by means of a firm and delicately curved throat. Her complexion had that pale and ardent tone of white brunettes; her face, with the same softness of lines, was suggestive of the naive human purity of the virgins of Italian primitive painters.]

Here we have perfect examples of bipolar contrast between villain and heroine. Good and evil are personified as opposites not subject to compromise. The subsequent chapters only confirm what was set out in this first one, with the bipolarization taken to extremes. María de las Angustias is the good, genuine, honest, passive, suffering, emotional, and wealthy female; while Alfredo is the evil, false, dishonest, cunning, insensitive, rational, calculating, insolvent male. Similar bipolarizations can be found at the beginning of *El extranjero*; indeed, many of de Burgos's feminist novellas start in this way. The moral epithets used in the above examples are another feature of melodrama, through which ethical conditions are made manifest and operative, through bipolarization (Brooks 1985: 36).

This bipolar world view is reproduced in melodrama's rhetorical features. According to Brooks, the manichaeism of melodrama alerts us to 'what much criticism has simply dismissed from embarrassment: the overstatement and overemphasis of melodrama, its rhetorical excess. These are not accidental but intrinsic to the form' (Brooks 1985: 36). Characters in melodrama say what they think, clearly, directly, and explicitly. Everything is spelt out, nothing implied. The genre's *raison d'être* is the possibility of saying everything, of expressing emotions that are almost overwhelming. '¡Dios mío, dios mío! ¿Por qué no he de poder yo romper este lazo?' [Oh my God, oh my God, why can I not sever this tie?] (1921: 11), the heroine of *El artículo 438* laments on finding herself trapped in an unhappy marriage. Later, she exclaims to her lover: 'Maridito, maridito mío: guárdame tú escondida dentro de tu corazón, y no tendré miedo de nada' [My little husband, my little husband, keep me hidden in your heart and I'll be afraid of nothing] (1921: 32).

Women in de Burgos's melodrama are not silenced, they speak out with melodramatic clarity although society would want them to assume the stereotypical role of silent martyr. In *El artículo 438*, de Burgos has her heroine openly criticize two bastions of male-dominated society: marriage—'¡Qué felices deben ser las naciones donde existe el divorcio!' [How happy those nations must be that have divorce!] (1921: 38)—and the notion of the asexual, maternal angel of the hearth—'¿Para qué ese absurdo de pretender que la maternidad borre nuestra ánsia de amar?' [Why this absurd supposition that motherhood eliminates our yearning for love?] (1921: 43). More importantly, the feminist narrator, by explicitly intervening to question phallocratic society's written or unwritten rules, makes the reader aware of its absurdities. Such interventions complement the emotionalism of the characters' rhetorical excess by requiring an intellectual response on the part of the reader—one made urgent by the use of overstatement, as in the closing invective of the narrator of *El artículo 438* which rails against the infamous article 438 of the Penal Code, which sanctioned the husband's murder or attempted murder of an adulterous wife:[3]

---

[3] The text of article 438 is faithfully reproduced by Carmen de Burgos at the beginning of her novella as an epigraph, and reads as follows:

El marido que, sorprendiendo en adulterio á su mujer, matase en el acto á ésta ó al adúltero, ó les causara alguna de las lesiones graves, será castigado con la pena de destierro. Si les causara lesiones de segunda clase, quedará libre de pena. Estas reglas son aplicables á los padres en iguales circunstancias, respecto de sus hijas menores de veintitrés años y sus corruptores, mientras aquéllas viviesen en la casa paterna. El beneficio de este artículo no aprovecha á los que hubieren promovido ó facilitado la prostitución de sus mujeres ó hijas.

[The husband who, surprising his wife in an act of adultery, kills either her or the adulterer, or causes either grievous bodily harm, will be punished with banishment. If he causes them assault and battery he will go unpunished. These rules are applicable in the same circumstances to fathers with regard to their daughters under the age of 23 and their corruptors, while they remain living in the family home. The benefits of this article do not apply to those who may have encouraged or facilitated the prostitution of their wives or daughters.]

For the original legal text and its commentary, see *Código Penal de 1870* (1889: iv. 578–98). For further details on the punishment of *destierro*, see *Diccionario enciclopédico Salvat universal* (1969: ix. 99). It should be noted that *destierro* here does not mean 'exile' but 'banishment' from the home town or region; it is thus the most lenient punishment on the scale for serious crimes, ranging from six months to six years. In the 1928 reform of the Penal Code there was an amendment whereby article

Alfredo estaba incluído, por entero, en el artículo 438. Había matado para lavar su honor mancillado, en el paroxismo de la pasión y de los celos, exasperado al descubrir la traición de su mujer y de su amigo. Era un gesto gallardo y simpático en un país que conservaba el espíritu calderoniano. [. . .] La ley promulgada por hombres, favorecía siempre á los hombres y humillaba á las mujeres. Ningún artículo del Código les daba á ellas aquella facilidad de asesinar á los infieles; ni siquiera el funesto artículo 438 decía: 'cualquiera de los dos esposos que sorprendiera en adulterio al otro', sino: 'El marido que sorprendiese en adulterio á su mujer'. Era sólo un privilegio masculino. Los jueces se cuidarían mucho de no quebrantar aquel principio, la lección indirecta que daban ellos mismos á sus propias mujeres. (1921: 55)

[Alfredo was fully covered by article 438. He had killed to cleanse his stained honour, in a fit of passion and jealousy, exasperated on discovering his wife's and his friend's betrayal. It was a gallant, endearing gesture in a country where Calderón's spirit lived on. [. . .] The law made by men always favoured men and humiliated women. No single article in the Code offered them the possibility of killing an unfaithful husband; even the fateful article 438 did not say: 'The spouse who surprises the other in the act of adultery' but: 'The husband who surprises his wife in the act of adultery'. It was an exclusively masculine privilege. The judges would do their utmost to uphold that principle, in an implicit lesson to their own wives.]

Excess, in terms of bipolarity and rhetoric, is thus achieved through the characters' statements and, most importantly, through the narrator's intervention. This preoccupation with clear, unambiguous messages is useful in a mass-produced medium aimed at a popular and largely uneducated readership. Melodramatic excess is used by Carmen de Burgos in a generalized Brooksian sense to confront readers with what they prefer to avoid thinking about. But as I now wish to show, this process is taken further through the co-option of the feminist potential of romance and the Gothic.

In her study of mass-produced fantasies for women, Tania Modleski divides popular fiction into romance and the Gothic novel, pointing out that these correspond to different stages in a woman's life: courtship and marriage. In romance the preoccupation is with getting a man; in the Gothic novel it is with the relationship itself (Modleski 1984: 61). Excess can be found in *El extranjero* in the

523 also allowed wives to kill the adulterers. In the 1932 reform, with the new divorce law in force, adultery was reclassified as a civil rather than criminal offence and hence article 438 of the Penal Code was repealed (López-Rey 1932: 67–8; Machado Carrillo 1978: 49).

guise of an excessively romantic disposition and in *El artículo 438* in the form of paranoia as an almost Gothic extreme state of being.

In the classic romance novel, a young, innocent heroine meets a seemingly cynical, hostile, brutal hero. By the end the misunderstanding is cleared away, they love each other and live happily ever after. The price for this happiness, however, is feminine selflessness: the heroine can achieve happiness only by undergoing a complete loss of identity (Modleski 1984: 36). Taking this romance formula and subverting it, de Burgos depicts her heroines as young, innocent, and selfless; but, unlike their 'luckier' counterparts in traditional romance, their courtship adventures go drastically wrong. One of the most radically feminist examples of a premarital affair going wrong is *El extranjero*, in which Matilde's excessively romantic disposition is a key issue.

El extranjero tells the story of Matilde who falls madly in love with an Italian called Alfredo and, after a short courtship, they have an affair. Soon after she gives herself to him, he gets bored with her, starts using her, then deserts her, and she, by then pregnant, lives unhappily ever after. Having to grow up quickly after the death of her father, Matilde reacts in two ways: responsibly by getting a job to support her brothers and sisters, and by escaping into an imaginary world. When she meets Alfredo she treats him with the same combination of realism and fantasy:

En el fondo, ella se sacrificaba; cerraba los ojos para no verle bien y mantener su ensueño. Para no fijarse más que en los ojos grandes, en la tragedia de su semblante y en aquella voz melosa que le acariciaba recitándole versos y hablándole en el lenguaje que alimentaba su pasión romántica. [. . .] Y su buen gusto sufría un golpe de rechazo con la indumentaria descuidada de Alfredo; á veces sentía la repugnancia de él, que en seguida vencía. Una lucha entre su espíritu noble, que parecía percibir la verdad, y su ansiedad de amores, su romanticismo que le hacía querer continuar su ensueño. (1923: 17)

[Deep down she sacrificed herself, closing her eyes so as not to see him as he was and thus maintain her fantasy. So as not to focus beyond his big eyes, that tragic appearance, and that syrupy voice that caressed her, reciting verses and speaking to her in a language that nourished her romantic passion. [. . .] And then suddenly her good taste would be repelled by Alfredo's unkempt dress; sometimes she felt disgusted by him, a reaction she instantly overcame. A struggle between her noble spirit, which seemed to perceive the truth, and her yearning for love and romanticism which made her want to keep up the illusion.]

The conflict between her accurate perception of reality and her romantic outlook on life is constant throughout the novella. From the start, Matilde projects the image of her ideal suitor onto Alfredo. To complete the perfect image of her hero, he is an artist. Predictably, Matilde makes love to him for the first time immediately after the successful first night of one of his plays:

Así la noche que Alfredo consiguió, al fin, estrenar su comedia, y ella le vió salir triunfante entre aplausos al palco escénico, sin ver la galantería que existía en aquellos aplausos de *clac* y de amigos para el extranjero; cuando le vió buscarla entre su triunfo con los ojos en el palco que le había ofrecido, ella se creyó elevada sobre todas las mujeres por el amor de un Dante, de un Petrarca, de un artista admirable. Olvidó su vulgaridad, la fealdad que á veces veía, á pesar suyo. [. . .] Le vió transfigurado, le pareció que todas las mujeres le miraban, se lo disputaban, y sintió prisa de hacerle suyo. Se le entregó aquella noche, [. . .] sin hacerle prometer nada, sin pedirle nada, sin exigirle nada, dichosa de ofrecérsele, de confiarse en él. Hallando un placer en el sacrificio de verle dichoso, dominando la repulsión de una intimidad que le hacía oler la suciedad de su ropa, una camiseta sudada y unos terribles calzoncillos largos, de rayas azules, blancas y negras, amarrados con cintas, sujetas al ojal y al botón, para no tener que abrocharlos. (1923: 24)

[Thus it was on the night that Alfredo finally managed to première his comedy and she saw him emerge triumphantly onto the stage without perceiving the courtesy implicit in that applause for the foreigner by an in-group of critics and friends; when she saw him, in his triumph, seek her out, his eyes trained on the box that he had offered her, she felt herself raised above all women by the love of a Dante, a Petrarch, of an admired artist. She forgot his vulgarity, the ugliness that she sometimes saw, against her will. [. . .] She saw him transformed, it seemed to her that all women looked at him, that they fought for his affections, and she made haste to claim him for herself. That night she gave herself to him [. . .] without making him promise anything, without asking anything of him, without demanding anything from him, happy to offer herself up to him, to confide in him. Finding pleasure in the sacrifice of seeing him happy, overcoming the disgust of an intimacy that made her smell his dirty clothes, his sweaty shirt, and his dreadful long underpants with their blue, black and white stripes, held up with tapes tied to the button and buttonhole, so he did not have to bother to do them up.]

This passage makes it clear that Matilde is not so much in love with Alfredo, as with her own fantasy. She is obsessed with making her dream of a romantic love affair come true. Every time this fantasy clashes with reality, Matilde has to close her eyes in order to enable herself to stay in her daydream. She even overlooks the repulsion his lack of personal hygiene produces in her, which makes it clear that she is not even physically attracted to him. The final disillusionment comes when Alfredo blames her for not accepting the fact that their relationship is over. Then she wakes up: 'Le veía tal como era, no como le había fingido su ensueño, y sentía repulsión y asco por aquel hombre' [She saw him as he was, not as she had imagined him to be in her fantasy, and she felt repulsion and disgust for that man] (1923: 56). Yet despite this eye-opener she immediately overcomes her disgust, negotiating this total failure of judgement on her part by reverting to romantic mode:

Aquel no era Alfredo; estaba frente á una de esas novelas en las que el héroe bueno es asesinado por el lacayo que usurpa su nombre. Su Alfredo había muerto y estaba suplantado por aquel otro Alfredo falso, que no le dejaba ni siquiera el refugio de un recuerdo santo, de algo de su pasado que venerar. (57)

[That was not Alfredo, she was faced with one of those novels in which the hero is murdered by some underling who usurps his name. Her Alfredo had died and been supplanted by this other false Alfredo, who had not even left her the refuge of a blessed memory, of something from her past to worship.]

It could be argued that the root of Matilde's problem lies in her withdrawal into the world of romance as a compensation for having had to care for her siblings at so young an age. Here de Burgos is echoing standard complaints about how reading romances is bad for women. She is, of course, doing so in a melodramatic novella, using the very medium that is criticized. Some feminist critics have tried to rescue romance, at least in part, from such complaints. Modleski, for example, compares religious suffering to 'romantic suffering', concluding that both are 'at the same time an *expression* of real suffering and a *protest* against real suffering' (1984: 47–8). Hence Matilde's excessive reading of romances could be interpreted as a protest as well as an escape. Alison Light argues in a similar vein: 'Romance imagines peace, security and ease precisely because there is dissension, insecurity and difficulty. In the context of women's lives, romance reading might appear less a reactionary reflex or an indication of their victimization by the capitalist market, and more a sign of discontent and a technique for survival' (Eagleton 1986: 143).

In her article ' "Returning to Manderley": Romance Fiction, Female Sexuality and Class', Light discusses the prevalent notion that romance works ideologically to keep women in a socially inferior place. In her opinion, this notion denigrates the reader: 'It also treats women yet again as the victims of, and irrational slaves to, their sensibilities. Feminists must baulk at any such conclusion which implies that the vast audience of romance readers (with the exception of a few up-front intellectuals) are either masochistic or inherently stupid' (Eagleton 1986: 141). Ann Barr Snitow also argues that romance allows women their one socially acceptable moment of transcendence: 'When women try to picture excitement, the society offers them one vision, romance. When women try to imagine companionship, the society offers them one vision, male, sexual companionship. When women try to fantasize about success, mastery, the society offers them one vision, the power to attract a man' (Eagleton 1986: 138).

Romance then obeys a dual impulse, feeding women's desire for empowerment at the same time as it contains that desire by giving it a phallocentric form. This dual impulse is articulated in *El extranjero* in the two levels of readership involved. First, within the text, Matilde is a reader of romances; and secondly, outside the text, the reader engages in reading a melodramatic story about Matilde. Matilde's own reading has disastrous consequences. She takes her reading at face value, expecting real life to be the same. To paraphrase Light, Matilde thus appears to be a 'victim of and irrational slave to her sensibilities' as well as being masochistic and stupid. The reader of Matilde's story is, however, placed in a different position. As Modleski argues, the reader allows herself emotional identification with the heroine partly because she does not have to suffer the heroine's confusion and can thus rationally distance herself. Furthermore, readers can enjoy outwitting the heroine by guessing the hero's true motives since they clearly understand the situation when the heroine does not (Modleski 1984: 41). Reading Matilde can therefore be seen as a distancing act as much as an identification. 'The reader of romances', Modleski continues, 'is engaged in an intensely active psychological process. Each novel [. . .] is as much a protest as an endorsement of the feminine condition' (1984: 58). *El extranjero*, then, can be read as such a protest against the feminine condition. In using melodramatic excess, de Burgos creates 'subversive romances' engaging her readers in an active psychological process which—given the excessiveness of the heroines' statements and her own explicit narratorial intrusions —of necessity produces protestation.

In the Gothic novel, melodramatic excess is achieved through the classic narrative structure confronting a fragile young girl who appears to be frightened with 'a handsome, magnetic suitor or husband who may or may not be a lunatic and/or murderer' (Modleski 1984: 61).[4] In Gothic novels the woman suspects the husband or lover of trying to drive her insane or to murder her (Modleski 1984: 60). Her feelings towards her husband turn from love into fear. Unlike the reader of romance, the reader of Gothic novels shares the heroine's uncertainty and is, as a result, as powerless in her or his understanding as the heroine.

Before analysing the use of Gothic conventions in El artículo 438, a brief plot summary may be helpful. As previously mentioned, the novel's title refers to the paragraph in the Spanish Penal Code in force throughout the nineteenth century until its removal in 1932, which condones a husband's killing of his adulterous wife. Thus the novella deals with the premeditated killing of the wealthy María de las Angustias by her nasty, insolvent husband Alfredo. The former feels trapped in her marriage and finally succumbs to her feelings for Jaime, starting an affair with him in her husband's absence. Alfredo, suddenly returning home, catches the couple *in flagrante*, kills his wife, and lives happily ever after on her money.

Most features of the classic Gothic plot can be found in El artículo 438. After an initial feeling of love towards Alfredo, María de las Angustias, the young, beautiful, fragile wife, is soon frightened of him. Alfredo, certainly the handsome husband, does not try to drive her insane so much as to 'corromper su espíritu' [pervert her spirit] (1921: 15). However, the reader does not share the heroine's uncertainty as regards her fate. The title, and more importantly the quotation of article 438 of the Spanish Penal Code as the novella's opening epigraph, gives us an almost certain prediction of the outcome. So it is the reader rather than the heroine who suspects the husband of attempting to murder his wife.

The Gothic novel usually deals with married couples. Why does marriage cause some women to become fearful, suspicious, and even paranoid? According to Modleski, social isolation is a major contributory factor to paranoia (1984: 62) and that is certainly so in the case of María de las Angustias. Modleski, however, also argues that another factor might be the disappointment women feel as their dreams of marital bliss conflict with harsh reality. Modleski, quoting Alexandra Symonds, argues that the key problem in marriage is the

---

[4] The Gothic novel is also discussed by Brooks (1985: 19–20).

declaration of dependence by women who look for a socially acceptable way to rely on somebody else: 'If for any reason the marriage
does not seem to be all they expected they are in panic and they cling
even more' (1984: 78). The panic then turns to phobia. The woman
deals with this situation by projecting her fear onto her husband,
making him the villain: '[It] appears as though all her troubles would
be over if only she had a different husband or if someone else would
get her husband to change' (Modleski 1984: 78–9). One of the typical Gothic formulas, then, is that the woman has got involved with
the wrong man, and the right man comes along and saves her from
the villainy of the first man. This holds true for *El artículo 438*: María
de las Angustias became involved with the wrong man, her marriage
is a big disappointment, and in comes Jaime, the lover, to 'save' her.

   Modleski calls the Gothic novel a paranoid text, in the sense that,
in a paranoid state, the aggressive component of a person is projected
onto someone else who is then seen as an agent of blame. The blaming of the self becomes a blaming of someone outside and one can
easily regard oneself as the victim (Modleski 1984: 83). Thus the
heroine colludes in her own disempowerment by a phallocentric society. In *El artículo 438*, however, the issue of victimization is more
ambivalent than in the classic Gothic novel. María de las Angustias is
quite obviously a victim of Alfredo, but she is also, up to a point,
fighting against those 'forces'. When Alfredo demands more money
from her to finance his expensive lifestyle, she resists as much as she
can, argues endlessly with him, and it is only the threat of rape that
finally 'convinces' her to succumb to his wishes. However, it could be
argued that, in her relationship with her 'saviour' Jaime, María de las
Angustias does put herself in the role of victim, or at least inferior
partner, becoming more subservient than she was to her husband.
She sees Jaime as her saviour and the solution to all her problems.
Interestingly, Jaime refuses to accept this power given to him. So the
dependency here comes from María's 'perpetuation of the cycle of
victimization', as Modleski puts it: 'In other words, the Gothic has
been used to drive home the "core of truth" in feminine paranoid
fears [. . .]. It has been used to show how women are at least potentially "pure victims", but how, in coming to view themselves as such,
they perpetuate the cycle of victimization which occurs between
fathers and mothers, mothers and daughters' (1984: 83).

   However, María de las Angustias is not only a victim of her own
(paranoid) imagination but is the 'real' victim of a vile man, who

'really' does kill her. Women *are* persecuted, as Modleski notes, and the Gothic heroine is not destined to turn the persecution into triumph (Modleski 1984: 83). Modleski's conceptual model of the Gothic novel works on two levels in *El artículo 438*: the first level is the cycle of victimization which is carried over to the relationship with Jaime, and thus one could argue that María de las Angustias displays features of paranoia. By happily putting herself into the weaker position again, by externalizing her fears, she makes herself a potential victim of the next man as well. However—and this is the second level—the novella, despite the Gothic features of tension and suspense, is not a completely paranoid text, since María de las Angustias's fears are all too well founded.

In this essay I have discussed two texts which indulge in excessive emotionalism. But what, after all, is wrong with that? Excessive emotion is often used as a major distinguishing factor between high and low culture, the latter being decried for its appeal to 'cheap emotionalism', seen as the response of those who are not educated enough to be capable of a detached, 'aesthetic' reading. Jane Shattuc argues that feminist critics should take this position to task. In her excellent article 'Having a Good Cry over *The Color Purple*', she analyses a problem that feminists have failed to address: the affective power of the melodramatic text. Feminist analysis usually ignores emotional responses in favour of more intellectual interpretations which distance the reader from the affective power of the text. According to Shattuc, feminists have had a constant love/hate relationship with melodrama. She argues for a different approach:

> We too need to look to how 'the intellectual feminine voice' has served to undercut the political power of melodrama texts that invoke the pleasure of tears and political change, rather than the policing effect of intellectual distance. What is it that middle-class feminists fear that causes them to support intellectual distance over emotion? Is it fear of blacks and working-class women being 'out of control' and therefore outside 'our' control? (Bratton, Cook, and Gledhill 1994: 149)

I propose that there is another fear operating here: the fear of objections from male intellectuals. By succumbing to that fear, feminist critics reproduce the axioms of phallocentrism. The notion that we must intellectualize everything and must not have emotions is dangerously close to the phallocentric world view which feminists have so criticized. Modleski consequently argues that, in assuming an attitude of dismissiveness or flippant mockery towards melodrama, it is not so much our emancipation from romantic fantasy that we assert as our acceptance of the masculine contempt for sentimental (feminine) 'drivel'. 'Perhaps we have internalized', she continues, 'the ubiquitous male spy, who watches as we read romances or watch soap operas, as he watched Virginia Woolf from behind the curtain (or so she suspected) when she delivered her subversive lectures at "Oxbridge" ' (Modleski 1984: 14).

WORKS CITED

Bratton, J., Cook, J., and Gledhill, C. (eds.) (1994). *Melodrama: Stage, Picture, Screen*. London: British Film Institute.

Brooks, P. (1985). *The Melodramatic Imagination: Balzac, Henry James, Melodrama, and the Mode of Excess*. New York: Columbia University Press.

Burgos, C. de (1904). *Divorcio en España*. Madrid: Viuda de Rodríguez Serra.

—— (1921). *El artículo 438*. La Novela Semanal 15. Madrid: Prensa Gráfica.

—— (1923). *El extranjero*. La Novela Semanal 94. Madrid: Prensa Gráfica.

Código Penal de 1870 (1889), ed. A. Groizard y Gómez de la Serna. Salamanca: Esteban Hermanos.

Código Penal de 8 de septiembre de 1928 (1928). Madrid: Boletín Jurídico-Administrativo.

Davies, C. (1998). *Spanish Women's Writing 1849–1996*. Women in Context. London: Athlone Press.

Delgado Iribarren, F. (1932). *El divorcio, ley de 2 de Marzo de 1932: antecedentes, discusión parlamentaria, comentarios, doctrina, jurisprudencia, formularios para su aplicación*. Madrid: Revista de Derecho Privado.

Diccionario enciclopédico Salvat universal (1969).

Eagleton, M. (ed.) (1986). *Feminist Literary Theory: A Reader*. Oxford: Blackwell.

Gerould, D. (ed.) (1980). *Melodrama*, vol. vii. New York: New York Literary Forum.

Gledhill, C. (ed.) (1987). *Home is Where the Heart is: Studies in Melodrama and the Woman's Film*. London: British Film Institute, 43–69.

González Calbet, M. T. (1988). 'El surgimiento del movimiento feminista, 1900–1930', in P. Folguera (ed.), *El feminismo en España: dos siglos de historia*. Madrid: Fundación Pablo Iglesias, 51–6.

López-Rey, M. (1932). *La reforma del Código Penal Español: 5 de noviembre de 1932*. Madrid: Revista de Derecho Privado.

Machado Carrillo, M. J. (1978). *El adulterio en el derecho penal: pasado, presente y futuro*, Colección de Criminología y Derecho Penal. Madrid: Universidad Complutense.

Modleski, T. (1984). *Loving with a Vengeance: Mass-Produced Fantasies for Women*. London: Routledge.

Sainz de Robles, F. (1966). *Espíritu y letra*. Madrid: Aguilar.

Scanlon, G. (1986). *La polémica feminista en la España contempóranea 1868–1974*. 2nd edn. Madrid: Akal.

7

Good Girls go to Heaven:
The Venerable Mari Carmen González-Valerio y Sáenz de Heredia (1930–1939)

JESSAMY HARVEY

A SMALL devotional card distributed by a convent of the Discalced Carmelite Order in Aravaca, Madrid, features the portrait of a solemn little girl, around 4 years old, under the phrase: 'El mejor adorno en una niña es la virtud' [The greatest embellishment in a little girl is virtue]. Printed on the reverse of this card is a prayer of intercession for divine graces or favours to be channelled through the Venerable Mari Carmen González-Valerio y Sáenz de Heredia (1930–9), a Spanish child whose heroic virtues were approved in Rome in 1995, and who was declared Venerable[1] by Pope John Paul II the following year. The devotional card attempts to resemble in appearance an illuminated manuscript; the initial letter of the pre-scriptive phrase is an ornate calligraphic design of multicoloured leaves on a vellum-tinted background. This collaboration between words and image serves an eternalizing function bridging religion, history, and femininity, and because the card is an example of what David Morgan (1998) calls 'visual piety'—the process of social con-struction that is encoded in the visual culture of religion—it is a primary document in understanding the construction of a particular identity: the good Catholic girl. A devotional card is part of the

---

[1] At present, the first stage of the canonization process is to award the title of Venerable, should the person under consideration merit this in the eyes of the Church. This means that she or he is now officially worthy of private veneration. All the docu-mentation prepared and reviewed up till this point, which is considerable, is 'in view of the Church, the product of rigorous human investigation and judgement, but fallible nonetheless' (Woodward 1991: 84). What is required to merit beatification and, there-after, canonization is signs of God: miracles. In Mari Carmen's case, data are still being gathered to substantiate claims that the requisite miracles have taken place.

liturgy of daily life for a believer. Morgan notes that 'the believer prays to a saint with whom he or she feels a special affinity, related perhaps to age, gender, profession, nation, ethnicity, namesake, family history, or particular circumstance' (1998: 70). Therefore this card, as any other devotional card, can be understood not only as a way and means to reach God, but as an expression of identity—both of the believer, who 'subscribes' to a saint of his or her choice, and of the saint (or aspiring saint, such as a Venerable or a Blessed) who is fashioned by the promoters of his or her cause.

This essay will analyse the material culture—visual and textual—promoting Mari Carmen as an exemplary figure for Catholic girls in order to shed light on the ways in which she has been represented, how her exemplary status has been established and sustained, the manner in which her life and personality has been imaginatively reconstructed, and to what purpose. Geoffrey Cubitt defines an exemplary life as one that is 'valued and admired not merely (or even necessarily) for its practical achievements, but for the moral or ethical or social truths or values which it is perceived both to embody and, through force of example, to impress on the minds of others' (Cubitt and Warren 2000: 2). As a mere child, whose short life yields very little in terms of practical achievement but presents many anecdotes that attest to her virtue, Mari Carmen is a particularly interesting exemplar, fulfilling's Cubitt's definition of a person whose existence 'is endowed by others, not just with a high degree of fame and honour, but with a special allocation of imputed meaning and symbolic significance—that not only raises them above others in public esteem but makes them the object of some kind of collective investment' (Cubitt and Warren 2000: 3). Sainthood is an eminently social phenomenon: saints are made, not born. Holy people in all times, places, and religions are the product of historically specific environments in which certain models of behaviour, out of a much larger repertoire available in their cultural tradition, are recommended for imitation. As Pierre Delooz observes: 'for nearly 2000 years, a social group, the Roman Catholic Church, has been recognizing certain persons as saints. The study of these persons is likely to teach us something about the group which selected them' (Delooz 1983: 189). So two questions are raised at this juncture. First of all, which social group selected Mari Carmen González-Valerio y Sáenz de Heredia as an exemplary model? And secondly, what is the model of behaviour that is being recommended for imitation?

GROUP CHARISMA

Mari Carmen was born into a noble and militant Catholic family: a family background which harks back to a medieval model of sainthood when 'the vast majority of the saints came from the wealthy noble and urban elite which governed Europe' (Goodich 1973: 286), reflecting 'the church's desire to reward a faithful clan rather than an outstanding individual' (Goodich 1973: 289). The willingness of the González-Valerio y Sáenz de Heredia clan, and the willingness of those around them, to view each member of their family as special and due public recognition is linked to the historical context: the Spanish Civil War, the triumph of the Nationalists, and the subsequent National-Catholic social order. The family were members of a social group which felt that it could claim superior grace and superior virtues as an eternal gift, by contrast with those groups defeated in the Civil War whom they, for that reason, felt entitled to condemn. They had what Norbert Elias calls, after Max Weber, 'group charisma'; whereas the defeated were culturally understood as having negative attributes or being tainted with 'group disgrace'. Even the most recent hagiographies and promotional material speak from the perspective of a 'charisma group' which feels entitled to condemn those they perceive as 'others': specified in the literature about Mari Carmen as 'rojos' [reds], 'judíos' [Jews], and masons.

Mari Carmen's grandmother, Carmen de Manzanos y Matheu, Marquesa de Almaguer, had very strong connections with the hierarchy of the Catholic Church, partly due to her social position and partly due to her work promoting the cult of the Sacred Heart, for which she spent time and money distributing devotional material from an office in her home (González-Valerio 1997: 52). The political implications of this cult are explored by William A. Christian who notes that the Sacred Heart was a 'defiant badge of activism for all mobilized Catholics' (1992: 4) to protest against liberal government policies which, they felt, eroded their moral values and religious beliefs. This political-religious militancy practised by the Marquesa de Almaguer is not the family's only connection to anti-liberalism, as she was also related, through marriage, to the Primo de Rivera family. The Marquesa's only daughter, also called Carmen, spent her childhood in the company of José Antonio and Pilar Primo de Rivera, her second cousins who, as is well known, became leaders of Falange Española (the Spanish fascist party) and its Women's Section (Sección

Femenina) respectively. In fact, when Carmen married Julio González-Valerio, second son to the Marqués de Casa Ferrandel, in 1928, the dictator Miguel Primo de Rivera—father of José Antonio and Pilar—witnessed the ceremony.

After a couple of years of marriage, Mari Carmen, their second child, was born—on 14 March 1930. Her baby record book, which gives an account of the girl's first years of life as recorded by her mother, is kept in the archive of the Convent of the Discalced Carmelites at Aravaca (Madrid), which is at the centre of the campaign for her canonization.[2] In having preserved all the telegrams and cards welcoming Mari Carmen into the world, the book functions as a roll call of illustrious names from the European nobility: 'entre tanto personaje se encuentra el nombre del tío de Carmen, el Marqués de Estella, Don Miguel Primo de Rivera, que la felicitó desde París pocos días antes de su mortal "angina de pecho" ' [among these many illustrious figures is the name of Carmen's uncle, Don Miguel Primo de Rivera, Marqués de Estella, who sent his congratulations from Paris a few days before his fatal *angina pectoris*] (González-Valerio 1997: 41).

Mari Carmen was born and lived through a historical period marked by socio-economic tension and fierce and violent power struggles between political ideologies and belief systems which would culminate in the Spanish Civil War. Growing up within a family whose world and identity would have felt deeply threatened by the changes wrought by the Second Republic of 1931–6, Mari Carmen's short life was irrevocably altered by the outbreak of the war. Her father Julio González-Valerio was arrested by a militia group, known as 'Milicias del Radio Sur' (González-Valerio 1997: 78), and executed on 29 August 1936. His death, like that of countless other Catholic men and women who, in some way or another, supported values that eventually nourished the ideology of National-Catholicism during the Franco regime, was and continues to be

---

[2] This archive is closed to researchers who are not members of a religious order. The sources used are, therefore, all hagiographical. However, two of the documents are of interest: Mari Carmen's younger sister Maria de Lourdes González-Valerio y Sáenz de Heredia's hagiography, *La niña que se entregó* (1997), which functions as both the biography of a family and a spiritual text; and M. Guadalupe Lucía Bertoglio's *Mari Carmen: la fuerza del perdón* (1999), which is the translation of the *Informatio super virtutibus*, a theological document prepared as part of the canonization process.

interpreted as martyrdom, a direct result of religious persecution.[3] Though it is never made clear that the family link to the Primo de Riveras may have been one of the reasons that Julio was executed, this link certainly endangered the family's life during the Civil War. In fact, Pilar Primo de Rivera mentions that Julio's wife Carmen sought refuge in their home at some point prior to the execution (Primo de Rivera 1983: 70–1). After the execution, Carmen and her children were sheltered in the Belgian Embassy, before they could flee to safety in San Sebastián, which had fallen to the Nationalists in October. Mari Carmen was sent, at that point, to a boarding school, Colegio de las Madres Irlandesas RR. De la Bienaventurada Virgen María [School of the Reverend Irish Mothers of the Blessed Virgin Mary], in Zalla. Her school notebooks still survive, and facsimiles of these pages are published in the various hagiographies. It can be read that she, and her contemporaries, wrote down sentences such as 'Dios me vé en todas partes' [God sees me everywhere], 'al cielo van los buenos' [the good go to heaven], and 'modestia que consiste en esa finura noble y digna de una niña verdaderamente cristiana' [modesty which consists in the noble, refined dignity of a truly Christian girl] (González-Valerio 1997: 115–18). These texts show how Mari Carmen's education enforced manners and morals for growing girls. Mari Carmen, it was hoped, would grow up to become 'la futura dama española, continuadora de las virtudes de la familia y encarnación completa y perfecta del tradicional espíritu cristiano en las mujeres de España' [the future Spanish gentlewoman, responsible for continuing the virtues of the family and the total, perfect incarnation of the traditional Christian spirit in the women of Spain] (Sánchez 1960). But, by April 1939, after the end of the Civil War on the 1st of that month, when Mari Carmen and her family could begin to

---

[3] This interpretation of the deaths of Catholic men and women during the Civil War is shared by the Vatican. On 7 March 1999, Pope John Paul II beatified eight Spanish Civil War martyrs: the diocesan priest Manuel Martín, and Vicente Soler and his six Augustinian companions. On 11 March 2001, John Paul II further beatified the archpriest José Aparicio Sanz and 230 other Spaniards plus two Uruguayans (priests, members of religious orders, members of Catholic Action, and lay people) who were killed during the Civil War. Present among the pilgrims witnessing this ceremony was Cardinal Antonio María Rouco Varela who actively supports the canonization of Mari Carmen: he has contributed to the Convent's newsletter and written the introduction to Bertoglio's Mari Carmen: la fuerza del perdón (1999). The Pope's message 'Capella Papale per la beatificazione di 233 Servi di Dio' concerning the mass beatification can be found (in Castilian only) at the Vatican's website www.vatican.va (2001).

contemplate returning to their home in Madrid, she was already terminally ill.

MARTYR

Mari Carmen lived only just over nine years, dying of scarlet fever in the summer of 1939. It was the severity of the complications that contributed to her death. Scarlet fever is an acute contagious disease prevalent among children that is characterized by a sore throat, nausea, and vomiting; because of the child's high fever, delirium may be present. The name of the illness is related to the changes it works on the body of the patient: a punctate scarlet rash spreads across the surface of the body and, later, a desquamation of the skin occurs in large flakes or casts. The period of incubation is short, around forty-eight hours, but the illness can last for weeks. Mari Carmen, after these initial symptoms, also suffered from otitis media, nephritis, operative mastoiditis, phlebitis, gangrene, and septicaemia. All of these were common complications developing from scarlet fever before the availability of antibiotics. There is no doubt that Mari Carmen suffered great pain and distress in the final weeks of her life. Those around her—her school-friends, the Sisters and staff at her boarding school, members of the medical profession, and her family—will have witnessed her agony and the gradual, but dramatic, corruption of her small body as it appeared to decay long before death. Although countless other children have died in this way, the spectacle of their suffering is often unrecorded, a private affair. However, Mari Carmen's family was well connected; as members of the ruling classes their power networks extended across noble, political, and ecclesiastic spheres. Shortly after her death, it was proposed that Mari Carmen was an exemplary figure: her short life had been marked by holiness and her agonizing death demonstrated heroic virtue. People within this small but powerful network began to suggest that Mari Carmen had been so good—both in everyday life and in the face of death—that she must be a saint. The child's illness and death was, therefore, recast not as a tragedy or loss but as a difficult, painful, but joyful journey of spiritual enlightenment. Furthermore, the discovery of a secret diary after her death, in which she had written 'me entregé [sic] en la parroquia del Buen Pastor 6 de Abril 1939' [I offered my life in the Parish Church of the Good Shepherd on 6 April 1939], a few days before falling ill, gave her death a meaning and a function. The Archbishop of Madrid, Excelentísimo Sr. D. Antonio Ma. Rouco Varela, states that Mari Carmen, in imitation of Christ, offered her life 'por la salvación de los pecadores' [for the salvation of sinners]; these sinners are specifically 'aquellos que asesinaron a su padre en la persecución religiosa durante la Guerra Civil española' [those who murdered her father in the religious persecution during the Spanish Civil War] (Carmelitas Descalzas 1999: 2). It is claimed that Mari Carmen gave her life for the conversion of one sinner in particular, Manuel Azaña y Díaz, Spanish Minister and President of the Second Republic (Verd 1986: 420–34; González-Valerio 1997: 108–10). But also, it is maintained, Mari Carmen offered her life to expiate the death of her father, for her secret diary records the message 'por papá —7-5-1939—Domingo' [for Daddy, Sunday, 7 May 1939] (Sánchez 1960: 50).

Her father's death was interpreted as religious martyrdom by the clergy, but his canonization process failed at an early stage, his daughter taking on the role of expiatory victim more successfully. On her deathbed she is supposed to have exclaimed, '¡Papá murió mártir! Pobre mamá. Y yo muero victima' [Daddy died a martyr! Poor Mummy! And I die a victim] (Sánchez 1960: 63; González-Valerio 1997: 132). The word 'victim' has to be understood here as having the sense of a theological virtue: 'hay también quienes se ofrecen especialmente como víctimas, a la manera del mismo Jesucristo, y se entregan en holocausto de expiación por los pecados del mundo' [there are also those who offer themselves up specifically as victims, as did Christ, and who give their lives in sacrificial expiation of the sins of the world] (Verd 1986: 93). Mari Carmen's exclamations were witnessed by Doctor Blanco Soler, a renowned paediatrician, also a supporter of the Nationalist cause, who would serve as a witness for the canonization process (González-Valerio 1997: 129).

Mari Carmen died on 17 July 1939. Her funeral, which should have been the following day, was delayed because the streets of Madrid were blocked due to the third anniversary celebrations of the military uprising led by Franco in 1936. A post-war schoolbook, in which the National-Catholic feast days are listed, calls this day the 'día del valor' [day of courage]: 'Fecha gloriosa en que los buenos españoles, capitaneados por Franco, se alzaron en armas para eliminar las influencias marxistas y extranjerizantes que dominaban la vida nacional y lograr que en España renaciera su ancestral sentimiento católico' [The glorious day when good Spaniards, captained by General Franco, rose up in arms to extirpate the Marxist and foreign influences dominating national life and to secure the rebirth of the nation's ancestral Catholic sentiments] (Dalmau Carles n.d.: 358). Mari Carmen lived between 1930 and 1939: though she was not a casualty of the Civil War, the events of her life are interpreted by those who support her cause for canonization as inextricably connected to this traumatic period. The date of her voluntary self-sacrifice or 'entrega', recorded in her secret diary as 6 April 1939, is so close to the 'día de la Victoria' [Victory Day] on 1 April; just as her death is on the eve of another crucial National-Catholic commemoration. (It can be noted that the word 'entrega' was also used at the time of the 'sacrifice' of the heroic Fascist warrior who gave his life in battle.) The private grief of her immediate family is transformed, through the canonization process, into an act of political and historical consolation. Mari Carmen's death has a meaning and function for the Spanish Catholic Church; to remember her is to remember the Spanish Civil War.

MAKING SAINTS

The Catholic Church has a formal, rationalized way of recognizing saints: the canonization process. At present, the first stage of the canonization process is to award, should the person under consideration merit this in the eyes of the Church, the title of Venerable. To reach this point, several activities must already have taken place. A group recognized by the Church—in this case the Discalced Carmelite order based in Aravaca, Madrid—anticipates the formal process by organizing financial and spiritual support on her behalf. Kenneth Woodward describes how at this stage 'a guild is formed, money is collected, reports of divine favors are solicited, a newsletter is circulated, prayer cards are printed, and, not infrequently, a pious biography is published' (Woodward 1991: 79). Today the memory of Mari Carmen is promoted in many authored hagiographies, prayers, and poems as well as via the distribution of her image on religious artefacts such as holy cards, medals, colouring books, car plaques, pill boxes, silver-plated trays with her childish signature engraved,[4] and, oddly enough, plastic cigarette cases.[5]

The canonization process involves interviews, lengthy appeals, and bureaucratic procedures that require the demonstration of an exemplary moral life and, for sainthood, the proof of posthumous miracles. The process, therefore, demands that the devotion to the figure of Mari Carmen, a child who died of scarlet fever in 1939 aged just over 9 years old, be maintained over decades, beyond a single generation of initial enthusiasts, by a dedicated international institution which has the resources and the desire to keep her memory alive. William A. Christian has noted how these institutions make use of forms of mass communication to stimulate and sustain devotion: 'the history of the industrial propagation of particular saints, critical for the survival of shrines and the growth of the saint's prestige, goes back to the very beginning of mass-produced literature', for 'in the first years of the sixteenth century, religious prints were being sent from Flanders to Spain in the tens of thousands at a time' (Christian 1991: 175) and by the late nineteenth century the publication of regular magazines, or 'mail-order shrines' as Christian quips, had begun to circulate across diocesan and international boundaries.

The magazine dedicated to Mari Carmen, prepared by the Discalced Carmelite order based in Aravaca, Madrid, is published twice a year and is posted to believers in Spain and abroad. Issue number 33, dated May 1999, is printed on glossy paper; a hand-tinted photograph of Mari Carmen taken on the day of her First Communion is inset alongside the title *La niña que se entregó a Dios* in pink cursive lettering. The main body of the text is formed by letters from supporters giving details of 'favours' granted by God via Mari Carmen's intercession. Although some may appear to a non-believer to be quite banal and therefore dismissable, these 'favours' demonstrate the way faith operates in contemporary Catholic culture. Amparo Romero, for example, understands both her husband's positive exam results and her new job 'con un horario adecuado, compatible para el cuidado de mis hijas' [with the right hours allowing me to look after

---

[4] Carolyn Steedman notes that there is a fetishistic aspect to the facsimile publication of a child's handwriting, as 'it allows some adults to believe that they have penetrated the very heart of childhood' (1982: 61).

[5] These and similar objects—what Colleen McDannell has called 'Jesus junk. Holy hardware. Christian kitsch' (1995: 222)—can be acquired for modest prices from Carmelitas Descalzas, Carretera de Húmera s/n, Aravaca, 28023 Madrid.

my daughters] as a direct response to her prayers, and indicates the special position that Mari Carmen holds in her belief system: 'es como si fuera el Ángel de nuestra guarda' [she's like our guardian angel] (Carmelitas Descalzas 1999: 4).

Mari Carmen, thus, has an afterlife that extends beyond the members of her immediate family and contemporaries. The real girl, whoever she may have been, has been thoroughly encased in the straitjacket of conventional hagiography.

HAGIOGRAPHIES AS SCRIPTS OF FEMININITY

Hagiographies are powerful and persuasive documents. They communicate much more than the life and death stories of their protagonists; they also incorporate social values in a divine, and therefore unassailable, context. All manner of social directives are couched in holy language. Those hagiographies which focus on the childhood of a saint, or which are specifically about child saints, by their very nature as 'record' of an early life emphasize domestic and private virtues such as familial duty, personal integrity, and social benevolence, through examples of good conduct and Christian virtue. Projected in the multiple hagiographies devoted to Mari Carmen is a role model for Catholic girls to emulate: that of a child who takes to the extreme limits of altruism the virtues of filial love, obedience, and self-discipline. Should Mari Carmen ever be recognized as a saint, her name will be added to the canonical list, one consequence being that a child considered exemplary and promoted as a model by a minority will be invested with sacredness. In the hagiographic texts, Mari Carmen is a model Catholic girl who bears many similarities to the nineteenth-century ideal of the virtuous 'charity girl'. Lynne Vallone, in *Disciplines of Virtue*, describes the ideal of the charitable female thus: 'the paradigmatic white middle-class lady-in-training prescribed in conduct books and brought to life in conduct novels, gives money, goods, and time to the poor' (1995: 10). In similar vein, it is written that Mari Carmen gave away her toys and other gifts: 'Mira, mamá, que este año con la guerra, no se van a atrever a venir los Reyes Magos, y se van a quedar sin regalos aquellas pobrecitas. Todos los míos, mamá, quiero que sean para ellas' [Just think, Mummy, how this year, with the war, the three kings will be afraid to come and all those poor little girls will be left without a present. I want all my presents to be for them, Mummy] (Sánchez 1960: 40). Another hagiography declares 'la hucha de Mari Carmen era el pequeño tesoro de los pobres' [Mari Carmen's piggy bank was a little treasury for the poor], adding somewhat ludicrously that 'algunos guardan como recuerdo o reliquia aquellas monedas' [some of them have kept those coins as a memento or relic] (González-Valerio 1997: 101).

Mari Carmen did not only practise the virtue of charity but is reported to have been modest, tidy, obedient, helpful, and profoundly religious. In the hagiographies devoted to her, children are admonished to focus on the religious meaning of the everyday, and the merits of sacrifice are illustrated by easily imitable anecdotes, such as Mari Carmen's act of immediately dropping her doll to do her homework, at her mother's request: 'Ahora los deberes? Menudo rollo!, hubierais pensado vosotros. Pero Mari Carmen pensó que podía ofrecer este sacrificio a Jesús' [So now it's time for homework? What a bore, you would probably have thought. But Mari Carmen thought that she could offer that sacrifice to Jesus] (González Sáez de Paylos 1984: 5–6). The absence in the narratives of any traces of great or practical achievements by Mari Carmen could, in fact, be considered a bonus for, as Rosemary Mitchell has noted: 'the truly Good Woman would surely efface herself too fully to leave evidence of her life sufficient to justify a biography' (Cubitt and Warren 2000: 160). This statement is equally valid in relation to the model of the good girl that is presented in Mari Carmen's hagiographies for edification and imitation.

Mari Carmen is perceived as saintly not only because she died well—'Carmencita lo sufria todo en silencio' [little Carmen endured all her sufferings in silence] (Sánchez 1960: 52)—but because she internalized discipline to correct her own faults through the practice of Christian virtues: 'Sus maestras nos hablan de la seriedad de la pequeña para el estudio, de su afán en la práctica de la virtud y, principalmente, de la generosidad de su corazón para con los pobres y menesterosos. Y todo esto no era simple casualidad, sino que respondía a un programa que María del Carmen se trazaba de antemano. Ella aspiraba a ser santa, y para conseguir la santidad era preciso "chincharse"' [Her teachers talk of the little girl's serious dedication to study, her eagerness to do good, and above all her generous heart. These things corresponded to a plan of action that María del Carmen had set herself in advance. Her goal was to be a saint, and to be a saint she had to 'grin and bear it'] (Sánchez 1960, 93). Mari

Carmen may or may not have expressed a desire for sainthood in her life—we will never know, as the real child is lost to us and what remains is a mythical being that stands for many different ideas—but it is possible to discern from the constructions of the Venerable Mari Carmen González-Valerio y Sáenz de Heredia that the standards of goodness and saintliness demanded of Catholic girls during her lifetime were based on a sacrificial economy. Promoted as an exemplary figure, worthy of emulation, Mari Carmen is what every good little Catholic girl should mould herself into, or at least aim to approximate. As Paz García Alajarín (12 years old) writes, cited on the back-jacket of the hagiography for children, *La florecilla de la Virgen* (Aragón 1992): 'estoy encantada con el libro de *La florecilla de la Virgen*. Lo he leído varias veces y su lectura, además de gustarme mucho, me ayuda a ser mejor e intentar parecerme a Mari Carmen, sobre todo en su amor a la Virgen y en su "entrega total" ' [I love the book of *The Virgin's Little Flower*. I've read it several times and, apart from enjoying it, it helps me to be better and to try to be like Mari Carmen, especially in her love of the Virgin and her total self-sacrifice]. This publication urges the Catholic girl to be well behaved, modest, humble, charitable, and an active participant in church rituals. The book acknowledges that the ultimate sacrifice, death, is not requested of all Catholic children, but declares that 'los niños obedientes son santos. Esto lo entiendes muy bien porque para ser obediente tienes que vencer la testarudez, el capricho, el orgullo, la pereza. Reprimir la impaciencia... Hay que saber sacrificarse y para eso hay que amar mucho a Jesús' [obedient children are saintly. That's easy for you to understand because, to be obedient, you have to overcome stubbornness, capriciousness, pride, and laziness. And suppress impatience... You have to be capable of sacrificing yourself and to do that you have to love Jesus] (Aragón 1992: 50). Lynne Vallone, analysing the complex ideologies manifest in girlhood culture, notes that 'each girl must decide how to conquer and then channel her girlish nature—characterized by desire, hunger, anger, ignorance, and aggression—into valuable, beautiful womanly conduct' (Vallone 1995: 5). Hagiographies are an important element of girlhood culture. Edifying books on saints for children have been in circulation in Spain from the 1880s to the present day, enjoying a heyday from the 1930s to the 1960s, though books for young girls are still being published today that portray sainthood as a state to which one should aspire. One of these, *Unas santas a tu edad*:

selección biográfica de niñas y jóvenes santas [*Saints at your Age: Selected Biographies of Girl Saints*] (1980), states in the introduction: 'para que no creáis que eso de ser santas es algo fuera de vuestro alcance, he querido escoger este manojo de flores fresquísimas y fragantes' [I've put together this bouquet of fresh, fragrant flowers so you won't think that being a girl saint is beyond your reach], and urges the reader to take note as 'en todos los estados y condiciones de vida hallaréis modelos de santidad que imitar y seguir' [in all aspects and conditions of life you will find models of saintliness to imitate and follow], adding '¡Ojalá que vuestros actos puedan llenar páginas como éstas!' [Let us hope that your acts will fill pages like these!] (Sanz Burata 1980: 1). These books can be considered 'scripts of femininity', because they reaffirm and reiterate cultural narratives that Catholic girls must follow in the process of becoming 'woman'.

SACRIFICIAL ECONOMY

The 'scripts of femininity' of any place or period constitute a system of ideas against which women have to measure their behaviour; they thus help us understand the meanings of their compliance or defiance. Models of sainthood, too, serve as behavioural scripts. How, then, might one define the dominant idea of sainthood in Spain in the early part of the twentieth century? William A. Christian, in his study *Visionaries: The Spanish Republic and the Reign of Christ*, notes that an ethos of female sacrifice was prevalent in Spain during the 1930s (1996: 96–103). With civil war felt to be inevitable, parishes in the north of Spain were preparing men to accept martyrdom as their fate: that is, death at the hands of other men as a result of religious persecution and in defence of their faith. Christian is attuned to the gendering of sainthood, noting that the complementary programme for women stated that God would take women's lives directly. They would be victims and stand for the sins of others. In this economy of substitute pain, Catholic women were granted the expiatory role. Christian finds that this ethos pervaded popular religious literature from the period; mystics such as Gemma Galgani and Thérèse of Lisieux became role models, their lives and deaths exalted as examples of passive sacrifice, voluntarily assumed in order to redeem the sins of the world. Certainly, the cult of suffering and sacrifice is embedded in Christianity and the figure of the victim is highly valued.

However, although the ideal of self-sacrifice has been put before men and women alike, it is to women that it has been most rigorously applied. And it is women who have been singled out to expiate the sins of men. This concept of a sacrificial economy, based on the notion of substitution, facilitates an understanding of the ways in which Mari Carmen's death is today being remembered by the Catholic Church. For if Mari Carmen enjoyed the 'privilege' of having her life taken by God directly, it was so that she might play the role of sacrificial lamb to expiate the wartime deaths of men at the hands of other men.

WORKS CITED

Anon. (1999). 'Madrid, la diócesis del mundo que tiene abiertas más causas de beatificación y con más casas religiosas'. Teletipo Europa Press y ¡Olé!. http://teletipo.ole.es/1999/08/09/19990809121950-CYS-SUC.html (accessed Jan. 2001).

Aragón, A. M. (1992). La florecilla de la Virgen. Madrid: Carmelitas Descalzas-Aravaca.

Bertoglio, M. G. L. (1999). Mari Carmen: la fuerza del perdón. Madrid: Ediciones Palabra.

Carmelitas Descalzas (1999). La niña que se entregó a Dios. No. 33. Madrid: Gráficas Don Bosco.

Christian, W. A. (1991). 'Secular and Religious Responses to a Child's Potentially Fatal Illness', in E. R. Wolf (ed.), Religious Regimes and State-Formation: Perspectives from European Ethnology. New York: State University of New York Press, 163–80.

——(1992). Moving Crucifixes in Modern Spain. Princeton: Princeton University Press.

——(1996). Visionaries: The Spanish Republic and the Reign of Christ. Berkeley and Los Angeles: University of California Press.

Cubitt, G., and Warren, A. (eds.) (2000). Heroic Reputations and Exemplary Lives. Manchester: Manchester University Press.

Dalmau Carles, P. (n.d.). Enciclopedia cíclico-pedagógica: grado elemental. Gerona: Talleres Gráficos.

Delooz, P. (1983). 'Towards a Sociological Study of Canonized Sainthood in the Catholic Church', in S. Wilson (ed.), Saints and their Cults: Studies in Religious Sociology, Folklore and History. Cambridge: Cambridge University Press, 189–216.

Elias, N. (1998). 'Observations on Gossip', in S. Mennell and J. Goudsblom (eds.), On Civilization, Power, and Knowledge. Chicago: University of Chicago Press, 249–52.

González Sáez de Paylos, M. (1984). *Mi Primera Comunión*. Madrid: Carmelitas Descalzas-Aravaca.

[González-Valerio y Sáenz de Heredia, M. de L.] (1997). *La niña que se entregó a Dios: vida de la venerable María del Carmen González-Valerio y Sáenz de Heredia*. Madrid: Carmelitas Descalzas-Aravaca.

Goodich, M. (1973). 'Childhood and Adolescence among the Thirteenth Century Saints', *History of Childhood Quarterly: Journal of Psychohistory*, 2: 285–309.

Granero, J. M. (1984). *Víctima*. Madrid: Carmelitas Descalzas-Aravaca.

John Paul II, Pope (2001). 'Capella Papale per la beatificazione di 233 Servi di Dio'. http://www.vatican.va/cgi-bin/w3-msql/news_services/bulletin/news/8723.html?index=8723&po_date=11.03.2001&lang=it (accessed Apr. 2001).

McDannell, C. (1995). *Material Christianity: Religion and Popular Culture in America*. New Haven: Yale University Press.

Morgan, D. (1998). *Visual Piety: A History and Theory of Popular Religious Images*. Berkeley and Los Angeles: University of California Press.

Primo de Rivera, P. (1983). *Recuerdos de una vida*. Madrid: Ediciones Dyrsa.

Resusta, T. (1993). *Mari Carmen*. Madrid: Carmelitas Descalzas-Aravaca.

Sánchez, E. (1960). *La niña que se entregó*. Barcelona: Publicaciones ACI.

Sanz Burata, L. (1980). *Unas santas a tu edad: selección biográfica de niñas y jóvenes santas*. Seville: Apostolado Mariano.

Steedman, C. (1982). *The Tidy House: Little Girls Writing*. London: Virago Press.

Vallone, L. (1995). *Disciplines of Virtue: Girl's Culture in the Eighteenth and Nineteenth Centuries*. New Haven: Yale University Press.

Verd, G. M. (1986). *Mari Carmen González-Valerio, una niña hacia los altares*. Madrid: Carmelitas Descalzas-Aravaca.

Woodward, K. (1991). *Making Saints. Inside the Vatican: Who Become Saints, Who do Not, and Why....* London: Chatto & Windus.

8

Victoria Abril: The Sex Which Is Not One

PETER WILLIAM EVANS

As Pam Cook (1985), Paul McDonald (1995), and others have argued, star studies has moved through four different but related stages over the last twenty years or so: semiotics, intertextuality, psychoanalysis, and audience reception (McDonald 1995: 80). In what follows I want to consider the significance of Victoria Abril above all in relation to the first three categories. My relative neglect of the fourth is motivated not by lack of interest but by as yet rudimentary preliminary research.

SEMIOTICS

Part of the difficulty of applying Richard Dyer's seminal work (1979) in this area to analysis of Victoria Abril arises from her appearance in different categories of film, some of which—especially early on in her career—could loosely be termed popular, with the majority probably best classified as art or auteurist films. I am not interested here in theorizing the disparities or resemblances between popular and art/auteurist film, merely in arguing that while Dyer's focus on the specific features of individual stars—voice, gesture, looks, role, etc.—is perfectly suited to analysis of European stars who move between the popular and the auteurist, his notion of Hollywood stars as constructs designed to resolve ideological contradiction is in this context more problematic, since in many of the films in which Victoria Abril appears (some of Aranda's, all of Almodóvar's), the exposure, not the resolution, of contradiction is the text's primary ideological justification.

Indisputably one of Spain's top two or three female stars, rivalled perhaps only by Carmen Maura or Ana Belén but with more international recognition than either of them, Victoria Abril, 'hermosa, peleona, discutidora, libertaria, chula, imparable y contradictoria' [beautiful, feisty, argumentative, liberated, raunchy, unstoppable, and contradictory], as she has been described by Juan Rioyo (1995: 33), has at first glance the aura of an elfin, pubescent, undeveloped waif. Yet for all her little girl's face and adolescent body, the determined gaze and rough, slightly husky voice and unladylike mouth express the confidence and assertiveness of a precocious maturity. Never a stranger to controversy off-screen, even though her on-screen roles often ultimately stress her girlishness, demanding eventual accommodation with the social order, Abril is the essence of experiment and transgression. The off-screen Abril's notorious awkwardness, her abrupt treatment of paparazzi who refer to her as 'la fiera' (fiery) (Rivera 1996: 96), as well as her outspokenness and sometimes outrageous demotic interviewee's prose, bring steel to the air of innocence displayed in her role as hostess for the TV game show *Un dos tres*, making her seem sometimes like a cross between the angelic Marisol (the hugely famous child and later teenage star of the 1960s) and the diabolical Lola Gaos (the son-devouring mother in films by Buñuel and Borau); a Buñuelian Devil's daughter, the 'fille terrible' not just of French cinema (a significant number of her films have been made in France), but of Spanish cinema as well; a woman of obvious intelligence but also, as José Luis de Villalonga remarks (1994: 106), 'peligrosa como una carga de dinamita a punto de estallar' [as dangerous as a stick of dynamite about to explode].

INTERTEXTUALITY

The meaning of the Abril persona, as of any star's, is not, of course, solely determined by the films in which she appears. Her presence is conditioned by information about her life off-screen—her relations with paparazzi; her two marriages; her recent separation from her French cameraman husband Gérard de Battista; her recent dispute with Víctor Aranda, the director of so many of her Spanish films—as well as by the impact of ideas or texts in circulation on gender, sexuality, and subjectivity, though it is always of course very difficult to pinpoint precisely which have exerted the greatest influence. Although Abril's first film *Obsesión* (Francisco Lara Polop, 1974) appeared before the expiry of the *ancien régime*, her major films have all been made since the transition to democracy. The intertextual discourses, therefore, that have helped define the Abril persona are not, say, the antique psychology of a López Ibor (perhaps the best known of conservative sex theorists in the Franco period), or the bulletins of the Comisión Episcopal de Ortodoxia y Moralidad which in the early Franco period even condemned as a 'peligro grave' the holding of hands by *novios*, but the work published by the Instituto de la Mujer, the dissemination of texts by other European and American feminists, key articles and books by Spanish feminist psychoanalysts like Silvia Tubert, the novels, poems, and films by writers like Almudena Grandes, Pilar Miró, Ana Rossetti, and many others, as well as the clear visibility in public life of women like Carmen Alborch and Cristina Alberdi (Socialist Ministers of Culture and Social Affairs respectively), or (in journalism and literature) Ángeles Caso and Rosa Montero, and so on. These texts, with a predominantly feminist perspective, have had to compete for attention with the post-dictatorship availability of pornography and the rise of magazines like *Interviú*, whose problematic definitions of femininity have not failed to affect the representation of women in even auteurist films (some of Bigas Luna's films come to mind). *Interviú* has even published a still of the disrobed Abril from *La muchacha de las bragas de oro* [*The Girl in the Golden Knickers*] (Aranda, 1979), a film discussed at length below.

In sociological terms the rise of Victoria Abril, a star formed partly by residual processes of objectification and partly by the new assertiveness, has also of course coincided with what Anny Brooksbank Jones has termed the post-1970s 'social and politico-juridical institutionalization of the less controversial assumptions of the 1970s explosion of feminism' (1995: 387). The Abril persona has developed in this climate, and even in her less assertive roles emerges largely untouched by dependency, passivity, low esteem, incompetence, or inhibition. Typically, the Abril character—fiction here merging with fact—is a risk-taker, a nonconformist, a transgressor against most forms of convention: against the family in *Cambio de sexo* [*Sex-Change*] (Aranda, 1976), *La colmena* [*The Hive*] (Mario Camús, 1982), *Las bicicletas son para el verano* [*Bicycles are for Summer*] (Jaime Chávarri, 1983), *Amantes* [*Lovers*] (Aranda, 1991), as well as *La muchacha de las bragas de oro*; against what Adrienne Rich calls

Fig. 4. Victoria Abril in the film *Río abajo* (Borau, 1984)

compulsory heterosexuality in *Gazon maudit* (Josiane Balasko, 1994) and *La muchacha de las bragas de oro* (Aranda, 1979); against a variety of bourgeois norms in *Río abajo* [*Downstream*] (José Luis Borau, 1984) (see Fig. 4), *El Lute, camina o revienta* [*El Lute, Walk or Die*] (Aranda, 1987), and *Si te dicen que caí* [*The Fallen*] (Aranda, 1989). The adolescent look perfectly matches her transgressive roles, adding a touch of playful self-consciousness to roles given their most satirical form in *Kika* (Pedro Almodóvar, 1993), a film that at some levels explores media manipulation of identity. In keeping with the spirit of the times, the Abril persona, not content with domestic roles, colonizes public spaces, but even in private ones her role is less narcissistic than code-breaking. And yet, her body and her provocative sexuality are key features of the persona.

CINEPSYCHOANALYSIS

There is no space here to summarize the copious work done in this area on the identifications between spectator and star as either object of desire or wish-fulfilment fantasy. Edgar Morin initiated it, but since his early and largely unacknowledged book *Les Stars*, Christian Metz, Laura Mulvey, Christine Gledhill, Mary Ann Doane, Judith Mayne, and many others have developed this tendency, most interestingly in recent years in the direction of gender studies. As Paul McDonald argues (1995: 86), 'For psychoanalytic film theory, the formation of the subject creates division and lack, and this motivates its desire. Desire is seen as the pursuit of that which will fill the lack, and so make the subject whole and complete.' The spectator identifies with stars on the screen who become either ego-ideals or objects of desire. Mulvey's interest in cinepsychoanalysis drew the discussion of Hollywood stars towards the view that pleasure is determined by patriarchal assumptions and positionality. But, in summary, this argument led subsequent feminist theorists to criticize its failure to take account of the female spectator's pleasure and the text's resistances to dominant ideology. Mary Ann Doane's work on female spectatorship—adapting Joan Riviere's theory of the masquerade—and later work by Barbara Creed, Judith Mayne, Christine Gledhill, and others looking at the instabilities of the texts and the cross-gendered shifts of identification have opened up the debate even more rewardingly. Abril's persona exemplifies the complexity of identification. Two films, one relatively early, *Cambio de sexo* (1976), and a later one, *La muchacha de las bragas de oro* (1979), provide the blueprint for the invariable fusion in her films between the narrative's deconstruction of gendered sexuality and the star persona's polymorphous perversity, something that Abril has not disavowed in interviews both in Spain and abroad.

The display of the body in these films is, of course, at one level, voyeuristic. Abril is very much an eroticized star, surprisingly so according to José Luis de Villalonga (1994: 106) given her diminutive stature: 'lo que más llama la atención en Victoria es que un cuerpo tan diminuto pueda encerrar tal carga de erotismo' [The most striking thing about Victoria is the way such a tiny frame can hold such a powerful erotic charge]. Almodóvar (1995: 34) echoes the point, comparing her to Jennifer Jason Leigh, Holly Hunter, Jodie Foster, Juliette Binoche, and Helena Bonham-Carter as 'mujeres diminutas e ígneas [. . .] dotadas especialmente para caracterizaciones terribles, personajes extremos, torturados física o mentalmente' [diminutive and fiery women [. . .] especially suited for playing extreme, terrible characters, tortured physically and mentally]. In the same interview, Almodóvar stresses Abril's natural uninhibitedness: 'se desnuda con la naturalidad del que inhala humo de un cigarrillo. Sin duda, Victoria Abril es la actriz que mejor rueda escenas eróticas. Para ella no hay tabúes, ni barreras' [She strips with the ease of a smoker inhaling smoke. Victoria Abril is undoubtedly the best actress for erotic scenes. There are no taboos or barriers for her] (1985: 34).

And yet Victoria Abril is clearly more than *Interviú* centrefold material in these films. There is a world of difference between her *déshabillé* moments and, say, the frivolous posing nudity of the *destape* (soft porn) stars Ágata Lys, Nadiuska, Bárbara Rey, and the others. In the casual display of her body she often seems to exemplify Irigaray's notion of the sex which is not one; that is, not one because defined in relation to the male, and more than one or multiple like female sexual pleasure: 'what they desire is precisely nothing, and at the same time everything. Always something more and something less besides that *one*—sexual organ, for example—that you give them, attribute to them. The desire is often interpreted, and feared, as a sort of insatiable hunger, a voracity that will swallow you whole. Whereas it really involves a different economy more than anything else, one that upsets the linearity of a project, undermines the goal-object of a desire, diffuses the polarization towards a single pleasure, disconcerts fidelity to a single discourse' (1977: 29–30). Like the woman of Irigaray's imaginary, Victoria Abril is protean, a visual emblem of 'écriture féminine', an exploded and reconstructed double syntax of the feminine, whose sexuality is less indebted to a secularized ideology's enthralment with the gym culture than to redefinitions of desire, demasculinizing it, challenging the association of the female body with lack.

It is appropriate that in *Cambio de sexo* Abril is the star chosen to mutate from male to female in a sexual odyssey that remains like that of well-known Spanish TV personality Bibi Andersen—also appearing in the film—a transsexualism never wholly carrying conviction. Interestingly, the part was first offered to Ángela Molina, who eventually rejected it. Aranda now reflects that although Abril was admirable in the role—the start of a long collaboration with him— Ángela Molina would have made the transformation from male to female more dramatic. In his view her femininity is more pronounced than Abril's (Vera 1989: 115; Kinder 1999: 142). Abril is more androgynous, more flexibly gendered, less sexually defined.

In *La muchacha de las bragas de oro*, the geography of Abril's body is as it were recreated to become eternally self-generating and fulfilling, a body which, when Mariana announces to her uncle (Lautauro Murua) that she is retiring to her room to masturbate, recalls Irigaray's reminder that a woman 'touches herself in and of herself without any need for mediation, and before there is any way to distinguish activity from passivity. Woman touches herself all the time, and moreover no one can forbid her to do so, for her genitals are formed of two lips in continuous contact' (Irigaray 1977: 24). This auto-eroticism, part of the woman's strategy for reclaiming authority over her own body, is plainly radically different in nature from the furtive practice of that other great masturbator of the screen, Woody Allen, whose characteristic joke, 'masturbation is having sex with someone I love', is a regression to narcissism, a flight from women he can no longer control. Allen's alter egos on screen represent the Law of the Father, on the run; the Abril character's presence represents the forces from which that Law is in retreat. The scene in which Abril—moving on from auto-eroticism and lesbianism—attempts to seduce the person who she imagines is her uncle, but who is discovered to be her natural father, draws attention to this changing pattern of submissiveness and dominance. With due acknowledgement of the sometimes problematic attitudes of Aranda and Marsé, the 'authors' of the film based on Marsé's novel, towards gender and the relations between the sexes, the appearance of Abril in the role offers new possibilities of identification between star and women spectators. The feminist discourse of post-dictatorship Spain displaces male-centred projections of femininity in the Abril persona.

Fellating the father here is readable, at one level at least, as symbolic triumph rather than as Freudian seduction. The scene provides one of the clearest examples of the Abril persona's refusal to seek either complicity or theft of normative masculine qualities of power to compensate for the deficiencies of an aberrant femininity. The gesture records not submission to the rule of the father—here identified as a broken man with suicidal tendencies—but liberation from patriarchy.

The refusals and assertiveness of the Abril persona, often negotiating difficult accommodation with the narrative's more conservative drives, remain in evidence and are further developed in her more recent films: the assault on heterosexual exclusivity in *Gazon maudit*; the combative identification with Republicanism—and its wider socio-sexual libertarianism—in *Libertarias* [*Anarchist Women*] (Aranda, 1996); and the appropriation of the look in *Amantes* (1991), where often the female is seer and the male seen. *Amantes* develops strategies from earlier Abril films, especially *Átame* (Almodóvar, 1989) where, as Paul Julian Smith has remarked, 'the parody of the male gaze is supplemented by a space between women, which is not ironised' (1994: 109). In this film, too, the self-conscious identification, through costume and especially *mise-en-scène*, with the *femme fatale* of classic Hollywood *noir* narratives, like Gloria Swanson's Norma Desmond in *Sunset Boulevard* (1950) and above all Barbara Stanwyck's Phylis Dietrickson in *Double Indemnity* (1944), stresses the Abril persona's cross-cultural alliance with transgression.

Of her recent films, *Nadie hablará de nosotras cuando hayamos muerto* [*No One Will Mention Us When We're Dead*] (Agustín Díaz Yanes, 1995) is especially interesting from the point of view of its self-conscious degradation of the Abril persona. Once again the sexual aura of the star is highlighted, but here less affirmatively. Sexual appeal has its price, the film seems to argue, and the Abril character is made to pay for it, making her a victim: first as prostitute (as previously in *Río abajo*), and then as the target of brutal Mexican gangsters. But even here the Abril character's suffering—climaxing in the scene of the corskscrew being driven into her leg by the sadistic Mexican hitman—is to some extent alleviated by her self-protective streetwise resilience, for Gloria will agree only to oral sex with her clients, an idiosyncratic gesture of defiance affirming her desire to limit the public boundaries of a body in which she is determined to retain some private, untrespassed spaces. This attitude is in keeping with the growing feistiness of the Abril persona, heightening the impish will-power of the waif, developing the single-mindedness and determination of the character which even in its early youthful stages masked a steely resolve beneath an exterior of vulnerability. This film moves the Abril character beyond the overt sexual *jouissance* of so many of her roles to develop other potential. No seductive *noir*-defined *femme fatale* here, the Abril character is never seen disrobed even in scenes where she services her eager clients. Sex here is a means to an end in a tough world where only the fittest survive. There is no eulogy here of the naked Abril body, as on the front cover of *Cinemanía* or the more torrid scenes of *Átame*. Rather, as Gloria discards the tight miniskirt and tottering high heels of her carnal trade for the leggings and other dreary practical clothes of a working woman, we are offered in close-ups the spectacle of a haggard face, of pale, hollow cheeks, weary but decisive eyes, and the gradual transformation of a body from sexual commodity to vehicle of practical efficiency. The mutation from whore to thief, trucker, and mature student is the measure of her victory as a woman over inner demons and external pressures. For all its bleakness, the film affirms the Abril persona's inner strength, allowing it to display its many attributes beyond the realm of sexual pleasure.

CONCLUSION

Victoria Abril's films have invariably been extremely successful commercially. The reasons are many, and may sometimes be governed more by the reputation of the director than by that of the star, though by now of course Abril's economic value is considerable and her signature usually guarantees healthy box-office takings. Much work remains to be done on the actual as distinct from the theoretical identification of spectators with stars. The work of Jackie Stacey on the impact of Hollywood stars of the 1940s and 1950s on contemporary audiences (1994) provides a useful model. It would be instructive to measure the ways in which since the transition Victoria Abril, as one of the most important stars of the Spanish cinema, has offered audiences new models of identification.

WORKS CITED

Almodóvar, P. (1995). 'Victoria Abril', *Cinemanía*, 2 (Nov.): 34.
Brooksbank Jones, A. (1995). 'Work, Women and the Family: A Critical Perspective', in H. Graham and J. Labanyi (eds.), *Spanish Cultural Studies: An Introduction*. Oxford: Oxford University Press, 386–93.
—— (1997). *Women in Contemporary Spain*. Manchester: Manchester University Press.
Cook, P. (ed.) (1985). *The Cinema Book*. London: British Film Institute.
Creed, B. (1993). *The Monstrous-Feminine: Film, Feminism, Psycho-analysis*. London: Routledge.

Doane, M. A. (1988). *The Desire to Desire: The Woman's Film of the 1940s.* London: Macmillan.

Dyer, R. (1979). *Stars.* London: British Film Institute.

Gledhill, C. (ed.) (1991). *Stardom: Industry of Desire.* London: Routledge.

Irigaray, L. (1977). *The Sex Which Is Not One*, trans. C. Porter. Ithaca, NY: Cornell University Press.

Kinder, M. (1999). 'Sex Change and Cultural Transformation in Aranda and Abril's *Cambio de sexo* (1977)', in P. W. Evans (ed.), *Spanish Cinema: The Auteurist Tradition.* Oxford: Oxford University Press, 128–46.

McDonald, P. (1995). 'Star Studies', in J. Hollows and M. Jancovich (eds.), *Approaches to Popular Film.* Manchester: Manchester University Press, 79–97.

Mayne, J. (1993). *Cinema and Spectatorship.* London: Routledge.

Morin, E. (1960). *The Stars.* New York: Grove Press.

Mulvey, L. (1989). *Visual and Other Pleasures.* Basingstoke: Macmillan.

Rioyo, J. (1995). 'Victoria Abril', *Cinemanía*, 2 (Nov.): 22–33.

Rivera, A. (1996). 'Victoria Abril', *El País* (14 Jan.).

Smith, P. J. (1994). *Desire Unlimited: The Cinema of Pedro Almodóvar* London: Verso.

Stacey, J. (1994). *Star Gazing: Hollywood Cinema and Female Spectatorship.* London: Routledge.

Vera, P. (1989). *Vicente Aranda.* Madrid: Ediciones JC.

Villalonga, J. L. de (1994). 'Victoria Abril', *El País Semanal* (18 Dec.): 106.

9

Sex, Lies, and Traditions:
La Cubana's *Teresina, SA*

JOSEP-ANTON FERNÀNDEZ

THE marriage of tradition and modernity is a central aspect of modern Catalan culture, an issue that virtually every generational movement has had to address, because what is at stake in it are the twin issues of social cohesion and national difference. No other period has been more successful in this respect than *Noucentisme*, the conservative, Catholic, neoclassical movement of the first two decades of this century, which played a major role in the institutionalization of Catalan culture, and which sought to modernize Catalan society through a set of reformist policies in order to avoid a revolutionary fracture.

Noucentisme's agenda claimed to be firmly rooted in the Catalan popular tradition; but, as art historian Robert S. Lubar (1994) has argued in an essay on the use of landscape in *Noucentista* art, the popular tradition was in fact a trope used by the movement's artists and intellectuals to construct a cultural myth that ultimately denied its popular origins; a myth which was addressed to the urban bourgeoisie, which excluded the people in which it had supposedly originated, and which aimed at containing the excesses of the industrial working class; a myth which was underwriting a reactionary, patriarchal, and elitist cultural and political agenda. The epitome of this discursive strategy is Eugeni d'Ors's 1912 novel *La Ben Plantada* (d'Ors 1983), whose protagonist, Teresa, is a woman who encapsulates all the essential features of the Catalan character: she is order, elegance, discretion, irony, moderation, proportion, beauty—and reproduction. Teresa, in short, is not an anecdote, but, to use Ors's own terminology, a Category that sums up all the virtues of the Catalan tradition—and, as nice girls do, at the end of the book she gets engaged.

The 1980s and 1990s are a comparable period to that of *Nou-centisme*, in the sense that Catalan society is engaged in a process of national reconstruction also termed 'normalization'. This time, however, the marriage of tradition and modernity can only take place through the mass media, within a highly fragmented audio-visual space, and before a mass audience. The sitcom I examine in this article, *Teresina, SA*, is a good example for discussing the terms of this new marriage, and I will attempt to do so by focusing on one of the episodes.

Produced and broadcast by Televisió de Catalunya (TVC)—the Catalan public broadcasting corporation—in the spring of 1992 (during prime time, after the evening news), and written, performed, and directed by the theatre company La Cubana, *Teresina, SA* consists of thirteen episodes of twenty-five minutes' duration. The series is set in the present time in a flat in carrer Verdi, a real street of Gràcia, a traditional working-class area of Barcelona; the fiction covers a time span of a year, from August to August. As the title indicates, the programme is very much character-based: indeed, the protagonists of the series are the Teresines, three unmarried sisters in their sixties and late fifties who have the same name, Teresa, although they have been each named after a different St Teresa (of Ávila, of Portugal, of Lisieux), and each of them is known by a different nickname: Teresina, Maria Teresa, and Tere. The Teresines work in the underground economy: their living room doubles as a workshop in which they produce the objects commissioned from them. Each episode is named after a popular tradition or an important moment in the calendar, and the Teresines work on something related to that month's tradition: in May, for example, they hand-paint First Communion cards, in June they make red scarves for San Fermín, at Christmas they assemble nativity scenes, etc.

There is always too much work to do, so they hire their neighbours who, obviously, keep quiet about their illegal economic activities. The Teresines' living room thus becomes a tightly knit social universe in which women are strong, and men are either gay and assertive or weak and immature. Much gossip circulates while work is being done, and most of it is about the neighbours' social status and sex life; at the same time, however, the characters attempt, unsuccessfully, to keep up appearances. Thus, for example, neighbour Montserrat, who managed to marry in her late forties, constantly boasts about her wedded bliss and advises the Teresines to get married too, but we will discover that her husband's performance is not exactly first class.

Angelina, who has delusions of grandeur, pretends that she goes to work with the Teresines not because she needs the money, but because she is bored at home. And the Teresines not only try to avoid the taxman's gaze, but also to maintain the pretence that, if they never married, it is because they never wanted to.

Teresina, SA combines the parodic and hyperbolic style characteristic of La Cubana with the realist *mise-en-scène* which is required by the sitcom genre, and these two elements are in turn combined with a self-reflexive slant (all the episodes contain sequences of television within television). At the same time, the series combines the genre's attention to women's lives with the representation of the interplay between the private and public spaces in Catalan society, and with a discourse on popular traditions.

Television is perhaps the main mediator, in contemporary society, between the public and the private. Television, claims Patricia Mellencamp (1992: 264), 'both traverses *and* maintains' the divide 'between the public sphere and the private home'. Television traverses this divide because it brings both terms, the private and the public, into each other's view; but it also maintains the divide because it defines the boundaries between private and public spaces. The situation comedy, however, has a specific role in this process; as Frances Gray (1994: 41) argues, '[w]hile other programmes seek to provide a (not always transparent) window on the public world which we view from our domestic space, sitcom brings the private space into the private space'. However, it could be argued that, if this is the case, it is because the sitcom, like any other dramatic genre, relies on an illusion of immediacy: when we watch the Golden Girls eating cheesecake or Edina and Patsy (from BBC's *Absolutely Fabulous*) drinking Bollinger in the kitchen, nobody has opened the door to us, we just suspend our disbelief and pretend we can see. The opening credits of *Teresina, SA*, however, immediately call this illusion into question. The credits, combining animation and video, start with the camera approaching the Teresines' door, moving on to a close up of the spy hole, and leading into the theme song. While the three protagonists sing, we see them in various rooms in their flat, engaging in their everyday activities, such as getting up in the morning, trying clothes on, or working, before they close the door of the flat.

The opening credits thus start with the audience intruding into the private space, and end with an interpellation: in the song, the Teresines introduce and define themselves (they are resourceful, independent, hard-working, and above all good neighbours), and finish saying: 'Som unes Teresines, i potser | tu també' [We are Teresines and perhaps | you are too]. On the other hand, the self-reflexive character of the show produces a closely related effect: in the first episode, the Teresines and their neighbours are watching a chat show in which La Cubana (the real theatre company) are being interviewed. The company's director, Jordi Milan, describes the Teresines, who are thereby simultaneously constructed both as an audience and as a subject of discussion in the public sphere (and importantly, Milan claims that anybody who shares their values can be a Teresina, irrespective of age, gender, or class: the Teresines are not anecdotes but a Category). The Teresines' previous interpellation of the audience ('perhaps you are a Teresina too') corresponds to their own identification and self-recognition ('look, they're talking about us'). The boundaries between public and private are thus blurred, but at the same time denaturalized and made visible.

This blurring of boundaries is carried forward by the setting of the programme. Critics often note that sitcoms are usually set either at home, the domestic space assigned to femininity, or at work, the public space where women usually find themselves in problematic positions (Bowes 1990: 132–4).[1] In the case of *Teresina, SA*, however, the private space of the home is also the workplace: as opposed to the Golden Girls, the Teresines do not just gossip but also work; but as opposed to Murphy Brown or Edina Monsoon (from *Absolutely Fabulous*), they are not young and successful professional women. They are more like female *bricoleurs*, as their work is not circumscribed to one particular product or to one set of skills—they will accept almost any order, and will learn any new techniques they need to complete it; their motto is, 'Si aquella pot fer-ho, jo també' [If she can do it, I can too]. On the other hand, this sitcom is not centred around a traditional, nuclear family, as in Antena 3's *Farmacia de guardia* [24-Hour Chemist], for example, but focuses on the everyday life of the whole community.

But as I have suggested earlier, what makes this sitcom different from others is the fact that the work being done in the Teresines' living room is inextricably related to popular traditions and the traditional calendar. The series thus represents some of the old and not so

---

[1] Patricia Mellencamp (1992) has brilliantly analysed this dynamic in American sitcoms. On specific American sitcoms, see also Frazer and Frazer (1993) and Kaler (1990).

old traditions to a mass audience through the highly technological medium of television, and at the same time traditions are shown in the context of an advanced capitalist economy. Every episode of *Teresina, SA* begins with a conversation about the meanings of the relevant tradition, focusing on how much things have changed, and giving information about the basic 'procedures' of the tradition.

The episode I will discuss in detail, 'Rams' [Palm Sunday], is no exception. The action takes place in March, and the Teresines are weaving the palms that children carry on Palm Sunday. As usual, some of the neighbours are helping out, among them Angelina and her daughter Conxiteta, who married just two months earlier and is already proudly looking like a fully-fledged housewife. During the conversation, Conxiteta expresses her desire to become a mother, so her child can carry one of these palms, because children look so cute with them. Marieta, an elderly neighbour, then explains that it is the godmother who buys the palm, and that on Palm Sunday girls carry the small, very elaborate *palma*, whereas boys carry the larger, more natural, and rather phallic *palmó*. It could be assumed that most Catalans of a certain age (thirty years and over) and with a Catholic background (the overwhelming majority of the population) would already know the information given in this conversation. The same would apply to the rest of the series, which features mainstream traditions such as Christmas, All Saints, the Falles, and Sant Jordi. However, the commercial success of the recent book by journalist Salvador Alsius, *Hem perdut l'oremus* (1998), a dictionary of idioms and sayings of Catholic origin in the Catalan language, might indicate that the speedy modernization and secularization experienced by Catalan society in the 1980s and 1990s has resulted in a hiatus in the transmission of the cultural codes (mostly originating in Catholicism) necessary to understand the meanings of popular traditions. But whether or not there is empirical evidence that the audience of *Teresina, SA* (especially younger viewers) does not share these cultural codes is perhaps less important, I would argue, than the fact that the series, as the initial dialogues suggest, assumes that the viewers have virtually no knowledge of basic aspects of the cultural heritage; therefore a break with the past is also assumed, one brought about by modernization.

The dialogues at the beginning of each episode thus provide a pretext for representing and reframing popular Catalan traditions. Could we go further and suggest that *Teresina, SA* is in fact reinventing these traditions? As Eric Hobsbawm has famously argued, invented traditions are 'a set of practices, normally governed by overtly or tacitly accepted rules and of a ritual or symbolic nature, which seek to inculcate certain values and norms of behaviour by repetition, which automatically implies continuity with the past' (1992: 1). The practices Hobsbawm refers to are modern inventions (to be distinguished from the practices of traditional society) that establish a fictional continuity with the past. However, the traditions featured in *Teresina, SA* would depart from Hobsbawm's definition in two ways.

First, in most cases they are indeed old traditions, with some exceptions, such as Gràcia's Festa Major (episodes 1 and 13), Sant Jordi (episode 9), and the episode devoted to tourism (episode 12). Secondly, these traditions are all very much alive, and this is shown precisely by their commodification which ensures them a role in modern society. Yet what is assumed here is a lack of continuity with the past. I would suggest that the function of this fictional discontinuity with the past is precisely to allow the values and social norms underwritten by these traditions to be openly discussed. Importantly, as the example of the *palma* suggests, to a great extent these values and norms have to do with traditional gender roles—which is precisely what the characters in this sitcom are struggling with.

The open discussion of social behavioural norms is what allows the public sphere to exist in the first place, and the negotiation of the role cultural tradition should play in a modern society is a key element in this process. As Seyla Benhabib writes with regard to Habermas's model of the public sphere: '[T]he appropriation of cultural tradition becomes more dependent upon the creative hermeneutic of contemporary interpreters. Tradition in the modern world loses its legitimacy of simply being valid because it is the way of the past. The legitimacy of tradition rests now with resourceful and creative appropriations of it in view of the problems of meaning in the present' (Benhabib 1992: 104). Indeed, legitimacy is at the centre of *Teresina*'s dynamic, because the legitimacy of tradition is the yardstick by which the characters measure their problematical social standing in the public arena. It is not coincidental that marriage is the crucial problem for most of the characters. The 'Rams' episode brings the issue of legitimacy and marriage to the fore.

The comic situation of this episode revolves around Pepe and Rafa, the middle-aged, openly gay couple living on the fourth floor. As the others are weaving the palms, Pepe and Rafa come downstairs to ask the Teresines a very special favour. Rafa is not out to his brother Gregorio, who lives back in Guadix, Granada. During all the years Rafa has been living with Pepe in Barcelona, he has led his brother to believe that Pepe was married. After relentless pressure from Gregorio, Rafa even told him that he had a girlfriend, who was the sister of Pepe's wife. The problem is that Gregorio is getting married in a couple of days, and he and the bride Rosario will come to visit on their way to their honeymoon in Majorca. The special favour Rafa and Pepe ask is for the three Teresines to play the roles of Pepe's wife, Rafa's girlfriend, and their mother, so that the five of them can make, in Rafa's words, 'una familia tradicional' [a traditional family] during the day their visitors will spend in Barcelona.

Thus, this episode follows a typical sitcom plot in which a character, confronted with a dilemma, stages an elaborate lie that in the end will not hold water. In this case, however, the plot becomes complicated by sexuality, so the Teresines' flat is transformed into a tasteful closet, and the door featured in the credits becomes the door of the closet, a door through which people come in rather than out. Here gay men and spinsters will share a fantasy of normality and recognition that will make them unlikely bedfellows, a fantasy which vividly contrasts with their lack of legitimacy. The Teresines are worried about their unsuitability for the role, as they are in their late fifties and early sixties; but Rafa's plan also offers them a chance of fulfilling their dream of being successfully married women, even if it is just for one day. On the other hand, Rafa and Pepe—described as a ' "matrimoni" ' in the character profile produced by TVC (n.d.: [29]) —are becoming straight for a day, which will allow them to taste the honey of legitimacy, even if it is at the cost of going back into the closet.

The characters' fantasy will therefore be a carefully staged performance. The day the visitors are expected, the Teresines are theatrically made up by Pepe, Rafa teaches Pepe how to behave like a traditional male, and the flat is cleansed of any signs of work, so it becomes a purely domestic space: the living and dining room abandons its traditional working-class decoration style and acquires a camp nuance thanks to Rafa's candelabra and white carnations. The whole group nervously rehearse their roles: Teresina, dressed in a black sequinned frock, will play Pepe's mother-in-law; Maria Teresa, who wears an exotic black dress with frills and big white polka dots, will be Pepe's wife; and Tere, renamed as Úrsula, will be Rafa's girlfriend. In turn, Rafa tells Pepe off for being unable to repress his effeminate demeanour, and prompts him to rehearse once again the greeting to Gregorio: Pepe spreads his legs apart, places his hands in his pockets, and utters in a deep, masculine voice, 'Hola, Gregorio, ¿qué tal por el pueblo, todos bien?' [Hi Gregorio, how's things back in the village, everyone OK?]. The Teresines look on approvingly, but Pepe, who is unable to sit down in a masculine way, finds his performance 'molt antinatural' [very unnatural].

Shortly afterwards, and after a false alarm, the bell rings. Rafa runs to check the spy hole: in a point-of-view shot, we see Gregorio and Rosario, unsuspecting of what is happening behind the door. Each member of the new family goes to their positions, and Pepe opens the door. In his carefully rehearsed voice, he delivers his 'Hola, Gregorio' greeting, after which he returns to his usual camp gesturing. After awkward introductions, the visitors are taken on a tour of the Teresines' flat, Pepe and Maria Teresa's pretend love-nest. But when they arrive in the bedroom, painted pink, Rosario remarks that there are three beds; Teresina, to justify this, says that Maria Teresa is expecting a child:

Teresina: Es que están esperando un hijo.
Pepe: No, un hijo no!
Gregorio: ¿Un hijo?
Maria Teresa: Que sí, un fill!
Gregorio: Hombre, Pepe, pues me alegro por ti, ¿eh?, porque en el pueblo todo el mundo se pensaba que eras de la acera de enfrente.
Pepe: No, hombre, no, si eso no me... no digas que... [*hands akimbo and legs apart*] Hola, Gregorio, ¿qué tal por el pueblo, todos bien?
Rafa: ¿Y por qué no vamos a ver el comedor, que os gustará mucho?

[Teresina: They're expecting a baby.
Pepe: Oh no, not a baby!
Gregorio: A baby?
Maria Teresa: Yes, a baby!
Gregorio: Well, Pepe, I'm really glad for you, because, you know, in the village everyone thought you were a bit of a poof.
Pepe: No, no, that's not my... you don't mean... [*hands akimbo and legs apart*] Hi, Gregorio, how's things back in the village, everyone OK?
Rafa: Why don't we go and see the dining room? You'll love it!]

Three points arise from this long scene. First, the performativity of gender is here linked up to tradition as a set of repeated and ritualized acts: if Rafa, Pepe, and the Teresines are to look like a traditional family, Pepe (the 'husband') must behave like a *macho ibérico* [traditional Iberian male]. But in this particular space (a space in between the public and the private, in which legitimacy is suspended), traditional gender codes are no more functional than the Teresines' make-up. They are constantly repeated, but their repetition marks their failure: rather than a ritual that establishes both a continuity between sex, gender, and sexuality, and a continuity between a traditional past and a heterosexual present, Pepe's 'Hola, Gregorio' becomes a magic formula that does not work. Secondly, the importance of the spy hole is again stressed, as the interface between the private and the public: the inspecting eyes of the legitimate couple (whose conformity to heterosexual norms makes it visible in the public sphere, as opposed to Rafa and Pepe) want to look through it, but the spy hole is also a window into the public space that serves as a defensive barrier for the private space. And finally, Gregorio's gaze is not that innocent; as he himself says, in the village everybody thinks Pepe is gay anyway, so his suspicions may well correspond to our suspicions that his visit is for disciplinary purposes: here is the legitimate couple, demanding its social reproduction wherever it goes.

What this episode shows is a situation in which communication is not possible: Gregorio's unsuccessful attempt to get Rafa to conform to social norms is met by Rafa's unsuccessful attempt to keep up appearances (this is a pattern many episodes in the series follow). In fact, the problem here is that Rafa feels he cannot come out to a brother who, being suspicious as to the nature of Pepe and Rafa's relationship, keeps putting pressure on Rafa to do the right thing, like himself, and get married. Thus, what is at stake in this episode's narrative is the conflict between the imposition of social norms and the interests of those who fall outside the legitimacy given by these norms. According to Jürgen Habermas, in a modern, democratic society this kind of conflict is resolved through engaging in practical, rational discourse; and such discursive exchange is governed by a universal pragmatics. Steven Connor sums up Habermas's theory of communicative action as follows:

Habermas argues that discursive exchange has as its ideal outcome the achievement of rationally based consensus [. . .]. Agreement depends on the degree of validity claimed and accomplished in four different ways: the comprehensibility of what is being said, the truth of what is being said, the sincerity of the speaker and the appropriateness of fit between what is said and

the social context in which it is said. To be rational and legitimate, such consensus must be unforced, which is to say, free of every kind of duress, dis-
tortion or constraint, and must be governed by no strategic or purposive
intention other than that of establishing truth. (Connor 1992: 104–5)

At this point, it might be useful to compare Habermas's 'ideal speech
situation' to the actual discursive exchange in the Teresines' flat. The
whole group are chatting around the dinner table after lunch, once
Gregorio and Rosario have been taken to visit Rafa and Pepe's flat
(Tere/Úrsula and Teresina's 'home'). The following dialogue ensues:

Maria Teresa: I què, els ha agradat el pis de dalt? Les ha gustado?
Gregorio: Ah, sí, el piso de arriba nos ha gustado mucho. Ya se lo he comen-
    tado a Úrsula [Tere] cuando bajábamos, que es mu fino, mu arreglao, se
    nota que viven dos mujeres allá arriba. [*The Teresines laugh.*]
Teresina: Doncs Mallorca els hi agradarà molt, mucho. Bonito, Mallorca,
    mucho.
Gregorio: Mallorca, sí, dicen que está mu bien, señora.
Pepe: Ai, aquello es precioso. Pensa que el Rafa y yo fuimos un año y aque-
    llo...
Gregorio: ¿Cómo? ¿Estuvisteis en Mallorca?
Pepe: Bueno, sí, pero... en... bueno, lo que pasa es que... estuvimos allí...
Gregorio: ¿Pero quiénes, Rafa y tú solos?
Pepe: No, todos, todos!
Tere: ¿Que les ha gustado el café?
Rosario: Pues sí, estaba mu rico el café, sí.
Tere: ¿Y allí cuánto pagan, allí?
Rosario: Pues en el economato lo pagamos a unas quinientas cincuenta o así,
    el torrefacto, que mira qu...
Tere: Més barato que aquí, eh?
Gregorio: Pero oye, Rafael, tú a ver cuándo te animas y te casas.
Rafa: ¡Cómo me voy a casar, tonto!
Tere: Sí, l'any que ve!
Rafa: ¡Sí, el año que viene me caso!
Gregorio: Ah, el año que viene. Pues cuando lo diga en el pueblo se van a lle-
    var una alegría.
Teresina: No, no, de moment no digui re, en el pueblo, no, no, en su
    momento, la sorpresa, la sorpresa...
Maria Teresa: La sorpresa... Ai...! [*To Rosario*] I vostè, de què es va casar,
    vostè? Se casó de blanco?

[Maria Teresa: So, did you like the flat upstairs?
Gregorio: Oh, yes, the flat upstairs, we loved it. I was telling Úrsula [Tere] as
    we were coming downstairs. Very elegant, very nicely decorated. You can
    tell two women live there. [*The Teresines laugh.*]

Teresina: You'll really like Mallorca. Really nice, Mallorca, very nice.
Gregorio: Mallorca, yes, they say it's great.
Pepe: Oh, it's gorgeous. Just think that Rafa and I went there one year and...
Gregorio: What? You were in Mallorca?
Pepe: Well, yes, but... I mean... well, you see... we were there and...
Gregorio: But who, just Rafa and you?
Pepe: No, no, all of us, all of us!
Tere: So, did you like the coffee?
Rosario: Why sure, it was really nice, yes.
Tere: And is coffee very expensive where you live?
Rosario: Well, in the co-op it's about 550 pesetas, the special roast, mind you...
Tere: Cheaper than here, isn't it?
Gregorio: But listen, Rafael, when are you going to tie the knot yourself?
Rafa: Me get married? Don't be silly.
Tere: Yes, next year!
Rafa: Sure, I'll get married next year!
Gregorio: Ah, so next year. Good. When I tell everyone back home, they'll be really glad to hear.
Teresina: No, no, don't say anything yet, no. Wait till the time's ripe. It'll be a surprise.
Maria Teresa: A surprise... Oh my God... [*To Rosario*] And tell me, what was your wedding dress like? Was it a white dress?

This dialogue, with all its gaffes and interruptions, could not be further away from the ideal conversation towards which all discourse should tend. In fact, it violates every single pragmatic rule set out by Habermas: agreement would be impossible, as Gregorio does not master both linguistic codes (Castilian and Catalan), most things being said are false, none of the speakers is sincere, and the dialogue follows the strategic purpose of concealing the truth. Nevertheless, even though communication (in the sense of a discursive exchange that aims at reaching truth) seems to have broken down in this episode, as we shall see later 'truth' is reached in the end, and Gregorio accepts that Rafa is gay and already 'married'. In order to understand this paradoxical result, an agonistic model might be better than a communicational one; and the distinction between strategy and tactic proposed by Michel de Certeau in *The Practice of Everyday Life* (1988) might prove more fruitful than that of Habermas between communication and strategy.

For de Certeau, a strategy is 'the calculation (or manipulation) of power relationships' that is launched by a subject 'with will and power' from a space appropriated as one's own, a place which de Certeau calls the proper. Strategy involves mastery of time through place, as having one's own, proper place 'allows one to capitalize acquired advantages, to prepare future expansions' and therefore to gain 'independence with respect to the variability of circumstances'; and it is also a 'mastery of place through sight' (de Certeau 1988: 35–6). I would suggest that Gregorio's own, proper place is the legitimate couple, that is, the institution of heterosexual marriage: he only visits Rafa once he is married, and with the full weight of legitimacy behind him. As a visitor in transit, he is able to control time, and through visual inspection he tries to transform what he sees into something readable.

By contrast, Rafa, Pepe, and the Teresines' behaviour could be better described, I would argue, in terms of de Certeau's concept of tactic, defined as:

a calculated action determined by the absence of a proper locus [. . .]. The space of tactic is the space of the other. Thus it must play on and with a terrain imposed on it and organized by the law of a foreign power [. . .] it is a maneuver [. . .] within enemy territory [. . .] It takes advantage of 'opportunities' and depends on them, being without any base where it could stockpile its winnings, build up its own position, and plan raids [. . .]. In short, a tactic is an art of the weak. (de Certeau 1988: 37)

Rafa, Pepe, and the Teresines act out their tactic in a symbolic space that does not belong to them, that of the traditional family; and whereas Gregorio and Rosario have a degree of control over time, the others have to make things up as they go along: hence the changes of subject, the improvised lies, the contradictions, and all the other tricks.

At this point, and before I can discuss the outcome of the protagonists' tricks and the logic behind it, I need to turn briefly to a trick played by the series itself, which has to do with the sequences of television within televison that are a feature of every episode. Generally speaking, these sequences play an important role in denaturalizing the realism of the *mise-en-scène* (of the series as a whole, not of this episode in particular) and of the language used by the characters, and also in defusing the stereotyping that is the base of humour in the series; this is achieved, I would argue, by constructing the characters as an audience by the close-ups of the TV sets, which render visible our own spectatorial position (we are indeed watching television).

But some of these sequences reveal that an additional trick is being played on the audience, which consists in concealing inversion behind parody. This becomes noticeably clear in episode 10, 'Al maig, comunions' [In May, First Communions]. At one point, the Teresines and their brother Tomàs are watching the Eurovision Song Contest, and we are shown (framed by a white TV set) the Spanish entry: a song about three sisters who are looking for love, happiness, and marriage. Shortly afterwards, a highly comic parody of the Eurovision voting ritual takes place, with the festival presenter—dressed in a very low-cut, flamboyant, shocking pink strapless frock and big costume jewellery—translating with a strong accent the vote of the Portuguese jury, from 'United Kingdom, ten points (le Royaume-Uni, dix points)', to 'the Netherlands, four points (les Pays-Bas, quatre points)', to, finally, with a grimace of disdain on her face, 'Spain, one point (l'Espagne, un point)'.

This parody obtains much of its comic effect from the use of clichés, such as the bilingualism of the festival, Spain's pattern of poor performance, or the tradition, shared by both Iberian neighbours, of acknowledging each other's existence but giving each other the lowest possible vote. However, at the same time the parody inverts the order in which Eurovision votes are announced. This would be irrelevant were it not for the fact that there are other instances of inversion in the series, which suggests an in-built logic of inversion which affects, for example, the chronological order of the episodes: the one entitled 'Holy Innocents' goes before 'Christmas', and most importantly 'Easter' goes before 'Palm Sunday'. (At the end of the series we learn that Conxiteta, the girl who has recently married and who so wants to have a baby, has given birth to a two-months premature baby weighing 6.5 kg, confirming suspicions that, as we say in Catalan, she has celebrated Easter before Palm Sunday; that is, she became pregnant before marriage.) The series even inverts carnivalesque inversion: the episode in which Conxiteta gets married (not for one day, like Pepe and Maria Teresa, but for ever, and legitimately) is entitled 'Carnestoltes' [Carnival].

The inverted Eurovision vote, however, is also an inversion of values which places the emphasis not on the winner, but on the losers. This should bring us to question the extent to which the gay couple's closeting performance was in fact designed to succeed. The 'Rams' episode concludes with Rafa and Pepe at home that evening, discussing the events of the day: embarrassing as the situation was, and despite the fact that their elaborate hoax made Gregorio furious at

Rafa, the former finally came to accept the latter's sexuality and his relationship with Pepe. The two gay lovers end up laughing almost hysterically at everybody's reaction during the visit—especially at Gregorio's and Rosario's.

But this dialogue is prompted by another parody in which a red TV set frames a camp setting with huge plants, a fake classical sculpture, and a long, red carpet with foliate patterns draped over the backdrop. A large female figure, clad in red lamé and wearing long purple gloves and an exuberant blonde wig, starts lip-synching to Gilda's 'Amado mío' while she sensually caresses herself walking down the stairs. Cut to Rafa and Pepe, who are sitting on the sofa watching television. The camera pans away from them and shows their living room, featuring excessive blue velvet curtains, Japanese fans, two Chinese lanterns hanging from the ceiling, candelabra with red candles and a putto's head on the coffee table, and lush, leafy plants all around. Rafa and Pepe, both wearing brightly coloured kimonos, are darning socks, and the following dialogue ensues:

Rafa: Ay, siempre me ha gustado, a mí, esta canción.
Pepe: Ai, sí.
Rafa [*singing*]: Amado mío... te quiero tanto...
Pepe: Ai, aquesta és d'aquella pel.lícula de la Rita Hayworth, de la *Gilda*.
Rafa: No, que ésta no es la Rita Hayworth, Pepe.
Pepe: No, ja ho sé, home. Si això és un home!
Rafa: No es un hombre, es una mujer. Lo que pasa es que va muy bien maquillada.

[Rafa: Ah, I've always loved this song.
Pepe: Ah, yes.
Rafa [*singing*]: Amado mío... te quiero tanto...
Pepe: It's from that Rita Hayworth movie, *Gilda*.
Rafa: No, Pepe, that's not Rita Hayworth.
Pepe: I know that. It's a man.
Rafa: That's not a man, that's a woman. It's just that her make-up's really convincing.]

What the TV shows is assumed to be a female impersonator, but as Andy Warhol (1977: 41) asks, 'a female impersonator of what?' Of Rita Hayworth, of course, but that is not the point. The point is that the female impersonator is not a man but a woman: 'It's just that her make-up's really convincing.' The prevailing logic of gender is thus inverted, and most importantly, it is the gay couple who finally have the definitional authority: they have the last word. It is also they who evaluate the events of the day: their elaborate performance was a total disaster, but the tactic did the trick and achieved the most desirable outcome. Not only that: as in most other episodes of the series, in the end those deprived of legitimacy (the butt of all the jokes) have the last laugh. It is perhaps not by chance that there is no canned laughter in the series: it has been replaced by the characters' own laughter.

Teresina, SA points to a new marriage contract between tradition and social change, one which maintains a role for tradition in a global, transcultural economy, but which also opens up a space for the values and norms derived from tradition to be discussed and reformulated, so that the articulation between public and private spaces, between social norms and everyday practices, can be examined and called into question. Rather than creating myths that contain essential truths, this new contract acknowledges that social dynamic is based on fictions, but that these fictions can and should be simultaneously disavowed and tolerated (as opposed to American sitcoms like *The Golden Girls*, here the Teresines have no problem in accepting that people need to believe their own lies to make life bearable). If the Teresines constitute a myth, it is one that inscribes difference within the same (as their own name indicates), and the origin it postulates is not one but inherently plural. Finally, *Teresina, SA* mobilizes an effort to revise the social practices of everyday life and the rules of the game of Catalan society; the new marriage contract towards which it gestures is open to change and socially inclusive, since anyone can be a Teresina: like Eugeni d'Ors's Teresa, La Cubana's Teresines are also a Category, not an anecdote. But Teresa la Ben Plantada has now become an economically independent, resourceful, working-class, televisual and not high culture, relatively *hortera* [kitsch], and occasionally bitchy spinster. The new marriage between tradition and modernity is now one outside legitimacy, that is, a 'marriage'.[2]

WORKS CITED

Alsius, S. (1998). *Hem perdut l'oremus*. Barcelona: La Campana.
Benhabib, S. (1992). *Situating the Self: Gender, Community and Post-modernism in Contemporary Ethics*. Cambridge: Polity.

[2] The author wishes to thank La Cubana and Televisió de Catalunya for kindly providing him with material for research.

Bowes, M. (1990). 'Only When I Laugh', in A. Goodwin and G. Whannel (eds.), *Understanding Television*. London: Routledge, 128–40.

Certeau, M. de (1988). *The Practice of Everyday Life*. Berkeley and Los Angeles: University of California Press.

Connor, S. (1992). *Theory and Cultural Value*. Oxford: Blackwell.

d'Ors, E. (1983) [1912]. *La Ben Plantada; Gualba, la de mil veus*. Barcelona: Edicions 62.

Frazer, J. M., and Frazer, T. C. (1993). '*Father Knows Best* and *The Cosby Show*: Nostalgia and the Sitcom Tradition', *Journal of Popular Culture*, 27.3: 163–72.

Gray, F. (1994). *Women and Laughter*. Charlottesville: University Presses of Virginia.

Hobsbawm, E. J. (1992). 'Introduction: Inventing Traditions', in E. J. Hobsbawm and T. Ranger (eds.), *The Invention of Tradition*. Cambridge: Cambridge University Press, 1–14.

Kaler, A. K. (1990). '*The Golden Girls*: Feminine Archetypal Patterns of the Complete Woman', *Journal of Popular Culture*, 24.3: 49–60.

Lubar, R. S. (1994). ' "La carn del paisatge": Tradició popular i identitat nacional en el noucentisme', in A. Suárez, M. Vidal, and M. Peran (eds.), *El noucentisme, un projecte de modernitat*, exhibition catalogue. Barcelona: Enciclopèdia Catalana and Centre de Cultura Contemporània, 281–7.

Mellencamp, P. (1992). *High Anxiety: Catastrophe, Scandal, Age, and Comedy*. Bloomington: Indiana University Press.

Televisió de Catalunya (n.d.). *Teresina, SA*, series outline and character profile. Barcelona: Televisió de Catalunya.

Warhol, A. (1977). *The Philosophy of Andy Warhol: From A to B and Back Again*. New York: Harcourt Brace Jovanovich.

10

Not Writing Straight, but Not Writing Queer: Popular Castilian 'Gay' Fiction

CHRIS PERRIAM

THE 1990s saw the beginnings of a mini-boom of publication and consumption of paperback novels about and for men who have sex with men in Spain. Like many narratives of the more established traditions of Valencia and Barcelona (Fernàndez 2000; Guasch 1991: 80–1; Smith 1992: 42–128), the three Castilian first-person narratives which I take as examples here break with the 'difficult', exoticizing, and florid narratives (by, respectively, Juan Goytisolo, Álvaro Pombo, Luis Antonio de Villena, Antonio Gala, Terenci Moix—in part) which began selling homosexual lives, or, rather, structures of feeling, to middle-class readers in the 1980s. My focus will be on Carlos Sanrune's 1992 *El gladiador de Chueca* [*The Gladiator of Chueca*] (published by Laertes—promoters of Alberto Cardín and Lluís Fernàndez among others—and classed in the 1998 catalogue of Madrid lesbian and gay bookshop Berkana as their top seller), Antonio Jiménez Ariza's 1996 *La sinfonía de los veleros varados* [*Symphony of Stranded Sailboats*] (published by Berkana and Barcelona-based Cómplice's new offshoot company Egales), and Miguel Martín's 1997 *Diario de una impostura* [*Diary of an Imposture*] (again, Laertes). In choosing these texts, my intention is in part to extend the recent pioneering literary historical project undertaken by Martínez-Expósito (1998): the establishing of the parameters and dynamics of a Spanish genre of writing conformed by and about homosexuality. In that all three narratives struggle to affirm a life and a voice—a subject position—for their non-heterosexual narrators in opposition to heterosexist discourses, their authors and narrators are 'escribas furiosos' [scribes possessed]: possessed, that is, by the divine fury which drives them to tell a rebellious 'truth' (Martínez-Expósito 1998: 14–15 and *passim*). Like those narrators studied by Martínez-Expósito, they respond to, construct, and transmit a radical discourse of dissent. However, I am mainly interested in examining the problematic and contradictory ways in which these texts deploy the conventions of popular fiction to target *en masse* a specific readership—here, the constructed community of consumers of 'gay culture' in Spain—positioned in substantial part outside the popular mainstream. My aim here is to explore how the normative strategies in these conventions adapt to or resist being deployed to tell queer stories.

Before moving on to the specifics of such telling, and a brief excursion into terminology, it is worth pausing on the question of the target audience just raised. Of the three texts discussed here only one, that by Jiménez Ariza (paradoxically the one with an exclusively lesbian and gay publisher), has clearly advertised middle-brow literary pretensions of the sort to recommend it to a general novel-buying public; its title echoes that of an earlier novel by the renowned high-brow writer of more or less lesbian narratives, Esther Tusquets— *Varada tras el último naufragio* [*Stranded*] (1980)—and the extract on its cover (discussed later in this essay) is very writerly. The other two (although their publisher's speciality is dissidence rather than gayness specifically) home in more or less exclusively on two distinct sorts of gay reader: those earnestly interested in the *angst* and personal politics of coming out and with a thirst for a gay history (Martín's text); and those eager for amusement, light sensationalism, and some homoeroticism (Sanrune's). Sanrune's text is the only one which has made a significant showing in any other than alternative bookshops (no doubt because of the similarity of its subject matter to that of a number of texts forming part of the commercially successful Sonrisa Vertical series of erotic narratives). These then are texts of special interest, in two senses: of interest precisely because of the application of mainstream structures—of narrative, representation, and marketing—to apparently micro-cultural concerns and a tightly focused constituency of consumers.

Martín's text—set in the early 1980s—uses questions of gay identity and liberation politics to ground its narrative: its narrator is obsessed by his difference and apparent incompleteness as he comes both to recognize his sexual attraction to men, the existence of 'constraining normative structures' (Seidman 1994: 116), and the (mistily perceived) possibilities of resistance through community in a gay movement; he 'comes out' into a new self and a new-found community, into a gayness classically defined in terms of personal identity, cultural difference, and 'identity-based interest-group politics' (Seidman 1994: 117). Jiménez Ariza's text is, potentially at least, part radical queer in that it emphatically rejects the commercial scene and lifestyle politics of late 1980s gay Madrid, in moves similar to those summarized in a specifically Spanish frame of reference by Llamas (1998: 371–85) in his succinct exploration of the politics of a plural, Spanish 'Tierra Bollera/Mundo Marica' [Dyke-Land/Queer-World]. However, the narrator's rejection, or ignorance, of a political explanation for his being emotionally marooned is owing in part to a conservative-romantic belief in monogamous love as the sole provider of meaning and motive: it mingles egocentric fantasy with a sporadic but powerful critique of arriving at identity through signing up for gayness. Sanrune's text, as well as being the most ludic and agile of my three examples, is the most explicit and fluid with regard to the terminologies which organize same-sex sex. In particular it responds to a Spanish politics of *entendimiento* (literally, being in the know) which I want to argue invites a reading whose politics resist the narrative's otherwise reactionary pull. In all three texts radical moments are come upon as if by accident. Plucked in curiosity and excitement from the shelf—this publishing phenomenon is relatively new in Spain—and read on balcony, park bench, beach, or bed, their hints and discontinuities can, I want to argue here, accrete certain emphases at the moment of reception which make them productive, as Earl Jackson, Jr. (1991: 112) has argued of queer texts in other contexts, of 'other forms of subjectivity as well as an alternatively eroticized body': forms constructed in opposition to the binarisms and dichotomies of hegemonic, hierarchized, phallocentric constructions of reality.

Articulations of homosexual culture and politics in Spain (and certain sectors of Spanish-speaking America) have occasionally been looked to by outside commentators through the 1990s for evidence of difference from Anglo-Saxon and northern European paradigms. Spain has been seen as a nation with a sophisticated understanding of gender, nationality, and homosexuality which sets it apart from Anglo-Saxon models of sexual political resistance (Smith 1994: 3). Because of a historic absence in Spain of identity politics (and early engagement with French theories of identity formation), and a tendency to avoid segregated social space and identity labels, Bergmann and Smith (1995: 10–12) suggest that non-heterosexual Spanish cultures produce themselves as queer rather than lesbian and gay. For Ellis (1997: 16) 'gay Spanish politics [and] culture reveals an anti-essentialist thrust'. However—and all those just cited would recognize that they did not mean to speak of Spain in general—within Spain it has been noted that queer politics as an agency for social change must be looked for at the micro-level, within minority groups (Llamas and Vila 1997: 223); and Aliaga and Cortés find themselves having to isolate instances of radical gay cultural production from a general context of lack of consciousness in the community of its formative history (1997: 60), of changes in social attitudes happening only slowly (1997: 112–13), and of the prevalence of homophobic discourses in representations of homosexuality by both gay and straight (1997: 61–73, 152–6). One instance of the latter tendency is, indeed, Sanrune's text, which they see as doing no more than reinforcing a heterosexist perspective on a homosexual world (153–4); but, as I have suggested, its engagement with the term of *entendimiento* promises otherwise.

For Óscar Guasch (1991), the terminology of *entendimiento* offers similar possibilities of an effective, Spanish sexual politics of change as for Llamas and Vila later (1997) do *bollera* (dyke) and *maricón* (queer, though with less of the positive and political connotation of the English term). The rise post-1977 in Spain of a 'modelo gay', while offering wider affective and political potential, was and is limiting for Spanish men who have sex with men. Its redefinition of homosexuality in terms of virility moves away from one powerful site of specifically Spanish activism, that of *locas* (queens) and transvestites; and an imported Anglo-Saxon-style politicization ('institucionalización') of homosexuality based around the emergence of specifically gay spaces, including the commercial scene, has little to do with the activism of the revolutionary left. Guasch prefers *entendido* to *gay* (1991: 160–5) as it is indigenous, carries no pejorative connotations, and is open enough to be applicable to men who have sex with men, a grouping who constitute 'una realidad intercultural, pluriforme y heterogénea' (a multicultural, plural, and diverse reality) (1991: 160–1).

The main narrator of *El gladiador de Chueca* (Chueca is Madrid's gay village) is a rent boy whose picaresque life story is being transcribed from a series of audio tapes. He is conscious, as Martínez-Expósito observes (1998: 48), both of the image of himself that he is creating and of his authentic self. In particular he is articulate and naively sincere about the sentimental and sexual education which has led to his self-avowed status as *entendido* (Sanrune 1992: 150) and (for Guasch it would be 'but') sharp on what differentiates him from *mariquitas* (effeminate queens), *locas*, and any men who are not straight-acting. This exclusive—phobic—differentiation is necessary: for self-protection at school and in military service, and to maintain a saleable image as a prostitute (48–9, 77, 94, 108). What he reveals here is a wisdom and self-awareness superior to that of the client reader—'¿O tú no lo hacías?' [I suppose you never did that?] he asks apropos of adolescent group jerk-off sessions (25)—and a sense of the social constructedness of oppression: the Francoist morality of the priests at his state boarding school, panic-stricken maternal interventions when two boys get too close (36, 78–81, 156). On the other hand his consciousness of image—identity—is a homophobically inflected fatalism. His first big teenage love affair, presented in orthodox manner as fulfilling, romantic, and special ('de putamadre, como en las pelis ¿no?' [fucking great; like in films, yeah?] [49]), is wrecked by the other boy's guilt and withdrawal transferring itself onto him as shame and impotence (53–4): 'como si [él] dijera ahí te mueras, cacho mariconazo' [like he's said you can drop dead, you bent bastard], he muses (54). A second affair, sabotaged by family interference, 'fue una bola cantidad de auténtica y legal, una historia de amor de esas que, si hubiésemos sido tío y tía, habría terminado en boda y en familia numerosa, pero no, como todos los rollos entre julais, terminó mal' [was a dead genuine, proper thing that we had going, a real love story like if we were a bloke and his girl would've ended up with a wedding and a big family; but no, it ended badly like it always does when it's guy meets guy] (76). In his teenage years, in fact, the censorship is explicit and he imagines as the instrument of self-control (in fact, self-oppression) a pair of scissors which cut through any thoughts of sex with men 'como si se tratara de una película de cine, ¿no?' [like it was a roll of film, see?] (37; also 63 and 68). An association is built up between this imagined film, the long monologue, and the spools of tape through the use throughout the text of the word *rollo* (which can signify all these things); the reader thus becomes aware of the proximity of both censorship and self-censorship in the story of young gay love and in the story of disavowal of which it is part.

It is through these perceptions of internal and external homophobia, the half-consciousness of the constructedness of identity and desire, and the awareness of the destructive capabilities of name-calling that the tale comes close to being queerly readable. Structurally this is also the case: the text's reinscription of the picaresque is subversive and innovative (the generic deflationary critique of society being specifically targeted now on heterosexism and closetry). The bravura monologue recorded on the audio tapes not only silences his (pay)master's voice, but also makes him the mere passive scribe, and inferior in his lack of street wisdom and sexual experience. The client's—and potentially the reader's—classist assumptions and patronizing *nostalgie de la boue* are critically highlighted as the narrator notes disbelief on his face when talking about books he has read, including the anonymous nineteenth-century homoerotic narrative *Teleny*, which he considers, incongruously enough given its archness, as 'cantidad de cachondo' [a good, raunchy laugh] (139): 'yo sé que a vosotros os gusta que los chaperos hablemos así, como muy barriobajeros y muy manguis. ¿A que os pone cachondo un tío buenazo como mi menda, que marca paquete cantidad y que, encima, os hable así? ¿O no, colega? Pues eso, tío' [I know you lot like us rent boys to talk that way, you know, all low life and criminal sounding. It gets you all worked up, yeah? A hunk like me, with a nice prominent packet and talking like that too. Am I right or am I right? Enough said] (139).

On the other hand, as with Luis Antonio de Villena's more complex rent boy's tale *Fácil* [*Easy*] (1996), there is no politicization of prostitution, its fuller social contexts, or its concomitant subject positions; it celebrates a hidden, forbidden, and yet institutionalized status quo. What the narrator wants (credibly enough) is stability, love, some sense to come out of his account. Furthermore, the narrative projects these desires onto its readership taking for granted the satisfactions of such certainties: represented as unmediated, spontaneous, and transparent, the (linear) narrative interpellates the reader as intimate friend and co-protagonist as well, not least, as client. The reader is reminded of the underlying political economy of his book consumption (he has paid to have a story told to him), is made privy to sensational and original material, and has the thrill of the reality effect of sitting across the kitchen table, sharing a beer (166) with this glamorous, sporadically intelligent, free spirit and his frequently emphasized physical endowments. This (relatively) widely read text then is complicit, *ma non troppo*.

While the story of the 'gladiator' is in a flawed way a quest for a meaningful identity and a recuperation of authentic affection through spontaneous monologue, Martín's *Diario de una impostura* is about achieving authenticity, and the possibility of love, through writing. Set in a much more solemn microcosm, it exploits an archetypal site—a monastery in a right-wing *pueblo* in central Spain—for the working through of guilt and repression and eventual self-discovery. The narrative—which can interestingly be read in relation to the subgenre of homoerotic 'relatos de sacerdotes' (priests' tales) explored by Martínez-Expósito (1998: 109–35)— takes the form of the diary of a 19-year-old novice monk, Miguel, covering September 1982 to October 1983 and, according to its first-person narrator, based on real events (Martín 1997: 11). The diary narrative is framed by a first-person analysis and meditation on the diary's main period of coverage by the older Miguel, now a layman living (we suppose) in Madrid.

Here we might posit two main groups of reader. One would be a problematically identifying reader, who like Miguel is perhaps 'un joven con deseos confusos y no aceptados' [a boy with confused, unacknowledged desires] and who like him might say 'me hubiera gustado ser *normal*' [I would have liked to be *normal*] (40), someone who feels 'confuso, reprimido' [confused, repressed] (44), 'dividido' [divided] (68). The other would be a more knowing and already some way out-of-the-closet subject whose reading is able to add to the twinges of recognition of the dilemmas and anxieties of the narrator a *blasé* admixture of sympathy, superiority, and slightly amused impatience. In making coterminous the subject's becoming 'gay' and his becoming monogamous through finding 'alguien como yo' [someone just like me] (181), this text flees the uncertainties of desires which fragment the sense of self; but it also can be seen, quite obviously, to denounce the structures of power (the monastery's rule and the Church) which simultaneously nurture and condemn homosexual desire. The community is a clichéd model of repressed and released desires: Miguel is caressed on cheeks and fondled on thigh by one monk (37); two others are in jealous rivalry over a young lay brother (who works topless in the steamy laundry and exploits this provocatively) (145–6); there are rumours of 'sadomasoquismo conventual' [monastic S&M] aided by 'cilicios y juguetes varios' [hair shirts and other toys] (71); a young novice gets drawn into solitary self-harming in the showers and falls seriously ill (92–4); and Miguel, at a retreat at Taizé, on Good Friday, tormented by desire for naked and semi-naked companions in the shared dormitory (83–5), ends up in a toilet with a glory hole and confronted by the emerging penis of a man he has already identified as the Prior and therefore by the appearance 'poco a poco' of 'el concepto de la doble moral, doble vida, hipocresía' [double standards, double lives, hypocrisy] (88). This, and his readings in the monastery archives about the Church's attitudes to queers and heretics and about the tortures inflicted on their bodies in the past, make him finally aware (so his later narrating self says) that he is, in effect, constructed in relation to the exercise of power within the context of 'la mentalidad esencialmente heterosexual y machista de la Iglesia' [the essentially heterosexist and *macho* mentality of the Church] (175).

Miguel (as if all the activity described above was not enough) is terrified of his wet dreams, of '[mis] genitales [que] me reclaman que les preste más atención de la que les estoy concediendo' [my genitals demanding I pay them more attention than I have been doing] (46); he is obsessively, hydraulically, aware of his body, of his need to 'vaciar[se]' [empty himself] (44). Were it not for the double shadow of guilt thrown over the narration by the past and present Miguel, this would be fertile material for Almodovarian excess, and queer fractures do indeed open up under the pressure of overdetermination. Soon after the first of the (many) passages on sexual frustration the book's love story begins, and Miguel's own exacerbated awareness of his own body finds dramatic transference onto the object of his desire Juan, another novice, in a single, breathless entry in the diary:

Convento, 15 de diciembre 1982
¡Ha sido espectacular la entrada en escena de Juan—pensando que no le veía nadie—al bajar por las escaleras para ir a la sacristía! Arremangándose el hábito para no tropezar como en otras ocasiones, se asemejaba a la protagonista de «Lo que el viento se llevó», Escarlata O'Hara, descendiendo por las lujosas escalinatas de Tara, la fastuosa mansión sureña. (47)

[The Monastery, 15 December 1982
Juan's entrance when he came down the steps to go to the sacristy—thinking nobody was looking—was spectacular! Lifting the skirts of his habit so he wouldn't trip up as before, he looked like Scarlett O'Hara, the protagonist of *Gone with the Wind*, descending the magnificent steps of the sumptuous Southern mansion Tara.]

This inscribed self-liberation, within the confines of diary and cell, allows the penetration into the institutions of oppression of Juan's body as both gay icon (in the reference to the movie) and pagan challenge: during a visit with Miguel to the top of the bell-tower at sunset in high summer (the clichéd frame quickly allowing most readers to register a camp effect), Juan's body is subversively exalted: 'Ante esa luz irreal los hábitos de Juan, su rostro, sus manos [. . .] cobraron matices mitológicos. [. . .] su contemplación supuso un firme competidor al dios Helios' [in that unreal light Juan's habit, his face, his hands [. . .] all took on mythological hues [. . .] To contemplate him was to see him as a strong match for the god Helios] (142).

These two representations of the bodily presence of Juan, one popular in reference, the other cod-classical, both reveal what is for the queer reader an immediately recognizable flirtation—through a ludic, odd juxtaposition of references—with surrender to femininity in the one case and exaggerated elevation of desire in the other. They offer simple cases of identity slippage in which the earnest young monk frees up another subject for himself. His recognition of the interlocking power over the body of Church and state coincides tellingly with his discoveries of the perturbations caused by the presence of Juan's body, whether in his habit or naked in the showers: 'en su presencia me siento distinto, muy distinto. ¿O quizás más yo? Sus ojos, deben ser sus ojos... ,' he decides, coyly, '¡Me pierdo en sus ojos!' [in his presence I feel different, very different. Or perhaps more myself? His eyes, it must be his eyes. I'm losing myself in his gaze] (118). Giving in becomes a way of winning out, and the violent alienation of homosexuality in legal and ecclesiastical history translates into being and feeling 'different, very different', both politically (bit by bit) and physically (as his eyes, hands, and feelings are drawn to Juan's body). The desire for Juan makes him realize that 'no tengo una crisis de vocación. Lo que he sufrido es una crisis de identidad. [. . .] Las piezas del rompecabezas de mi vida comienzan a encajar [. . .]. Deseo ver la imagen completa' [it's not my vocation that's in crisis. It's my identity. [. . .] The pieces of the puzzle which makes up my life are at last coming together [. . .] I want to see the whole picture] (181).

Such a search for 'the whole picture', confirmed in an earlier entry for 28 June (Gay Pride Day), has impeccable queer credentials in that it ostensibly mingles the construction of sexuality with the idea of self as a process marked with pride: 'Mi propio criterio, mi propio conocimiento de mí mismo, mi creciente autoaceptación hacen que camine deseoso hacia la palabra «gai», y todo ese nuevo valor lleno de dignidad que encierra...' [my own criteria, my own self-knowledge, my growing acceptance of who I am, are all letting me positively want to move towards that word 'gay' and towards the courage and fresh dignity it contains...] (134). However, the pre-postmodern emphasis on repairing the fragmentary rather than celebrating plurality (nothing of the often mooted diversity of modern cosmopolitan Spain emerges from this journey into gayness), the fixation on salvation as monogamous similitude, the cautious double domestication of the term gay through spurious orthographical Hispanization and quotation marks, all these inflect the statements of the diary with a conservative politics. 'Dignity' evokes more the politics of rights than that of difference, the struggle for new identity formation shades over into new-age inflected individualistic identity politics, and the diary risks narrating the substitution of one lifestyle for another in that familiar, problematic 'metaphysics of identity' which depends on 'seemingly fundamental distinctions and the inevitability of a symbolic order based on a logic of limits, margins, borders, and boundaries', on inside and outside, same and other (Fuss 1991: 1).

Jiménez Ariza's *La sinfonía de los veleros varados* (1996)—characterized in an early review as having 'espléndidos momentos literarios, muy intimistas y sin embargo, comprensibles para todos' [splendid literary, inward moments, but nonetheless accessible to everyone] (Ferrándiz 1996)—takes as its pivotal moment the death, two years back from the narrative present, of Tomás, wealthy, older ex-lover of the narrator, one-time member of Catholic Action, once married, and never able to see his lovers as anything but objects (if the narrator is to be believed). It is 'inward' in its episodes of intense meditations on love and obsession; and (despite some virtuoso disruptions of linear chronology) its accessibility comes from its chronicling of the lives of a group of gay friends in 1980s to 1990s Madrid and Benidorm in a combination of AIDS-literature elegy (in mode if only implicitly in content), queer *novela rosa* [romantic fiction], and realist critique of the contemporary commercial and affective scenes.

Stock types of character and relationship and specific, recognizable institutions of Spain offer occasions for engaging the reader through satirical realism: the intellectual whose partner is a frivolous shopaholic and cottage queen using El Corte Inglés and the nearby toilets for both activities (26); the aged grandfather, 'mariquita reprimida [que] se fue liberando a medida que el dictador agonizaba' [a repressed queen [who] the nearer the dictator got to death the more liberated s/he became] (49) and now seeing in the pages of *¡Hola!* magazine 'los nietos de quienes un día, hombres y mujeres, cayeron rendidos a sus pies víctimas de sus encantos' [the grandchildren of those men and women who had once fallen at his feet smitten by his charms] (86); or embittered Fernando, 'un personaje clave en el mundo de las mariquitas malas' [a key player in the world of evil queens] (79). A description of mass in Benidorm at the end of the 1980s prompts explorations of the close interrelationship of a certain manifestation of Spanish homosexuality with the apparatus of Catholic worship and control, but also rests on the laurels of camp comedy and once again invokes the logic of inside and outside, of them and us:

en aquel pequeño horno que era la iglesia, los mariquitas no cesaban de abanicarse ni conseguían que sus ojos se quedaran quietos por un momento. Auscultaban todo cuanto se movía: el aire, la mosca, el insecto de una tarde de verano, el ángel que desplegaba sus alas sobre las cabezas de los concurrentes y el Cristo que, semidesnudo, bajaba a saludarlos. [. . .] En realidad nadie sabía de qué hablaba el cura [. . .]. Esperábais, esperábamos, que el cura dijera algo sobre nosotros, pero el cura sólo hablaba del hambre, de la sequía, de la Virgen de Carmen y de los pescadores que tenían su flota amarrada. (52–3)

[In that cramped oven of a church, the assembled queens never ceased fanning themselves nor were able to keep their eyes from roving for a moment. They monitored every moving thing: the afternoon air, a fly, a summer insect, the angel whose wings spread out over the congregation's heads, the Christ figure who stepped down naked from his cross to greet them. [. . .] Nobody really knew what the priest was talking about [. . .]. You were all—we were all—waiting for the priest to say something about us, but the priest only talked of famine, drought, the Virgin of Carmen, and the fishing fleet, holds bare, at anchor.]

The wry acceptance, and the reassuringly familiar details of that world which has nothing to do with 'us' (but which perhaps Jiménez Ariza supposes will strike a chord in many *pueblo*-fixated Spanish readers), as well as the exploitation of a stock Spanish narrative scene (mass attended by dissident protagonists and the topos of stifling heat), make this (nicely achieved) representation as integrationist (safely enfolding the difference of the queer congregation into a cultural convention) as it is parodic.

The commercial gay scene back in Madrid is the establishing frame for the whole novel, and the narrator's distance from it. The

following is part of the passage (oddly) used as publicity material for
the book on its back cover and in the bookshop Berkana's 1998
catalogue:

Algunos sábados bajábamos a Chueca y tomábamos unas copas en el Blanco
y Negro. Allí los mariquitas se detienen y el tiempo pasa sobre ellos como una
apisonadora. Caen atrapados en esta tela de araña que entre todos tejen, pero
de la que se consideran a salvo [. . .]. Allí la fauna nocturna se detiene, carga
motores y devora la noche. Pero la verdad es que la noche les devora a ellos.
(11)

Sometimes on Saturdays we would go down to Chueca and have a few drinks
in Black and White. There the queer boys pause and time passes over them
like a road roller. They fall caught up in the spider's web they all weave
together but from which they think they are safe [. . .]. There the creatures
of the night pause too, rev motors and devour the night. But in fact the night
is devouring them.]

This postmodern Gothic (spider's web and motorbikes) very briefly
opens up interesting possibilities of an empowering, deconstructive
parody of the gay ghetto—which Aliaga and Cortés (1997: 185–98)
suggest is as dominant and as multivalently coded as elsewhere in the
West—but, rather than constructing a queer refusal to live in such a
space, the novel (very effectively) fully portrays it as, even if destructive, at least familiar, and as the site of the narrator's formation of his
identity. Madrid in the 1980s, as well as in the 1950s—when the narrator's ex-lover Tomás had preyed on 'jóvenes y delgados estudiantes
de tez pálida, durante el día hijos modelo del régimen y de la familia'
[young, slim, pale-skinned students, model sons of family and state
by day] rather cinematically keeping their photos in a shoe box on top
of his wardrobe (44)—supplies the vital other territory against and
within which can be formed the narrator's sense of redeemed one-
ness. '[Y]o conocí el amor contigo,' he tells Tomás, 'contigo amé y
follé. Pero ser marica es algo más que todo eso. Ser marica es sentir'
[with you I once knew love; with you I loved and screwed. But being
queer is more than that. Being queer is about feeling] (57). Once
again, here is a point which might serve as pivot between the reactionary and the queer. 'Being queer is about feeling,' while on the one
hand a self-indulgent restatement of the homosexual as sensitive
queen, on the other is potentially an approximation to the radical,
late 1970s counter-masculinist tactics (and counter-old left politics)
of *locas y travestis* described by Guasch (1991: 78–83) and the

importance of '[una] mayor visibilidad de lo femenino' (1991: 81) [a greater visibility for the feminine]. Giving in to feeling, again, might be a classic opening up.

Indeed a certain melodramatic ecstasy reveals itself in structure as well as plot here. Having fallen in love with the male hustler Rudy on the island from which he writes his chronicle, the narrator intersperses the text with numerous declarations of the following type: 'amo unos ojos, el sonido de una voz, un nombre... El perfume de un cuerpo' [I am in love with a pair of eyes, the sound of a voice, a name... With a certain body's scent] (101). Like the young monk Miguel, here is a narrator whose structuring account of himself is distracted by the desire for corporeal presence and a loss of self into the other. However, this surrender leads also to conventional hyperbole and positions the narrator in a scenario borrowed from the tradition of romantic fiction: 'Caí de nuevo. Me atraparon las redes del amor, sedosas, y casi me ahogaron. Fui feliz de nuevo. En sus ojos yo veía la luz que iluminaba mi vida. Pero esta luz se apagó. Los ojos se cerraron. [. . .] ¡Qué difícil el amor!' [Fallen once more. The silken nets of love trapped and almost suffocated me. Once more I was happy. In his eyes I could see the light of my life. But that light died out. Those eyes closed. [. . .] How hard love is!] (131).

Some strenuous reverse reading would need to be deployed in order to render queer a passage like this, unmarked as it is with any hint of self-awareness or distancing from complicity with what is at base, albeit at several removes, a heterosexist and patriarchal model of swooning dependency. However, the narrator does himself salvage from the emotional morass and contradictory positions of the text a crucial moment of political awareness; it is one based on *superación*, on a reclaiming of his ex, Tomás's, sexual adventurousness and turning its emptiness into resonance. If he had never met Tomás, the narrator realizes, he (like a number of the older minor characters) would have grown up and got married, put off having sex with his wife, and spent his afternoons watching boys in the square below (114). Meeting Tomás has led to being 'yo, real, auténtico' [myself, real, authentic], to tasting 'el dulce sabor de la libertad. De la Libertad' [the sweet taste of freedom. Of Freedom] (114). What queer readers could have in this text is a melodramatic narration of the progress towards authenticity which activates a politics that stands in opposition to the institutions of heterosexuality and that is inflected by the sensual: by tears and outpourings, nets of silk, a body's perfume, by flexible and cumulative sentence structures, and unashamed obviousness (as in that emphatically achieved 'Freedom').

To some extent, then, these texts and the bodies with which they are concerned respond to the ways in which, as Seidman (1994: 105) has remarked, 'contemporary lesbian and gay male cultures evidence a heightened sensitivity to issues of difference and the social formation of desire, sexuality, and identity' and their narrators 'know what it means to be treated as different'; they approach their 'bodies, desires and identities with a deliberateness often lacking in mainstream straight society'. Yet none of them, any more than the more up-market texts by Gala, Moix, and Villena, could be said thoroughly to '[shake] the ground on which gay and lesbian politics have been built, taking apart the ideas of a "sexual minority" and a "gay community"' (Gamson 1996: 395). Rather, they revel in the fascinations of uniqueness, yearn for identity in relation to a special community. Their themes and narrative strategies are in the main conventional (the interspersed arias of *La sinfonía de los veleros varados* notwithstanding), their characters are stock ones, the goal of their stories self-discovery. Readers are drawn into sympathetic relationship with a narrator posited as full, special, and interesting— in a meeting of bourgeois subjects—and they are given pleasure and relief, not difficulty and challenge. It is possible, by refocusing on the issue central to each—what to do with, and how to think from, the body—to resist the movements towards settlement, complicity, and closure which these texts successfully (and with commercial good sense) deploy; to posit, for example, Pablo Pedro's exploited body, Miguel's self-definition in relation to Juan's body gazed upon and embraced, the romanticized 'perfume de un cuerpo' and the 'difficulty' of love in Jiménez Ariza's text as far more liberating and liberated than their narrators ever imagine. But these emphases on subjectivity and a metaphysical body, emphases which I mentioned at the start, are not necessarily, or—to hypothesize—often, those of book-buying Spanish *entendidos* reading for leisure. As this new market expands—creating as it unquestionably does a new, politically liberating visibility for the subjects of what we can so far still only call Spanish 'gay' fiction—the extent to which it could construct and represent a new 'queer' Spanish cultural space (while erasing the colonializing, hegemonic potential in such a transplanted and increasingly commercialized term) will, no doubt, come out into the open.

WORKS CITED

Aliaga, J. V., and Cortés, J. M. (1997). *Identidad y diferencia: sobre la cultura gay en España*. Barcelona: Egales.

Bergmann, E., and Smith, P. J. (1995). 'Introduction', in E. Bergmann and P. J. Smith (eds.), *¿Entiendes? Queer Readings, Hispanic Writings*. Durham, NC: Duke University Press, 1–14.

Ellis, R. R. (1997). *The Hispanic Homograph: Gay Self-Representation in Contemporary Spanish Autobiography*. Urbana: University of Illinois Press.

Fernàndez, J.-A. (2000). *Another Country: Sexuality and Nationality in Contemporary Catalan Gay Fiction*. Leeds: Maney/MHRA.

Ferrándiz, J. L. (1996). '*La sinfonía de los veleros varados*', book review, *¿Entiendes?* (Nov.): 59.

Fuss, D. (1991). 'Inside/Out: Introduction', in D. Fuss (ed.), *Inside/Out: Lesbian Theories, Gay Theories*. London: Routledge, 1–10.

Gamson, J. (1996). 'Must Identity Movements Self-Destruct? A Queer Dilemma', in S. Seidman (ed.), *Queer Theory/Sociology*. London: Blackwell, 395–420.

Guasch, Ó. (1991). *La sociedad rosa*. Barcelona: Anagrama.

Jackson, Jr., E. (1991). 'Scandalous Subjects: Robert Glück's Embodied Narratives', in T. de Lauretis (ed.), *Queer Theory: Lesbian and Gay Sexualities*, special issue of *Differences: A Journal of Feminist Cultural Studies*, 3.2: 112–34.

Jiménez Ariza, A. (1996). *La sinfonía de los veleros varados*. Barcelona: Egales.

Llamas, R. (1998). *Teoría torcida: prejuicios y discursos en torno a 'la homosexualidad'*. Madrid: Siglo XXI.

—— and Vila, F. (1997). 'Spain: Passion for life. Una historia del movimiento de lesbianas y gays en el estado español', in X. Buxán (ed.), *Conciencia de un singular deseo: estudios lesbianos y gays en el estado español*. Barcelona: Laertes, 189–244.

Martín, M. (1997). *Diario de una impostura*. Barcelona: Laertes.

Martínez-Expósito, A. (1998). *Los escribas furiosos: configuraciones homoeróticas en la narrativa española*. New Orleans: University Press of the South.

Sanrune, C. (1992). *El gladiador de Chueca*. Barcelona: Laertes.

Seidman, S. (1994). 'Identity and Politics in a "Postmodern" Gay Culture', in
  M. Warner (ed.), *Fear of a Queer Planet: Queer Politics and Social
  Theory*. Minneapolis: University of Minnesota Press, 105–42.
Smith, P. J. (1992). *Laws of Desire: Questions of Homosexuality in Spanish
  Writing and Film 1968–90*. Oxford: Oxford University Press.
—— (1994). *Desire Unlimited: The Cinema of Pedro Almodóvar*. London:
  Verso.

Part III

Popular Culture

Editor's Introduction

STEREOTYPES again figure largely in the essays in this section, where the stress is on their manipulation for both strategic and tactical purposes (see the introduction to Part I for de Certeau's distinction between these terms). Parsons reminds us that, with changing attitudes to modernity, the notion of the 'typically Spanish' (*lo castizo*) shifted from an original close association with Madrid's urban underclasses to a diametrically opposed and politically motivated association with the Castilian peasant; but that, nonetheless, the original meaning of the term continued in popular cultural forms such as the *zarzuela* and the *sainete*, reclaimed by popular audiences in an appropriation of the stereotypical image of themselves. Parsons's essay on poster art necessarily deals in stereotypical images since the poster requires instant recognition by the viewer. As Parsons notes, the commercial poster has been neglected by cultural historians, who have concentrated on the political posters of the Spanish Civil War, whose links with commercial advertising were in fact recognized by poster artists at the time (for example, Josep Renau, mentioned by Parsons, who had himself worked as a designer of commercial posters before the war).

In fact, the very simplicity and boldness of commercial poster design allows it to make important statements about cultural identity since—as shown by Santaolalla's discussion of contemporary advertising in Part I—identification is a central strategy in advertising, making it essential to ask who is advertising what to whom. In this case, the advertiser is the Madrid City Council, allowing a reading of the fiesta posters studied as an index of changing institutionally sanctioned representations of the city's identity. Crucial to poster art is the fact that it is a visual medium: the importance of visual culture in this volume is not coincidental for, if Simmel (1991) and Benjamin (1983) saw visual spectacle as the defining feature of urban modernity, this has intensified in the postmodern period with the dominance of the electronic media. The Republican posters discussed also raise the issue of the relationship of popular culture and of urban modernity to the feminine. The early Francoist posters studied raise the question of the extent to which it is licit to read subversion into generally reactionary popular cultural forms: a question that is also relevant to Labanyi's essay in this section on early Francoist cinema. Parsons's generally positive evaluation of the promotion of fiesta culture by Madrid's post-dictatorship Socialist City Council can usefully be read in the context of Raphael Samuel's controversial defence of the heritage industry (1996). Parsons's emphasis on the subversive potential of the party-going street culture of modern urban Madrid, revived in the heady days of the Madrid *movida* discussed in Allinson's essay, additionally raises the issue of the extent to which pleasure and licence have an oppositional value, especially when they are promoted by the municipal authorities. Central to Parsons's essay is the question of the institutional management of culture— which figures also in Allinson's essay on the institutionalization of the original subversive potential of Spanish punk, and in de Toro's essay on the historical evolution of the management of popular Galician music.

A subject that recurs in all four essays in this section is that of the management of culture via competitions: those for Madrid fiesta posters, the radio contest in the 1941 film *Torbellino* discussed by Labanyi, the bagpipe competitions instituted in late nineteenth-century Galicia, and even the *erecciones generales* in Almodóvar's *Pepi, Luci, Bom* (whose subversive potential is considerably diminished by being added to this list). Competitions allow reconciliation of institutional control with a populist appeal to democracy since anyone can enter the competition (provided they obey the rules which, as de Toro notes in the case of late nineteenth-century Galician bagpipe competitions, were stringently prescriptive); they also raise the important question of the co-option of popular culture for high-cultural purposes—the famous 1922 flamenco competition organized by Falla and Lorca is the classic example here (Mitchell 1994: 160–77). But, at the same time, such contests by definition allow an element of contestation: the subject of Labanyi's essay on the contests dramatized in the early Francoist *folklórica* between popular, mass, and high musical forms. Like several essays in this volume, this essay points to the equation of popular culture with the feminine, and examines the complexity of the identification processes whereby audiences are invited to assume certain subject positions. Like the essay by Parsons, it also raises the question of the perception of the popular classes as performers; here there is a link with the discussion of the performance of ethnic stereotypes in the essays in Part I.

Allinson's analysis of the career of the stage performer Alaska deals with performance in its literal sense of a stage act, rather than the performance of everyday life—though the anti-artistic stance of punk was an attempt to collapse the two, also making life a matter of (resolutely anti-aesthetic) style. Allinson treats punk, in its Spanish and British variants, as a subculture heavily reliant on fashion. Here he argues that Spanish punk lacked the political edge of its British model: this raises important questions about what happens to a counter-cultural movement (like the Madrid *movida*) when it coincides with a period of affluence and (pink) socialist government. Allinson's discussion of the institutional management of the *movida* by Madrid's Socialist City Council suggests, unlike Parsons's more optimistic account of its promotion of popular culture, that institutionalization necessarily implies co-option—though one cannot help feeling that the openness of Madrid's City Council in co-opting counter-culture for its civic project was preferable to the Thatcherite philistinism which ensured that British punk remained politicized.

The last essay in this section by de Toro considers the different process of institutionalization that occurs in the construction of a non-state national identity. His historical survey shows how the fabrication of a Galician national identity has played with stereotypes of a rural, melancholic Galicia—epitomized by the bagpipes—that are imposed from the centre and also cultivated from within as a way of resisting the colonizing impulse of the modern nation-state. Conversely, this essay shows how the Franco dictatorship was able to co-opt the Galician bagpipe—as it did with regional folk music generally—for its own anti-modern state-nationalist project, to the extent that the anti-Franco opposition was reluctant to re-admit it as a symbol of Galician nationalist aspirations. This essay shows particularly well the importance of culture—and especially of popular culture—for the negotiation of collective identity: a point that is also central to Labanyi's essay on the folkloric film musical. Folk music, as a survival from pre-modern oral culture, is particularly suited to the fabrication of a concept of 'organic' community: a concept usually elaborated by intellectuals, as de Toro, following Hobsbawm, shows. The co-option of popular music by Galician intellectuals also raises the question of purist fossilization (almost always the stance of intellectuals) versus innovation and hybridization (almost always the stance of the musicians themselves, from the nineteenth century to today's globalized World Music scene). Like Allinson with regard to the Madrid *movida*, de Toro argues that the punk element in the Galician *movida* was defused through institutionalization, though it seems significant that the avant-garde experimentalism of Antón Reixa, which originated out of the high-cultural medium of poetry, has retained its counter-cultural potential, despite his co-option by television.

The theoretical frameworks used in this third section are grounded solidly in the British tradition of cultural studies, exemplified by Raymond Williams (used by de Toro), which has drawn heavily on Gramsci's unorthodox Marxist stress on the centrality of culture as a tool for negotiating political consensus. Gramsci's insights are valuable for analysis not only of early Francoism (to which they are explicitly applied by Labanyi) but also to the late nineteenth-century nation-formation process discussed in the Galician context by de Toro (who here relies on Hobsbawm's analysis of nationalism as a cultural construct), and to the promotion of culture by the late twentieth-century Socialist government, discussed by de Toro, Allinson, and Parsons. The essay by Parsons is grounded in theories of modernity and modernism and their relation to the experience of the modern city. Like Evans in Part II, Allinson argues against the use of star theory in the Spanish context, particularly when dealing with non-mainstream cinema; instead, like Mateo's essay on second-generation Spanish migrant culture in Part I, he draws on the analysis of subcultures developed by members of the Birmingham Centre. The end of the last essay by de Toro raises the question of contemporary Spanish (in this case, Galician) culture's insertion into postmodernity in a way that allows it to be simultaneously local and global: an issue that will be developed theoretically in Part IV.

WORKS CITED

Benjamin, W. (1983). *Charles Baudelaire: A Lyric Poet in the Era of High Capitalism*. London: Verso.

Mitchell, T. (1994). *Flamenco Deep Song*. New Haven: Yale University Press.

Samuels, R. (1996). *Theatres of Memory*. London: Verso.

Simmel, G. (1991). 'The Berlin Trade Exhibition', *Theory, Culture and Society*, 8.3 (special issue on Simmel): 119–23.

11

Fiesta Culture in Madrid Posters, 1934–1955

DEBORAH PARSONS

IN the 1980s, particularly under the Socialist government of Felipe González (1982–95), Spain was at the forefront of a continental trend towards investment in heritage and cultural regeneration. Even before the Socialist Party's national electoral victory, the Socialist City Council of Madrid, under its charismatic mayor Enrique Tierno Galván (1979–86), revived the city's celebrations for *carnaval* and expanded the Fiesta de San Isidro to involve a variety of both traditional and new cultural events. Such contemporary regeneration has also prompted an interest in the history of popular culture, and in 1991 Madrid's Museo Municipal presented an exhibition of over one hundred posters designed to advertise the city's fiesta celebrations under the Republic and from 1947 to the present. These offer a vivid chronicle of cultural heritage in its popular and public form, and its role within the self-identity of Madrid in the mid- and late twentieth century (in the Franco period, as we shall see, the identity of Madrid will be submerged beneath the construction of a 'universal' and timeless 'Spanishness'). This chapter will analyse the changing representation of fiesta celebration in the posters from the early and mid-1930s and from the early years of the Franco dictatorship, and the images of *madrileño* and, in the later period, Spanish identity that they construct and mediate.[1] Concentrating on the images of foolery, disorder, and urban modernity in the *carnaval* and *verbena* posters

[1] The exhibition of 118 posters comprises three main categories: sixteen pre-war posters for *carnaval* and *verbenas* (1931–6, most of them from 1934–6, though not all are precisely dated); ten pre-war posters for Madrid City Council's social aid organizations, *Asistencia Social* and *Junta de Beneficiencia* (1931–6, no exact dates); and then the majority for the Fiesta de San Isidro (annual for 1947–90). See Museo Municipal (1991). I concentrate here on the posters for *carnaval* and *verbenas*, and on the first sixteen for San Isidro issued 1947–53.

issued under the Republic, I compare these with the religious and folkloric imagery in the early Francoist posters for the Fiesta de San Isidro issued a decade later, investigating their different functional and ideological agendas. The contemporary celebration of *carnaval* in Spain has been well studied by Mintz (1997) on Cadiz and Gilmore (1998) on Seville; however, both focus on present-day celebrations in rural areas with a specifically Andalusian focus. The status and modes of celebration of carnival and other types of fiesta in the large cities remains a largely unresearched field.

As an aesthetic practice, poster art both exemplifies and articulates the conditions and experiences of modernity: mass-reproduced for mass consumption, designed for the street rather than the elite gallery, and directed towards a new mode of sensory perception. The use of a contemporary aesthetic idiom for the representation and advertising of local fiesta customs also serves to blur the boundaries or to mediate between tradition and modernity, and to highlight the continuity of the urban and the modern within popular cultural expression. For the poster, as an urban art form and register of urban subcultures, is in a sense an extension of the aesthetic style of the city carnival and *verbena*, and of the Spanish café-concert (*café cantante*) and music hall (*teatro de varietés*). As I will illustrate, the popular identity of Madrid employed in the thematic motifs of particularly the pre-war 1930s posters is drawn from a palimpsest of cultural representations, the construction of a cultural stereotype of the *madrileño* at play in the urban theatricals of the late nineteenth century being utilized and manipulated for the posters of the period. Such phenomena constitute, I argue, what Miriam Hansen has lucidly termed 'vernacular modernism', referring to cultural practices in dialogue with the experiences of modernity that connect 'the dimension of the quotidian, of everyday usage, with connotations of discourse, idiom, and dialect, with circulation, promiscuity, and translatability' (1999: 60).

Graphic art flourished in the commercial and technical environment of the modern city across Europe in the 1880s and 1890s, including Madrid where poster design was promoted by the initiation of various annual competitions for advertisements for the city's fiesta programme, most notably the Círculo de Bellas Artes' competition from 1900 for its *baile de máscaras* [masked ball] in celebration of carnival (Vela in Círculo de Bellas Artes 1993: 7). An art of the street, the poster, advertising a wide range of popular entertainments and consumable products, was a space for social and cultural broad-cast, innovative design, and the manifestation of an experimental modern aesthetic, manifest in the work of Madrid's leading early exponents Rafael de Penagos, Francisco Rivas, and Salvador Bartolozzi, but also in the work of later artists of the 1920s and 1930s such as Serny (Ricardo Summers Ysern). I argue that the designs of the early 1930s posters in the Museo Municipal collection consis-tently acclaim the position of Madrid as a city of social and aesthetic modernity with graphic eloquence. The cessation of the fiesta posters after 1936 is explained first by the outbreak of Civil War, the city being under siege by Nationalist troops from October 1936 until they entered the city on 27 March 1939, five days before the war's official end; and subsequently by the Francoist regime's prohibition of carnival celebrations and favouring of traditional rather than new art forms (Mintz 1997; García Rodero 1992). It was not until the end of the 1940s that competitions for poster design were again inaugur-ated, although now highly subject to censorship and promoted for the purpose of disseminating conservative, traditional ideology as opposed to encouraging innovative, modern art. The San Isidro posters in the Museo Municipal begin in 1947 as a result of one such new competition organized by the Comisión Municipal Permanente del Ayuntamiento to promote the fiesta after the austerity of the war years. The Círculo de Bellas Artes restored its own poster com-petition the following year, reinstating its masked ball and holding it on the original date of the banned *carnaval*, but under the new name of 'Gran Baile de Exaltación del Traje Regional' [Grand Ball in Celebration of Regional Costume]. We thus see local government and a bourgeois high-cultural institution negotiating a compromise that enables them to bow to popular tradition while overtly com-plying with state censorship—a move that can also be read as the licensing of carnival in order to promote the illusion of a return to civil 'normality', masking the reality of continued repression.

A comparison between the pre- and post-war fiesta posters reveals limitations imposed by censorship but also strategies of visual articu-lation that avoid proscription. The capacity of the poster to convey messages powerfully through simple, direct, and vivid forms lends itself to mass political as well as to mass commercial or civic com-munication, and the Republican propagandist culture programme championed popular and mass culture as forms of communication most accessible to the general public. Although short-lived, the five-month appointment of Communist poster artist Josep Renau as Director of Fine Arts in 1936, after the outbreak of war, not only highlighted the artistic status accorded this modern mass art form but perhaps more significantly eased a transition in emphasis from the aestheticism of the avant-garde to a more politically expedient function for art and culture. As previous studies have indicated, the potential of such a medium for the promulgation of ideology to the masses was fully recognized during the Spanish Civil War and, although the Republic remained in control of the major cities where the publishing and printing industries were located, poster art was effectively utilized for both the Republican and the Nationalist cause (Tisa 1980). In both cases, whether clumsily dogmatic or more sophisticatedly influential, design was subordinated to political function. What is distinct about the posters in the Museo Municipal collection is that they are intended to perform a commercial function on behalf of the civic institution of the Madrid Ayuntamiento [City Council], advertising seasonal festivities.

Advocating leisure, consumption, and public entertainment, the pre-war *carnaval* and *verbena* posters are particularly significant because they evoke exactly the climate of play and the consumption of enjoyment that the city of modernity advocates, whilst reconciling this commercial secularism with the continuation of folkloric elements in the Spanish fiesta tradition. The Republican posters I shall discuss are either loosely dated as some time between 1931 and 1936, or, when they bear a specific date, were issued in the years 1934–6. While the whole of the Republican period was characterized by immense political ferment, the years 1933–6 were characterized by particular political instability with the entry of the mass Catholic party CEDA (Confederación Española de Derechas Autónomas [Spanish Confederation of the Autonomous Right]) into a coalition government after its success at the November 1933 elections—a swing to the right reversed by the victory at the February 1936 elections of the Popular Front alliance of Republicans and Socialists. Nevertheless, the 1934–6 posters remain comparatively free of socialist or reactionary propaganda. Their symbolic focus is instead based in popular images of *madrileño* culture: urban, witty, and frivolous. By contrast, the expurgated subject matter and conservative stylistic arrangement of the early post-war posters in the Museo Municipal collection manifest the Franco dictatorship's censorious power over cultural production, advertising a traditionalist narrative of Spanish identity as much as the annual fiesta. Yet as the posters are created for competition, an important element of the artist's intention is necessarily to display conceptual originality, aesthetic skill, and typographic craft. During this period the context of the competition makes for an interesting negotiation between the aesthetic and the ideological demands of the judges, and I suggest that, at the same time as acceding to the Francoist censor, some of these later posters subvert the 'Hispanic' ideology they purport to advertise, emphasizing the specific vernacular of the festival and its relation to non-Nationalist myths of *madrileño* urban identity.

The significance of processes of negotiation, bargaining, and compromise between dominant and subaltern social groups, highlighted by the work of Antonio Gramsci in the context of fascism in Italy, illuminates, as noted elsewhere in this volume, discussion of cultural practices and their equivocal control under the Franco regime. Reading Madrid fiesta posters in the context of this politicization and marketing of a particular brand of Spanish culture allows us to appreciate their role in asserting, but also to a degree disputing, the regime's ideology. The simple images of the posters belie layers of significance that expand their eloquence beyond the function of advertisement or propaganda, and the visual images they present for a mass audience often make implicit reference to broader issues of cultural identity and struggle. *Carnaval*, the *verbenas*, and the Fiesta de San Isidro become spaces of negotiation between the regime and Madrid's urban subcultures, sites where social, ethnic, and class boundaries are symbolically and geographically contested.

MADRID, MODERNITY, AND PUBLIC CARNIVAL

During the first decades of the twentieth century, continuing the process of migration to the cities and urban redevelopment which characterized the late nineteenth-century modernization process, Madrid experienced a rapid expansion in size and economy, encouraged by an influx of money resulting from the loss of its remaining colonies and returning investment in the home nation, and the capitalization by industry on Spain's neutral stance during the First World War (Fernández Cifuentes 1999; Carr 1980: 16–30). Between 1900 and 1930 Madrid's population doubled to almost one million (still relatively small for a capital city), less than half the population being indigenous to the city itself (Serrano 1973: 196). Far from a 'Castilian' capital, Madrid was becoming a socially magnetic city of modernity, increasingly secular and cosmopolitan. At the same time however, the individual but loyally *madrileño* identities of the *barrios* [neighbourhoods], characterized by their localized nature and vivid everyday streetlife, intensified. Collective, public festivity remained a significant aspect of *madrileño* self-identity in this expanding and modernizing city, incorporated into the everyday life of urban modernity rather than regarded as a nostalgic tradition that was opposed to it. The colour and vitality of this lower-class urban culture pervades descriptions of the city's fiestas, and particularly of the street parties of the summer *verbenas* indigenous to the *barrios*. Integral to the mythology of Madrid's *castizo* social identity, it is constantly represented throughout the poster collection.

Translatable as 'authentically' or 'genuinely Spanish', the adjective *castizo* (and the generic term *lo castizo* referring to the sum of all those things that are *castizo*) was in mid-nineteenth-century *costumbrista* literature—disseminated thanks to the newly developing newspaper and book-publishing industry—applied to popular Spanish 'types' in general, but most particularly to Madrid's urban underclasses thanks to the popularity of the *Escenas matritenses* [*Madrid Scenes*] (1842) of Ramón Mesonero Romanos who, in addition to proposing various detailed plans for the modernization of the city, was in 1864 appointed Cronista de la Villa [City Archivist]; the library of records and books on Madrid which he built up in this capacity came to form the basis of the library of the Museo Municipal, which holds the posters discussed in this essay. The term is thus associated with the modernizing nation-formation impulse, but at the same time it denoted a class—and to a certain extent ethnic and racial—marginality. The term was resemanticized at the turn of the century by the writers of the 'Generation of 1898'—most notably Unamuno and Azorín—who, in their reaction against urban modernity, relocated 'typical values' to the supposedly unchanging peasant of the Castilian hinterland. It was this latter meaning that was incorporated into Francoist discourse in its visceral rejection of all cultural manifestations of modernity; indeed, the appropriation of the term *castizo* by Francoist rhetoric has resulted in a tendency to neglect its *madrileño* and marginal connotations, and to use it in reference to any aspect of nationalist, Castilian ideology. I shall use the term here in its earlier nineteenth-century sense, in contrast to the nostalgic Francoist construction of an 'authentic' Spain that represses the class, ethnic, and racial marginality in which the term originates.

An urban identity similar to that of the London cockney, *lo castizo* is in its specifically *madrileño* dimension principally associated with the working-class inhabitants of the plebeian *barrios bajos* of La Latina, Lavapiés, and Embajadores, and partly derives from an earlier cult identity regarded as indigenous to the area, *majismo*. The *barrios*, low-lying districts near to the Manzanares River on the southern outskirts of the city centre, and in close proximity to the original southern entrance of the Puerta de Toledo, originated as the outer-city settlements of Madrid's Jewish and Muslim inhabitants, but were later occupied in the seventeenth and eighteenth centuries by a pre-industrial trade and servant class (tailors, milliners, domestic servants, builders, and tradesmen) that quickly came to dominate the cultural identity of the city. Their urban street culture, and reputation for a social temperament and public attitude of saucy wit, self-assured arrogance, and resourceful disingenuity, were constructed into the widely disseminated popular representation of *majismo*, frequently characterized in the early paintings of Goya (Tomlinson 1994). Late nineteenth-century popular theatre drew on this cult identity in the creation of a new dilettante image of the urban underclasses of modernity, which became the embodiment of *lo castizo* in the popular imaginary. The strong cultural heritage within the *madrileño* imagination of public performance, raillery, and diversion, prominent in the posters, was exemplified at the turn of the century by the hugely popular *zarzuela*—a light-hearted, hybrid musical genre, with a dramatic plot across one or more acts in the manner of operetta but somewhat similar to music hall or variety in musical style—and *sainete*—a one-act popular theatrical comedy of Madrid lower-class types, often with musical interpolations—that regularly and sentimentally portrayed the streets, stereotypical characters, *verbenas*, and the *castizo* spirit of the *barrios*.[2] The repertoire of images, narratives, and types constituting *lo castizo*, and its predecessor *majismo*, thus provides a model

---

[2] In 1890 for example, ten of the city's theatres regularly presented *zarzuelas*, most famously the Apolo, where *La Verbena de la Paloma*, which became a classic of the genre, opened on 17 Feb. 1894. See Gubern (1998).

of the cultural configuration of urban identity, enacting the interconnection of artistic, literary, and theatrical culture and the creation of
a metropolitan personality and temperament within the narrative
spaces of canvas, newspaper, book, stage, and street—particularly
the last two.

The cultural legacy within collective public memory of the stereotype of Madrid's fun-loving and witty *castizo* underclasses is frequently
apparent in the pre-war *carnaval* and *verbena* posters in the Museo
Municipal collection, which, in accord with the *zarzuela*, combine
elegant, crafty, and buffoonish characters, frivolous play, popular
culture, and satiric or crude comedy, against a backdrop of recognizable city landmarks, within a modern and urban art form. Numerous
studies of turn-of-the-century urban performance and theatre associate variety, music-hall, or cabaret entertainment with the Simmelian
model of modernity, in which a battered and benumbed urban human
psyche is in constant need of ever-changing and ever-shocking stimu-
lation (Segel 1987; Rifkin 1993). However, despite its status as a
genre emanating from and responsive to the conditions of urban
modernity, the light-hearted *zarzuela*, with its common theme of
romance and lovers' quarrels, proffered a picturesque construction
of the lower classes as carefree urban types with only trivial worries
and romantic dilemmas rather than as a collective working class
with social and political demands. Although late nineteenth-century
Madrid was not an industrial city, the still small proletariat had started to
organize politically after the 1868 Revolution, causing—particularly
in the wake of the Paris Commune—anxieties about possible social
revolution: the picturesque representation of Madrid's urban underclasses in the *zarzuela* can be seen as a disavowal of such fears. The
second group of posters that I will go on to discuss, those dating
from 1947 and advertising the Fiesta de San Isidro, utilize this more
reactionary role of the turn-of-the-century *zarzuela*, depicting historical stereotypes of the lower (and bourgeois) classes dressed in
their finery, and offering a construction of social life that edits out
the social and political conditions of dictatorship. The two sets of
posters—pre-war and post-war—thus each draw on different aspects
and functions of the ideological and cultural construction of *lo
castizo*, the first to emphasize an ideology of exuberant, energetic,
and party-spirited modernity, and the second to portray a nostalgic
narrative of pre-industrial Spanish life. Although the competing
definitions of *lo castizo* as 'urban modern' and 'rural pre-modern'

conflict, both utilize a romanticized, symbolic iconography that elides the socio-historical actuality.

CARNAVAL AND VERBENA

Carnival—pagan in origin—is traditionally a pre-Lenten festival, celebrated during the three days preceding Ash Wednesday and culminating in the partying, masked street processions, grotesque pantomime, and parody of *Mardi Gras*. It remains widespread in Latin America and across southern Europe. A diary-style study of Spanish fiestas by C. E. Kany, written in Spanish for the Anglo-Spanish Society in 1930, notes, for example, that on the evening of Shrove Tuesday:

> Los paseos principales de la ciudad están llenos de parejas y comparsas de máscaras, príncipes, moros, diablos, guerreros, que hablan y ríen y cantan y gritan y chillan y tocan instrumentos ruidosos. Parece verdaderamente 'un gran manicomio con todos los locos sueltos'. (Kany 1930: 26)

> [The main streets of the city are filled with masqueraders, dressed as princes, Moors, devils, and warriors, that talk and laugh and sing and shout and scream and play noisy instruments. It truly seems 'a great lunatic asylum with all the madmen let loose'.]

The posters for *carnaval* evoke this atmosphere of mad frivolity. In one 1934 design by J. Pizarroso, the city shield forms the body of the marionette clown Punchinello. This type of figure occurs as a jester or buffoon in four of the *carnaval* posters, approaching life with a clownish mask of fun, pranks, and self-mockery, personifying carnival and identified with the city itself. The *máscara* (mask) is another primary motif, directly associated with the identity of the city through conjunction with the Madrid shield. In one 1934 design, for example, produced by the Escuela Municipal de Cerámica [Municipal Ceramics Training School] it is the shield itself that seems to be putting on a mask, and the symbols of authority that comprise the city emblem—the griffin, *madroño* [strawberry tree], and crown of thorns—disappear behind the clown's laughing mouth, rosy cheeks, and long red nose. This image is repeated in 1935 by Navarro, with the familiar shield glimpsed behind a domino mask, the crown of thorns metamorphosing into the laughing clown mouth which blows a paper trumpet. Emphasizing the hilarity, social disorder, and irreverence of the carnival, but also the city 'standard', the posters convey through their designs the ambiguity of authorized subversion that defines the very nature of carnival.[3]

Perhaps the most striking poster in the group is by the artist Ibáñez for the 1935 *carnaval*, dominated by a devil-like jester surrounded in a swirling cape and holding the city (symbolized by the *madroño*) in his hand (Fig. 5). The figure's jeering face, and the dark shadow thrown by his vivid green cape against a backdrop of typical '[s]erpentinas y confetti de mil colores' [streamers and confetti in a thousand colours] (Kany 1930: 26), evoke the atmosphere of frivolity and maelstrom that pervades carnival. Bakhtin's suggestion (1984) that the subversive potential of carnival is tamed under the institutionalizing influence of modernity, although I think quite accurate, bears little relation to this image. The jester is a subversive demigod, a carnival trickster directly associated with the temperament of the city itself, but behind whom the city shield is almost invisible. The dark blue of the background suggests a night setting, common also to the *verbena* posters but an aspect that ceases in the San Isidro advertisements of the 1940s and 1950s, characterized by daytime recreation. More similar to the Bakhtinian model is Kany's description of the Spanish fiesta as a space where revellers give vent to their frustration at what seems absurd, disagreeable, or lunatic about everyday life. As he states, '[t]odos llevan máscara que representa lo contrario de lo que son en la vida, manifestando así el descontento que lleva cada uno en el corazón' [everyone wears masks that represent their opposite in life, thus expressing the discontent they feel at heart] (Kany 1930: 26). Ibáñez's design however does not depict a man in the carnival mask, but a personification of carnival itself.

The pre-war posters advertising the *verbenas* differ in style and motif from those for *carnaval*, continuing the atmosphere of play but through the image of the modern woman and contemporary urban scene rather than the clown and city shield. The shift away from the use of the shield as a central subject within the poster design accords with the distinctively local as opposed to city-wide aspect of the *verbenas*: summer street fiestas that traditionally take place in the

---

[3] Rather out of character with the general boldness of colour and the typical motifs of the other posters, a second picture for 1935, by Tita, depicts an 18th-century couple in masquerade dress, a flowered border, and Gothic script for the word *carnaval*. In marked contrast to the capitalization and clear modern typography of the other examples, it evokes the elite masquerade ball of the past rather than a contemporary, classless frivolity. Within the eight posters in the collection, it is something of an anomaly.

Fig. 5. 1935 carnival poster by V. Ibáñez,
issued by the Ayuntamiento de Madrid

various different *barrios* of the city, famous for the fairground rides,
stalls of saccharine candy, colourful flowers, and flag bunting that
line the streets, and a general lack of the solemnity that marks the
more religious fiestas. The first is the Verbena de San Antonio on 13
June, in the eighteenth century a holiday for the city's seamstress
population and consequently famed as a day in which single women

seek a husband (Ministerio de Comercio y Turismo 1998: 29).
Numerous others include the Verbena de San Juan on the summer
solstice, which is immediately followed by the Verbena de San Pedro
on 29 June, and the most popular, the Verbena de la Paloma, on
15 July. The artist Maruja Mallo, who in 1927–8 painted a series of
four oil paintings under the heading *Verbenas*, later described, in a
lecture on 'The Popular in Spanish Art' given in Montevideo in 1937
and published in English, the spectacle of 'the crowds from around
the capital who came laden with branches, toys, almonds, rattles,
alms, jugs, jars, mats, baskets, wickerwork, marzipan, all made from
the land, the growing things and the skill of the peoples of Alcalá,
Ávila, Toledo, Colmenar, Cuenca and Tarancón' (Gómez de la Serna
1942: 45), and the mingling of this traditional aspect of the *verbenas*
with their modern funfairs of 'revolving Ferris wheels, stalls and
carrousels [. . .] a sky filled with fireworks, rockets' (Gómez de
la Serna 1942: 44). Kany, who reprints two of Mallo's paintings—
La Verbena de Pascua (1927), now lost, and *La Verbena* (1928)
(Kany 1930: 136, 92)—in his Anglo-Spanish society volume, similarly describes 'bailes, tíosvivos, columpios, plataformas de la risa,
organillos, fotógrafos, churreros y numerosas rifas' [dances, merry-
go-rounds, swings, amusements, hurdy-gurdies, photographers,
churro-makers, and numerous raffles], along with stalls '[de] rosquil-
los, de buñuelos, de almendras, de agua, de horchata y de licores
inconcebibles' [with pastries, doughnuts, almonds, water, tiger-nut
milk, and inconceivable alcoholic drinks] (Kany 1930: 91). For the
madrileño, each *verbena* is pervaded by the character of its specific
barrio locale and proudly asserted as unhomogenizable, distinct
from any other. For, although the *verbenas* are officially part of the
Catholic calendar, they are primarily secular events, their focus being
the local nature of the particular *barrio* with which a saint is associated and the gift that he or she bestows on the inhabitants. They are
thus 'street' parties in the literal sense, indigenous to named streets and
areas in the city. Significantly, unlike those for *carnaval*, each of the
five *verbena* posters—three for the Verbena de la Paloma, one jointly
advertising the Verbenas de San Juan y San Pedro, one for the Verbena
de la Moncloa—display the name of the *barrio* to which they are
indigenous: La Latina, El Congreso, and Moncloa respectively.

   The status of the urban fair as part of the vernacular of modernity
fascinated numerous writers and artists of the 1920s and 1930s—
most notably the writer Ramón Gómez de la Serna and the painter
Maruja Mallo—who turned to public festivity and the energies of

quotidian and/or technical cultural practices for the tools of avant-garde expression, appropriating the forms and subject matter of fiesta, carnival, and comedy as instinctive, physical, and thus revitalizing forces. As Richard Sheppard has noted, for many modernist intellectuals, 'the educated bourgeois [had] lost touch with the complexities of his own, most primitive nature and those of external Nature, and, simultaneously, much of his instinctive feeling for the myths, images and rituals which pictorialize the relationships between those two realms' (Sheppard 1983: 123), and their aim was to revitalize the immediacy and energy of both the individual and art. Part of a European avant-garde that, in seeking aesthetic innovation, initiated a deconstruction of the boundaries between high and popular cultures, Spanish writers and artists thus incorporated elements of popular song and dance, of the *zarzuela* and *commedia dell'arte*, of the circus and the cinema, into their art. Mallo, for example, highlighting a carnivalesque aspect of the Madrid *verbenas* in the socially marginal *barrios*, argued that they manifested 'the irreverence and grace, the parody and the creation of a society which rose up and confronted the ruling class, transforming it and mirroring it in a world of phantoms and dolls [. . .] "Verbena" ' (Gómez de la Serna 1942: 45). In her paintings, the *castizo* and the urban bourgeois elite, the city youth and older peasant figures come together in representative costume to enjoy local party traditions and modern machine rides in a montage of colour and movement. A close friend of Gómez de la Serna and of Ernesto Giménez Caballero (editor of Spain's leading avant-garde magazine, founder of the country's first film club, and reputedly the first Spanish writer to draw on Freud's theories), she was acclaimed by both as one of the foremost Spanish artists of the period, and one of her *Verbena* canvases was incorporated into the short documentary film *Esencia de verbena* [*Essence of the 'Verbena'*] made in 1930 by Giménez Caballero, with Gómez de la Serna figuring as animated fairground exhibit. The film depicted a series of *verbenas* at different sites in the city, utilizing the disorienting viewpoint from various rides to experiment with camera perspective.[4]

---

[4] In her first Madrid exhibition, organized by Ortega y Gasset's *Revista de Occidente* in 1928, Mallo displayed the *Verbenas* and a series of urban prints entitled *Estampas* or 'Aspects', which Gómez de la Serna described as 'cinematic' in style (Pérez de Ayala and Rivas 1991). Giménez Caballero devoted an essay to Mallo as 'queen of the verbena' in his 1929 *Julepe de menta*). Giménez Caballero also used the poster as an avant-garde art form and in 1927 published a collection of essays called *Carteles* [*Posters*] (Giménez Caballero 1994).

The hugely successful 1894 *zarzuela La Verbena de la Paloma*, by Tomás Bretón and Ricardo de la Vega, was also adapted in an equally popular 1935 film version by Benito Perojo, again associating the *verbena* with the cinema as a new, specifically urban art form. The film is notable for its thematic and stylistic juxtaposition of tradition and modernity, historical exactitude and experimental cinematic technique, in its representation of the *verbena* fairground. Perojo's earlier film *La condesa María* (1927) had also included a sequence shot at a Madrid *verbena* where merry-go-rounds whirl amidst the traditional local dances and dress (Gubern 1994: 269). In *La Verbena de la Paloma* Perojo emphasizes the social and physical dynamism of the fair, with its swings, merry-go-rounds, big-wheel, and shooting galleries set to the sound of the fairground organ, in order to present the romantic comedy within a vanguard style. Playing on the formal structures and motion of the vertically revolving wheel and horizontally revolving carousel, he merges these into a montage with the revolving wheels of Julián's printing press and Susana's sewing machine. Colour is introduced, for the first time in Spanish film, to emphasize the vitality of the fairground scenes. At the same time, such experimentalism was combined with the costume, scenery, and music of 1890s Madrid, evocatively recreated by scenographer Santiago Ontañón's sets for cafés, bars, upper-class salons, and working-class dwellings, as well as in the street scenes of children dancing to the organ grinder. The medium of film provided Perojo with the means to register the social and spectacular vitality of the fair and to highlight the conjoining of different social classes in the space of the *verbena*, the local life and popular culture of the *madrileño* being expressed through avant-garde techniques of expression. The balance of the past and the modern, and the apt association of fairground and film, was widely recognized and commended, Antonio Barbero for the newspaper *ABC* commenting for example that '[l]a evocación histórica de tipos y costumbres viene felizmente conjugada con lo que es técnica artística privativa del cinema: el juego de las figuras y la colocación de la máquina' [the evocation of historical characters and customs is skilfully linked with the specific technical aesthetic of the cinema: the play of shapes and the positioning of the machine] (Barbero 1935). It is primarily this technical aesthetic that allows Perojo to capture the vital and anarchic chaos 'de la movilización de masas, de la impresión bulliciosa, abigarrada y multiforme, de la verbena, de la fiesta y cortejo nupcial, del tumulto callejero' [of the mobilization of the crowd, of the hustle and bustle, jumbled and multiform, of the *verbena*, of the *fiesta*, and of the wedding party, of the street], as the reviewer for the film magazine *Cinegramas* noted (Merino 1935).

The *verbena* posters held by the Museo Municipal register the significant generic aspects of carnival and *verbena*, articulating a social and public space of modern vitality and change in which past and present, tradition and modernity merge, regional and folkloric images coinciding with modern elements such as the swinging boat or carousel. They turn the city into a performance space, an open-air gallery for poster art just as it is a theatrical stage for the *verbena*, and emphasize an aesthetic of 'variety', the physical senses, and visual spectacle—an aesthetic associated with popular performance rather than bourgeois or elite art forms. Certain images recur in the designs, such as fairground rides, urban buildings, and, most prominently, the young and fashionable modern woman, and in each the locality of the *verbena* is coupled with the new modernity of the city. In Esteban's design for the 1933 Verbena de la Paloma for example, an elegant, slightly arrogant young woman stands in front of a silhouette of the Puerto de Alcalá and a wildly rocking swing-boat. The woman herself combines tradition with contemporary vogue, her aspect that of both the self-assured *maja* and the independent 'modern woman', and her Manila shawl and carnation complementing a 1930s couture-style gown. Another elegantly coiffured female figure appears in the Verbena de la Paloma poster of 1935 (anonymous), wearing a similar style of dress and shawl, riding a carousel horse side-saddle and eating *churros* (Fig. 6). The seemingly free-floating horse, the effervescence of the woman's diaphanous skirts, and the dark background used to mimic the quality of a photographic negative suggest the influence of Toulouse-Lautrec and his innovative representations of the American dancer Loïe Fuller.

The Antonio Cabrera poster for the Verbena de la Paloma (attributed to an unspecified date between 1931 and 1936) more directly appropriates the photographic genre, in a collage that includes a photograph of two *castiza* women amidst staves of *zarzuela* music and fairground streamers. Thus although the women themselves do not quite approach the *à la mode* appearance of their counterparts in the other posters, their modernity is emphasized through the technical medium through which they are represented. However, the musical notes of the song '¿Dónde vas con mantón de manila, dónde vas?'

Fig. 6. 1935 poster for the Verbena de la Paloma (anonymous),
issued by the Ayuntamiento de Madrid

[Where are you going in your Manila shawl, where are you going?]—
from the *zarzuela La Verbena de la Paloma*—imply another form of
urban identity to the women, capturing the doubled meaning of a
female 'streetwalker' who parades the city *barrios* in her finery. The

most overtly cosmopolitan urban image is that by Augusto (again dated loosely as between 1931 and 1936) for the Verbenas de San Juan y San Pedro, in which a young blonde woman this time sits astride a carousel horse, her dress pulled up above her knees, waving a flower in one hand. The light, bright colouring of the woman and the horse in the foreground is set against a darkened background of shadowy, menacing shapes that imply an industrial urban scene rather than the imperial monuments and elegant landmarks of the city centre. The juxtaposition is significant, implying a recognition of the industrialization on which the prosperity and leisure of consumer modernity is based, and perhaps also an acknowledgement of the opiate or 'distraction' provided for the working classes by mass-cultural entertainment. One thinks here of Frankfurt School theorist Siegfried Kracauer's concept of 'distraction', articulated in his numerous essays on the relation of urban experience, mass entertainment, and social politics (1995). Due to the lack of a specific date, it is impossible to confirm whether this poster derives from the 1931–3 period of reformist government, from that of the 1934–5 CEDA coalition, or from the post-February 1936 Popular Front period, but, regardless of how one reads it, its reference to industrialization brings in a political dimension noticeably absent from the urban images of the other Republican fiesta posters.

The concentration on the single, attractive woman in the foreground of all the designs—the remaining *verbena* poster in the series, Kamel's design for La Verbena de la Moncloa (1931–6), also depicts a voluptuous woman—can partly be explained by the specific connotations of the *verbenas* as celebrations of romantic superstitions and periods of public but non-spiritual holiday. The *verbenas* deal largely with sexual licence, and the implicit reference of all the images is to a party theme of light eroticism and flirtation, in contrast to the pagan misrule of *carnaval* or the religious reverence of San Isidro (García Rodero 1992: 25). Equally resonant, however, is that in a society in which women were achieving emancipation in politics and the divorce courts—the Republican Constitution of December 1931 granted women the vote, and its divorce law was passed in Feburary 1932—all but one of the *verbena* posters depict women who are solitary and unaccompanied. Moreover, the enticing eyes, displayed bodies, and inviting smiles of the women in the posters, wearing their Manila shawls to wander the streets, and in particular the suggestiveness of those whirling on mechanical horseback, one closing her eyes in the sensuous eating of *churros*, the other sat astride and flinging her arm behind her, evoke an atmosphere of urban sexuality within an unprohibited zone. In the *verbena* and the posters for the Verbena de la Paloma, the city and the woman of modernity become one.

SAN ISIDRO AND CONSUMABLE NOSTALGIA

The San Isidro posters, initiated in 1947 with a poster competition for the fiesta by the Comisión Municipal Permanente del Ayuntamiento de Madrid, manifest the influence of early Francoist propaganda, the iconic images being noticeably more traditionalist than their 1930s predecessors. Compared with the modern urban symbolism and experimental use of photography and of impressionistic and collage styles found in the earlier posters, these are predominantly picturesque in tone, static rather than dynamic, and atemporal rather than self-reflexively modern. What is particularly significant, as other studies have shown, is that even those artists working in innovative modern design styles in the 1930s produced substantially more conservative images during the early years of the Franco dictatorship (Vela in Círculo de Bellas Artes 1993: 18). From 1938, during the period between the two groups of Museo Municipal posters, all printed and broadcast media in Spain had been regulated by the Falange and obligated to 'the service of the state', a role that passed to the Church-controlled Ministry of Education in 1945, just prior to the first posters in the second group, and was finally assumed by the Ministry of Information and Tourism in 1951. These two institutional shifts indicated the government's cultural agenda: to educate the masses in Nationalist social dogma, and later to develop and exploit its international profile. The posters advertising San Isidro illustrate Francoist ideology and the control of print culture by the regime's rigid if arbitrary censorship, with artists left with little option other than compliance.

It is important to bear in mind this context of rigid if arbitrary censorship, given Mikhail Bakhtin's assertion (1984) of the importance of carnival celebration as a space of transgression in which authority is challenged, meanings renegotiated, and social controls and taboos relaxed. Much has been made of the simultaneously contestatory and reactionary potential of carnival, and it has become widely accepted as not just a period of festivity but as 'politics masquerading behind cultural forms' (Cohen 1993: 132). With carnival traditionally attacking most notably the restrictive bourgeois institutions of 'religion, fatherland [and] family culture' (Buñuel in Mellen 1978: 111) that dominated Spain and would become the buttress of Franco's dictatorship, the General's response was to suppress its existence. From 1937, one year into the Civil War, when the Valencian *fallas*, nicknamed the *Fallas Antifascistas*, burned paper effigies of Franco and other Nationalist figures in the city streets, Franco banned *carnaval* celebrations in the Nationalist zone and, after Nationalist victory in April 1939, in the whole of Spain until 1967. *Carnaval* had previously been banned during the 1920s under the earlier dictatorship of Miguel Primo de Rivera. The festival did gradually begin to reemerge during the 1950s and 1960s, however, if in a diluted form, under tolerant governors in certain areas of Spain such as Seville, Córdoba, and Málaga (Gilmore 1998: 12). The example of the *Fallas Antifascistas* makes explicit the political role of carnival celebration, but also its ambiguous significance as a space in which social authority is contested yet over which it is reasserted. The 'politics' of carnival can also be subtle and, although it delights in the violation of social hegemony, part of its very definition is that its dissidence is temporary, providing an outlet for disobedience that ultimately serves to sustain rather than overthrow the dominant order. What Bakhtin also recognized, and what is at risk of being overlooked in the claiming of carnival as a purely oppositional event, is that the ambiguity that is the essence of carnival culture extends to its sociopolitical function. It is this ambiguity that allows for both the embrace of carnival by subcultural groups and its cultivation and appropriation by the hegemonic authority. Despite proscribing *carnaval*, the Franco regime encouraged a suitably mediated observance of carnival tradition in religious celebrations and processions.

The Franco regime's agenda operated on a socio-cultural as much as a directly political level, with the Nationalist politics asserted in war articulated and upheld through control of all forms of public activity, in particular of popular culture. Cultural policy concentrated on mass culture, both in terms of censorship, as high art forms were assessed with greater leniency, and in terms of management, with popular and folk culture being selectively supported. As Marvin D'Lugo has described in relation to cinema of the period, folkloric rhetoric 'imaged a sanitized, provincial world of pure spiritual and moral values, implicitly opposing the milieu of moral corruption, sexual promiscuity, and heretical foreign ideas that was synonymous for the regime with urban culture' (Vernon and Morris 1995: 126). Concerned primarily with the political influence of art, it was the pervasiveness of popular culture that the government recognized as powerfully subversive or utilizable, the familiar codes of folk culture being especially prized as a means of instilling ideology within the minds of the populace. Differentiating a 'true Spain' from the recent past of the 'decadent', 'degenerate', modernizing turn of the century, the dictatorship marginalized the country from modernizing Europe and reasserted traditionalism through restrictive and limiting cultural policies. It promoted a traditional ideology that looked backwards to a past Spain of the Catholic kings, romanticized into a myth of a united, Catholic, heroic, imperial nation. Underlying this vague, 'quixotic' mythology was a belief in the superiority of a 'Hispanic' race. In contrast to the liberal Europeanism of Republican Spain, the early Francoist propaganda machine formulated a carefully cultivated but counterfeit *hispanidad*, defined by prescribed racial and cultural characteristics. Acutely aware of the power of popular community culture for ideological purposes, Nationalist cultural policy harnessed popular culture and entertainment to forward this new myth, judiciously employing certain regional practices to advertise the falsely singular and centralized identity of *hispanidad* whilst regulating or banning aspects that challenged its values. Although some fiestas, such as San Isidro, could be utilized as public media for the inspiration of the Castilian-based nationalism and religious ideology of the New State, others were regarded as threatening to the promotion of the new order and thus subject to government suppression (Mintz 1997; García Rodero 1992).

Carnaval, the *verbenas*, and San Isidro are classic examples of the selective condemnation, disregard, or condonement of popular and mass-cultural practice by the Franco administration. Whereas the first threatened the position and dogma of the dictatorship, and therefore required suppression, the Castilian saint provided an ideal figure for veneration. Unlike the localized *verbenas*, the fiesta in honour of Madrid's patron saint San Isidro during the second week of May, the principal celebration of the year, is focused at the heart of the city in the Plaza Mayor, culminating in a day-trip to the Pradera de San Isidro, the large meadow outside the city beneath the Palacio Real, for a mass fête and picnic. Rejecting the articulation of modernity that is central to the *carnaval* and *verbena* posters of the earlier period, the advertisements for San Isidro from the early years of Francoism frame Madrid within a closed Christian and romantic past. References to the city's medieval and Golden Age heritage, the selective use of early Goya, and images of exotic regionalism and a provincial peasant class construct a populist mythology. Spatial and temporal difference is homogenized into a vision of an eternal Spanish identity, *castizo* in the sense that it invokes nostalgic historical images of *madrileño* architecture, culture, and dress.[5] The atmosphere evoked is that of Spain's national heritage rather than its place within a twentieth-century Europe, and the images are literally those found in the Prado museum rather than in Madrid's contemporary streetlife.

Rural Spain of the 1940s remained a world closed off from European influence, and its Catholic population, unskilled and agrarian, was constructed as symbolically representative of the Nationalist 'true Spain', although not materially supported as such (indeed, widespread starvation in the rural areas broke up supposedly organic communities by forcing mass emigration to the cities, and later overseas). It is thus not surprising that the focus of the posters from the early Franco period should be the peasant, rather than his urban cosmopolitan popular counterpart. Elderly provincial couples approaching the city walls, bearing farm produce in honour of their saint, are conspicuous in examples from 1947, 1948, 1956, and 1958, referring both to the traditional status of Madrid as *la Corte*, a seat of monarchy and government sustained by commanding the produce and labour of its regional area (Ringrose 1996), and more implicitly to the contemporaneous role of the city as national capital of a highly centralized state to which the individual was bound in service. The *botijo*, a type of pitcher traditionally used by Spanish farm labourers, drinking from which is one of the rituals of the fiesta, is represented in 1951 and 1953. San Isidro himself, the labourer patron saint, is the subject in 1947, 1949, and 1952. The collective image refers to a Catholic, rural Spain, drawing on stereotypical constructions of identity based on a highly sanitized version of the

[5] The cultural nostalgia upon which such images capitalize is similar to the contemporary use of art and traditional culture in the ever-expanding heritage tourism industry. Comparison between the role of the Franco regime in promoting an internationally marketable 'Spain' for the tourist clientele of the 1960s and 1970s, and the recent trend in regional cultural tourism to Catalonia, Andalusia, and the Basque Country, for example, offers much potential for the study of constructions of national identity and their internal and international promotion.

Castilian provincial labourer. Aspects of regional cultures are, however, selectively incorporated, as in one of two posters from 1948 by Antonio Casero, which depicts exotic, gypsy-like young peasant women with olive skin and loose dark hair, offering a very different image of the rural populace from the staid and sombre Castilian peasant. In the universalized culture of Francoist ideology, the specificity of Madrid and its urban lower class is subdued or 'nationalized'. The result is a Nationalist identity based in traditionalist and gendered ideology, its restrictions masked by an advertised image of festivity and exoticism. The masses are depicted as peasants, and women as historical or regional types who always appear in pairs or as part of a couple, in contrast to the contemporary, autonomous, single figures of the pre-war posters. Both the masses and women—social groups of modernity that were perceived as threatening to the social order— are tamed by such representation. As a result the posters convey a rather subdued and picturesque symbolic representation of the fiesta, in contrast to the more vivid, participatory evocation achieved by the *verbena* posters' modern subjects and kinetic settings. Few of these posters evoke the *bullicio* [bustle] of the 1930 San Isidro witnessed by Kany: the rush for trams and taxis by the urban crowds making the conspicuously secular pilgrimage to the Pradera for the festival picnic, and the typical fairground entertainment of merry-go-rounds, games, and stalls selling wine, sweets, and nuts. The modern fairground of mechanical pleasure rides in the 1930s *verbena* posters has disappeared in favour of religious themes or images drawn from the past.

Seemingly colluding in promoting Francoist ideology through the religious, peasant image of San Isidro, several of the posters however utilize contesting visual codes, including references to modern urbanism and carnival that prompt complex processes of popular cultural association and succeed in problematizing nationalist constructions of folklore. For example, the articulation of local and marginal cultural practices of the *barrios*, under cover of acceptable iconography, highlights—inadvertently perhaps—the conflict between competing ideologies of nationalism and modernization, urbanism and regionalism. By emphasizing urban-*madrileño*, *castizo* culture, the city's individuality could be asserted, refusing the translation of its past into a universal identity and proclaiming its own difference from the ideological construction of a mythicized Castile. One of the most notable artists continuing to design from the 1930s into the Franco regime was Serny, who was awarded second and first prize respectively from the Círculo de Bellas Artes for posters for the *baile de máscaras* in 1933 and 1934, and who is also represented in the Museo Municipal collection with posters from 1947, 1949, and 1957. His prizewinning poster in the opening year of the competition, in compliance with the demands of censorship, presents a timeless traditional image of a light-hearted, classless young couple, a moderated and picturesque version of a *majo* and *maja*, set against a copy of Goya's 1798 *La Pradera de San Isidro* (Fig. 7). Yet Serny here seems to juggle the ambiguous connotations of the *zarzuela* as both conservative and picturesque in theme and plot, and urban and modern in genre. Although he exploits their nostalgic status within the cultural imaginary and de-emphasizes their subversive attitude towards social authority, at the same time he makes explicit reference to the working-class culture of the city and to the popular *zarzuela*. For the *madrileño*, the connotations of the *majo* and *maja*, however romanticized, as members of an urban lower class known for their satiric wit, and the use of Goya, a national artist but one whose early paintings are specifically associated with Madrid, reinstates the primacy of the city and its culture. Moreover, the conjunction of the pretty *maja* and the popular and recognizable Goya painting makes an implicit reference, for those familiar with the exhibits of the Prado museum, to the more notorious *Maja desnuda* (1797), itself a highly subversive work painted during the ban on images of female nudity in the last years of the eighteenth century (Marqués 1998: 39) and banned from exhibition in the Prado during the early Franco years.

The winning entry for the first San Isidro poster under the new regime also succeeds in circumventing the censor by combining the demands of Francoist ideology with reference to indigenous *madrileño* carnivality. For although it is the saint himself in the act of receiving his divine calling who dominates the foreground, behind him lies a blurred fairground scene. The cathedral spires that flank Isidro reach to the heavens alongside the brightly striped hot-air balloons catering to the fiesta's pleasure-seekers. Along with the manipulation of thematic symbolism, cultural negotiation of the atemporal and the modern, and the ruralist and the urban, could also be achieved through aesthetic form, as in Mairata Serrano's 1948 design of two young women dressed in Manila shawls, one carrying a carnation and the other a fan. Despite these traditional symbols the poster, marked by simple silhouetting and block colour, proclaims its

Fig. 7. 1947 poster for the Fiesta de San Isidro by Serny

formal and technical modernity, countering with its own medium the notion of a picturesque Spain. Such experimentation with typographic style and technique, however, remains uncommon during this period, and the sanitized, regulated heritage images in the 1940s and 1950s fiesta posters typically lack the immediacy of the pre-war *carnaval* and *verbena* posters. With the Franco regime's appropriation of religious fiestas for the construction of a homogeneous national culture, the status of fiesta as a space of free expression, public culture, and social and regional diversity was altered, the result being the affirmation of an ideological but also commercially marketable image, dictated by an authoritarian regime that rejected the cultural values of modernity but facilitated capitalist modernization (Richards 1995). Although some of the posters retain images recognizable to the *madrileño* as motifs of the city's own cultural myths of identity, one feels that it is an edited image of folkloric nationality for the outsider gaze that prevails, anticipating the promotion of a picturesque Spain for the purposes of consumer tourism that would ambiguously harness tradition and capitalist modernization—with counter-productive ideological results—in the later Franco period.

CONTEMPORARY CARNIVAL

The culture of the street celebrated by *madrileño* writer-*flâneurs* such as the early twentieth-century writer of *sainetes* Carlos Arniches, and the avant-garde chronicler, novelist, and literary host Ramón Gómez de la Serna, was a culture of immediacy and the everyday, and its language and atmosphere polyphonic and diverse. For both writers, the personality of the city lay in the experience of its streets, the poverty and the inferior conditions of the *barrios* and the city's basement and attic population, and in the temperament of *lo castizo*: a resistance to misery in determined public laughter and gregarious streetlife that they register as specific to Madrid and no other modern city. In the post-Franco era, the reconstruction of this identity has finally been promoted. Public festival and celebration are again a focal aspect of national, cultural, and economic politics, the numbers of feasts and fiestas having considerably increased in recent decades, particularly the 1980s. Such regeneration can be related to recognition of the commercial potential of heritage tourism but there is also evidence

that, at least in southern Europe, the reappearance of ritual celebration is partly connected with issues of identity and cultural memory.
Many fiestas have been reintroduced in Spain after suppression during the years of dictatorship, and perform a multiple role as tourist
magnets and as expressions of previously forbidden cultures. In addition, civic festival programmes have become influential markers of
cosmopolitan, cultural status within the move towards a newly collective Europe. Festival culture is regenerating and reasserting the
traditions and heritage of *lo castizo* but also evolving new aims and
events, providing space for the performance of multiple interests,
in which nationalism and Europeanism, tradition and innovation,
ritual and commerce come together in varying states of contestation
and connection. Madrid is again a city famed for a lively and energetic culture of night-time street partying, and it is interesting to
note that the images for the contemporary fiestas of the 1980s that
close the Museo Municipal collection indicate a return to those of
the beginning: for example, dominating the 1987 triptych depicting
carnaval, San Isidro, and the *Veranos de la Villa* are a masked figure,
a slender *maja* in Manila shawl, and a chic modern woman, all set
against a darkened background. The secular *Veranos de la Villa* (a
new series of summer fiestas instigated under Tierno Galván) constitute a period of art festivals in the new-Europeanist mode organized
by the City Council. Although coexistent with the summer *verbenas*
they differ by taking an aesthetic rather than popular cultural focus,
and are promoted for the whole of the city ('la Villa') rather than
within the local *barrios*. The carnivalesque, the religious, and the
newly established arts festival are thus in the 1987 design accorded
equal significance in the self-promotion of the city's public cultural
agenda: an example of institutionally managed, but also initiated,
public culture.

The success of this championing of cultural activity was evident in
the choice of Madrid as 'Culture Capital of Europe' in 1992. (Tierno
Galván did not live to see the event, dying in 1986; his importance to
the people of the city was commemorated by the massive numbers
who lined the streets for his funeral.) Posters for contemporary fiestas
have taken on a new ideological function, to promote the city's culture within a new identity of the 1990s 'Eurocities'. Taken as a whole
the Museo Municipal collection provides a record of the assertion,
negotiation, and manipulation of local and national symbolism in the
metamorphoses of *madrileño* tradition and identity from the 1930s

to the present day. As registers on which the national and local identities of the city are mapped, they perform a complex dialectic between orchestrated cultural propaganda and aesthetic resistance, marked by conflicting ideals, requirements, and influences. They register the ways in which the Madrid fiestas have been institutionally promoted for differing purposes, from the support for local popular cultural manifestations in the pre-war years, through the manipulation of selected aspects of religious and regional iconography during the early Franco regime, to the regeneration of public entertainments within the 'cultural capitals' of 1990s Europe.

WORKS CITED

Amorós, A. (1991). *Luces de candilejas: los espectáculos en España 1898–1939*. Madrid: Espasa Calpe.

Bakhtin, M. (1984). *Rabelais and his World*, trans. H. Iswolsky. Bloomington: Indiana University Press.

Barbero, A. (1935). Review of *La Verbena de la Paloma*, ABC (24 Dec.).

Carr, R. (1980). *Modern Spain 1875–1980*. Oxford: Oxford University Press.

Círculo de Bellas Artes (1993). *Carnavales*. Madrid: Círculo de Bellas Artes.

Cohen, A. (1993). *Masquerade Politics: Explorations in the Structure of Urban Cultural Movements*. Oxford: Berg.

Fernández Cifuentes, L. (1999). 'The City as Stage: Rebuilding Metropolis after the Colonial Wars', *Arizona Journal of Hispanic Cultural Studies*, 3: 105–27.

García Rodero, C. (1992). *Festivals and Rituals of Spain*. New York: Harry N. Abrams.

Gilmore, D. (1998). *Carnival and Culture: Sex, Symbol, and Status in Spain*. New Haven: Yale University Press.

Giménez Caballero, E. (1930). *Esencia de verbena* (film).

——(1994). *'Carteles literarios' de Gecé* (exhibition catalogue). Barcelona: Universitat de Barcelona/Madrid: Museo Nacional Centro de Arte Reina Sofía.

Gómez de la Serna, R. (1942). *Maruja Mallo: 1928–1942*, English text by Lawrence Smith. Buenos Aires: Editorial Losada.

Gubern, R. (1994). *Benito Perojo: pionerismo y supervivencia*. Madrid: Filmoteca Española.

——(1998). 'Benito Perojo's *La Verbena de la Paloma*', in S. Zunzunegui and J. Talens (eds.), *Modes of Representation in Spanish Cinema*. Minneapolis: University of Minnesota Press, 49–57.

Hansen, M. (1999). 'The Mass Production of the Senses: Classical Cinema as Vernacular Modernism', *Modernism/Modernity*, 6.2: 59–77.

Kany, C. E. (1930). *Fiestas y costumbres españolas*. London: Harrap.

Kracauer, S. (1995). *The Mass Ornament*. Cambridge, Mass.: Harvard University Press.

Marqués, M. B. M. (1998). *Goya*. Madrid: Fundación Amigos del Museo del Prado/Alianza Editorial.

Mellen, J. (ed.) (1978). *The World of Luis Buñuel*. New York: Oxford University Press.

Merino, A. G. (1935). Review of *La Verbena de la Paloma*, *Cinegramas*, 68 (29 Dec.).

Ministerio de Comercio y Turismo (1998). *Fiestas de España*, brochure. Madrid: Ministerio de Comercio y Turismo.

Mintz, J. (1997). *Carnival Song and Society*. Oxford: Berg.

Museo Municipal de Madrid (1991). *Carteles de Fiestas en la Colección del Museo Municipal 1932–1991*. Madrid: Ayuntamiento de Madrid.

Pérez de Ayala, J., and Rivas, F. (1991). *Maruja Mallo*. Madrid: Guillermo de Osma Galería.

Richards, M. (1995). ' "Terror and Progress": Industrialization, Modernity, and the Making of Francoism', in H. Graham and J. Labanyi (eds.), *Spanish Cultural Studies: An Introduction*. Oxford: Oxford University Press, 173–82.

Rifkin, A. (1993). *Street Noises: Parisian Pleasure 1900–40*. Manchester: Manchester University Press.

Ringrose, D. (1996). *Spain, Europe, and the 'Spanish Miracle', 1700–1900*. Cambridge: Cambridge University Press.

Salaün, S., and Serrano, C. (1991). *1900 en España*. Madrid: Espasa Calpe.

Segel, H. B. (1987). *Turn of the Century Cabaret: Paris, Barcelona, Berlin, Munich, Vienna, Cracow*. New York: Columbia University Press.

Serrano, C. (1973). *Sociedad, literatura y política en la España del siglo XIX*. Madrid: Guardiana de Publicaciones.

Sheppard, R. (1983). 'Tricksters, Carnival and the Magical Figures of Dada Poetry', *Forum for Modern Language Studies*, 19.2: 116–25.

Talens, J., and Zunzunegui, S. (1998). *Modes of Representation in Spanish Cinema*. Minneapolis: University of Minnesota Press.

Tisa, J. (1980). *The Palette and the Flame: Posters of the Spanish Civil War*. London: Collet's.

Tomlinson, J. (1994). *Goya*. London: Phaidon.

Vernon, K. M., and Morris, B. (eds.) (1995). *Post-Franco, Post-modern: The Films of Pedro Almodóvar*. Westport, Conn.: Greenwood Press.

12

Musical Battles: Populism and Hegemony in the Early Francoist Folkloric Film Musical

JO LABANYI

IN this article I should like to analyse the Spanish cinematic genre of the folkloric film musical, which enjoyed massive popularity with lower-class and especially female audiences in the early Franco period, in terms of Gramsci's key concepts of the 'national-popular' and 'hegemony'. The genre has generally been dismissed by Spanish film directors and critics, reflecting the unfortunate tendency in Spanish film criticism to scorn popular cinema. The proliferation of folkloric film musicals in the 1940s and early 1950s has encouraged perceptions of it as mindless escapism serving the early Francoist political project. Of the two books on the subject, Pineda Novo (1991) consists in trivializing anecdote about its hugely popular female stars; while Moix (1993) lays the ground for a contestatory reading by reclaiming the genre for gay spectators. I should like here to develop the possibilities for a contestatory reading—without forgetting the genre's obviously conservative plot structures—on the assumption that the popular and especially female audiences who enjoyed these films were not simply duped by them but found in them resonances that struck a chord with their own life-experiences, needs, or aspirations. Gramsci's theories have formed the basis of British cultural studies, as developed by Raymond Williams and the Birmingham Centre for Contemporary Cultural Studies, because—unlike Adorno's and Horkheimer's tendency to view popular culture as the culture industries' manipulation of the masses—they credit popular audiences with discrimination and the ability to resemanticize the cultural products they consume for their own ends.[1] One of

---

[1] A good outline of the development of cultural studies as a discipline is given by During (1993: 1–25).

the unfortunate cultural consequences of Francoism is that it encouraged opposition critics to adopt an orthodox Marxist position which viewed popular culture as little more than ideological manipulation —a view which at the time was excusable given state censorship and control of the media (though one must remember that the film industry remained in private hands). Curiously, the acknowledged debt of the Spanish oppositional cinema that developed in the 1950s to Italian neo-realism, itself based on Gramsci's theories of the 'national-popular', did not lead to the assimilation of Gramsci's unorthodox Marxist analysis of culture, which to this day remains largely ignored by critics of Spanish culture.

There are, in fact, many reasons why Gramsci's theories should be applied to Spanish culture. First, Gramsci was analysing another Mediterranean culture (Italy), marked by the dominant influence of popular and official Catholicism, and by a north–south divide. Coming from undeveloped Sardinia, Gramsci was keenly aware of the divorce between the state and the mass of the southern Italian peasantry, whose incorporation into the nation he regarded as a political priority. Here Gramsci was rejecting what he called bourgeois 'voluntarism'; that is, the co-option of select individuals moulded in the image of their 'superiors': a cultural strategy that has typified Spanish liberalism. Ortega y Gasset's emphasis on the need to create 'select minorities' is the clearest example; but the taking of bourgeois culture to 'the people' also characterized the cultural efforts of the late nineteenth-century Krausist liberal reformers and their heirs, educated at the Krausist-founded Institución Libre de Enseñanza, under the Spanish Republic of 1931–6—for example, the taking of high-cultural art forms to the rural hinterland by the Misiones Pedagógicas and La Barraca. For Gramsci, education was rather a means of enabling the subaltern to articulate their own cultural aspirations. His aim was not to co-opt the peasantry but to empower them through an interactive process of cultural alliances and contestation: what he famously termed 'hegemony'. It is important to remember that, for Gramsci, hegemony was not so much a negative description of the way the dominant classes had used culture to manipulate the people, as a political theory designed to enable the Italian Communist Party, of which Gramsci was leader when arrested in 1926, to secure a mass political voice. For, even when hegemony is exercised by the traditional ruling classes, the need to negotiate consent by cultural means leaves a space for subaltern groups. It is also important to remember that Gramsci's concept of hegemony insists on culture as a plural site of struggle between competing constituencies, which are internally heterogeneous and fractured, and which relate to each other through a double process of collusion and contestation. Indeed Gramsci notes that collusion can be a strategy for survival: subversion and subordination overlap. There is no place in this cultural map for binary oppositions.[2]

Gramsci's theories are particularly salutary when dealing with early Francoism, whose manichaean rhetoric has tended to fool critics into supposing that the period was one of relatively straight-forward opposition between victors and vanquished. This is what Gramsci suggestively calls a 'melodramatic' representation of history, according to which the oppressors simply impose their rule on the oppressed, constituted as passive victims. In her book *Film, Politics, and Gramsci*, Marcia Landy (1994: 32) notes that this melo-dramatic conception of history characterized fascism. Despite its rhetoric of exclusions, fascism was as concerned with incorporating the people into the nation as was Gramsci. Indeed, Gramsci developed his notion of the 'national-popular' as a cultural strategy for securing hegemony through his analysis of Italian fascism during his years in prison under Mussolini 1926–37. Gramsci's theories are thus directly relevant for an analysis of early Francoism. Spanish fascism had always been ideologically closer to Mussolini than to Hitler, and the fact that Francoism was an alliance of disparate extreme-right forces, of which the Spanish fascist party Falange Española was one, confirms Gramsci's insistence that even power blocs which present themselves as monolithic are a precarious amalgam of competing groups. A significant feature of Gramsci's writings is his understanding of the ideological strength of fascism because, contrary to the bourgeois capitalist exclusion of the masses and particularly of the rural populace which had no place in the capitalist scheme, fascism sought to construct an all-inclusive national culture based on an organic concept of 'the popular'.

This is not to underestimate the repressive effects of early Francoism which, like the Italian fascist state, sought to manufacture consent through the manipulation of popular culture, especially cinema. There are crucial differences between the fascist model

---

[2] My account of Gramsci's theories is taken from Forgacs and Nowell-Smith's anthology of his cultural writings (1991), and from Landy (1994) who is particularly helpful in showing the relevance of Gramsci's writings for the analysis of cinema.

of incorporation of the people into the nation, and that envisaged by Gramsci. As Landy notes, the fascist concept of the 'national-popular' is a hegemonic tool for incorporating the nation's diverse constituencies into a monolithic state; it is an 'organic' concept because it aims to subsume difference into wholeness, whereas the Gramscian notion of the 'national-popular' is concerned with incorporating the masses through a hegemonic process that allows the expression of cultural differences. But no matter how 'melodramatic' the fascist conception of history, in practice fascist populism sought to manufacture consent by dramatizing, in its cultural products, complex bargaining processes between dominant and subaltern groups, in which collusion and contestation coexist or blur. The romance plots of the early Francoist folkloric film musical (*folklórica*) are just such an example of manufactured consent, with the lower-class (usually gypsy) heroine who figures the people surrendering to the higher-class male protagonist (usually a landowner) only after using her seductive powers to secure his capitulation to her cultural values.

Gramsci is especially relevant to study of the *folklórica* because of the centrality in his writings of folklore. Gramsci rejects the prevailing 'picturesque' concept of folklore, produced by intellectuals who view the peasantry as 'foreign' and who frequently are themselves foreigners.[3] Instead he argues for an 'organic' concept of folklore whereby the intellectual allies himself with the peasantry by viewing their way of looking at the world from the inside. The fact that the heroines of the early Francoist *folklórica* are overwhelmingly 'other-race' (mostly gypsies or stereotypical Andalusians who have assimilated the marks of gypsy culture to the point of being virtually indistinguishable from them) on the one hand perpetuates the picturesque idea of the 'pueblo' as foreign; but the point of the plot is to assimilate the heroine, in return for her higher-class suitor assimilating, and being enriched by, her values; indeed, in several films, the higher-class suitor has been educated abroad, constructing *him* as foreign.[4]

---

[3] Hobsbawm (1990: 103–4) notes that the folkloric 'rediscovery' of 'the people', which typified the rise of European nationalism from the late 18th century through the 19th century, was largely 'the work of enthusiasts from the (foreign) ruling class or élite'.

[4] For a more detailed analysis of the racial dynamics of the *folklórica* than can be given here, see Labanyi (1997, 2000).

Gramsci notes that, while folklore—in this sense of the peasant world view—is largely opposed to officialdom, it incorporates elements from official culture, including cultural relics from the past. Indeed, as he acutely observes, it is 'a repertory of clichés' (1991: 378) bordering on pastiche. The lower-class heroine of the early Francoist *folklórica* is, without exception, a performer, who expresses herself by mimicking a mixture of popular and high-cultural forms. This is both because the popular cultural traditions represented are already hybrid mixes of high and low (as well as mixes of traditional rural culture and modern urban mass culture), and also because the bargaining process which secures her final marriage to the landowner involves her mimicking his habits and speech. However, it also involves her higher-class suitor, despite the fact that he is not a performer and is acted in a 'straight' if not wooden acting style, to an extent mimicking the cultural signs of *her* class. The populist use of folklore in the early Francoist *folklórica*, despite some ethnographic touches, makes relatively few gestures to the 'purist' concept of folklore cultivated by 1920s avant-garde artists like Falla and Lorca and by 1950s Francoist intellectuals, for, in opting for the modern mass-cultural medium of film as a tool for manufacturing national consensus, early Francoism is accepting a concept of the 'national-popular' marked by hybridity and by modernity.[5] The genre thus echoes Gramsci's insistence that popular culture is always touched by official culture and by historical change. Indeed, the lower-class heroines frequently triumph in the modern city (in Spain and abroad) as performers. The resourcefulness of the genre's lower-class female protagonists, and even of the caricaturesque work-shy gypsy males, supports Gramsci's view that folklore contains 'various strata: the fossilized ones which reflect conditions of past life and are therefore conservative and reactionary, and those which consist of a series of innovations often creative and progressive [. . .] which are in contradiction to or simply different from the morality of the governing strata' (1991: 190). Above all, the *folklórica*'s use of hybrid forms of popular song and dance as the subaltern's strategy for seducing the dominant classes, in a double process of collusion and subversion, illustrates Gramsci's view that all forms of popular song, whether or not composed by or for the people, are 'adopted' by the people

---

[5] For a critique of the primitivist co-option of flamenco for the purposes of high culture by Lorca and Falla, and by 1950s intellectuals, see Mitchell (1994: 160–77).

'because they conform to their way of thinking and feeling' (1991: 194) and thus serve as a strategy for survival. Gramsci also notes that popular songs are commonly recycled for different purposes (1991: 352); this recycling is a characteristic of the *folklórica* genre, with many films of the early Franco period being built around a song that had enjoyed previous popularity, often under the Republic, thus carrying over considerable cultural ambivalence.

The romance plot of the *folklórica* is an attempt to secure, with the final marriage, the fascist dream of a society transcending capitalist class conflict, which differs from the egalitarian socialist dream of Gramsci (or indeed of the Spanish Republic which first promoted the *folklórica* as a 'national-popular' genre) in its vertical ordering: higher-class male marries lower-class female. Nevertheless, in the process class relations are shown to be complex, interactive bargaining processes between different cultural groups that are internally heterogeneous and contradictory. In an article drawing parallels between Gramsci's notion of hegemony and Bakhtin's notion of heteroglossia, Craig Brandist (1996: 103) notes that Bakhtin outlines two hegemonic principles whereby discourses seek to bind other discourses to themselves 'either by establishing a relation of authority between the enclosing and target [i.e. subaltern] discourses or by facilitating the further advancement of the target [i.e. subaltern] discourse *through* the enclosing discourse'. In principle, the former ('establishing a relation of authority between enclosing and subaltern discourse') corresponds to the populist project of the early Francoist *folklórica* and the latter ('facilitating the further advancement of the subaltern discourse *through* the enclosing discourse') to Gramsci's Marxist political project. In practice, the *folklórica* blurs the difference between Bakhtin's two categories, since the lower-class heroine's surrender to the embrace or 'enclosing authority' of the higher-class male protagonist takes the form of her seduction of him and of the spectator.

For Bakhtin, like Gramsci a linguistics scholar, hegemony is effected via the negotiation process that he termed 'dialogism' or 'heteroglossia'; that is, a contest of voices. In a large number of *folklóricas*, the romance plot takes the form of a contest between popular music (personified by the heroine, usually a gypsy flamenco singer) and either some form of classical music (associated with the male protagonist) or else nineteenth-century operetta or modern cabaret, represented as urban, bourgeois, and foreign-influenced (sometimes personified by the male suitor but more often by a treacherous female rival). There is space here only to outline these musical battles but it should become clear that the transactions involved are complex and by no means a knock-out competition between cultural opposites. What emerges is a view of culture that, far from monolithic, is inter-active and dynamic. By representing relations between popular and bourgeois musical forms as a contest—which necessarily involves contestation—the *folklórica* genre provides a self-reflexive com-ment on early Francoist populism as an attempt to secure hegemony through a process of cultural negotiation. John Kraniauskas (1997) describes the Peronist populist promotion of Evita as lower-class movie star as a case of 'the State meets the culture industry'; the same could be said of the populist project enacted in the early Francoist folkloric musical.

This contestation process is particularly well illustrated by a key sequence from *Estrella de Sierra Morena* [*Estrella of the Sierra Morena*] (Ramón Torrado, 1952) which runs through a gamut of performance styles. The sequence starts with a spectacularly choreographed formal display of eighteenth-century-style classical flamenco, performed by a dance ensemble at the Provincial Gov-ernor's ball, where Lola Flores (brought up by bandits and not knowing she is his daughter) is impersonating his niece as a ploy to get her bandit adoptive father freed from jail; in the process she falls for an army officer in the Provincial Governor's entourage. Bored by this aestheticized high-cultural entertainment and incapable of the piano-playing expected of a bourgeois lady, Lola first performs a mildly saucy song, typical of the music hall which emerged out of the late nineteenth-century modernization and urbanization process (Salaün 1990) and which incorporated traditional popular song, including flamenco, into its repertoire. In the course of her rendition of the song, we see her wink at a comic bandit disguised as a bour-geois, showing that her performance is a strategy of collusion for subversive ends; indeed, she weaves her clandestine message to him —'meet me in the garden'—into the lyrics. At the end of the sequence, she bursts into an openly defiant performance of popular flamenco dance (*bulerías*) whose provocative physicality leaves the assembled bourgeois guests shell-shocked. The bourgeois ladies present— whose crass stereoptying constitutes a send-up of bourgeois taste— comment in horror that her unrestrained dancing style shows she has been educated abroad. The stock comedy here conceals a serious critique of bourgeois culture's dismissal of popular culture, which the

ladies regard as 'foreign'. Lola Flores's flamboyant, seductive performance ensures that audience identifications are entirely on the side
of popular culture, as they are in another of her films, made with
the same director the previous year, *La niña de la venta* [*The Girl at
the Inn*] (Ramón Torrado, 1951). Here Lola dances 'spontaneously'
at the tavern of her *padrino* [adoptive father], contrasting with the
suave, modern cabaret singer Raquel, billed as 'La Venus de Tánger'
[The Venus of Tangiers], hired to distract the police chief from the
locals' smuggling operations. Predictably Raquel turns out to be a
spy. She is Lola's rival in song as well as love; the local audience is un-
enthused by her cool jazz-inspired crooning which constructs them as
passive audience, unlike Lola's folkloric singing and dancing which
fires them all to join in: popular music constructs community. There
is a third musical scenario in the film: the gypsy camp, whose inhabitants are filmed almost ethnographically as a 'native tribe'. This
serves to construct Lola as a musical hybrid: 'spontaneous' by comparison with the cabaret singer but a performer by comparison with
the 'raw' dancers at the gypsy camp. Like most *folklóricas*, this film
promotes flamenco as a source of national-popular identifications
not so much in the sense of a return to natural, rural origins as in that
of popular culture as performance. While this could be viewed as an
orientalist reduction of the lower classes to spectacle, it can also be
seen as a demonstration of how performance can be used by the
subaltern as a strategy for their own ends: the innkeeper and Lola
put on a performance to put the police off the scent, Lola gets her
higher-class man by performing a stunning drum routine on oil cans
outside his window.

   In *El sueño de Andalucía* [*Dream of Andalusia*] (Luis Lucía, 1950),
the star Carmen Sevilla is similarly pitted against a treacherous
female rival in the form of a Viennese operetta star, who performs to
an entourage of ballet dancers dressed in tutus and hussars' uniforms,
the pretentiousness of which is exposed by a comic chase scene, reminiscent of music-hall bawdy, when the Andalusian *gracioso* [comic
side-kick], dressed in female costume to evade pursuit by a jealous
Mexican, gets mixed up with the performers on stage, finally triumphing with a flamenco *zapateado*. Andalusian song and dance are in
this film promoted as a source of national-popular identifications,
not because they are 'natural' by contrast with the tackiness of
Viennese operetta, but because they are *more* polished and glitzy:
Carmen Sevilla's hairdo and toothpaste-advert smile are straight
out of Hollywood; the male singing lead Luis Mariano was a star of

French operetta. The self-reflexivity of this film—typical of its director Luis Lucía—is notable, with its outer narrative frame converting
the drama into a 'film within the film'. The film opens with Luis
Mariano playing himself as acting star in his Paris theatre dressing
room, signing the contract for *El sueño de Andalucía* and starting to
read the script, which slips into voice-over as the start of the film
proper appears on screen. At the narrative's climactic moment, we
cut to the actors in the Paris film studio; on finishing filming, they
decide to go off to Andalusia to see 'the real thing' and we follow
them touring Seville, ending in the film-set version of the city used in
the main narrative. The effect is to construct Spanish popular culture
—figured by an exotic Andalusia staged explicitly for the benefit of
foreigners—as performance. Indeed, the resolute lack of realism of
the folkloric musical genre as a whole can be seen as promoting an
almost postmodern notion of the performance of everyday life, with
everyone assuming roles for different tactical ends.

In *Gloria Mairena* (Luis Lucía, 1952), Juanita Reina plays an
internationally successful performance artist, who performs polished
versions of Andalusian song to her husband's classical guitar accom-
paniment. When she dies, he becomes a priest and music teacher in
the school attached to Seville Cathedral where he had been a choir-
boy, bringing up their daughter (also played by Juanita Reina) in an
all-male environment where she is forbidden to sing. However, the
unconscious memory of her mother's singing asserts itself in Gloria
Junior and she triumphs as a singer, winning the love of a successful
pianist who, having failed as a classical musician, has turned to the
mambo; the Carmen Miranda look-alike who performs with him is
the treacherous rival in this film. Juanita Reina is left cold by the
mambo, and converts him to 'Spanish song' by getting him to perform with her the song her father had written for her mother to the
music of Granados's fifth Spanish Dance. The film ends with the couple triumphing worldwide, after a rapid cut to the seminarist previously in love with Gloria sublimating human passion by conducting
a choir of turbaned little boys as a missionary overseas. This colonial
scenario throws another kind of music into this film's particularly
complex contest of musical styles, whose function is to raise popular
Andalusian song to high-art status. The fact that Gloria 'cannot help
singing' despite the paternal prohibition does not so much construct
Andalusian song as natural as construct her as a 'born performer'; the
pull of maternal origins is the pull of performance.

In *Canelita en rama* (Eduardo García Maroto, 1942) Juanita Reina plays a somewhat similar role as a gypsy girl who has lost her mother and who is educated to be a lady by the landowner who has been tricked by her gypsy family into thinking he is her father. Again, she 'can't help singing' because it is in the blood. However, here the rural setting of her father's Andalusian estate is filmed with ethnographic precision, constructing her song as tied to the land. She sings mostly in the open air, though on the first occasion she says she'd like the pony-trap to have a radio but, since it hasn't, *she* will be the radio; later we hear her singing along to jazz music on the radio or record-player: 'natural song' is linked with modern means of mass reproduction. The film is an indictment of the upper classes' dismissal of popular song as in bad taste; Juanita Reina's singing wins everyone over, including the landowner's Oxford-educated son, to the extent that he starts taking guitar and singing lessons from her stereotypically work-shy male gypsy relatives. Here we have a double carnivalesque reversal, as the work-shy gypsies mimic the lifestyle of the *señorito* [landowner's son], reclining in armchairs, smoking cigars, and commenting that as gentlemen they wouldn't dream of working, while he mimics their musical prowess, provoking the nicely subversive comment from one of the gypsies speaking in thickest 'andalú' [Andalusian]: 'hombre, que no, que me destroza el castellano' [not like that, you're mangling Castilian]. What is important in this carnivalesque scene is that lower and upper classes are both engaged in a process of cultural negotiation; the *señorito* may have the land and he gets Juanita Reina (only after his conversion to flamenco, which she lays down as a condition), but the film shows that she and her trickster relatives are able to use the stereotypes associated with popular culture to considerable advantage.[6]

Carnival figures explicitly in *Bambú* (José Luis Sáenz de Heredia, 1945), set in Cuba during the independence struggle.[7] The film's protagonist, a failed Spanish avant-garde composer, finds musical

---

[6] González-Medina (1997), in an otherwise excellent analysis, sees the film as a mouthpiece of Francoist populist ideology, failing to appreciate the complexity of the bargaining processes dramatized in it.

[7] Sáenz de Heredia, a cousin of the founder of the Spanish fascist party José Antonio Primo de Rivera, had in 1941 been chosen to direct the ghastly Nationalist panegyric *Raza*, scripted under a pseudonym by Franco. At the same time that he was making *Raza*, Sáenz de Heredia was writing the lyrics for Celia Gámez musical revues: an indication of the cultural complexity—particularly in terms of the relations between high and low culture—of the early Franco regime.

regeneration through his love for Cuban mulatto singer Bambú, whose song, proclaiming the fruit she sells, constructs her as the nourishment provided by the colonies to a decadent bourgeois Europe. In this capacity, she is contrasted on the one hand with the Pay-Pay cabaret where the singers prostitute themselves for money, and on the other with the composer's initial Spanish upper-class fiancée who wants him only for the prestige expected of him as a classical composer. One of Bambú's musical appearances is with the Afro-Cuban carnival singers who 'invade' the Governor's palace singing 'El Gobernador no permitió el carnaval' [The Governor banned the carnival] in a tolerated ritual of subversion, which recurs in the final syncretic musical masterpiece—choreographed and filmed like a Busby Berkeley fantasia—which the male protagonist composes in his head as he dies in a *Liebestod* with Bambú, both shot by the rebel Cuban troops. No matter how seductive Bambú's singing, the only kind of subversion permitted here is, it seems, that which colludes—as she does—with Spain's colonial presence: the function of Afro-Caribbean music is to enrich the Western classical musical tradition. Bambú is, of course, played by a Spanish star (Imperio Argentina, who was actually half-British, her father being from Gibraltar) and the film's wonderful musical score is by Ernesto Halffter, the principal composer of the 1927 Generation who developed Falla's syncretic brand of cultural nationalism.

A similar plot occurs in *Serenata española* [*Spanish Serenade*] (Juan de Orduña, 1947), a fictionalized biopic of the classical composer Albéniz based on the play by Eduardo Marquina, which has the composer derive his inspiration from his love for a gypsy singer (Juanita Reina), conveniently murdered by a jealous gypsy suitor so that Albéniz can go on to triumph unencumbered by her presence. This entirely spurious plot allows Albéniz to be rescued from his multinational musical formation (and from his Jewish origins, never mentioned), by giving him an indigenous source of inspiration. Juanita Reina's musical and amorous rival is a foreign classical singer. In another syncretic musical fantasia, Albéniz imagines Juanita Reina performing a balletic version of flamenco against a theatre backcloth depicting the Giralda, an iconic representation of Andalusianness. Here the balance between ballet and flamenco is on the side of the latter, albeit staged. By contrast, flamenco metamorphoses completely into ballet in the climactic moment of *Lola la piconera* (Juan de Orduña, 1951), again with Juanita Reina, set in Cadiz during the

Spanish War of Independence against Napoleonic occupation. In this sequence, the performance-artist heroine (a product of urban mass culture, since she runs a *colmado* or cabaret) and her French officer lover first watch the highly choreographed but raw dancing of some gypsy nomads, which then slips into their 'dream' of a world where national enmities can be overcome by love; that is, where cultural heterogeneity can be turned into homogeneity. At this point, the costumes and choreography become balletic, with non-diegetic choir and orchestra taking over from the previous diegetic guitars and drums, climaxing in a spectacular musical fantasia set against tropical plants and exotic backcloth. In this film too, Juanita Reina dies, showing the utopian dream of syncretic fusion to be a mere fantasy; the narrative dramatizes, not the achievement of fusion, but the tensions and conflicts that occur along the way. The film is based on a play by José María Pemán, cousin—like Sáenz de Heredia—of the Spanish fascist party's founder José Antonio Primo de Rivera (both were from Cadiz), and head of the early Francoist Comisión Depuradora [Purification Committee] which purged Republican teachers and cultural workers. The film's patriotic exaltation of flamenco as a popular cultural form associated with 'spontaneous' female emotion (the heroine dies a martyr to the Spanish cause) betrays Pemán's anti-intellectual stance, but the film's elevation of popular song and dance to high art also betrays his association with official culture: the credits bill him as 'D. José María Pemán de la Real Academia Española' [Don José María Pemán of the Spanish Royal Academy] (he was in fact its President).

In the penultimate film I wish to discuss, *Torbellino* [*Whirlwind*] (Luis Marquina, 1941), the contest between popular and classical music is weighted in the opposite direction. Estrellita Castro plays a humble girl from Seville who dreams of being a radio star: we see her singing to a parrot perch functioning as makeshift microphone, foregrounding the mimicry involved in the hegemonic process of cultural negotiation and contestation. In a complicated intrigue where collusion and subversion blur, she impersonates the niece of the dour director of a Madrid radio station, which is floundering thanks to his insistence on broadcasting gloomy classical music. He hates 'la alegría' [fun] and 'lo populachero' [the lowbrow], despite his involvement in the modern mass media: his 'modern-style' office combines an art-deco mural of a gigantic radio transmitter with a portrait of Beethoven. The plot revolves around a 'concurso' between competing radio stations, figuring hegemony as a struggle between competing cultural claims. Estrellita Castro saves the day for her supposed uncle (converting him to 'lo andaluz' [Andalusian culture] as well as winning his hand) by exposing the treacherous defection to a rival radio station of the Italian opera *diva* he had contracted, and by fixing the controls so her own performance of Andalusian song goes out on the air for the competition—winning, of course—instead of the programmed classical broadcast. A particularly interesting sequence occurs midway through the film, as Estrellita Castro breaks into the radio station at night to enact her fantasy of being a radio star. As she manipulates the radio controls, her fantasy image as singing star (also played by Estrellita Castro) materializes and performs before her eyes, separated from her by the glass window of the control room. This sequence is interesting on several counts. First, because it throws into relief the film's self-reflexivity as a film about the radio; that is, the culture industry commenting on itself. Secondly, because in this fantasy sequence the mass media invest her popular 'andalucismo' with an aura of glamour, as she appears with ball gown and full orchestra, dramatizing the hybridization process resulting from the meeting of popular and mass culture.[8] Here the song is popular while the orchestration is classical: in a telling shot, Estrellita Castro as fantasized radio star is filmed with the harp—a visual icon denoting classical music—in the foreground. Popular culture is here subsumed into high culture, in a populist move typical of early Francoism; but this process allows the underclasses (Estrellita Castro as 'little poor girl') considerable scope for agency: she takes the plot entirely into her hands, manipulating and outwitting everyone as a popular trickster figure. Thirdly, this sequence is significant because it illustrates the 'double-voiced discourse' which Bakhtin opposed to 'the verbal and semantic dictatorship of a monologic, unified style' (Brandist 1996: 103). We see Estrellita Castro reacting as stage-manager and spectator to the spectacle of her persona as performer: her two incarnations as 'little poor girl' and radio star alternate on screen in classic shot/reverse-shot mode, constructing them as in dialogue with one another. The sequence ends with a travelling shot going a full 180 degrees, as the camera sweeps from Estrellita Castro in the control room to her fantasy persona performing before her eyes in the studio.

[8] Rowe and Schelling (1991: 8) note that, when the culture industry coincides with the nation-formation process, as it has in countries where modernization occurred late, the former takes on some of the 'aura' of high culture.

It is important that a travelling shot and not a dissolve is used here: the two class personae do not merge but form a continuum in which they retain separate identities. Indeed, the precariousness of this populist fantasy of cross-class alliance is immediately exposed as the controls start to smoke and then blow a fuse, bringing the fantasy to an abrupt end. Estrellita Castro may at the end of the film win the hand of the radio station's owner, but she does so on her terms: his conversion to popular culture is also figured as his conversion from misogyny to an appreciation of the feminine. The romance 'happy end' of marriage is one in which the partners will clearly continue to bargain and negotiate (we see them still arguing), and in which the woman—representing popular culture—will be the driving force.

I hope to have shown how, in these films, 'the people' are constructed not as 'natural' but rather as 'natural or born performers'. The notion of the 'born performer' undoes any belief in the essential qualities of 'the Spanish people'; indeed, any belief in the essential qualities of Woman, for in these films 'the people' are without exception figured by the female protagonist. While this allows the popular classes and women a measure of subversion, it also marks them out as inherently untrustworthy: tricksters. The notion that men create and women imitate has a long history, going back to Aristotle. I should like to end on a less positive note with a brief discussion of Carlos Serrano de Osma's 1947 *Embrujo* [Bewitched]: an attempt to turn the folkloric musical into art cinema by psychologizing it. At the end of the film, Lola Flores's dancing talent turns out to be the psychological projection of her dancing and singing partner Manolo Caracol's unrequited love for her.[9] At the moment he collapses and dies (from advanced alchoholism), her talent deserts her and her professional career is ended; he, in other words, initiates and she merely follows. Indeed, in this film, he is the singer while she dances, without a voice. The attempt to raise the folkloric musical to the status of high art masculinizes the genre, and in the process 'castrates' the female protagonist: at the end, we see a now frail, grey-haired Lola feebly recounting her past, her threatening seductive vitality as a performer drained away. The dignification of flamenco is illustrated by the ballet-like choreography (with dancers from Barcelona's Teatro Liceo, Spain's equivalent of Covent Garden); and, in the sequence of

---

[9] Lola Flores and Manolo Caracol's off-screen tempestuous adulterous relationship was well known to audiences.

Manolo's funeral, by the fusion of popular song with religious choral music (the religious variant of flamenco, the *saeta*, has always enjoyed high-cultural status). In Lola's final fantasy performance, a projection of Manolo's voice from the grave at the moment of his burial, flamenco is again given high-cultural status through the avant-garde backcloth. This appropriation of flamenco for high-cultural purposes requires the replacement of popular carnival by tragedy: Lola is 'emasculated', Manolo dies, and the subversive potential of the genre disappears—ironically since Serrano de Osma, though not a member of the Spanish Communist Party, had made propaganda films for it during the Civil War and remained culturally marginalized throughout the 1940s. It is worth noting that the moments in *Serenata española* and *Lola la piconera* when flamenco slips into ballet, thus acquiring high-cultural status, occur in both cases just before the female protagonist's death.

I do not want to deny the conventionalism of the more popular folkloric musicals, whose sudden reversals and ethos of sacrifice echo fascism's melodramatic vision of history. But their attempt to create a national-popular imaginary through their dramatization of contests between competing musical forms is anything but manichaean or monologic. In all of them popular song is privileged, but the alignment with the varied repertoire of other musical forms is different in each case. What is common to all these films, as musicals about musical contests, is their self-conscious dramatization of the hegemonic process. My discussion of the films does not follow the order in which they were made for, contrary to what one might have expected, there is no overall chronological movement from the privileging of the popular towards its incorporation into elite culture. Despite the historical differences between early 1940s and early 1950s Spain, throughout the period we find the two tendencies coexisting. Indeed, they overlap since, in every case, we have the dramatization of a process of cultural hyridization, in which binary oppositions do not hold. It is commonly said that early Francoism did not have a coherent cultural project. I would reformulate this to argue that early Francoism had a sophisticated understanding of hegemony, precisely because it appreciated that this involves complex, shifting negotiations between heterogeneous cultural forms. The fact that, in the films discussed, these heterogeneous cultural forms relate to each other, not through conflict, but through mimicry, on the one hand signals the Francoist desire to transcend the class struggle generated by capitalism and promoted by socialism; but on the other hand it confirms Gramsci's contention that mimicry can, for the subaltern, be an effective—if ambiguous—means of access to power.

WORKS CITED

Brandist, C. (1996). 'Gramsci, Bakhtin and the Semiotics of Hegemony', *New Left Review*, 216: 94–109.
During, S. (ed.) (1993). *The Cultural Studies Reader*. London: Routledge.
González-Medina, J. L. (1997). 'E. G. Maroto's *Canelita en rama* (1943): The Politics of Carnival, Fascism and National(ist) Vertebration in a Postwar Spanish Film', *Journal of Iberian and Latin American Studies (Tesserae)*, 3: 15–29.
Gramsci, A. (1991). *Selections from Cultural Writings*, ed. D. Forgacs and G. Nowell-Smith. Cambridge, Mass.: Harvard University Press.
Hobsbawm, E. J. (1990). *Nations and Nationalism since 1780: Programme, Myth, Reality*. Cambridge: Cambridge University Press.
Kraniauskas, J. (1997). '*El fiord*: The State and Literary Form', paper to LASA conference, Guadalajara (17–19 Apr.).
Labanyi, J. (1997). 'Race, Gender and Disavowal in Spanish Cinema of the Early Franco Period: The Missionary Film and the Folkloric Musical', *Screen*, 38.3: 215–31.
—— (2000). 'Miscegenation, Nation Formation and Cross-racial Identifications in the Early Francoist Folkloric Film Musical', in A. Brah and A. Coombes (eds.), *Hybridity and its Discontents: Politics, Science, Culture*. London: Routledge, 56–71.
Landy, M. (1994). *Film, Politics, and Gramsci*. Minneapolis: University of Minnesota Press.
Mitchell, T. (1994). *Flamenco Deep Song*. New Haven: Yale University Press.
Moix, T. (1993). *Suspiros de España: la copla y el cine de nuestro recuerdo*. Barcelona: Plaza & Janés.
Pineda Novo, D. (1991). *Las folklóricas y el cine*. Huelva: Festival de Cine Iberoamericano.
Rowe, W., and Schelling, V. (1991). *Memory and Modernity: Popular Culture in Latin America*. London: Verso.
Salaün, S. (1990). *El cuplé*. Madrid: Espasa-Calpe.

13

Alaska: Star of Stage and Screen and Optimistic Punk

MARK ALLINSON

THIS essay analyses the iconic status of punk figure and pop star Alaska (Olvido Gara) as used by Pedro Almodóvar in his first commercial feature, *Pepi, Luci, Bom y otras chicas del montón* [*Pepi, Luci, Bom, and Other Girls on the Heap*] (1980). Measuring the persona of Alaska against the model of star study (and quickly acknowledging its limitations here), the aim of the essay is to situate Alaska as a representative icon of the subcultural forms of punk and Madrid's *movida*, using a cultural studies theoretical framework. The work of the Birmingham Centre for Contemporary Cultural Studies of the 1970s will be applied to Spain's (sub)cultural scene of the late 1970s and 1980s. The comparison of Almodóvar's use of Alaska as cultural icon with British film-maker Derek Jarman's use of UK punk figures Jordan and Toyah in his 1978 film *Jubilee* both contextualizes the British-born cultural debates, and offers explanations for Spain's relationship to them.

The study of subcultures—the context for much of the academic work on punk and other youth or urban cultures—is founded on neo-Gramscian hegemony theory, which informs culturalist and ethnographic debate, and on Barthesian semiology, which informs structuralist debate. The seminal Birmingham Centre essay on subcultures in the 1975 volume *Resistance through Rituals* attempts to deconstruct some of the 'mythologies surrounding [youth cultures]' taking 'culture' as 'the practice which realizes or *objectivates* group-life in meaningful shape and form' (Hall and Jefferson 1976: 9–10). The struggle between the subculture and its dominant or 'parent' culture is an emblematic hegemonic one, related to class and to consumption (music, fashion). Key concepts in the signification of subcultures are homology and bricolage. Homology investigates items in terms of how they reflect 'structure, style, typical concerns, attitudes and feelings of the social group' (Willis 1978: 178). Bricolage is the 're-ordering and recontextualization of objects to communicate fresh meanings', an idea formulated first by Lévi-Strauss.[1] Most widely read of the studies in subculture is Dick Hebdige's 1979 book *Subculture: The Meaning of Style*, which takes punk as its case study. In its analysis of punk's 'spectacular' subcultural style, it points to two ways in which the style can be recuperated into the dominant culture: the conversion of subcultural signs into mass-produced, commodity objects, and the labelling of deviant behaviour as dangerously 'Other' by dominant groups (Hebdige 1988: 94). The example of Alaska (in comparison with Jarman's Toyah and Jordan) demonstrates that, in the Spanish context, the commodification of subculture by the dominant culture is such that the labelling of subculture as deviant is rendered unnecessary. This in turn can be related to the precise social, historical, and cultural context of the irruption of punk onto the Spanish cultural scene.

   With so little work done on the subject of stars in Spanish cinema, it may seem unusual to begin with a figure such as Alaska. The application of a Hollywood phenomena to Spain already implies the move from mainstream to marginality, but the choice of Alaska goes beyond this: while Spanish cinema has often taken its actors from the theatre, its real stars are more likely to emerge from television or music, a point frequently made about British cinema (Petley 1985: 113). Movie stars—in the Hollywood sense—are rare in post-Franco Spanish cinema. National film actors are respected as professionals, rather than adored as celebrities—a fact doubtless accounted for by the fact that the Spanish film industry takes its auteurist role seriously, often spurning mass popularity altogether. Alaska is a phenomenon of music or pop culture who has also shown herself to be adept at self-publicity and is frequently seen on television. But in the late 1970s both Alaska and her director Pedro Almodóvar were unknown outside the inner circles of Madrid's *modernos*. Many of the characteristics of star study, as applied to Hollywood by Richard Dyer (1979) and others, are inappropriate when applied to marginal cultural products like *Pepi, Luci, Bom* or *Jubilee*. The distinction

---

[1] Lévi-Strauss's *The Savage Mind* (1966) and *Totemism* (1969) are cited by John Clarke in his essay 'The Creation of Style' in Hall and Jefferson (1976: 177).

between the 'production' of stars to be launched into fame and the 'consumption' of established stars as selling commodities is lost in marginal film production where the actors are made up of personal friends of the director, people who were simply there at the time, whether significantly or not. And the effects of the profoundly conservative value system of the Hollywood industry on stars are diametrically opposed to the roles of Alaska, Jordan, and Toyah in the films under analysis. While the phenomenon of stars purposefully devalues acting abilities in general terms in favour of the construction of a whole star persona, here it is not Alaska's performance which holds greatest significance in *Pepi, Luci, Bom* but rather how she is used as a cultural product, an icon. Thus, where the construction of the star persona Alaska along Dyer's lines is problematic, a subcultural analysis of her status as a punk icon is more revealing.

If Alaska is a cultural product, her factory (in industrial and Warholian senses) was the *movida madrileña*. Discounting the ambiguous and polemical nature of the term, the *movida* can be taken as the formerly underground cultural activity in Madrid which gained prominence in the late 1970s and evolved until its almost unanimously agreed death around 1984–5. Alaska is intimately related to the *movida* and illustrates as well as any the link between it and British punk. Spain's best-known writer on pop music, Jesús Ordovás, describes her thus: 'Una de las chicas que más despunta tiene sólo trece años y acaba de llegar de Méjico. Le gusta el punk, David Bowie, el Glam, Los Ramones' [One of the girls who most stands out is only 13 years old and has just arrived from Mexico. She likes punk, David Bowie, Glam rock, the Ramones] (Ordovás 1986: 195). And Diego Silva (1984: 24) adds that Alaska was the first to sport a safety pin as punk arrived in Spain. She formed part of Madrid's first punk band Kaka de Luxe, and by 1978 she was calling herself Alaska Vómito Popelín. Almodóvar is among those who remark that Alaska could neither play nor sing, recalling, 'En aquel momento no había grabado ningún disco, ni siquiera era cantante. Ella era la guitarrista de Kaka de Luxe. Cantó por primera vez en la película. "Yo no canto," me dijo. Pero la convencí de que el personaje tenía que cantar y cantó' [At that time she hadn't recorded anything, she wasn't even a singer. She was the guitarist in Kaka de Luxe. She sang for the first time in the film. 'I don't do singing,' she told me. But I convinced her that the character had to sing, and sing she did] (Vidal 1988: 29). A lack of musical abilities was in itself a prerequisite for punk band formation, as recalled by Steve Jones about the Sex Pistols in the 1996 BBC documentary on punk *Dancing in the Streets*: 'That's why we sounded like we did. Johnny couldn't sing and I couldn't play the guitar.' The do-it-yourself culture of punk is mirrored in the music of the *movida*. Paco Martín, chronicler of the musical life of the period, explains how groups produced their own discs with no record company support (1982: 11). The amateurishness of this production not only affected the quality of the sound, but also acted as a leveller in both punk and *movida* culture. Anyone could make music and the *movida*, like punk, attracted all social classes.[2] Similarly, both punk and the *movida* took music as their departure point, but their effects were felt in the plastic arts and in fashion. Steve Redhead (1993: 3) asserts that 'Punk style was much more likely to have originated in the arts schools rather than the "street".' Dave Laing (1985: p. viii) sums up the way punk is made up of far more than music: 'The events of punk were both the live performances of the era and certain other key incidents,' and he cites the examples of the notorious television interview with the Sex Pistols, concert cancellation, and acts of censorship. The *movida* can also be seen as a series of events, including the famous performances of Alaska, Fabio McNamara, Almodóvar, and others, but also an event like the filming of Almodóvar's first commercial feature.

Aside from the do-it-yourself culture of punk, Laing lists two other fundamental definitions, in terms of opposition to mainstream music culture. The first is the challenge to the orthodoxy about what constitutes artistic excellence, and the second is the 'aggressive injection of new subject-matter into the lyrics of popular songs, some of which broke existing taboos' (Laing 1985: 14). Both aspects can be seen clearly in the unspoken and unwritten manifesto of the *movida*. Alaska's first band Kaka de Luxe, though brief in its existence, was a direct challenge to the music of the time and led to the creation of some of the most significant bands of the 1980s in Spain. And the punk-inspired proliferation in nasty or bad-taste lyrics coincided with Spain's new-found freedoms and excesses. The lyrics of Alaska's 'Murciana marrana' in *Pepi, Luci, Bom* are certainly not the stuff of the average Spanish pop hit of the period, but neither are they as aggressive and disturbing as some of the punk lyrics. Thus they illustrate both the

---

[2] This, of course, distinguishes punk from many earlier youth subcultures which were heavily class-based.

debt to punk and the departure from it. Even more than this, they illustrate how Almodóvar et al. took up the punk posture of parody and exploited it for humour rather than for subversive satire:

Te quiero porque eres sucia
Guarra puta y lisonjera
La más obscena de Murcia
Y a mi disposición entera

Sólo pienso en ti, Murciana
Porque eres una marrana

Te meto el dedo en la raja
Te arreo un par de sopapos
Te obligo a hacerme una paja
Soy más violenta que el GRAPO

Te voy como anillo al dedo
Conmigo tienes orgasmos
Si en la boca te echo un pedo
Me aplaudes con entusiasmo

Me perteneces, Murciana
Porque a mí me da la gana

[I love you because you're dirty
a disgusting, flattering whore
The most obscene of all Murcia
and at my beck and call

I can only think of you, Murciana
Cos you're a dirty pig

I stick my finger up your slit
I slap you about a bit
I force you to wank me
I'm more violent than the GRAPO[3]

I'm a perfect match for you
With me you have orgasms
If I fart in your mouth
You applaud me enthusiastically

You belong to me, Murciana
Because I like it like that][4]

[3] GRAPO: Grupos de Resistencia Antifacista Primero de Octubre, anti-fascist terrorist group.

[4] 'Murciana marrana' was composed by Almodóvar and Los Pegamoides and performed by Bomitony (alias Alaska and Los Pegamoides).

While punk and the *movida* have in common the connotations of disruption of convention and normality, their contexts and trajectories are different. British punk can be seen as a reaction to conservative forces in the music industry and in society at large. Economic, aesthetic, and ideological forces interact to produce a culture which rejects the mainstream and actively works to undermine it. The classic example is, of course, the Sex Pistols' reaction to the Queen's Silver Jubilee of 1977. If not actually propagandistic, punk is subversive of mainstream politics and culture. Thus, in Hebdige's terms, the need to 'bring back into line' the behaviour of these groups by labelling it as deviant (1988: 97).[5] The position of Madrid's underground version of punk culture is different in several important aspects. First, it is derivative, finding its inspiration in British punk and attempting to copy it. As Ordovás puts it, 'El punk es el revulsivo que abre nuevas puertas a docenas de grupos y personajes que tienen cosas que decir' [Punk is the detonator which opens new doors to dozens of groups and artists with something to say] (1986: 195). Secondly, the *movida* is selective in its appropriation of punk's cultural baggage. The aesthetic of punk and the element of bad taste and corrosive humour are taken up, but largely without the political or moral significance. In Silva's words, 'No olvidemos que el punk, en este país, [está] desprovisto de toda la carga política que ha tenido en otras partes de Europa' [Let's not forget that in this country punk is without the political weight that it has had in other parts of Europe] (1984: 22). Gonzalo García Pino and Borja Casani take this point further, in the round table organized by José Luis Gallero:

García Pino: Está claro que en Inglaterra, el movimiento punk tenía una raigambre de protesta social, de agresividad...
Borja Casani: España es una sociedad más amable, y también más frívola. La movida coincide con un momento muy positivo económicamente. No se produce en una situación de crisis... (Gallero 1991: 16)

[García Pino: It's clear that in England, the punk movement had a tradition of social protest, of aggression...
Borja Casani: Spain is a more indulgent and more frivolous society. The *movida* coincides with a very positive moment economically. It doesn't come into being in a crisis situation...]

---

[5] As a means to contain and neutralize this deviant behaviour, Hebdige offers Barthes's strategies for dealing with the Other in his 1957 *Mythologies*.

The context of a free and fast-developing post-Franco Spain largely accounts for the lack of bitterness in its adoption of certain punk modes and attitudes. As we shall see, the 'pessimistic punk' of Jarman's apocalyptic premonitions in *Jubilee* contrast with the 'optimistic punk' of Almodóvar's political *pasotismo* in *Pepi, Luci, Bom*.[6] And the positions in the films of Jarman's punk actors and of Alaska also reflect the trajectories of punk in the UK and the *movida* in Spain. Where Jordan, an emblematic figure in the London punk scene of the 1970s, represents the past and present of punk in *Jubilee*, Alaska represents in Almodóvar's film almost exclusively the future. Of the actors in Jarman's film, it is Toyah who represents the future, both in film and in music. The trajectory of these stars runs parallel to those of the scene which gave birth to them. While British punk maintained its marginality and died, the *movida* came out of the underground and onto the street. Alaska, Almodóvar, and the *movida* itself all moved from marginality to mainstream, their underground culture forming the basis of Spain's most successful cultural enterprise of the 1980s. Borja Casani, editor of the emblematic *movida* magazine *La Luna*, separates the *movida* into the three phases of coming out, becoming mainstream, and becoming commercial and international (Gallero 1991: 248). The mainstream, here, not only signifies culturally and commercially, but also politically. Moncho Alpuente recalls how the Socialist City Council in Madrid became the friend and promoter of the *movida*. He cites the anecdote of the local authority-sponsored concert by La Polla Record [Record Prick] or the City Council financing of the magazine *Eyaculación precoz—Revista de Alcobendas* [*Premature Ejaculation—Alcobendas Magazine*] (Ripoll 1988: 32, 61). Whereas in the UK the neutralization of punk's subversive power takes both of Hebdige's forms (commodity, through market appropriation; and ideological, through labelling as 'Other'), in Spain the dominant social and political group embraces the subculture, thus negating any dangerous qualities of 'Otherness'.

Before looking in more detail at the iconic use of punk figures Alaska, Jordan, and Toyah, I should like to point to certain parallels which exist between Almodóvar's and Jarman's films. Two aspects stand out: the debt both owe to gay culture, and the production contexts of the films which leave their mark on stylistic elements. The

---

[6] 'Pasotismo' roughly translates as a 'couldn't care less' attitude, a posture adopted by rebellious teenagers especially in the late 1970s and 1980s.

association with circles in which gays are prominent proved to be a constant in Jarman while Almodóvar largely moved away from gay characters. But in the two films under analysis here, both gays and transvestites are fully integrated into the frenetic worlds of chaos-ridden London or labyrinth-of-passion Madrid. This, in turn, relates to the *movida* and to punk in more general terms. Borja Casani has said that gay culture was the first and foremost to take advantage of the *movida* (Gallero 1991: 248). Redhead writes of punk's debt to gay culture (1993: 5). And gay styles certainly influenced at least the fashion side of the British punk scene, partly through the S & M effect on Malcolm MacClaren and Viviene Westwood's Chelsea shop 'Sex'. The Sex Pistols themselves were very much a part of the sexual ambiguity which characterized early punk, gay culture playing an important part, until fame and commerce necessitated otherwise. As Jon Savage puts it, 'The sexual fluidity, or denial, would quickly go sour. [. . .] Once defined, the Sex Pistols became a Rock band and rock bands are not usually tolerant of homosexuality' (1991: 190).

Jarman's vision of punk and its relationship to gay culture is of course very personal. In isolation from his other films, the gay-coding of *Jubilee*, with lesbian relationships and a homosexual incestuous relationship between Angel and Sphinx, seems part and parcel of the taboo-breaking element of punk. In Almodóvar's Madrid too, the apparently heterosexual men who prostitute themselves for older gay clients are only a part of the general sexual licence of the film (a sign that in post-Franco Spain, unlike in the UK, sexual taboos were broken already). The inclusion of transvestites parallels the general differences in tone between the two films. The character of Roxy, played by Almodóvar's friend and co-performer Fabio, is played entirely for laughs. In *Jubilee*, the transvestite Lounge Lizard who performs 'Paranoia Paradise' is grotesquely murdered by Bod, watched by Mad and Amyl. Both in the *movida* and in the punk era, the emergence of gay and transvestite cultures is linked to a more general opening up of previous subterranean groups into the mainstream. This same movement applies to both film-makers (though Almodóvar can be said to have moved much further into the mainstream than Jarman did).

Apart from the evident underground origins, and the fact that they began working in a doubly marginalized context (not Hollywood, not mainstream or respectably auteurist European cinema), they are also both self-taught film-makers, with much experience in Super 8 film. Both films originated as Super 8 projects. *Jubilee* is Jarman's second commercial feature but, like *Pepi, Luci, Bom*, it has much of the self-consciousness that comes from the sheer difficulty in making a film. This self-reflexivity is a direct result of the do-it-yourself culture common to both punk and the *movida*. The result, in both films, is a constant sense of incipient parody. Hebdige refers to punk's wilful fulfilment of society's worst fears as 'parodying alienation' (1988: 79), and *Jubilee* is a documentary of such parody. In *Pepi, Luci, Bom* self-consciousness is expressed in the conceit of having character Pepi herself writing the story of Luci and Bom, and telling them that they cannot simply be themselves, but actually have to act. One can almost hear Pedro himself here, telling his early 'chicas Almodóvar' that merely being in front of the camera is not enough. And of course, Almodóvar appears in the role of compère to the *erecciones generales* [General Erections] contest, directing the show (just as he appears directing in *Laberinto de pasiones* [*Labyrinth of Passion*] (1982), *¡Qué he hecho yo para merecer esto!* [*What Have I Done to Deserve This?*] (1984), and *Matador* (1986), each time parodying himself). Derek Jarman more modestly appears only as a bystander in *Jubilee*. But he does make reference to the process of creativity, albeit in more general artistic terms through the painter Viv who tells Angel and Sphinx that 'artists deal the world's energy' in one of many self-reflexive moments which turn characters into Jarman's own authorial voice.

Self-consciousness can also be seen in the style of each film, though, once again, the effect is somewhat different. In Jarman, the combination of inexperienced actors and director leads to a generalized overacting performance which proves one of the most engaging aspects of the film. Jordan sounds like a home counties sixth former in a school play declaiming Shakespeare, Toyah like a violent brat dominating the play of other children. In Almodóvar, the self-consciousness is expressed in Alaska's performance by an unwillingness to act at all. Again this is made into a virtue. Pepi (Almodóvar's alter ego as director of the film-within-the film) criticizes Bom (Alaska) for appearing not violent, but simply 'antipática' [unpleasant]. Indeed, much of Bom's disdain in the film is expressed by a distinct lack of reaction.

The absence of a standard narrative-led structure to these films gives them an episodic feeling which contributes to their status as underground. The episodic structure of *Pepi, Luci, Bom* centres on the idea of a pop product, hence the breaking up of the action to include the hilarious advert spoofs. In Jarman, the interludes are more rhapsodic, with Jordan's ballet performance and Viv's meditation on art and the artist. One final anecdotal parallel is worth mentioning. *Pepi, Luci, Bom* opens with the pop song 'Do the Swim' by Little Nell, singing co-star of Jim Sharman's cult 1975 film *The Rocky Horror Picture Show*. And Little Nell also shows up in *Jubilee*, in the role of Crabs, over-the-top artiste. Homage is paid to *The Rocky Horror Picture Show* by both directors, not only in the appearance of this singer, but in the camp extravagance and stagy self-consciousness of their films.

Pepi, Luci, Bom y otras chicas del montón was shown the day after Julian Temple's punk film *The Great Rock N Roll Swindle* at the 1980 San Sebastián Film Festival. Though *Pepi, Luci, Bom* does not constitute a documentary of Spanish punk, it does have resonance in its 'radical concepto amoral' [radically amoral conception] (Hardinguey 1980: 31) and most of all in its co-protagonist Alaska. Almodóvar himself reflects on his iconic use of Alaska in *Pepi, Luci, Bom* as follows: '*Pepi*... corresponde a la época del punk. Aunque estéticamente no es punk sino pop, popísima. Cuando empecé a escribirla partía de la ideología del punk, la agresividad, la corrosividad social que tenía el punk y que estaba representado por el personaje de Alaska' [*Pepi*... belongs to the punk era. Though aesthetically it isn't punk but rather pop, very pop. When I began to write it, it started out from a punk ideology, the aggressive, corrosive attitude of punk which was represented by the character of Alaska] (Vidal 1988: 36). Comparing the role of Alaska as Bom in *Pepi, Luci, Bom* with Jarman's punk actresses in *Jubilee*, Jordan and Toyah as a composite (present and future) of the punk star correspond to Alaska's trajectory from optimistic punk to star of stage and screen. All three play punk music stars in their respective roles, displaying the expected punk traits of violence (physical and verbal), rebelliousness, and nonconformity. Both Bom (Alaska) and Mad (Toyah) enjoy boxing (Fig. 8) and they are involved in sadistic lesbian relationships. But here already there are differences. In Jarman's film, Mad boxes for real, the fight leading to the spilling of blood. In Almodóvar, Bom fights only with a punchball—only a parody for this *pasota* punk. And where Mad carves the word 'LOVE' with a knife into the back of her lover Bod, the most Bom can manage is the famous 'golden shower' scene or obliging Luci to eat the contents of her nose. At other times, Bom's sadism seems no more than a fashion accessory, as when she has Luci on a dog's lead. Clearly, there is a difference between the disturbing sadomasochism of the British film and its outrageous but hardly disquieting form in the Spanish film.

In an interesting parallel, both Bom and our two UK punks are seen enacting vengeance for acts of violence committed by the police on friends. Mad and Amyl take revenge on the police for the murders of brothers Angel and Sphinx. This episode is filmed in a realistic mode, without incidental music, and the repaid violence is emotional (note the hysterical tears of Mad). In contrast, the scene in which Bom and her group carry out the planned attack on the policeman who had robbed Pepi of her marketable virginity is a parody of violence. The frivolous morality of this justification (commercial violation rather than sexual and psychological) is matched by the extravagant theatricality of the attack. The marked difference in tone between these sequences is partly accounted for by the music which accompanies Bom's group attack. The *zarzuela* [Spanish popular operetta] *La Revoltosa*—the title means *Female Rebel*, albeit in a reassuring *Taming of the Shrew* sense—provides the theatrical tone in a carefully staged scene, the performance using playback rather than real singing actors. This also allows the director the indulgence of including traditional popular elements in the pastiche of his art, offsetting a national musical product against the tribal aggression of the punks. There is something of the absurd in the spectacle of the punk in full *zarzuela* costume. The resulting parodic stand on national culture is playful rather than politically subversive. This is not the case for the similar parodying of national music in *Jubilee*. The use of the hymn 'Jerusalem' for the orgy scene in *Jubilee*, which takes place in Westminster Cathedral, proved deeply offensive to conservative nationalists and Catholics alike, leading to death threats for Jarman himself on *Jubilee*'s first screening on British television.

The parodic (and satirical) stances on national institutions by Jarman and Almodóvar are quite different in intention. Two sequences from *Jubilee* stand out, both commentaries on the national obsession with the Queen's Silver Jubilee in 1977. The scene in the Palace of Heavenly Delights, the name given to Westminster Cathedral by its new owner, media tycoon Borgia Ginz, plunges the event into hedonistic sexual pleasure, with orgy scenes and gay sex between policemen in uniform (multiple challenges to national institutions, the police, and to heterosexual orthodoxy). The other key scene is

Amyl's rendition of 'Rule Britannia', an obscene parody of a national anthem. Amyl manipulates Britannia's staff between her legs (complete with suspenders), wearing a Union Jack plastic dress. The song is given a contemporary electronic backing track and interspersed with Hitler's speeches. The equivalent scene in *Pepi, Luci, Bom* takes the national obsession with the new-found institution of democracy and deflates it with parody and the breaking of sexual taboos. The 'erecciones generales' scene (in which the player with the biggest member gets to do whatever he wants with whoever he pleases for the rest of the night) formed the core of Almodóvar's original story and was the film's first working title. After the contest (compèred by the famously headless Almodóvar himself in a technical lapse seen here for the first and last time in his films), the resulting prize-giving obliges Luci to perform fellatio on the winner. Luci hesitates. Bom's reply is sublime, combining the tone of sadomasochistic tormentor with the content of a nagging mother: 'Vamos, come antes de que se te enfríe' [Come on. Eat up before it gets cold].

At every opportunity, Almodóvar exploits Alaska's ambivalence, caught between a second-hand punk culture which is fading fast, and the new kitsch pop which she will soon come to embody in her real life public persona. Her only stage performance in the film, as compared to that of Mad (Toyah) in *Jubilee*, gives an indication of what lies in the future for Alaska. Where Mad's performance in her audition is aggressive and offensive in true punk style (she ends the audition by spitting onto the camera lens), Bom's number is only pseudo-aggressive; the bad taste of the lyrics an entertainment; and the music decidedly pop. This scene anticipates Alaska's live performances (recorded for TV), the colourful Fabio presenting the show. And at the end of the film, Bom's look (a combination of punk remnants and kitsch pop) is exactly the look which she sports on the cover of Alaska y los Pegamoides' first album. The changing times are signalled in the film itself. Bom bemoans the stagnation of the music scene and Pepi suggests she become a singer of *boleros*. Thus the film ends with the kind of sentimental song which will characterize Almodóvar's future films in which *boleros* will figure much more frequently than musical parodies with scatological lyrics. Although this film is very much a product of its time—an idea consonant with Almodóvar's description of the film as 'un documento que se aguanta muy bien' [a documentary which has stood the test of time] (Vidal 1988: 15)—Almodóvar is already predicting the changing popular culture scene of Madrid, and his film signals the ephemeral nature of the *movida*'s crazed (and parodic) punk stance.

Almodóvar made only one more film which could be considered a recording of a particular contemporary Madrid music culture scene. The film *Laberinto de pasiones* has acquired much more status as a cult film depicting an era about which a whole generation of Spaniards are now nostalgic (whatever their attitude at the time, it seems). And he has not made another film with Alaska. Indeed, she has not herself appeared in any further films, preferring to concentrate on developing a pop personality which is now firmly established in Spain's hall of fame. Once again, the comparison with our two UK punk actors is revealing. Jordan appeared with much the same iconic status in *Jubilee* as Alaska in *Pepi, Luci, Bom*, lending a touch of authenticity to the contemporary scene. But Jordan, a prominent figure in the punk scene in the 1970s, frequently seen in the Chelsea shop 'Sex' and in the many photographs which record the era, did not make a mark in the celebrity world. On the other hand, Toyah, who like Alaska made her debut in the films under discussion, went on to stardom (in that modest British sense which affords television a greater role even than the movies for home-grown stars). In the year after *Jubilee*, Toyah had a role in the cult music film *Quadrophenia* (Franc Roddam, 1979), and she has since had three major film roles, and many television appearances, presenting both *The Good Sex Guide* and occasionally an episode of a quasi-religious programme, *Discovering Eve*. In the late 1970s and early 1980s she had appreciable success with her music career and she has acquired a cult following in recent years.

Alaska has formed the most high-profile component in the groups with Los Pegamoides, Dinarama, and lately with Fangoria, her music ranging from the tongue-in-cheek pop of early hits like 'Horror en el hipermercado' [Horror in the Hypermarket], through the dance-influenced 'Bailando' [Dancing] and 'Mi novio es un zombi' [My Boyfriend is a Zombie] to the mix of techno and pop which characterizes Fangoria. Even here there remains the tendency to humorous lyrics which are reminiscent of the old days with songs like 'Hagamos algo superficial y vulgar' [Let's Do Something Superficial and Vulgar]. But she has been a constant presence on television, known to all children as the presenter of the series *La bola de cristal* [*The Crystal Ball*]. More recently she has identified herself with the cause of Spanish drag queens, appearing on television chat shows as 'la reina de los drag' [The Queen of the Drag Queens]. The compromise between punk rebel and celebrity was identified by Alaska herself: 'Yo tenía dos referencias antagónicas. Por un lado, el punk—que me incita, a los 14 años, a hacer lo que creo que hacen las estrellas: subirse a un escenario—y por otro lado, Hollywood' [I had two opposing frames of reference. On the one hand, punk—which when I was 14 drove me to do what I supposed stars did: get up on a stage—and on the other hand, Hollywood] (Gallero 1991: 374). Interestingly, Alaska here conflates punk stage figure and Hollywood star persona, in her adolescent ambition. She is right to point to the mutual incompatibility of the Hollywood star and the punk attitude. For the great majority, such goals would be unreconcilable ambitions. But here too lies a possible resolution to the question of the study of star personas outside the great unifying edifice of Hollywood: stars from marginalized cultures can be approached in terms of their *difference* from the Hollywood star persona (hence star study has only a limited value for European or otherwise marginal figures); and where star study *per se* cannot adequately account for such marginal cultural products, then comparative subcultural analysis can provide a useful theoretical approach.

WORKS CITED

BBC (1996). *Dancing in the Streets* (TV documentary).
Dyer, R. (1979). *Stars*. London: British Film Institute.
Gallero, J. L. (ed.) (1991). *Sólo se vive una vez*. Madrid: Ardora.
Hall, S., and Jefferson, T. (eds.) (1976) [1975]. *Resistance through Rituals*. London: Hutchinson.
Hardinguey, Á. S. (1980). Review of the San Sebastián Film Festival, *El País* (26 Oct.): 31.
Hebdige, D. (1988) [1979]. *Subculture: The Meaning of Style*. London: Routledge.
Laing, D. (1985). *One Chord Wonders: Power and Meaning in Punk Rock*. Milton Keynes: Open University Press.
Martín, P. (1982). *La movida: historia del pop madrileño*. Madrid: Paco Martín.
Ordovás, J. (1986). *Historia de la música pop española*. Madrid: Alianza.
Petley, J. (1985). 'Reaching for the Stars', in M. Auty and N. Roddick (eds.), *British Cinema Now*. London: British Film Institute, 111–122.
Redhead, S. (1993). *Rave Off: Politics and Deviance in Contemporary Youth Culture*. Aldershot: Avebury.

Ripoll, A. J. (ed.) (1988). *La gloriosa movida nacional*. Avilés: Casa Municipal de Cultura.

Savage, J. (1991). *England's Dreaming: Sex Pistols and Punk Rock*. London: Faber & Faber.

Silva, D. (1984). *El pop español*. Barcelona: Teorema.

Vidal, N. (1988). *El cine de Pedro Almodóvar*. Barcelona: Destino.

Willis, P. (1978). *Profane Culture*. London: Routledge.

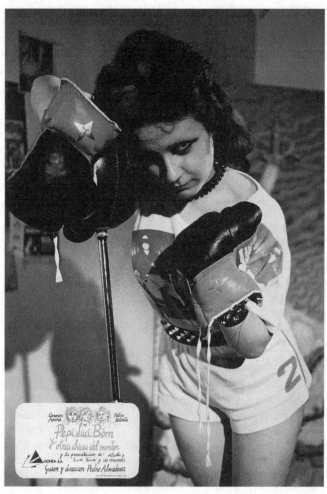

Fig. 8. *Pepi, Luci, Bom*: punk Bom (Alaska) loves boxing

14

Bagpipes and Digital Music:
The Remixing of Galician Identity

XELÍS DE TORO

NESTES intres que vivimos, nos que Galicia está a loitar pra tirar co xugo dun colonialismo imposto, compre recuperar, dun xeito total, a gaita, o noso instrumento musical nacional.

[At this moment in time, as Galicia struggles to set itself free from the yoke of an imposed colonialism, it is necessary for us fully to reclaim the bagpipe, our national musical instrument.]

(Manuel María in Foxo 1982: 6)

With the granting of autonomy to Galicia in 1981, questions of identity became less focused on nationalist politics and were incorporated into more open public debate. Activities seen as representing a kind of Galicianness started to enjoy official support in order to give an impetus to the new institutions of the Xunta de Galicia. Symbols and marks of identity formerly used only in Galician nationalist discourse started to be appropriated, and in some cases reformulated and refashioned, by the new institutions which throughout have been under the control of the conservative Partido Popular. The resulting process, centred on the written language, national symbols, and even the names of the new institutions, has been complex and dogged by controversy (Cores Trasmonte 1986). Within this context, the playing of bagpipes has experienced a steady growth, becoming prominent in Galician music of the 1990s.

Ever since the beginnings of the discourse on a distinct Galician identity in the mid-nineteenth century with the Rexurdimiento Galego [Galician Revival] (frequently called the Rexurdimiento Literario [Literary Revival], privileging the literary as the bestower of national identity)[1] and the development of a regionalist political movement, the bagpipe has been seen as the 'true expression' of the 'Galician soul' (Vicetto 1865: 99; Milladoiro 1998: 339). For most of this period, the main mark of Galician identity has been the Galician language. But in the mid-1990s, after steady growth in popularity through the 1970s and 1980s, the bagpipe acquired a position of dominance in Galician music, becoming a battleground for competing definitions of tradition and identity. Various key events need to be mentioned at the outset, before entering into detailed discussion.

First, although Galician folk music—epitomized by the bagpipe —started to be marketed in the 1970s, and although by the 1980s the band Milladoiro had already gained international recognition, it was in the mid-1990s that Galician folk came to be perceived as commercially successful in the Spanish and international arena. The bagpiper Carlos Núñez obtained a gold record in 1996 with 'A irmandade das estrelas' [The Brotherhood of the Stars], made with The Chieftains and Ry Cooder; the band Luar na Lubre toured with Mike Oldfield with their joint show Tubular Bells Three; and again in 1996 The Chieftains obtained a Grammy with the record 'Santiago', made together with Carlos Núñez and based on Galician music throughout.

Second, in the field of non-commercial folk music, a new type of bagpipe band emerged, incorporating new styles of dress and bagpipe design, new musical arrangements, and a military marching style contrasting with the festival ambience of 'traditional' formations. This produced a split in the Asociación de Gaiteiros [Bagpipers Association] between 'purists' and 'innovators', provoking a lively public debate, taken up by the Galician media, known as the 'guerra das gaitas' [bagpipe war] in which issues of tradition and authenticity were at stake (Alfonso de la Torre Núñez 1995). The new bands were criticized for copying Scottish bagpipe formations; the fact that they were supported by public funding, thus occupying an institutionalized musical space, made them doubly controversial.

Third, the President of the Xunta de Galicia for the conservative Partido Popular, Manuel Fraga Iribarne, helped to bring the bagpipe

---

[1] The key texts of the Rexurdimiento Literario are Rosalía de Castro, *Cantares galegos* (1863); Eduardo Pondal, *Rumores d'os pinos* (1879); and Curros Enríquez, *Aires da miña terra* (1880). In fact, a number of texts were written in Galician from the start of the 19th century, but these have tended not to be seen as part of the Galician Revival by critics who have dismissed them as having a political rather than aesthetic intent.

to the forefront of cultural debate by celebrating his 1993 and 1997 election victories with gatherings of around 2,000 bagpipers, in an event that came to be known as the 'gaiteirada'.

In the first part of this essay, I will explore the role played by the bagpipes in the Galician imaginary, and how they came to be part of our sense of identity. I shall trace their move from their original context of rural community celebrations to a new mass-market scenario: that is, a shift from one sort of popular music to a very different kind. Here I shall draw on work in the field of cultural history which problematizes notions of tradition and identity. In the second part, I will show how some musicians have used the bagpipes to challenge notions of stable, fixed identity and home. The importance of the diasporic experience for Galicia, with its history of mass emigration, has created a strong association between the bagpipes and the concepts of place, land, and home. Here my analysis will be based on postmodern theories of performance.

The bagpipe's role as an expression of Galician identity is inextricably linked to its image as a traditional instrument. Tradition is usually presented unproblematically as that which has been preserved through the ages until the present. This notion has been problematized by Hobsbawm and Ranger in their classic collective volume *The Invention of Tradition* (1983), which among other things famously demonstrates that the supposedly traditional Scottish kilt is a product of modernity, 'invented' in the nineteenth century. Marfany (1996: 322–47) has made a similar point about the invention of the *sardana* as the national dance of Catalonia. The case of the Galician bagpipe is not quite the same, since it really was widely played in Galicia in earlier centuries. The bagpipe was not, then, an 'invented tradition' but it underwent a similar process of ritualization and symbolization. Stuart Hall has outlined the problematic nature of the term 'tradition':

Tradition is a vital element in culture; but it has little to do with the mere persistence of old forms. It has much more to do with the way elements have been linked together or articulated. These arrangements in a national-popular culture have no fixed or inscribed position, and certainly no meaning which is carried along, so to speak, in the stream of historical tradition, unchanged. (Storey 1998: 450)

It is this process of linking, articulating, and conferring meaning on the practice of bagpipe playing that allows the bagpipe to be seen as traditional. The development of the instrument has been subject to a double movement: on the one hand, players have innovated to keep abreast of new musical trends and popular tastes; on the other, defenders of tradition have striven to keep the practice unchanged as proof of the persistence of a specifically Galician culture and 'Galician soul'. In this essay I am mainly concerned with the shifts undergone by bagpipe music since the mid-nineteenth century and particularly in the last decade of the twentieth. These shifts will be traced by identifying changes in the markers of 'place' and 'occasion' which Raymond Williams (1981: 131) has seen as crucial to the study of art as a social form. It is important to note that such shifts in performance styles and public perception do not mean that previous practices disappear: all the different practices outlined below coexist in the present.

The earliest recorded references to the bagpipe suggest that it was played by a solo *gaiteiro* on feast days and at fairs, country markets, and similar events.[2] As one would expect of pre-modern forms of social organization and entertainment, music is incorporated into communal activities and celebrations. The *gaiteiro* was a well-known member of a local community, like the *matarife* [slaughter-man], the *curandeiro* [healer], and the *cacique* [local political boss]. Williams's markers of 'place' and 'occasion' are paramount here: bagpipes were played in communal spaces like the market square or outside the church to mark local occasions such as events in the family life cycle or agricultural calendar. The bagpiper mingled with the public, with no distinction between the space of the performer and that of the spectators: the latter are thus constructed as participants rather than as audience.

It was in the second half of the nineteenth century, with the Rexurdimiento Literario, that the bagpipe started to attract attention as a specifically Galician instrument. The struggle for the legitimization of the Galician language, the definition of Galicia as a Celtic country, and the defence of rural culture seen as the basis of the Galician character were the main features of this discourse aimed at 'inventing' a Galician identity. Urbanization and industrialization—the former significant in Galicia but the latter very limited although a matter of discussion generally at the time, showing how, with the

---

[2] The earliest record is a legal document of 1374 which refers to a *gaiteiro* as a witness. Some 16th-century documents refer to a contract between a bagpiper and a guild to play on a feast day (Torres Regueiro in *No país das gaitas* 1995: 4–6).

advent of a national press, local concerns are inflected as much by national (and international) debate as by local circumstance—were perceived as a threat to traditional ways and customs. The bagpipe was incorporated into this discourse as an authentic element of a rural culture threatened by modernity, being seen as an emblem of resistance to change. Indeed, the book generally seen as marking the start of the Rexurdimiento Literario was entitled *A gaita galega* (1853). Key literary figures of the Rexurdimiento followed suit by publishing poems about bagpipers which established the founding trope of the bagpipe as the metonymic signifier of the 'Galician soul' and home. For example, Rosalía de Castro included the poem 'A gaita galega' in her 1863 *Cantares galegos*, the publication date of which (17 May) is now celebrated as the Day of Galician Literature. The poem answers an earlier poem by Ruiz de Aguilera which asks if the Galician bagpipe sings or cries; Rosalía's poem affirms that it cries. Valentín Lamas Carvajal, editor of one of the first newspapers written in Galician, published in it—and possibly authored— satirical texts criticizing bagpipers who departed from tradition. His book *Saudades galegas* includes the poem 'O anxiño', in which a bagpiper plays at a child's funeral. In 1877 Curros Enríquez was awarded first prize at the Certame Literario de Ourense for his poems 'Unha boda en Einibó' and 'O gueiteiro', both featuring bagpipes and subsequently published in his *Aires da miña terra* (1880).

The bagpipe, as an instrument made of wood and cloth, and the bagpiper as a member of the rural community participating in communal activities, were perfectly suited to represent the rural, nature, and landscape: the places where Galician identity was supposedly to be found. The association between the bagpipe and nature and landscape runs deep in the Galician imagination, evoking powerful resonances still, as we can see in the words of the internationally successful musician Carlos Núñez in a 1997 interview in *El País* significantly entitled 'Carlos Núñez, un gaiteiro en Manhattan': 'El árbol sigue vivo en la gaita' [The tree lives on in the bagpipe] (Rivas 1997: 58). But, if the bagpipe was to play a part in the construction of Galician identity, it had to be promoted, legitimized, and preserved. In the late nineteenth century, several competitions were launched whose organizers—for example, at the competitions of 1887 in Ourense and of 1906 in Betanzos—found it necessary to produce guidelines for competitors explicitly prescribing adherence to traditional dress and bagpipe design. Regionalist writers—for example, Lamas Carvajal in 1888; the magazine *A Monteira* in 1889; and Camilo de Cela in 1897—criticized the innovations introduced by some bagpipers (Torres Regueiro in *No país das gaitas* 1995: 12). In practice, the value attached to the bagpipe by these competitions and by regionalist writers helped to create a new vision of the instrument, no longer seen as one played just at local and religious festivals, but as a valuable activity whose 'authenticity' had to be preserved and policed so that it could represent the 'Galician soul'.

Despite these attempts at fossilization, bagpipers continued to introduce innovations in performance mode and musical style. The nineteenth-century predominance of the bagpiper as solo musician, or accompanied by a single drum, had by the end of the century given way to a preference for two bagpipes and two drums: this quartet formation came to be regarded as the traditional mode of performance. At the start of the twentieth century, new formations appeared introducing other instruments such as the clarinet, accordion, and violin. These new formations also enlarged the repertoire to include new rhythms and lyrics (Luengo in Milladoiro 1998: 171–6). At the same time, the old way of playing the bagpipe known as 'dixitación pechada'—alternating the fingers so that one is lowered as the other is raised, allowing complementary notes to be heard—was dying out (Fernández in *No país das gaitas* 1995: 23), while individual bagpipers continued to innovate with regard to dress, bagpipe design, and repertoire. For example, Lamas Carvajal criticized the bagpiper of Ventosela for replacing the traditional *monteira* with a new kind of hat with gold trimmings, for using a bagpipe with keys like those of a saxophone, and for playing waltz and mazurka rhythms (Torres Regueiro in *No país das gaitas* 1995: 12).

The bagpipe remained central to Galician nationalism in the 1920s. The major 1920s Galician intellectual, Vicente Risco, writing in the first issue of the nationalist cultural magazine *Nós*, talked of 'O fundo mesmo de todol-os pensamentos e de todol-os sentimentos da y-alma galega. E como a nota grave, sostida, monótona do ronco, sobre da que se deseñan logo os sinxelos arabescos da gaita' [The ground of all the thoughts and feelings of the Galician soul. Like the deep, sustained drone of the *ronco* [part of the Galician bagpipe] which underlies the bagpipe's simple arabesques] (Risco 1920: 4).

In accordance with the stress in nationalist discourse of this period on the distinctness of Castilian and Galician, the Galician bagpipe was posited as the polar opposite of the Castilian guitar. The caption to a cartoon by the major politician and artist of the so-called 'nationalist period' (1920–36), Castelao, reads: 'para a tocar a gaita fan falla máis folgos que para tocala guitarra' [to play the bagpipe you need greater lung power than to play the guitar].[3] When, in 1924, Avelino Cachafeiro was named the best Galician bagpiper by Galician intellectuals, Castelao called him a 'prototipo da rexeneración gaitística' [prototype of the regeneration of the bagpipe] (Calle in Milladoiro 1998: 101–7). In his article 'O nazonalismo musical galego', the Galician intellectual Jaime Quintanilla (1920: 5–7) equated the music of the *zanfoña* and bagpipe with that of the Galician soul, and encouraged new musicians to create a Galician classical—i.e. high-cultural—music based on traditional and religious musical forms, in a similar vein to the Spanish musical nationalism of Santiago Tafall and Eladio Oviedo (Costa Vázquez-Mariño in Milladoiro 1998: 251–92). During this 'nationalist period', bagpipe bands started to perform at nationalist meetings, signalling a decisive shift in the marker of 'occasion': that is, the entry of the bagpipe into the political arena.

This trend was reversed during the Francoist period (1939–75) as bagpipe bands were promoted as 'folklore', seen as an unthreatening manifestation of Galician regional (as opposed to nationalist) culture. Indeed, it was the Sección Femenina (women's section of the Spanish fascist party, Falange Española) that pioneered such folkloric conservation activity. While the public use of Galician language and literature was banned, the bagpipe was co-opted into official Francoist culture as a way of incorporating into the nation-state an ambiguous, undefined Galician identity which posed no threat to Spanish hegemony. During this period, the red and yellow colours of the Spanish flag were introduced into bagpipe design. Bagpipes were incorporated into institutional activities and some institutions had their own bagpipe bands, the most important being the Rei de Viana, supported by the Diputación de A Coruña. Many community associations and schools also had their own bagpipe band or Escola de Gaitas, giving tuition in bagpipe playing. In the emigrant communities abroad, bagpipe bands were very popular, helping to maintain a

---

[3] A parliamentary deputy for the Partido Galeguista, Castelao was President of the Consello de Galicia in exile after the Civil War. He was also a cartoonist for the newspapers *A Nosa Terra*, *El Pueblo Gallego*, and *El Sol*. The cartoon cited here is from the 1920 album entitled—like the contemporaneous Galician nationalist cultural magazine—*Nós*.

sense of community and home. This new use of the bagpipe to achieve social integration and community led to increasingly large bagpipe bands, usually accompanied by dancing troupes. Towards the end of the Franco dictatorship, the most visible gathering of bagpipe bands was the annual competition Encontros de Folklore held at Santiago and sponsored by the Caixa de Aforros de Galicia, which brought together the bands of Galician emigrant centres overseas, local community groups, and official institutions.

An important shift occurred in the 1970s, intensifying in the 1980s, with the emergence of Galician folk. Estévez (in Milladoiro 1998: 202) sets the start of the process in 1975—the year in which Franco would die—with the creation of the Movimento Popular da Canción Galega, and the folk music festival held in Santiago in February of that year. In the last years of the Franco regime, a new type of musical formation emerged, mixing bagpipes with other traditional instruments and—in a shift back to the political—appearing at musical events staged by the democratic opposition. This was a gradual process since there was explicit resistance even from Galician nationalists as the bagpipe, thanks to its appropriation by Francoist officialdom, was seen as a regressive folkloric relic. To cite an interview with Nando Casal and Xosé Ferreiros, looking back at this period: 'estabamos nun canto perigoso, eramos xente que tamén loitaba polas libertades, comprometida politicamente pero que por outro lado ao mellor iamos vestidos de traxe de gaiteiro que sonaba folclórico no pior sentido da palabra e moitos progresistas non acababan de asumir o noso papel' [we were on dangerous ground, we were political activists fighting for democratic freedoms but sometimes we would be dressed in bagpiper costume, which was seen as folkloric in the worst sense of the word, and many people on the left were reluctant to accept us in that role] (No país das gaitas 1995: 25–6).

This incorporation of bagpipe music into the pro-Galician anti-Franco opposition struggle was matched by the introduction of new musical practices which developed into the new trend of Celtic folk. Estévez (in Milladoiro 1998: 204) sees the record 'Fonte do Araño' by Emilio Cao, which introduced the harp as an instrument, as the starting point for this Celtic fashion. Transcriptions of folk music were compiled by many of these groups, at the same time as they incorporated musical influences from what were regarded as fellow Celtic 'nations' (Brittany, Cornwall, Scotland, and especially Ireland), in a mixture of purism and hybridization. This musical trend, combining traditional folk music and Celtic roots, is best exemplified by the group Milladoiro and the Festival Internacional Celta de Ortigueira, which started in the mid-1970s with the participation of important Celtic singers and musicians such as Alan Stivell and The Chieftains. Once more there is a shift in the markers of 'place' and 'occasion', since performances took place at political or folk gatherings —and, most importantly, now on a stage, even when performed as part of a local celebration.

Here it must be remembered that, even at the height of the Celtic folk trend of the 1980s, it was still common to talk about the bagpipe in a derogatory manner and to see it as a metaphor for the inward-looking: Televisión Galega was known as the *telegaita*, and a scandal involving the Galician lottery was known as the *lotogaita*. And the folk movement was not hegemonic in Galician music; it had to compete with other trends (mainly pop-rock) for the public's favour. *Rockis* and *folkis* (as they came to be known) played alongside each other at music festivals, competing for the same space and public.

A change in the perception of the bagpipe occurred in the 1990s, prompted mainly by the factors mentioned at the start of this essay. Other factors also deserve attention. In the late 1990s, women bag-pipers like Mercedes Peón, Susana Seivane, and Cristina Pato started to gain recognition, performing in a field that has always been male-dominated. The trajectory of the band Milladoiro is paradigmatic here. Emerging out of the partnership of the two musicians Anton Seoane and Rodrigo Román, with their traditional ensemble of two bagpipers and two drummers, the band was formed in the mid-1970s. Its first record *A Galicia de Maeloc* (1979) incorporated Celtic instruments (ocarina, violin, harp); after a series of successful records in the Celtic folk vein, the band was signed up by CBS in 1982, and in 1986 it won the Goya Prize for best soundtrack of the year for its music for Gutiérrez Aragón's 1986 film *La mitad del cielo*. In 1990 it initiated a series of institutional collaborations, providing the music for the major exhibition 'Galicia no tempo' and for the exhibition of Maruxa Mallo's paintings which inaugurated the Centro de Arte Contemporáneo in Santiago. In 1994 it ventured into new territory with its orchestral composition *Jacobus Magnus*, made with the English Chamber Orchestra. This move from local folk to entry into the globalized market to institutional sacralization and finally classical music—performing at elite venues like the classical concert hall of the Auditorio de Galicia—marks a violent shift in the markers of 'place' and 'occasion', with the bagpipe's humble country-market origins left firmly behind.

The consequent changes of perception have been made possible by a reorganization of the musical landscape. In the field of mass-cultural entertainment, Galician folk—and with it the bagpipe—has benefited from the new interest in ethnic and world music, and a very lively promotion of new bands using traditional music now occupies centre-stage in the Galician popular music scene. However, while there is almost universal agreement that globalization has been beneficial for Galician music, now included under the broad label of Celtic music, anxieties have also been expressed about whether this makes Galician music too dependent on fashion and commercialization (Andrade and Sampedro 1999: 19–23), and also about the possible dilution of identity resulting from production for a global market. Carlos Núñez's 1999 record *Os amores libres* helped to stir the waters when he mixed Galician music with flamenco. Anton Seoane, one of the founder members of Milladoiro, has been the most outspoken critic of globalization and *mestizaxe* [hybridization] (in Milladoiro 1998: 235–51).

The rivalry that existed in the 1980s between *rockis* and *folkis* seems to have abated: the practice of featuring folk and pop-rock bands in the same concert has dramatically reduced, since it is now accepted that they have different publics and therefore should have separate venues. Not only is folk music at the forefront of Galician music but there are signs of diversification, with separate venues and modes of production and distribution for each trend. A particularly interesting trend emerging in the early 1990s was *rock bravú*, developing out of the broad group of bands that performed in Antón Reixa's TV series *Sitio distinto*, each with their own style but all singing in Galician in a medium dominated by Castilian. At first *rock bravú* was perceived as a cross between rock and folk; it later proved to be a more complex intersection of rock and folk, literature and music, politics and culture, enlarging the concept of traditional music by incorporating popular music played by *orquestas* at *verbenas*, which had never before been seen as part of Galician traditional music. The main voice for *rock bravú* has been the band Os Diplomáticos, whose leader recently published a couple of books that tried to give momentum to a literary trend called *literatura bravú*. Their defence of the Galician language and emphasis on notions of 'belonging' have made *bravú* bands frequent performers at nationalist festivals.

It was, however, in the field of traditional rather than commercial folk that the *guerra das gaitas* emerged. A new type of band, sponsored by the Diputación de Ourense, was criticized for copying Scottish bands. While in folk music Celtic influences were assimilated and seen as part of a common cultural legacy, in the bagpiper band circuit this new form of band was criticized from the start as 'alien' to the Galician tradition. The criticisms have been aimed at the new types of costume (kilts), drums, bagpipe design, musical arrangement, and especially the spirit of the playing which was seen as military. Indeed, critics referred to this new kind of band as the *gaita marcial* [military bagpipe]. The Director of the Real Banda de Ourense was expelled from the Asociación de Gaiteiros de Galicia and traditional bagpipers staged public protests at events in which the new bands were performing. The importance of the bagpipe as a symbol of tradition can be seen in the following statement by the Asociación de Gaiteiros de Galicia: 'Isto non é só unha liorta de gaiteiros: é algo que atinxe ó conxunto da sociedade, a aqueles que cren que Galicia ten que estar no mundo con voz propia' [This is not only a struggle among bagpipers: it is something that concerns society as a whole and those who believe that Galicia has to have its own voice on the world stage] (*No país das gaitas* 1995: 39).

There is, then, thus a double movement: an endeavour to ritualize and repeat a set of practices and markers that allow the bagpipe to be seen as traditional, and a continuous process of change that makes the bagpipe relevant to new audiences. We should remember here that, while there is a clear difference between a song played by a bagpiper at a communal celebration and a song performed on a vast stage by professional musicians, with modern arrangements combining new instruments for a mass audience who consume music in their leisure time, nevertheless the pleasure of the latter is enhanced by the knowledge that the music they are hearing has the 'added value' of past tradition. The two practices, however distinct their historical contexts, feed off each other.

I should now like to go on to show how the bagpipe, precisely because of its consecration as a symbol of Galician identity, has additionally become a site for challenging that identity. I shall do so by analysing two songs in which bagpipes are used to subvert stock notions of identity: 'Miña terra galega' by Sinestro Total (1984), and

'Galicia Sitio Distinto 2 parte' by Os Resentidos (1988; text published in Reixa 1994: 87–8). Both belong to a trend that emerged in the 1980s with influences ranging from punk and rock to hip hop and rap, and in various ways signifying a break with tradition; their use of the bagpipe is thus a counter-cultural one. These two groups were the main protagonists of the *movida viguesa* or *movida galega* which took over from the *movida madrileña* at the start of the 1980s as the latter declined, lasting till 1986 when the Universidad Menéndez Pelayo dedicated a summer exhibition to it: an institutionalization that, as in the case of the Madrid *movida*, could be seen as having defused its original counter-cultural energies.

Siniestro Total—a possible translation would be 'Beyond Repair' —first emerged in 1981 as a punk band. They denied the notion of the artist as individual creator by publicly performing acts of plagiarism. Most of their hits were undisguised classic R & B songs remade with different lyrics. They also denied the R & R narrative of 'working-class kid rebels and becomes rich and famous', engaging in mischievous role play and in certain periods performing almost as a Sex Pistols tribute band, but replacing the nihilism, self-destruction, and political revolt of the Sex Pistols with irony, cynicism, and a desire to shock. Many of their first hits were banned on commercial radio stations and they provoked criticism from feminists with lines like 'las tetas de mi novia tienen cáncer de mama' [my girl's tits have got breast cancer] (Siniestro Total 1982), and from gays with 'Más vale ser punkie que maricón de playa' [Better to be a punk than a beach queen] (Siniestro Total 1983). They also sent up Galician folk with the song 'Fa, fa, fa, fa' (Siniestro Total 1985). Their punk period ended when a member of the band was badly injured by a bottle thrown from the audience at one of their gigs, prompting the band to use motorbike helmets and cover the front of the stage with a net. Since then, they have toned down their performances with smoother, more elaborate songs. By the mid-1980s, they were one of the most successful bands on the Galician and Spanish scene, obtaining their first *disco de oro* in 1990, and one of the few bands to have survived from the 1980s *movida*. Their album *Cultura popular* issued in 1998 is a compilation of popular Spanish hits in retro mode.

Siniestro Total have rarely used Galician in their lyrics although many of their songs have Galician cultural references and deal directly with Galician subjects. Their use of the bagpipe is almost incidental but very interesting. They used the instrument's image very effectively on the cover of their 1984 maxi single *Me pica un huevo*, depicting a *gaiteiro* smashing his bagpipe in a remake of the famous cover of the 1979 album *London Calling* by The Clash, in which a member of the band smashes his guitar—this in turn being a remake of the cover of Elvis Presley's first record. The 1984 song 'Miña terra galega' makes constant reference to bagpipe music and other forms of Galician traditional music. The following words by Alberto Casal sum up well the place of Siniestro Total in the Galician and Spanish music scene:

Sempre vin en Siniestro Total unha sorte de grupo/aduana. Unha ben engraxada bisagra-rock entre o galego e o foráneo [. . .]. Abandeiraban a trincheira da barbaridade atlántica no Foro, caótica e críptica galeguidade en pé de guerra: na viaxe a conquista de España. Pero ó mesmo tempo aquí había quen consumía os seus contrasinais como se os cociñase á galega un grupo madrileño. (Casal 1995: 20)

[I always saw Siniestro Total as a kind of frontier group. A well-oiled rock-music pivot swinging freely between Galicia and the outside world. Waving the flag of Atlantic barbarism in the Forum [i.e. the capital Madrid], a chaotic, cryptic Galicianness on a war footing: out to conquer Spain. But at the same time here [in Galicia] some people consumed their battle cries as if they'd been cooked by a Madrid group in the best Galician style.]

'Miña terra galega' follows the pattern of many successful Siniestro Total hits. It is a remake of the blues song 'Sweet home Alabama' by Lynyrd Skynyrd, with new lyrics in Castilian and a chorus in Galician. The first part of the song includes almost every cliché of Galicianness: homesickness (*morriña*), a waiter far from home, grey skies, an emigrant crying as he listens to the *muiñeira*. There is also intertextual play with the Galician anthem: *morriña* is called 'el dolor de Breogán' [Breogan's sorrow] (in the Galician anthem, Galicia is referred to as the home and nation of Breogán, a mythical Celtic king who is supposed to have ruled Galicia); the phrase 'Donde se quejan los pinos' [Where the pines lament] refers to Eduardo Pondal's 1880 book of poems published under that title, which includes the poem which provides the words of the Galician anthem. But although this song strikes almost every chord of Galicianness, at the same time it unsettles the Galician listener. We know that the song talks about us and our home, but we do not know how to relate to it: whether we are supposed to feel sentimental, patriotic, or proud, or just amused at the pastiche. The second part of the song lists a series of things missed by the emigrant. The list is structured around a series of oppositions. First, 'zanfoñas de Ortigueira' (the 'zanfoña' or hurdy-gurdy is, like the bagpipe, widely used in traditional Galician and Celtic music; Ortigueira refers to the previously mentioned Festival Celta de Ortigueira which started in the mid-1970s) paired with 'los kafkianos del Jaján' (apparently a reference to a group of Kafka followers who used to gather at a mountain outside Vigo called Xaxan, which apart from being pretty nonsensical—Kafka, after all, represents the absurd—cannot be encapsulated within the constraints of Galician identity signalled—albeit in pan-Celtic mode —by the 'zanfoñas de Ortigueira'). The next pair of opposites is 'la Liga Armada Galega' and 'el pazo de Meirás': the former refers to a Galician armed nationalist organization of the 1970s; the latter symbolizes the Francoist presence in Galicia, being the manor house that once belonged to the late nineteenth-century novelist and feminist Emilia Pardo Bazán, which was given to Franco for his summer holidays by the Governor of A Coruña at the end of the Civil War. The bagpipes are not played in this song, but the *gaita* is present through the references in the lyrics to the *muiñeira* and by association through the references to other traditional instruments and musical forms such as the *zanfoña* and the *alalá* (an unaccompanied Galician song characterized by its refrain 'alalá'). The incongruous references in the song construct a contradictory, divided home, constituted by a range of incompatible marks of identity.

Before discussing 'Galicia Sitio Distinto 2 parte' by Os Resentidos, it is necessary to set this band in context. Its image is dominated by that of its lead singer Antón Reixa, the most versatile Galician artist of the last two decades: writer, video-artist, singer, and mass-media persona. Os Resentidos—which one might translate as 'The Angry Young Men'—initially grew out of Reixa's poetry group 'Rompente', whose performances turned into Os Resentidos' first records. In this early period, the group cannot be described as a rock band but was more akin to experimental, avant-garde groups such as The Residents and The Art of Noise. In their second period they developed new styles, assimilating varied influences such as South American rhythms, hip hop, and rap, their repertoire becoming a hybrid mix of cultures, styles, and instruments, rapidly making them a successful band in popular entertainment. Os Resentidos' work contains every stock ingredient of postmodernism: the decentring of the subject, the blurring of high and popular culture, pastiche, etc.

(Truett Anderson 1996: 18–25). An overall analysis of their work is beyond the remit of this essay, and I shall merely make some brief points and explain some concepts central to Reixa's and Os Resentidos' work that relate to the role in it of the bagpipes and digital music.

In their eclectic mix of styles and instruments, the bagpipes and digital music are constant ingredients, blending the traditional instrument associated with nature with music that is electronically produced and relayed. If the *gaita* is associated with popular Galician roots, digital music is rootless and nationless, belonging to science and technology. It provides no sense of belonging nor identity, looking forward to a fractured future rather than back to organic wholeness. An opposition, in short, between the 'authentic' and the synthetic. The ability of digital music to transform analogue sound into binary bits allows for the manipulation and 'quotation of sounds'. As Simon Frith observes (1996: 115), digital music 'has speeded up the process in which composition means quotation', thereby highlighting the 'performance of the quotation'. So, through their constant use of digital music, mixing and manipulating sounds and songs, Os Resentidos foreground the process of music-making, engaging us in the activity of decoding their songs. Bagpipes are part of this process whereby, through constant quotation, sounds become self-referential signs.

Os Resentidos' discourse is a counter-discourse on identity. Reixa defines the Galician as follows: 'Un galego é un refuxiado en terra de ninguén cunha estrela de David nos collóns e no centro da estrela as siglas da Organización para a Liberación de Palestina' [A Galician is a refugee in a no man's land with a star of David on his bollocks and in the centre of the star the letters PLO] (Reixa 1994: 71). It would be hard to find a quotation that better describes the sense of deterritorialization. Galicians, in Reixa's quotation, not only lack a home but get their symbols so mixed up that there is no hope of finding a 'home' through political mobilization. The 'differentness' of this 'Galicia Sitio Distinto' [Galicia a different place/the place of difference]—an implicit allusion to the 'Spain is different' slogan promoted in the 1960s by Manuel Fraga Iribarne (President of the Xunta de Galicia since 1982) when he was Francoist Minister of Information and Tourism—is eroded because this fictitious nation has no boundaries. It is similarly difficult to pin down 'Galicia Sitio Distinto 2 parte' as a piece of music. Included in the 1988 album *Fracaso tropical*, the song was also one of several performed in the 1990 thirteen-episode TV series *Sitio distinto*, all of which (apart from 'Galicia Sitio Distinto 2 parte') were reissued in the 1991 album *Delikatessen (Música tradicional da República de Sitio Distinto)*; 'Galicia Sitio Distinto 2 parte' was issued on its own as a promotional record and video.

Sitio Distinto is an imaginary nation conceived as the repressed underside of Galician nationalism: 'Galicia é un imperio e a República de Sitio Distinto é a súa colonia subconsciente' [Galicia is an empire and the Republic of Sitio Distinto is its subconscious colony] (Reixa 1994: 119). In the TV series, Sitio Distinto issued its own passports, had its own symbols (a cow patterned with camouflage), and its own food (*churrasco*, a typically Argentine way of barbecuing meat brought to Galicia by returning emigrants and now widely eaten 'at home'). The first line of the song's refrain 'tacón, tacón, tacón, punta tacón' [heel, heel, heel, toe heel] refers to the steps that have to be learnt in order to dance the *muiñeira*; its second line 'eu quero bailar nos autos de choque' [I want to dance in the dodgems] is glossed in the sleeve notes to the record: 'O ruído dos coches de choque da verbena e da miña banda de ritmo maltreito bloqueáme o pensamento e xa non penso máis e fumo e bebo e bebo aínda máis' [The noise of the fairground dodgems and of my band with its limping rhythm jam my brain and I stop thinking and keep on smoking and drinking and drinking]. The dancing of the *muiñeira* (the promotion video has some dancers in traditional costume) is performed against the background of the noise of the fairground dodgems, which figure prominently in the promotion video—a different kind of popular culture: modern, urban, and commercial. The lyrics end with two lists of place names (with capital letters suppressed): 'a coruña lugo ourense e pontevedra' and 'namibia palestina nicaragua e guatemala'; and after that a list of proper names (again, no capital letters): 'castelao nelson mandela e álvaro pino que comprou un vespino'. Reixa's songs frequently include lists placing Galicia alongside countries riven by ethnic, territorial, or class conflict (here Namibia, Palestine, Nicaragua, Guatemala), blurring the 'difference' between 'third world' and Europe.[4] In the same way Nelson Mandela, as internationally respected black leader, and the Galician political icon

---

[4] The song 'Abdul' from the 1985 album *Vigo capital Lisboa* lists the names of Galician hamlets and African countries. The song 'Camarada Sitting Bull', like 'Galicia Sitio Distinto 2 parte' included in *Fracaso tropical*, includes the Galicians in a list of native American tribes.

Castelao are listed together with the popular Galician cyclist Álvaro Pino (here demoted to a scooter), in a medley of culture heroes that testifies to media globalization.

Just as in 'Galicia Sitio Distinto 2 parte' geographical borders are eroded and different discourses (politics, mass-media, traditional) are mixed, so too different sound and instruments are combined to create something that is new. But as Simon Frith, writing about rap, reminds us, this mixing process 'is best understood as producing not new texts, but new ways of performing texts, new ways of performing the making of meaning' (1996: 115). Reixa displays his quoting and mixing, attracting attention to the new globalized, hybridized Galicia but also to the process of constructing it. Reixa's Sitio Distinto is not a place we can go to in order to be reassured of our identity; it is a place undergoing change and transformation. The words 'Arde galicia con lume forestal [. . .] arde galicia pero non queima' refer to the repeated forest fires in summer which destroy precisely the landscape and land identified with the bagpipe, serving in nationalist discourse as a 'nature reserve' for Galician identity.

To conclude, the bagpipe has been used in Galician culture both to reassert an idea of identity based on nature and traditional culture and to challenge this perception and create new modes of conceiving —and experiencing—Galician identity. In the first part of this chapter I tried to show how tradition is constructed by repeating certain signifiers—a process deconstructed by the foregrounding of repetition and citation by both Siniestro Total and Os Resentidos. The promotion video for 'Galicia Sitio Distinto 2 parte' shows some traditional images being photocopied and becoming something else. In Sitio Distinto there is no safe, secure, bounded home but a place in which home is constructed and deconstructed, through the mixing of bagpipes and digital music with each other and with the noise of the 'autos de choque'.

WORKS CITED

Alfonso de la Torre Núñez, J. R. (1995). 'La guerra de las gaitas', *La Voz de Galicia, Cultura*, 31 (Sept.): 2–4.

Andrade, L. R., and Sampedro, P. (1999). 'Panorama do folc en Galicia de Norte a Sur', *Tempos Novos*, 27: 19–23.

Casal, A. (1995). *Rock & grelos*. Santiago: Edicións Lea.

Cores Trasmonte, B. (1986). *Los símbolos gallegos*. Santiago: Velograf.

Foxo, X. L. (1982). *Os segredos da gaita*. La Coruña: La Voz de Galicia.

Frith, S. (1996). 'Music and Identity', in S. Hall and P. Du Gay (eds.), *Questions of Cultural Identity*. London: Sage, 108–27.

Hobsbawm, E. J., and Ranger, T. (eds.) (1983). *The Invention of Tradition*. Cambridge: Cambridge University Press.

Marfany, J.-L. (1996). *La cultura del catalanisme*. Barcelona: Empúries.

Milladoiro (ed.) (1998). *Galicia fai dous mil anos*, ii: *O feito diferencial na música*. Santiago: Museo do Pobo Galego.

No país das gaitas (1995). Special issue of *Cadernos A Nosa Terra*, 20 (Vigo).

Os Resentidos (1985). *Vigo capital Lisboa* (record).

—— (1988). *Fracaso tropical* (record).

—— (1991). *Delikatessen (Música tradicional da República de Sitio Distinto)* (record).

Quintanilla, J. (1920). 'O nazonalismo musical galego', *Nós*, 2: 5–7.

Reixa, A. (1994). *Viva Galicia beibe*. Santiago: Edicións Positivas.

Risco, Vicente (1920). 'O sentimento da terra na raza galega', *Nós*, 1: 4.

Rivas, M. (1997). 'Carlos Núñez, un gaiteiro en Manhattan', *El País* (11 May): 58.

Siniestro Total (1982). *Cuando se come aquí* (record).

—— (1983). *Siniestro Total II (el regreso)* (record).

—— (1984). *Menos mal que nos queda Portugal* (record).

—— (1985). *Bailaré sobre tu tumba* (record).

—— (1998). *Cultura popular* (record).

Storey, J. (ed.) (1998). *Cultural Theory and Popular Culture: A Reader*. Hemel Hempstead: Prentice Hall.

Truett Anderson, W. (ed.) (1996). *The Fontana Post-modern Reader*. London: Fontana.

Vicetto, B. (1865). *Historia de Galicia*, vol. i. El Ferrol: Texonera.

Williams, R. (1981). *Culture*. London: Fontana.

Part IV

The Local and the Global

Editor's Introduction

THE issues discussed in this section in many ways come full circle with those raised in the discussion of migrant identities by Santaolalla and Mateo in Part I, since the latter presuppose a globalized, multicultural world. All four essays show the local and the global to be connected in complex ways for, as postmodern theory rightly insists, the two are not in opposition but are enmeshed through the processes of late capitalism, which have mapped onto the model of the nation-state (which still remains in place) new macro and micro groupings. Spain's current *estado de las autonomías* has been deemed a success by all and sundry, as has its integration into the European Union. But of course the Basque Country remains a problem which is therefore fittingly discussed in the first essay here.

Gabilondo's focus on Basque identity takes a psychoanalytical focus—the only essay in this volume to do so—drawing on a politicized reading of Lacan which at the end explicitly engages with Žižek's reworking of Lacanian theory to examine political issues of collective fantasy as embodied, not in the individual unconscious, but in material reality. Thus Gabilondo applies the psychoanalytical notion of 'the uncanny', elaborated by Freud, to an analysis of the economic and institutional aspects of Basque cinema, as well as to an analysis of the representation in two very different Basque films of the gaze, which has played such an important role in film theory as the marker of desire and identification. (It may be noted that film provides the major source of Žižek's examples of collective fantasy projection.) The stress on the gaze in this essay could usefully be put together with the discussion of surveillance and spectacle by several contributors to this volume. Gabilondo's Lacanian framework produces an analysis of the relationship between Basque and Spanish identity which avoids binary oppositions because this is a system in which there are no 'selves' (and thus no possibility of identity politics) but only a series of others (and Others) arranged in a specular relationship, since for Lacan the self is always based on lack, being founded by seeing itself looked at by others (and by the metaphysical Other which is the sign of lack and castration). Gabilondo's notion of an 'othered' identity avoids the essentialist concepts of Basqueness which have been (and still are) important in political discussion, and posits the Basque and the Spanish as tied together in an uncanny repetition of something like Freud's *Fort/Da* principle, for the 'othering' of Basque identity means that adherence to it necessarily involves adherence to the Spanish state responsible for this 'othering'. Gabilondo reads the two films discussed as performing the negation of Basque identity in what can be seen, via Žižek, as a revenge on the Spanish state inasmuch as it breaks the latter's monopoly on the negation of 'other' identities. There is no postmodern celebration of cultural plurality and hybridization here (Mateo's essay in Part I warns against the tendency in much postmodern theory to celebrate cultural hybridity as if no power relations were involved) although Gabilondo suggests that the second film discussed (*Airbag*) negates Basque and Spanish identity by subjecting the desire of both to global others who refuse to enter this game of specular 'othering' by exploding all concepts of identity. The concept of pleasure in effecting—rather than suffering—one's own destruction allows a complex reading of the repeated attraction in Spain of the *Carmen* myth, in which the image of Spanishness—Carmen herself—is destroyed (interestingly, in the 1938 Spanish-Nazi co-production *Carmen la de Triana* she was not).

The notion of identity as specular play recurs in the essay by Sánchez, who examines the narcissistic structures whereby the citizens of Barcelona are (literally) invited to see themselves in the surfaces of its recent waterfront redevelopment. Like Gabilondo and de Ros, Sánchez examines local public cultural policy and its intersection with private enterprise, in this case to analyse a cultural development that deploys commercialization in order to enhance collective rather than individualistic identity formation. If Gabilondo examines collective rather than individual identity projections, Sánchez argues that postmodern architecture's use of narrative and citation constructs collective identity through a mirroring process which puts narcissism at the service of a civic project. Sánchez's emphasis on the ways in which public spaces are given meaning through the everyday life practices of those who use them is grounded in de Certeau's notion of space as 'a practiced place' (1988: 117), also fundamental to the essays by Nair and Mateo. Sánchez's analysis of buildings and public sites shows the importance of material culture for constructing a sense of identity, and how Barcelona's imitation of postmodern waterfront developments in other countries has been specifically geared to the construction of local pride and pleasure (although, as Sánchez notes, not everyone is included in the party). The importance of pleasure in producing subject positions is central, in different ways, in the essays by both Sánchez and Gabilondo.

De Ros's essay on the Guggenheim Museum Bilbao raises similar issues about the intersection of global and local economic interests, stressing the role of cultural policy but also that, as in the case of Barcelona's waterfront redevelopment, the project's success was in the end decided by the positive local popular response to the building. Thus an icon of high culture (an art museum) has become incorporated into popular culture through the practices of everyday life. The question of spectacle and specularity arises again here with the Guggenheim Bilbao's metal surfaces reflecting the surrounding waterfront environment, as does the question of architecture as narrative and citation, with the building's references to Bilbao's industrial past. Particularly interesting in this case is the use of an import to further a sense of Basque national identity in a way that breaks its dependence on the Spanish state—though at the cost of another kind of dependence. As de Ros notes, the building has allowed supranational high technology to be co-opted for the purposes of local identity formation, while also courting international tourism. In the process, art takes on the hugely important role of revitalizing not only the local economy but also a local sense of pride—though the building has become an emblem of the city of Bilbao rather than of the Basque Country in general. Nevertheless, de Ros argues controversially that the museum's construction has been infused with a sense of nationalist endeavour by the uncanny way (Gabilondo's term is pertinent here) in which the debate around it has mimicked previous representations of the creation of the modern Basque nation. Indeed, the whole process mimics the way in which nineteenth-century states constructed a sense of national identity by holding world exhibitions: we have here another example of the recycling of cultural processes that recurs in several essays throughout this volume.

The last essay in this section and in the volume challenges dominant apocalyptic notions of the triumph of globalization in late modernity, showing through discussion of recent developments in commercial Spanish television that in fact local production is keeping the multinationals afloat economically. Smith's positive appraisal of quality local programming fits well with Fernàndez's essay on Catalan TV in Part II; both essays examine the recycling for local purposes of established TV genres (in Smith's essay, the workplace drama series). As in Fernàndez's essay, Smith shows how the play on stereotypes of national identity can be used to construct new forms of identity, particularly here for women—though he notes that Telecinco's other locally produced workplace drama simply reproduces stereotypes for comic purposes. The point made in Part I by Mateo about the importance of irony in allowing a degree of control over the stereotypes imposed on one from without, through a distancing process, might be relevant here too.

Also important in Smith's essay is his insistence, drawing on recent theoretical work in television studies, on harnessing discussion of programme content to discussion of industrial concerns, and his particular attention to trade sources (including the Internet) for key statistical information on audiences and financial outlay, as well as on cultural policy. Here Smith argues for the need to combine humanities-based cultural analysis, including the ethnographic analysis of audiences which Evans's essay in Part II also called for, with social-science-based analysis of policy and of social and economic data. Analysis of policy and economic factors in fact figures in all four essays in this section, which between them call on the discourses of psychoanalysis, museum studies, postmodern theory in architecture, cultural geography, and media theory. If Gabilondo implies that Basque and Spanish national identites are forever locked in a specular relationship, de Ros, Sánchez, and Smith all give largely positive accounts of the construction of local identities, not in opposition to, but through the medium of global cultural corporations (in Barcelona's case, through the city's staging of the Olympics). The other side of this equation is that global corporations are, it seems, more sensitive to local cultural factors than they are often given credit for. The fact remains that culture is big business—but culture has always had an institutional backing and been economically motivated, from the medieval epics written to generate a tourist trade to a particular monastery onwards (I am of course referring to that foundational narrative of a supposed Spanish national identity, the *Poem of the Cid*). It should be remembered here that the modern bourgeois notion of the individual artist is an anomaly in the history of culture, and largely an illusion—though, as several essays in this collection show, implicitly confirming Žižek, illusions are powerful realities. Several of the essays in this volume—particularly the last one by Smith—point to the cultural snobbery inherent in the frequent supposition that commercial and institutional concerns are necessarily in opposition to cultural value. As Bourdieu (1986) has shown, the function of the supposedly disinterested aesthetic detachment that constitutes high-cultural taste is precisely to construct class distinctions: that is, identity formations. And the frequent association of popular culture with the feminine, illustrated in several essays in this book, has important consequences for the ways in which gender is conceptualized and experienced. Analysis of cultural institutions and industries is crucial to study of the processes whereby national, social, and gender identities are constructed, particularly when it is combined with attention to the identification processes that enable cultural products to engage with their varied audiences. The essays in this section, and in the volume as a whole, are intended to make a contribution to such analysis in the Spanish context.

WORKS CITED

Bourdieu, P. (1986) [1979]. *Distinction: A Social Critique of the Judgement of Taste*. London: Routledge.
Certeau, M. de (1988). *The Practice of Everyday Life*. Berkeley and Los Angeles: University of California Press.

15

Uncanny Identity: Violence, Gaze, and Desire in Contemporary Basque Cinema

JOSEBA GABILONDO

GENEALOGY OF A VIOLENT REPRESENTATION

IN the history of representations of Spanish national and ethnic identities, there is a text that, in its manifold transformations, has defined
the relationship between Spanish identities and the violence that has
characterized their history: Prosper Mérimée's *Carmen* (1845). What
originally was conceived as a French Romantic travel narrative that
violently reduced post-Napoleonic, post-Carlist Spain to a land of
new, romantic exoticism for the contemplation of the (capitalist,
male) European gaze, eventually turned into an opera (Bizet, 1875)
and developed a life of its own in the twentieth century with works
as different as Otto Preminger's *Carmen Jones* (1954) or Laurie
Anderson's '*Carmen*' (1994). In Spain, *Carmen* laid the ground for
the cinematic tradition known as the *españolada* which, after the
Franco dictatorship, was revived with a film that became one of
the biggest international box-office hits in Spanish film history:
Carlos Saura's *Carmen* (1983). In Evlyn Gould's words, the success
of Saura's *Carmen* made it 'a paradigm for modern European cultural identity' (1996: 9), thus coming full circle in the articulation of
Spanish identities.

Ironically enough, Saura's *Carmen* also represents the internal-
ization of the original violence inscribed by the European gaze on
the body of Carmen as Spanish other. To contextualize this saga of
national violence and representation, I should like to refer to another
rendition of *Carmen*: Basque director Imanol Uribe's *Días contados*
[*Running out of Time*] (1994). In the film, there is a brief sequence in
mise en abyme, which captures the street performance of *Carmen* by

an older woman and a disabled man in a wheelchair dancing to the karaoke recording of the opera in a boombox. This representational wink in a film where a Basque terrorist falls in love with a new 'Carmen' from the subaltern classes of Madrid is a direct reference to the fact that, in Mérimée's original *Carmen*, don José, a Basque soldier from Navarre, is seduced *in Basque* by the gypsy *femme fatale* Carmen. Don José introduces himself as follows: ' "I was born," he said, "in Elizondo, in the valley of Baztán. My name is don José Lizarrabengoa, and you are familiar enough with Spain, señor, to be able to tell at once from my name that I am a Basque and an Old Christian" ' (Mérimée 1989: 19). A few pages later, he confesses to his seduction by Carmen in these terms:

'*Laguna, ene bihotzarena*—companion of my heart,' she said suddenly, 'Are you from the Basque Provinces?' [. . .] 'She was lying, señor, as she always lied. I wonder whether that girl ever spoke one word of truth in her life; but whenever she spoke, I believed her—I couldn't help it. She spoke Basque atrociously, yet I believed her when she said she was from Navarre. You only had to look at her eyes, her mouth, and her complexion to tell she was a Gypsy. I was mad, I overlooked the most obvious things.' (Mérimée 1989: 23–4)

Días contados thus restores the original narrative of a fatal romance between the two Spanish ethnicities that, for the French Romantic traveller, were the most exotic: Basques and Gypsies—although this time the seduction takes place in Spanish. For the representation that defines and grounds the future *españolada* is structured around a national violence effected by, and on, two of its most 'distinctive' ethnicities. In short, *Carmen* is a European spectacle of (inter-)ethnic violence—inscribed misogynistically through a Basque male subject.

Uribe's new rendition of *Carmen* won public and critical acclaim: it was the top box-office hit of 1994 and was awarded eight Goyas in 1995. This reception is directly linked to the fact that *Días contados* successfully refashions the national memory of the inherited ethnic violence inscribed in *Carmen*. Furthermore, the film by contrast high-lighted Saura's own violence in reducing his *Carmen* to an 'essentially Spanish' national performance orchestrated around flamenco and gypsy culture, in which (inter-)ethnic tension and conflict disap-peared. Saura had to vacate Basque identity from his filmic version in order to present a 'coherent and homogeneous' representation of Spanish identity. In this sense Saura inadvertently followed the

national standards imposed by Francoism in its attempts to cater to
the most conservative perceptions of Spain in Europe and the USA.
By contrast, Uribe, from within Basque cinema, restored inter-ethnic
conflict to his own *Carmen*, reopening the cycle of violence that has
constituted the discourse on ethnic and national identities in Spain.
As I will argue here, this cycle can be best defined as 'uncanny'
because the moment Basque identity is violently erased it re-emerges
with a vengeance.

BASQUE CINEMA'S UNCANNY IDENTITY

Spanish representations of Basque ethnic and national violence are
not incidental, circumscribed to a single film, nor simply the alleged
products of a French Romantic tradition. This representational violence affects the entire group of cinematic texts that, in the last third
of the twentieth century, have come to be referred to as 'Basque cinema'. 'Basque cinema' occupies a distinctive position among contemporary Spanish discourses of subject formation. It is characterized by
an uncanny questioning of its own identity and existence which is
not found in, for example, Basque literature and art.[1] The question of
whether Basque cinema has an identity or even exists is still dogged
by controversy, sometimes bordering on violence. The history of this
cinematic debate is thus a privileged site from which to address the
issue of violence and identity in the Basque Country and Spain.

   Film had been produced intermittently in the Basque Country from
the beginnings of cinema through to the second Spanish Republic
of 1931–6. After the Spanish Civil War, Basque cinema was relegated
to a marginal position, continuing in exile or in the French Basque
Country. Although as early as 1933 the film *Euzkadi* (Ernandorena,
Aragonés, and Pujol) had triggered a short-lived journalistic discussion about the notion of 'Basque cinema', the concept became
a reality, albeit a problematic one, only at the end of the Franco
period (Zunzunegui 1985: 378–80, 399–400). At this foundational

---

[1] Basque literature (Atxaga, Urretabizkaia, Saizarbitoria, etc.) is marked out by its
use of *euskara* as unquestionably local as well as national, whereas literature written in
Spanish or French in the Basque Country has to date never considered itself fundamentally Basque. Art institutions and artistic production (the Guggenheim Museum
Bilbao, Oteiza's and Chillida's sculptures, etc.) are accepted as both Basque and international. In the field of television, the system is divided, with Basque and Spanish TV
channels clearly separated and organized independently by law.

moment, Basque cinema came into existence precisely via discussion of its non-existence. For example, at the first historic meetings of Basque film-makers in 1976, they devoted most of their energies to discussing a practice that was felt to be non-existent but necessary (Zunzunegui 1985: 378–97). The process of prescribing solutions to Basque cinema's non-existence lasted almost a decade (de Pablo 1996: 78–82; Unsain 1985: 7). In this phase, Basque identity over-determined a practice whose non-existence became uncannily recurrent. It must be noted that the (non-)existence of Basque cinema was at this stage of little concern to the Spanish public and critics. It was not till the mid-1980s, when a number of Basque films pioneered by Uribe's *La muerte de Mikel* (1984) became popular throughout the Spanish national territory, that the Spanish media and critics began to pay attention to the issue (López Echevarrieta 1984: 246). Indeed, it was foreign critics (Besas 1985: 204–8; Hopewell 1986: 233–4) who first acknowledged Basque cinema's incipient yet unclear existence.

In the 1990s the debate resurfaced in almost diametrically opposed terms. In the late 1980s, José María Caparrós Lera had claimed that Basque cinema was undergoing a crisis similar to that previously experienced by Catalan cinema (1992: 345). Once a new group of Basque film-makers such as Bajo Ulloa, Medem, Bollaín, Lazkano, de la Iglesia, Urbizu, and Calparsoro had been acknowledged as central to the Spanish film industry, the debate on Basque cinema re-emerged. But this time Basque cinema's existence was actively denied from various quarters, starting with the film-makers themselves (Martí Olivella 1999). Even on the academic front, monographs on Basque cinema set about denying its existence (Arocena Badillos in de Pablo 1998: 242). In this second phase, it was the supposed ethnic or national identity of Basque cinema that was denied. This time, a wide range of both Basque and Spanish practitioners and critics invested in the denial. Other film-makers and theorists on the periphery of the debate—for example, Juan Miguel Gutiérrez Márquez in the Basque Country or Jaume Martí Olivella in the United States—questioned the implications of this negation. Although the US critic Marsha Kinder concentrated on the Catalan case (1993: 388–440), her theorization of the micro-regional and the macro-regional implied that Basque cinema was also part of this new configuration. The uncanny historicity of this problem of identity is perhaps best captured by Martí Olivella (1999: 206) who concludes:

'Such a reaction is almost identical to the one expressed by many Spanish women writers and film-makers when faced with the concept of feminism concerning their work. In Spain, feminism and national-ism are two negative cultural and political signifiers. Rarely, if ever, have they been articulated as necessary and dynamic terms in the pro-cess of cultural and ideological construction.'

In recent work on Spanish cinema, the polarization between denial and affirmation seems to have increased. Two books in English by British and Spanish critics respectively are telling examples. Barry Jordan and Rikki Morgan-Tamosunas introduce their book by emphasizing the importance of 'questions of identity' (1998: 10) in post-dictatorship film-making. Although they dedicate the first two sections of their book to historical and genre film, the last two sec-tions focus on gender/sexuality and national identities respectively. Thus a quarter of their book is devoted to national identity, with Catalan and Basque cinema, as well as cinemas from other regions, discussed in detail. By contrast, Jenaro Talens and Santos Zunzunegui avoid any discussion of identity and instead introduce their volume by focusing on the question of historicity (1998: 1–45).

This essay will not be concerned with denying or affirming the existence of Basque cinema, for the fact that the question keeps coming back shows that there is no clear-cut answer. Rather, I shall explore the uncanny identity of Basque cinema as something that is simultaneously denied and affirmed—and indeed haunted by the impossibility of closing the question of its (non-)existence. As Freud explains, uncanny identity is a negative identity, an othered iden-tity that, in its negativity, returns to haunt the attempt to repress its being: 'among instances of frightening things there must be one class in which the frightening element can be shown to be something repressed which *recurs*. This class of frightening things would then constitute the uncanny' (1955: 241). Freud adds that the origin of the recurrence has to do specifically with the familiar or even fam-ilial origin of a repressed affect: 'we can understand why linguistic usage has extended *das Heimliche* ["homely"] into its opposite, *das Unheimliche* ["un-homely", uncanny]; for this uncanny is in reality nothing new or alien, but something which is familiar and old-established in the mind and which has become alienated from it only through the process of repression' (1955: 241). Hence, the uncanny is defined by the repression of a familiar affect that then recurs as repressed and consequently frightening. Following Freud's definition,

I shall argue that Basque identity and its filmic representations are uncanny in the sense that the Spanish state and its nationalist system (in which I include both Spanish and peripheral nationalisms) tend to repress them. As a result, Basque identity and its visibility recur with a violence that is clearly uncanny: familiar in its affect and yet frightening. In this essay I will discuss the violent cycle of negation and resurgence that constitutes Basque cinema's uncanny identity as a way of exploring the connection between subject formation and violence in Spain. My claim is that the logic of the uncanny affects most areas of Basque cinema's visibility: from its organization to the particular cinematic representations themselves.

AN 'UNHOMELY' ECONOMY

As far as the economics of cinema are concerned, and as most critics have pointed out, Basque cinema does not have an industrial and economic infrastructure of its own, unlike Basque television or literature. Basque films need to rely on the production infrastructure located in Madrid and Barcelona and thus do not have a 'home' of their own (Zunzunegui 1985: 399). In the 1980s, to palliate this situation, the Basque government started a new cultural policy of economic subsidy 'a fondo perdido' (no repayment required) for film. This policy was inaugurated with a subsidy to Uribe's *La fuga de Segovia* (1981) and eventually made possible the release of thirty-five feature films under the label 'Basque cinema' (de Miguel in de Pablo 1998: 218).[2] As de Miguel notes, this economic policy gave Basque cinema what now retrospectively can be considered its nationalist identity (de Pablo 1998: 224–6). However, Imanol Uribe had already pointed out in the mid-1980s that Basque cinema was a 'bubble' that might easily burst (Gutiérrez Márquez 1997: 215). As this cinema became known as Basque, the Basque government decided to tighten its control over production in the early 1990s, implementing idiosyncratic policies that ended up alienating most successful Basque filmmakers, who consequently turned to non-Basque sources of funding, as did younger directors like Alex de la Iglesia, Enrique Urbizu, Juanma Bajo Ulloa, and Julio Medem. Thus, in the 1990s, Basque

---

[2] For detailed discussion of the first law regulating Basque cinema and its progression through 1985, see Zunzunegui (1985: 270–9).

cinema lost its 'financial home'. Gutiérrez Márquez (1997: 215–17) blames this economic crisis primarily on the legislation on film subsidies passed in the 1990s by the new Media Institute of the Basque government, Euskal Media, SA, which promoted forms of co-sponsorship and co-production with little Basque participation. This new investment policy was attacked publicly by Basque film-makers in what Arocena Badillos (de Pablo 1998: 250) has described as a 'war'; that is, a form of violence.

Today 'Basque cinema' is produced outside the Basque Country and its majority audience is non-Basque Spanish. Nevertheless, Spanish audiences identify this film-making as clearly Basque in its modes of representation and subject matter, so much so that the uncanny haunting of its identity must be actively denied by both Spanish and Basque directors and film theorists. Basque cinema is *heimlich* but it does not have a home; it is unhomely—uncanny.

THE GAZE OF THE OTHER AND
THE PERFORMANCE OF VIOLENCE

Basque cinema's uncanny formation can also be traced in its contemporary filmic representations. Most critics agree that Basque cinema is defined textually by its representation of violence. As Martí Olivella notes (1997a: 90), the latter cannot be reduced to the issue of ETA terrorism, as critics such as Bermejo and Juaristi tend to do. This kind of reductiveness 'others' this violence by implying that it is 'only Basque' and not something affecting and implicating the entire Spanish state. I will argue here that violence becomes the ultimate unrepresentable moment of Basque cinema. It returns to haunt Basque cinema because it exceeds the Basque field of filmic representation and points to a larger reality: that of the Spanish state and its nationalist system. Although there are several Basque films in which violence is directly represented as a political problem—*La fuga de Segovia*, *El juicio de Burgos* (Uribe, 1979), among others—the majority do not situate violence within a standard political framework (political parties, police, terrorism). Basque cinematic violence follows an uncanny pattern that defies representation; that is, Basque cinema does not represent violence but rather *performs the violence of the process whereby its identity is represented as other*. This will be my central thesis in my analysis of two classic Basque films: Julio

Medem's *Vacas* (1991) and Juanma Bajo Ulloa's *Airbag* (1997, top box-office grossing film of the year). Although the two films are completely different, violence structures them in similar ways.

Vacas is known for its allegorical rendering of Basque history through the generational rivalry between two rural families from the last Carlist war (1875) through to the Civil War (1936), finally resolved through the union of their heirs. The film captures in a non-reductive way the natural, rural Basque environment from which Basque nationalism derives its foundational discourse. The suturing element that makes allegory filmically possible in *Vacas* is the camerawork, which constructs a point of view that cannot properly be called mythical or historical. The film camera literally enters sites of vision such as animal and human eyes, photographic cameras, etc. in order to construct a point of view that defies historical positionality. For example, the spectator sees a cow's eye looking at the camera and thus returning the spectator's look, and then enters this reciprocating gaze so as to occupy the place of the gaze on the screen. As a result, viewers find themselves looking back at themselves from behind the cow's eye and the various other reciprocating gazes in the film; sometimes the film uses this device as a bridge transporting the viewer to another time or place. The viewer thus occupies the gaze of the Other.

At this point it is necessary to make an excursus through Lacan's understanding of the Other and its gaze. Lacan claims that what is at stake in the specular gaze whereby we see others looking at us cannot in fact be explained in terms of a reciprocating look (1981: 84–5). For, as he stresses, the act of 'being looked at' is what constitutes consciousness and subjectivity in the first place: 'we are beings who are looked at, in the spectacle of the world. That which makes us consciousness institutes us by the same token as *speculum mundi*. Is there no satisfaction in being under that gaze [. . .] that circumscribes us, and which in the first instance makes us beings who are looked at [. . .]?' (1981: 75). Lacan thus implies that, behind the look of every other, the world is looking, although in Lacan the world assumes the form of the Other since desire and language are involved in this 'being looked at'. Indeed, according to Lacan, when the spectator is looked at by others, the resulting recognition and subjection work because desire is involved. Desire is the bridge between the (particular) others whom we see looking at us and the Other (the world) which looks at us from behind their gaze. (Throughout this essay, the terms 'other' and 'Other' will be distinguished in this way.

The human world is, in Lacanian terminology, constituted by language and representation, and thus is ultimately a Symbolic Order. The 'Other' is the law and referent that regulates the Symbolic Order of the human world, and all the others represented in it, through violence and desire.) Thus when the spectator is looked at by others, he or she becomes the subject of, and subject to, the desire of the Other. The Other looks only indirectly through the gaze of others for the Other is lack and violence, and thus cannot signify except through the mask of an other. In *Vacas*, the look of others—whether that of the cow or that of the human eye—is necessary to signify the Other standing behind. The gaze of others, as the mask of the Other, reveals the latter's ultimate lack and destructive power (1981: 118). Lacan has theorized this aspect of the Other as the Name and Law of the Father (1966: 277–9). What concerns me here is the double bind of desire and violence which structures the field of the Other (the Symbolic Order), for desire and violence always come together when the Other subjects the spectator to its desire through the gaze of others. In the last instance, the Other is the subjecting and objectifying effect of language, including the visual.

This Lacanian framework provides a way of reading the end of *Vacas*. In the film's closing sequence, the camera enters a final 'site of vision': a hole in the rotten trunk of a beech tree, which expands into a netherworld in a movement signalling the abject entrance into 'mother earth' and its gaze. The hole in the beech tree is also connected, through the gaze of the grandfather, with madness. Thus the film can be said to end in death and madness (Yraola 1995). This absolute violence destroys the basis of filmic representation: the film ends with a shot that literally blacks out the screen. At this point, violence moves beyond rural Basque 'mother nature' which till now has been represented as the origin and source of violence. The viewer can only speculate about the origin of this final extra-filmic recurrence of violence—extra-filmic because this is a violence that the film performs but can no longer represent. The gaze of the Other which the camera forces the viewer to confront and occupy throughout the film returns in this final instance in such a way that the gaze of the Other exceeds representation and reveals itself as lack—that is, darkness. This final recurrence of the gaze of the Other is not historical, mythical, or contained within the otherness of the Basque nationalist imaginary. It is the recurrence of an extra-Basque Other: the Other which subjects the Basque other to its objectifying and destructive gaze.

This final image of darkness, which violently annuls the representation of an 'othered' Basque imaginary, obliges the Spanish viewer to penetrate it, thus subjecting his or her desire to the desire of the Other. For Basque representations function as other only within the political order that gives rise to their formation and against which they are othered: that of the Spanish state and its nationalist system. This political order resulted from the clash between tradition and modernity which erupted in the nineteenth century precisely after, and as a direct extension of, the Carlist wars: the historical period portrayed in *Vacas*. Because Basque identity has been othered, the Other that regulates the film and its representations appears to be atemporal, ahistorical, even mythical. In effect, the desire created in the Spanish viewing subject by the Basque others whose viewpoint he or she repeatedly enters is the desire of the Other standing for the Spanish which is responsible for othering them in the first place.

However, in the final sequence, as the camera enters the hollow beech tree and the screen goes dark, the film calls into question the Spanish order which functions as Other behind the Basque others represented. When the screen blacks out the image of the Basque other ('mother earth' in this case), then the Spanish Other hiding behind it and responsible for its othering appears in the only way that it can: as wholly invisible. The film's end not only represents Basque violence—the Basque other as violent—but also confronts us with the violence by which Basque identity is othered. The film's end thus performs the violence of representation effected by the Spanish state as Other. The key point here is that this violence is performed rather than represented.

Moving now to the second film: *Airbag* takes as its starting point the traditional comedy situation of a planned wedding, following a well-established subgenre constituted by films as different as *The Philadelphia Story* (Cukor, 1940) and *My Best Friend's Wedding* (Hogan, 1997). In this case, the marriage represents the symbolic consolidation of Basque elite society through the union of two of its offspring. But first *Airbag* tells the story of a series of accidents, starting with the groom's loss of the wedding ring in a bordello a few days before the ceremony, and ending with a car chase from Portugal through Galicia to the Basque Country. At the end of the film, as the groom abandons the bride at the altar and takes off with the woman he met at the bordello, the chase continues, now transformed into a liberating flight from Basque elite society. The chase also functions as a narrative locating Spain and the Basque Country in the new global arena of international politics, commerce, and violence: the groom and his buddies have to deal with international (mainly Portuguese, Spanish, and Latin American) drug and prostitution cartels.

The title of the film refers to the airbags that the drug dealers use to transport cocaine. In the first part of the film, the Basque groom and his two buddies, while searching for the wedding ring, by chance end up driving a car with cocaine-filled airbags. As the car stops at a police checkpoint, the airbags pop up and, when the police shoot at them, cocaine lands on everybody's face. The car takes off leaving behind a white trail of cocaine powder that clouds the *mise-en-scène* till it covers the entire screen. In the ensuing chase, the three buddies drive through the Spanish landscape, leaving behind them a trail of cocaine powder and dust. This image is replicated in the film's finale as the three buddies and their respective partners drive off from the wedding party, leaving behind a trail this time of leaves and papers. There is no diegetic reason for the appearance of these flying papers, but the film provides a clue: the woman from the bordello sings a song playing on the double meaning of the Spanish word *polvo* ('powder' or 'dust' but also 'the sexual act'). Thus, the white trail of *polvo* represents not only the violent irruption of the global order (drugs) but also the road to pleasure and freedom (sex). Airbags, meant to serve as protection against accidents, become devices for triggering them, creating opportunities for freedom. This repeated image has a geopolitical component: the global violence symbolized by the drug trade, irrupting onto the scene via the exploding airbags, wreaks havoc on the national territory and bodies.

The film thus generates an unstable structure whereby the three-buddy posse is propelled in contrary directions by local and global impulses and pressures. However, the unstable relation between the local and the global is sutured at the end of the film by incorporating two ethnically marked subjects and their gaze into the Basque national order. At the wedding, a new president of the Basque Government is introduced: a male *lendakari* [president] of African or Middle Eastern descent, representing the new Basque and Spanish political and economic order (for this presidential appointment is part of the local and the national state apparatus) displaced here by the irruption of the global. Named Omar Urretabizkaia, the only words he utters are in Basque: 'eskerrik asko' [thank you very much].

At the same time, the protagonist jilts the Basque bride at the altar and drives off with the woman he met at the bordello, presented as ethnically marked. At the start of the film, she represents the dark-skinned prostitute with Caribbean accent: the contemporary Spanish stereotype of the exotic, sexualized woman (the bordello is decorated with stereotypical representations of Arab-Andalusian Spain, pointing to the continuation of the Carmen saga in a new postcolonial, global scenario). At the end of the film, she turns out to be 'really Spanish'. As such, she occupies the position of the object of national desire regulated by the protagonist, who is heir to the economic empire of one of the Basque Country's most powerful families. These two ethnically marked subjects, embodying the effects of the new global order, are mobilized to suture the film as Basque *and* Spanish, and thus seamlessly 'national'. In other words, at the end of the film the political identity and desire of the Basque Country are represented by global others who are further othered by being represented as both Basque and Spanish.

However, we are made aware that there is an act of violence involved in the othering of these two ethnically marked subjects, which is performed by Basque subjects. In the wedding scene just before the end, the camera cuts to a close-up of the protagonist and the wedding is left off-screen. The camera shows the protagonist's fantasy of being kissed by his pseudo-ethnic object of desire: the woman from the bordello. At that point, the film abandons the more or less realistic conventions of comedy and turns into a musical, with the wedding interrupted by cocaine coming out of the groom's pockets and accidentally landing on the priest's face. This accident—a recurrence of the previous airbag accidents—triggers a miraculous phone call from 'God', sung by the priest, ordering the protagonist to marry the woman from the bordello. At the same time, the ring flies out of the protagonist's body and lands on the hands of the pseudo-ethnic woman who has just arrived, and they kiss in 'reality'. A series of long and medium-long shots alternating high and low angles covers most points of view in this wedding-turned-musical, thus presenting the transformation of the protagonist's original fantasy into a collective 'reality' shared by the characters at the wedding and by the film-viewers. What starts as the Basque protagonist's individual fantasy thus becomes a collective Spanish 'reality'. At this point, the protagonist and his buddies take off, leaving behind the wedding party and the new *lendakari*. In a final high-angle long shot, viewers see the car and motorcycle being driven off by the three-buddy posse and their partners, leaving behind the unexplained white trail of flying papers.

Thus, the protagonist's desire for a pseudo-ethnic woman involved in prostitution—a desire which is not accepted by the Basque political order and cannot be resolved within the generic conventions of comedy—returns at the end of the film in the form of a musical fantasy. Within this musical fantasy, the protagonist's desire is fulfilled as the pseudo-ethnic woman sutures the film. The film effects a representational violence by shifting from the original comedy genre to the conventions of the musical, cheating the viewer of an end that—had the film remained within the conventions of comedy—would have had a critical function, precluding desire from materializing. The film can reach its conclusion only when the global others represented by the ethnically marked subjects are incorporated into a pseudo-ethnic Spanish fantasy contained within a musical. The musical—thanks to its ability to operate on a fantastic, hallucinatory plane, containing even a phone call from God—neutralizes ethnic and geo-political difference. At the same time, thanks to the conventions of the musical, the protagonist abandons his position within the Basque order, effecting the violence of negating his identity as Basque. At this point, the *lendakari* can be black, the protagonist's object of desire can be a Spanish prostitute with an ethnic look, and the protagonist himself becomes a Basque subject whose desire is no longer Basque. In this way, the three characters become others who no longer stand for a global or a Basque order, but for a Spanish order which appropriates both of these. As Spanish others—othered by a Spanish order which thereby appropriates them—these three characters become sites behind which the Other of the Spanish nationalist order stands. The film's celebration of hybridity is thus not a celebration of difference, but of its incorporation into a seamless Spanish order, effected via the film's scopic regime. The gaze exchanged by these three characters, returning the gaze of the camera, subjects the desire of the Spanish spectator. The desire of the protagonist and of the viewer becomes the desire of the Spanish Other.

However, the end of the film contains another moment that can be read as the uncanny return of Basque identity. The film's protagonist can also be interpreted as standing for the gaze of a global Other which threatens the Spanish order and its Other. The closing shot, showing the protagonist's posse as they drive away leaving behind a white trail of papers and leaves, can be read as a final recurrence of the film's emblematic image of *polvo* coming out of airbags, pockets, etc., clouding the mise en scène and blanking out the screen. In this sense, the film bursts open all containers, with the result that no gaze can contain or appropriate it. If *Vacas* enters a series of sites of vision in order to vacate the Basque other and reveal the gaze of the Spanish Other behind, *Airbag* repeatedly fills sites of vision so that it becomes impossible to see what lies behind. That is, the film obliterates any site in which the others that stand for the global Other—whether cocaine dealers, ethnic subjects, prostitutes, or Basques—might be contained and thereby confined to the role of being the others of the Spanish Other's desire. Thus the final white paper trail spilling out onto the road becomes an abject reminder of the impossibility of reducing the global Other to any Spanish order. The trail of *polvo* recurring throughout the film—a dispersal that is geographic (road dust), economic (drug trafficking), and sexual (*polvo* as sexual act performed on a pseudo-ethnic female body)—is a material but traumatic reminder of the irreducibility of the global Other to the Spanish order and its Other. This reading is reinforced by the film's opening: the title, in the shape of an airbag, explodes as if hit by a bullet. The film's final image can be read as the uncanny recurrence of this initial exploding image. At the end, the film explodes in the viewer's face, undermining any attempt to contain the global within the Spanish national order. This is also an explosion of Basque identity, whose signifiers have—in this road movie—become ethnically, economically, and geographically unstable.

Like *Vacas*, *Airbag* subverts the Spanish order, in this case by performing the violence and desire of the global Other which threatens it. Basque uncanny identity recurs, not from within Basque nature and history as in *Vacas*, but from without: that is, from the global world of politics and economics. In both cases, Basque filmic representations are haunted by an uncanny identity whose violence lies elsewhere and recurs as Spanish Other. Both of these Basque films simultaneously reveal and contest the Spanish Other and its gaze by performing its violence and desire without representing it. They do so by representing their own identity as uncanny: that is, repressed yet recurring, and recurring through the act of cancelling itself out.

STATE *JOUISSANCE*

I hope to have shown in the above analysis that the Spanish state is not only the guarantor of political order but also an order organized around otherness, desire, and violence. The formation of any identity other than the national-Spanish is othered by the state while also recurring as irreducible and uncanny. Joseba Zulaika and William Douglass state that 'the grip that terrorist discourse holds upon the collective imagination is far beyond what the phenomenon would merit in strictly military or destructive terms; the subjectively experienced potential terror becomes "real" independent of the actual violence' (1996: 29–30). What makes this 'independent terror' work, as Lacan reminds us, is desire. In other words, the moment the others (terrorism) are desired, they stand for the violence and the desire of the Other (the state). In this context, Basque cinema occupies a central position in understanding the effects of the state order and the uncanny recurrence of the othered subject positions which it produces.

Before jumping to hasty conclusions about the possibilities of a 'politics of the uncanny', it is worth recalling Slavoj Žižek's Lacanian reading of Althusser's theory of state apparatuses and ideological interpellation. As Žižek argues: 'Althusser speaks only of the process of ideological interpellation [. . .] [but] there is always a residue, a leftover, a stain of traumatic irrationality and senselessness sticking to it [. . .] this leftover, far from hindering the full submission of the subject to the ideological command [. . .] confers on the Law its unconditional authority' (1989: 43–4). Following Žižek, we have to conclude that the uncanny return of a repressed identity *per se*, rather than defying the state order, legitimizes it. In other words, the state order and its ideology need this uncanny, irreducible recurrence of the other, in order to justify themselves.

In Spain most new subject positions and identities, as soon as they are othered, become national noises and fractures that, nevertheless, are constitutive of the state order and its desire. This is the contradiction at the core of Basque cinema but also of other subjects: queers, immigrants, and women, for example.[3] If I began with a reference to

[3] Strict Lacanian theory would not allow women to be seen as subjects since, for Lacan, 'woman' is part of the lack that constitutes the Other. I do not subscribe to this position.

Carmen, I would like to return to it so as to understand the state order and its desire in their historical and genealogical complexity. There is an important difference between Uribe's and Saura's versions of *Carmen* that needs to be mentioned. At the end of Uribe's *Días contados*, both don José and Carmen die, whereas in the Saura version only Carmen dies, albeit in a clever play between reality and fiction. This suggests that the interplay between nationalities and gender in contemporary Spain is complex: the moment don José is nationalized as non-Basque Spanish, as in Saura's film, only Carmen dies; whereas when the play between national and ethnic identities—present in the original version—is rescued in its otherness, as in Uribe's film, then both protagonists, because of their newly regained otherness, die. In other words, in Saura's Spanish nationalist version, the male fantasy of killing the dangerous woman is salvaged, no matter how subtle the interplay between reality and fiction. But in Uribe's Basque version, the original fantasy of exterminating the uncontainable, sexually excessive woman is extended to include the extermination of the Basque subject—the newly restored other of the film. The double violence suggests that both the *femme fatale* and the terrorist share a similar fate in contemporary Spain: the fate of otherness. Žižek would add here that state *jouissance* is reinforced rather than weakened or subverted by the denunciation of a violence that affects more than one other—hence perhaps the film's popularity and critical acclaim in Spain.

In this sense, the active negation of their identity by many filmmakers and cultural practitioners—queer, women, Basque—points to this broader scenario involving state violence. Paul Julian Smith has documented Almodóvar's refusal to be categorized as a homosexual director (1994: 88–90). Martí Olivella registers the opposition of Arantxa Lazkano and Pilar Miró to his characterization of their film-making as feminist (1997*b*: 225). I suggest that these filmmakers negate their own identities strategically in order to effect a violence that, if effected by the state, would rob them of their identity and desire: that is, of their capacity for *jouissance*. For there is an element of enjoyment in negating one's own identity in order to break the state's monopoly on negation. It is important to recognize that Basque cinema adopts a similar strategy. Starting from its othered position, Basque cinema mobilizes its uncanny identity in order to perform state violence on its formation and representations. In so doing, Basque cinema takes *jouissance* away from the state.

WORKS CITED

Anderson, L. (1994). *Stories from the Nerve Bible: A Retrospective, 1972–1992*. New York: Harper Perennial.

Bajo Ulloa, J. (1997). *Airbag* (film).

Besas, P. (1985). *Behind the Spanish Lens: Spanish Cinema under Fascism and Democracy*. Denver: Arden Press.

Caparrós Lera, J. M. (1992). *El cine español de la democracia: de la muerte de Franco al 'cambio' socialista (1975–1989)*. Barcelona: Anthropos.

de Pablo, S. (ed.) (1996). *Cien años de cine en el País Vasco: 1986–1995*. Vitoria-Gasteiz: Diputación Foral de Álava.

—— (ed.) (1998). *Los cineastas: historia del cine en Euskal Herria: 1896–1998*. Vitoria-Gasteiz: Fundación Sancho el Sabio.

Freud, S. (1955). 'The Uncanny', in *The Standard Edition of the Complete Psychological Works of Sigmund Freud*, ed. J. Strachey, vol. xvii. London: The Hogarth Press, 216–59.

Gould, E. (1996). *The Fate of Carmen*. Baltimore: Johns Hopkins University Press.

Gutiérrez Márquez, J. M. (1997). *Sombras en la caverna: el tempo vasco en el cine*. San Sebastián: Eusko Ikaskuntza.

Hopewell, J. (1986). *Out of the Past: Spanish Cinema after Franco*. London: British Film Institute.

Jordan, B., and Morgan-Tamosunas, R. (1998). *Contemporary Spanish Cinema*. Manchester: Manchester University Press.

Kinder, M. (1993). *Blood Cinema: The Reconstruction of National Identity in Spain*. Berkeley and Los Angeles: University of California Press.

Lacan, J. (1966). *Écrits*. Paris: Seuil.

—— (1981). 'Of the Gaze as Object petit a', in *The Four Fundamental Concepts of Psycho-Analysis*, ed. J.-A. Miller, trans. A. Sheridan. New York: Norton & Co., 67–119.

López Echevarrieta, A. (1984). *Cine vasco de ayer y hoy: época sonora*. Bilbao: Ediciones Mensajero.

Martí Olivella, J. (1997a). '(M)otherly Monsters: Old Misogyny and/in New Basque Cinema', *Anuario de Cine y Literatura en Español*, 3: 89–101.

—— (1997b). 'Regendering Spain's Political Bodies: Nationality and Gender in the Films of Pilar Miró and Arantxa Lazcano', in M. Kinder (ed.), *Refiguring Spain: Cinema/Media/Representation*. Durham, NC: Duke University Press, 215–38.

—— (1999). 'Invisible Otherness: From Migrant Subjects to the Subject of Immigration in Basque Cinema', in W. Douglass et al. (eds.), *Basque Cultural Studies*. Reno: Basque Studies Program, 205–26.

Medem, J. (1991). *Vacas* (film).

Mérimée, P. (1989). *Carmen and Other Stories*, trans. and ed. N. Jotcham. Oxford: Oxford University Press.

Smith, P. J. (1994). *Desire Unlimited: The Cinema of Pedro Almodóvar*. London: Verso.

Talens, J., and Zunzunegui, S. (eds.) (1998). *Modes of Representation in Spanish Cinema*. Minneapolis: University of Minnesota Press.

Unsain, J. M. (1985). *Hacia un cine vasco*. San Sebastián: Filmoteca Vasca.

Uribe, I. (1994). *Días contados* (film).

Yraola, A. (1995). 'El discurso de la muerte en *Vacas* de Julio Medem', in G. Cabello-Castellet, J. Martí Olivella, and G. Wood (eds.), *Cine-Lit II: Essays on Hispanic Film and Fiction*. Portland: Portland State University, 163–8.

Žižek, S. (1989). *The Sublime Object of Ideology*. London: Verso.

Zulaika, J., and Douglass, W. A. (1996). *Terror and Taboo: The Follies, Fables and Faces of Terrorism*. New York: Routledge.

Zunzunegui, S. (1985). *El cine en el País Vasco*. Bilbao: Bizkaiko Foru Aldundia/Diputación Foral de Vizcaya.

16

The Guggenheim Museum Bilbao:
High Art and Popular Culture

XON DE ROS

CULTURAL icons are central to the definition of national heritage. They are instrumental in projecting the nation's image into a discursive space and are therefore the object of governmental attention and the subject of cultural policy. The emergence of a cultural icon is a complex phenomenon related to both public perception and the politics of nationalism. The issue becomes more problematic when the icon a society collectively comes to adopt as part of its cultural patrimony is an import, as exemplified in the controversies surrounding the public funding of foreign art. Cultural technologies such as the museum, the art gallery, and the exposition play an important role in the process of naturalization through public display. Their function in governmental programmes of social performance has been the object of recent studies which draw from a range of theoretical writings by Foucault and Habermas (Bennett 1995; McGuigan 1996; see also Bourdieu 1994). From this vantage point a case study of the Guggenheim Museum Bilbao, which brings together the notions of museum, art gallery, and exposition, and is in itself a cultural icon appropriated by nationalism, will provide a privileged site for exploring these dynamics.

The opening in October 1997 of the Guggenheim Museum in Bilbao marked the culmination of a process of redefinition of culture in terms of a cultural policy of urban regeneration. The process began with the transfer of responsibilities for social services from the central state and the subsequent creation of the Department of Culture by the Basque government in 1980. From then onwards the importance and relevance of cultural policy in the public sphere has steadily grown. With the implementation of the 1986 urban scheme or *Plan*

General, Bilbao joined the prevalent Western European trend for programmes of economic and physcial revamping, following American cultural policy initiatives. As elsewhere, the mobilization of culture for the purposes of marketing the city has been criticized for being at the expense of cultural activities that allow non-consumerist forms of popular expression and community participation (Julia González in Bianchini and Parkinson 1993: 73–89).

The Guggenheim venture which came of age in 1991, with the signing in New York by the Basque authorities and the Guggenheim Foundation of the pre-agreement, represents an attempt to reconcile economic development priorities with social and cultural demands. The refashioning of a city beset with recession and unemployment, and ravaged by the effects of terrorism, represents a milestone in the history of urban redevelopment. The project combined the economic logic of international business and finance with an aesthetic and cultural engagement with the local, with some allusions to the city's historical heritage. The Museum's location on a former industrial site, housed in a building which quotes from the past of its surroundings, is repeatedly highlighted in the unprecedented marketing and promotion campaign surrounding the project. The monumental construction in the form of a ship, made of Spanish limestone, titanium, and glass, was designed by the American architect Frank O. Gehry as a homage to the city's life as an industrial port (see Figs. 9 and 10). It stands on the River Nervión waterfront, the site of the former docks and steel foundries which were the source of the city's once flourishing manufacturing trade (the material originally chosen was steel but this was later discarded in favour of titanium). The first impression is that of a building that has collapsed upon itself. Its design, whose harsh, gleaming metal plates contrast with a structure where straight lines are scarce, suggests a representation of the dislocations of the present deindustrialization process. Be that as it may, the building's massive, distinctive profile has become a landmark and signature for the city, as was anticipated in the official discourse surrounding its inauguration.[1] The economic rationale behind the promotion of, and widening of access to, high-quality art is to foster private investment in general by encouraging its sponsorship of the arts, and to promote

---

[1] See the statement of Karmen Garmendia, Minister of Culture in the Basque government, in the press release issued at the 1997 Venice Biennale: 'The new museum will certainly become a landmark, a signature for our city that will be recognized across Europe and the world' (English original).

Fig. 9. Guggenheim Museum Bilbao

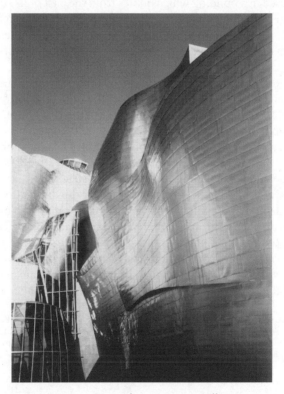

Fig. 10. Guggenheim Museum Bilbao

the services sector with the influx of tourism. Josu Bregara, President of the Regional Council of Biscay, was clear in this respect when speaking at the presentation of the Museum to the press at the 1997 Venice Biennale: 'The Administration's goal was to diversify the city's economic base and counteract an economic slump. A museum of modern and contemporary art was conceived as a major element of this plan' (Press release 1997). The role of culture as a vehicle for economic growth reflects a general shift in the field of cultural policy whereby 'the language of "subsidy" was gradually replaced by the language of investment' (Bianchini in Bianchini and Parkinson 1993: 13). In this sense, the slogan 'Juntos por amor al arte' [Together for the love of art] in the advertisment of the savings bank BBK Bilbao Bizcaia Kutxa saluting the opening of the Museum carries a bleak underlying irony. Disinterestedness is something that a society whose rate of unemployment was, at the time of the Museum's opening, nearly 25 per cent can hardly afford. A pointed illustration of this situation is the more than 40,000 applications received for the 73 jobs advertised at the Museum. However, three months after the opening the hotel and catering trade had already seen a twofold increase in business, even if limited to the Museum's surrounding area (*El Correo* 1998).

While the extent and quality of the economic benefits that the Museum can provide for the city is debatable, it is undeniable that it has changed Bilbao's image by its association with it. Gehry's masterpiece, praised by leading architects and hailed by many as the building of the century, has become an architectural flagship that overshadows the Museum's contents. The request for Picasso's *Guernica* to be housed in the Museum on loan, overruled by the curators of the Reina Sofía Art Centre in Madrid, was a strategy to counterbalance this fact. But, with or without *Guernica*, the real protagonist of the operation has been Gehry's work. This privileging of the container over the contents is a feature that characterizes the international exhibition or expo form. In this case, this is by no means accidental, since the whole enterprise was conceived in the form of the exposition event. The notion of Bilbao as host city was conveyed in the Basque Minister of Culture's official presentation of the Museum, which began with the following salutation: 'On behalf of the government and the people of the Basque Country, I should like to welcome the Guggenheim Museum to Bilbao' (Press release 1997).

The Museum is the centrepiece of the city's redevelopment programme, which includes other state-of-the-art constructions designed by some of the world's most renowned architects. The overall design appears to be based on the exposition policy of pavilion-making. Certainly, the behaviour of Bilbao's citizens seems to correspond to this principle. Visiting the 'fosteritos', as the metro stations designed by Norman Foster are popularly called, became a local pastime when the underground system first opened in 1995. Likewise, the Guggenheim has become the reference point for the Sunday stroll of many *bilbaínos*, as acknowledged by the local press commenting on a survey: 'los datos ponen de relieve que el Museo Guggenheim emerge como un importante polo de atracción y ocio para los ciudadanos' [the findings show that the Guggenheim Museum has become an important locus of attraction and leisure for the city's inhabitants] (*El Correo* 1997c). It is the paradox of international expositions that, while the display is meant to show the outside world the capacity of the host city to take on the challenge of modernity, reality proves that its most significant audience is the local public, which in turn enters into a kind of entropic relationship with its own city. From this perspective, the Museum is not only a Basque national and corporate pavilion standing among others, but in itself constitutes a micro-expo within the larger site of the expo that is the city. The aquatic park with Yves Klein's fountains of fire and Jeff Koons's Giant Puppy, combined with the striking shape of the building, give its exterior the air of a fairground more in tune with the traditional, spectacular format of the exposition than that of the museum.

Inside the building, the exhibition space is arranged in eighteen interconnecting galleries of a variety of shapes and sizes, distributed on three floors around a central atrium. Some of the galleries have names—'Nemo', 'Pez' [Fish], 'Zorro' [Fox]—as do other zones in the building—'el palio' [the canopy], 'la bota' [the wineskin], 'Potemkin' —thereby becoming installations on display, small pavilions in themselves. The access to the different levels is by a glass elevator, stairways, and curvilinear bridges open to the atrium which, together with the overlooking balconies, provide the visitor with ample vistas of the transit areas. Every subject becomes a potential object of vision, and therefore, in the context of the Museum, an exhibit. The principle of surveillance as a civilizing mechanism studied by Foucault with reference to the penitentiary system is equally relevant to cultural technologies of public instruction, and is particularly evident in the exposition where the emphasis is more on performance than on representation (Bennett 1995: 212). The behaviour recommended to the visitor by the Director General of the Bilbao Museum Foundation, Juan Ignacio Vidarte, reinforces this idea:

aconsejaría al visitante nuevo que se dejara llevar por sus propios instintos. Se trata de un centro de arte, de cultura, pero también un espacio lúdico que permite el disfrute de los sentidos y recorrerlo como se descubre una ciudad nueva, callejeando. En sucesivas ocasiones podrá realizar otros recorridos de carácter formal y con un rigor quizás cronológico o geográfico, pero, primero, yo le recomendaría que fuera intuitivo. (*El Correo* 1997*d*)

[I would advise first-time visitors to follow their instincts. This is an arts centre, a cultural centre, but also a ludic space which indulges the senses, and invites the visitor to stroll around it as if discovering a new city. On future visits they could follow a more formal itinerary, perhaps organized according to chronological or geographical criteria, but to start with I would recommend an intuitive approach.]

The exposition experience is exemplified in another aspect of the building, also highlighted in descriptions of the project. In the words of Juan Ignacio Vidarte: 'La obra ha demostrado la capacidad tecnológica del País Vasco' [The building has demonstrated the Basque Country's technological capacity] (Torres 1997). The coverage given to the new technologies used in the project is significant because it identifies the expo with the ideal of modernity which it celebrates. *Catia*, the computer programme used in the design process and originally developed for the aerospace industry, was instrumental in allowing the design to become a reality and made it possible for the project to stay within the construction budget allocated by the Basque administration. For some commentators it shares the accolades with the architect, since without it 'transformar garabatos en estructuras acordes con la ley de la gravedad sería un proceso menos espectacular y creativo' [the transformation of doodles into structures obeying the laws of gravity would be a less spectacular and creative process] (Villacorta 1997). Thus, the prestige associated with high technology is added to the aesthetic value of the building, which becomes not only a physical symbol of urban renaissance but also a symbol of the break with styles of the past through its identification with expanding economic sectors, from the world of design and high technology to the media. The local daily newspapers' lavish supplements

—'Territorios de la cultura', *El Correo* (3 Oct. 1997) and 'Guggenheim Museoa', *El Mundo del País Vasco* (18 Oct. 1997)—as well as the Museum website (http://www.guggenheim.org/bilbao.html) attest to these aspirations.[2] Both make reference to American waterfront developments, and of course to Frank Lloyd Wright's Solomon R. Guggenheim Museum in New York and to the prominent role of Guggenheim in the development of the European and American avant-garde, illustrated in the inaugural exhibition: 'The Guggenheim's Museums and the Art of this Century'.

One of the points of contention has been the indecisiveness on the Basque side with regard to exhibition programming and the acquisition of works for the Museum's permanent art collection. The advisory committee appointed by the Basque Department of Culture in 1992 was dismissed three years later before any purchases were made. The works acquired to date have been described by a foreign observer as a 'genuflection to the taste of the head office back in New York, as are the site specific works commissioned from Serra, Clemente and Holzer' (Sudjic 1997: 57). In the absence of an artistic director in Bilbao, responsibilities in this area were taken over by the Director of the Guggenheim Foundation, Thomas Krens, who was accused of cultural imperialism by the opposition. The suspicion that his agenda totally ignores Basque interests, and that it responds only to pressures to repay the rising debts incurred by his recent deals and to find an outlet for the overcrowded New York and Venice collections, was aired by the press and contributed to the resentment of Basque artists (*El Correo* 1997*a*). Discontent among the local art scene led to the September 1997 exhibition 'Prometeo encadenado', held in the Bilbao art gallery ARSenal under the motto 'Ongi Etorri Mr Guggenheim' (Welcome Mr Guggenheim), an allusion to Berlanga's well-known 1952 film comedy *Bienvenido Mr Marshall*, which satirized Spanish avidity for American financial aid. This exhibition showed the work of 123 artists with an emphasis on *Povera* styles ironically indicating their concern about the future of official arts subsidies (*El Correo* 1997*b*).

Their objections echoed the more alarming ones of Herri Batasuna (HB), on the radical left of Basque Nationalism, who in a letter addressed to Krens in 1992 had asked for the cessation of the

[2] I should like to thank Pablo Guimón for his help in collecting press material for this essay.

negotiations 'hasta que pueda llevarse a cabo un debate hoy por hoy hurtado a todos los sectores implicados en la política cultural' [until it is possible to hold discussions which so far have been denied to all sectors involved in cultural policy] (Tellitu 1997*b*). The memory of the tragic fracas of Lemoniz—the site on the Biscayan coast of a nuclear plant built in the 1970s by the hydroelectric corporation Iberduero, which became the target of a campaign of political protest and was abandoned after a series of terrorist attacks carried out by ETA—was in everyone's mind. Once again, HB's opposition led to widespread apprehension of an intervention by the terrorist group ETA. The fears proved well founded and ETA struck a few days before the inaugural ceremony in a failed attempt to sabotage the event with a massive explosion. The killing of a security guard, a member of the local police (the Ertzaintza), cast a shadow over the celebrations. Certainly, the leading article that the *New York Times* dedicated to the Museum was wary of the situation and not very conciliatory in this respect. Its opening paragraph reads:

If you want to look into the heart of American art today, you are going to need a passport. You will have to pack your bags, leave the U.S.A. and find your way to Bilbao, a small, rusty city in the northeast corner of Spain. The trip is not convenient, and you should not expect to have much fun while you're there. This is Basque country. A region proudly, if not officially, independent from the rest of Spain, it is also bleakly free from Spanish sophistication. Oh, and by the way, you may get blown up. (Muschamp 1997)

The main indictment however came from the US-based Basque anthropologist Joseba Zulaika. His well-informed and documented critical study of the project *Crónica de una seducción: el Museo Guggenheim Bilbao* (1997) argues that, behind the secrecy of the operation, the Basque taxpayer is being exploited. Indeed, by far the most controversial issue has been the draconian conditions of the financial agreement between the Guggenheim Foundation and the Basque administration. In exchange for the Guggenheim's European franchise and the loan of a proportion of the American collection, the Basque administration—the government of the Basque Autonomous Community and the Regional Council of Biscay—provides the financial resources for capital investment including construction costs and annual operating support. The land for the site was donated by Bilbao City Council. The total cost of the operation rises to 23,500 million pesetas: an exorbitant amount, particularly if we consider that in 1989 cultural expenditure by the Basque government in the city of Bilbao stood at an unprecedented 556 million pesetas. Then the cultural budget's priorities had been promotion of the Basque language Euskera on TV and radio, and conservation of the local cultural heritage.

The hostile reaction of Álava and Guipúzcoa, the two other provinces that comprise the Basque Country, came as no surprise, recalling the kind of inter-city rivalry that surrounds exposition events. The results of the June 1997 opinion poll by *El Correo*, according to which two out of three Basques had doubts or did not believe that the investment was justified, reflected the initial pattern of opinion across the various provinces. The opposition of Álava and Guipúzcoa was partly attributed to the roles nominally allocated to the different capitals, with Vitoria, capital of Álava and the site of the government, being considered the administrative centre; Guipúzcoa's San Sebastián, a tourist resort famous for its film festival, being seen as the centre for leisure and cultural activities; with Bilbao standing as the financial and commercial capital.[3] The official emphasis throughout the promotional campaign has been that the Museum will benefit the whole of the Basque Country but, if this could be argued in the case of Bilbao, it was obviously more difficult to ascertain the advantages for the rest of the community.

However, perceptions have changed since the opening. The percentage of Basques for whom the investment was not justified decreased from 35 per cent in May 1997 to 15 per cent in October 1997 (*El Correo* 1997c). Despite all the misgivings, the success of the Guggenheim Bilbao has surpassed all predictions. Operations in 1997 exceeded targets both in terms of visitors and of the number of corporate patrons, whether partners or sponsors. The income from contributions by the thirty-three associated companies, together with individual membership and admission tickets (at 700 pesetas per person), added to the proceeds from exploitation of the Museum's public spaces (the renting out of galleries, atrium, and auditorium) and the takings of the Museum's store and café, provides a level of self-financing which, should things continue in this manner, would be the highest of any European museum. But the prospective reduction

---

[3] According to this survey, 36% of Guipuzcoans and 31% of Álava's population had doubts, and 32% and 36% respectively were against the project (Torres 1997).

of the deficit and thus of public funding are not the only factors that have affected perceptions on the part of the Basque community. For certain aspects of the promotional campaign may have served to infuse a sense of national endeavour into what after all is a private-enterprise initiative.

From its inception, the Guggenheim operation had resonances whose symbolism recalled the birth of the modern Basque nation. The secrecy and apparent laboriousness of the negotiations finds a parallel in the secrecy and laboriousness with which, in 1979, the agreement for the Basque Statute of Autonomy was reached after long and fruitless discussions. On that occasion, success was attributed to the wiliness of the then Spanish President, Adolfo Suárez, and to the determination of the President of the PNV and the Basque General Council, Carlos Garaikoetxea, who subsequently became the first *lendakari* (president) of the new regional government. Krens's negotiating skills are acknowledged by supporters and critics alike, and the agreement signed by the current *lendakari*, José Antonio Ardanza, was preceded by a period whose description by the press could equally refer to the events of 1978–9: 'el proceso de negociación se prolongó durante un largo año, en secreto y bajo la sombra de la polémica' [The negotiation process dragged on for a whole year, in secret and beset by controversy] (Tellitu 1997a).

The language used by the press also evokes a more distant past: the Carlist wars of the nineteenth century, in particular the third war in which Bilbao was besieged by Carlist forces. Certainly, the soul-searching ruminations of the Carlist leader, General Ollo, on the siege of Bilbao in 1874 seem to resonate in many commentaries on the Guggenheim Bilbao in which the Museum's high cost is balanced against the international prestige it entails:

No alcanzo todavía las grandes ventajas morales y materiales que su conquista nos puede proporcionar. Aun dado el caso de que nos apoderásemos de Bilbao, cosa bastante problemática, careciendo de potente artillería, ¿no es verdad que necesitaríamos todos o casi todos los batallones hasta hoy organizados para su defensa? ¿No sería locura suponer que el enemigo nos dejase en pacífica posesión de la villa? Dicen que nuestro reconocimiento por las potencias europeas como beligerantes depende de la toma de Bilbao. (Clemente 1990: 143–8)

[I cannot envisage the great advantages, moral and material, that its conquest can provide. Even if we take Bilbao, which is highly problematic given that we lack strong artillery, would we not need all or nearly all our battalions for its defence? Is it not madness to assume that the enemy will let us take the town peacefully? They say that our recognition as a military force by the European powers depends on our capture of Bilbao.]

The news headlines covering the Guggenheim negotiations often acquired a Valle-Inclanesque tone. The following are found in the special supplements of *El Correo* (3 Oct. 1997) and *El Mundo del País Vasco* (18 Oct. 1997): 'Pacto de caballeros' [Gentlemen's Pact], 'Conspiración por fax' [Conspiracy by Fax], with subheadings such as 'División en el País Vasco' [Division in the Basque Country], 'Huída hacia delante' [Suicidal Escape] , 'Una locura' [Act of Madness], 'Ardanza se vende' [Ardanza is Selling Out], and elsewhere 'Bilbao resurge de sus cenizas' [Bilbao Rises Again from its Ashes], 'La guerra del "Guernica"' [Battle for 'Guernica'], 'Nostalgia de proyectos pasados' [Nostalgia for Past Projects], 'Más sombras que luces' [More Shadows than Lights]. In one of the reports there is a highlighted passage that seems, in the mode of its dramatization, to come straight from Valle Inclán's *Sonata de Invierno*, set in the Carlist wars:

'¿Sabe cuántas haciendas hay en la comunidad europea?'. La pregunta del duque le cogió por sorpresa a Krens, que se hallaba en un palacete de Madrid, en una sala rodeada de retratos de la familia real. 'Pues hay dieciseis. Están las haciendas de los doce países (estamos en 1991), más Navarra, Bizkaia, Álava y Guipúzcoa.' (Zulaika 1997*b*)

['Do you know how many treasuries there are in the European Community?' The Duke's question took Krens by surprise. He was in a palatial house in Madrid, in a large hall surrounded by portraits of the royal family. 'Well, there are sixteen altogether: one treasury for each of the twelve countries (this is 1991) plus those of Navarre, Bizkaia, Álava, and Guipúzcoa.']

The historical allusions did not only come from local newspapers. An article by Jon Jauristi in *El País Semanal,* recalling that it was in 1897 that Miguel de Unamuno published his first novel *Paz en la guerra*, an epic account of Bilbao's heroic resistance to the Carlist siege of 1874, went so far as to suggest that the opening of the Guggenheim Museum a century later signalled the reconciliation of Basque nationalism with the liberal city—a reconciliation which, according to Jauristi, implied the final victory of nationalism over

Bilbao (Jauristi 1997). The Catalan *La Vanguardia*, in turn, recalled that the site was a former Carlist graveyard (Batista 1997).

The two periods evoked by the press in relation to the Guggenheim have an interesting point in common. Both signified the loss of the Basque *fueros* (local customary law): through their abolition in 1876 on Carlist defeat and through the Basque Statute of Autonomy's disregard for them in 1979. The prerogatives enshrined in the *fueros* conferred economic and administrative autonomy on the Basques. The autonomy conjured up by the Guggenheim, however, is no longer attached to traditions of the national past but attuned to the international pace of modernity. It is precisely its configuration as exposition that brings together the ideas of the nation and of modernity. As Bennett observes in his seminal work on the subject, expositions are generally planned to coincide with national celebrations, thus 'inserting themselves into the symbolic rhythm of national histories' (1995: 209). That was certainly the case with the Seville Expo held in 1992 in association with the festivities of the quincentenary of Colombus' discovery of the Americas. However, as the example of Seville demonstrates, the relationship between the two events is by and large not one of symbolic identification but rather the opposite. In Bennett's words: 'Their simultaneity has more often served to mark the differences between them throwing into relief the contrivance of their association' (1995: 209).

The Carlist defeat of 1876 signalled the rebirth of Bilbao as an industrial centre which superseded its former trading economy and in turn helped to revitalize the life of the whole region. A symbol of this transformation was the transporter bridge, known as the *puente colgante*, between Portugalete and Las Arenas. It was the first of its type in Europe, and, significantly, its design was inspired by the Eiffel Tower, the figurehead of European modernity recently constructed for the 1889 Paris International Exhibition. The Guggenheim is equally symbolic of a new turning point in the history of the region after the final industrial debacle of the 1980s. In modelling itself on the idea of the expo, and thereby turning high art into popular culture, it has become a cultural icon which not only embodies the rhetoric of progress but, in an illustration of Foucault's concept of 'governmentality' (1991), serves also as a powerful instrument in government programmes of social performance.

WORKS CITED

Batista, A. (1997). 'Guggenheim ya vive en Bilbao', *Magazine La Vanguardia* (12 Oct.): 72–9.

Bennett, T. (1995). *The Birth of the Museum: History, Theory, Politics.* London: Routledge.

Bianchini, F., and Parkinson, M. (eds.) (1993). *Cultural Policy and Urban Regeneration: The West European Experience.* Manchester: Manchester University Press.

Bourdieu, P. (1994). *The Field of Cultural Production: Essays on Art and Literature*, ed. and trans. Randal Johnson. Cambridge: Polity Press.

Clemente, J. C. (1990). *Los Carlistas.* Barcelona: Istmo.

El Correo (1997a). 'Detractores tenaces: la mayoría de artistas vascos, encabezados por Oteiza e Ibarrola, ve en el Museo Guggenheim una nueva agresión del colonialismo cultural', special supplement *Territorios de la Cultura* (3 Oct.): 40–1.

—— (1997b) '123 artistas exponen en el ARSenal su obra anti-Guggenheim con un marcado carácter festivo e irónico' (12 Oct.) (http://www.diario-elcorreo.es/guggenheim/archivo).

—— (1997c). 'Juicio al Guggenheim' (26 Oct.): 60.

—— (1997d). Article on the Guggenheim Bilbao (27 Oct.): 31.

—— (1998). Article on the Guggenheim Bilbao (24 Jan.): 3.

Esteban, I., González Carrera, J. A., and Tellitu, A. (1997). *El milagro Guggenheim: una ilusión de alto riesgo*, prol. A. Muñoz Molina. Bilbao: El Correo.

Foucault, M. (1991) [1978]. 'Governmentality', in G. Burchell, C. Gordon, and P. Miller (eds.), *The Foucault Effect: Studies in Governmentality.* London: Harvester/Wheatsheaf, 87–104.

Jauristi, J. (1997). 'Bilbao: la metamorfosis de una ciudad', *El País Semanal* (1 June): 26–36.

McGuigan, J. (1996). *Culture and the Public Sphere.* London: Routledge.

Muschamp, H. (1997). 'The Miracle in Bilbao', *New York Times Magazine* (7 Sept.): 54–9, 72, 82.

Press release for the Guggenheim Bilbao issued at the Venice Biennale (1997).

Sudjic, Deyan (1997). 'Reflective Glory', *Tate Art Magazine*, 13 (Winter): 55–8.

Tellitu, A. (1997a). 'Operación Guggenheim', special supplement *Territorios de la Cultura*, *El Correo* (3 Oct.): 4.

—— (1997b). 'Atentado frustrado contra el Guggenheim', *El Correo* (14 Oct.): 14.

Torres, C. (1997). 'El Guggenheim intenta suavizar el rechazo al museo dos meses antes de su inauguración', *El Correo* (http://www.diario-elcorreo.es/guggenheim/archivo).

van Bruggen, C. (1998). *Frank O. Gehry: Guggenheim Museum Bilbao*. New York: Guggenheim Museum Press.

Villacorta, J. L. (1997). 'El sueño de Gehry: el proyecto', *El Mundo del País Vasco* (18 Oct.): 18.

Zulaika, J. (1997a). *Crónica de una seducción: el Museo Guggenheim Bilbao*. Madrid: Nerea.

—— (1997b). '... Y Xavier Arzalluz dijo sí', special supplement *Guggenheim Museoa*, *El Mundo del País Vasco* (18 Oct.): 14.

17

Barcelona's Magic Mirror:
Narcissism or the Rediscovery of
Public Space and Collective Identity?

ANTONIO SÁNCHEZ

THE architectural success of Barcelona's redevelopment has been widely acknowledged. The massive renovation began in the 1980s and gained new impetus with the city's selection as the site for the 1992 Olympic Games, putting the city under enormous pressure to meet the technological and urban requirements of such a large-scale public event. At the same time, this pressure provided a unique opportunity for transforming the city into an ultramodern yet human environment. This chapter explores the social repercussions of Barcelona's aesthetic reconstruction. To do so, it will locate this urban renovation within the global context of late capitalism and its reterritorialization of decaying modern urban spaces into what Mike Featherstone (1991) terms 'postmodern spaces': that is, theme parks, shopping malls, tourist sites, and leisure areas based on architectural eclecticism as their common feature and on consumption and leisure as their dominant cultural experience.

By contrast with the modern concept of the city as an ever-expanding structure, postmodern architecture and town-planning engage with a multiplicity of small projects of urban restoration. This strategy, vital to Barcelona's redevelopment, is exemplified by the revitalization of the former docklands and seafront and their incorporation into the city. It is evident also in the attempt to strike a balance between the city's old centre and its periphery, overcoming the atomization and dislocation produced by the zoning of the 1970s. Given that Barcelona's redevelopment comprises a broad range of urban projects, rather than attempt to give an overview I have chosen to focus on one particular project: the old dockyard Moll d'Espanya, now turned into a postmodern urban space visually dominated by the Maremagnum complex, comprising a shopping mall, aquarium, multiscreen cinema, and open public areas. However, my analysis of this specific redevelopment is in many respects applicable to Barcelona's overall urban renovation project.

For those familiar with Barcelona prior to its transformation during the 1980s, the contrast between the previous modern and the current postmodern environments is self-evident. The previous sight of decaying docklands and factories dating back to the period of capitalist modernization has been replaced by fashionable leisure and commercial sites, crowded with tourists enjoying the glitter of the city's latest restaurants and shops. The redevelopment of the docklands and their integration into the city has been central to official plans for revitalizing the old city centre (the Ciutat Vella).

Pedestrian access to the Moll d'Espanya is by the Rambla del Mar, a swing bridge whose mobility allows maritime traffic to pass through. Its high undulating rails, and its wooden boards reminiscent of a pier or boat deck, introduce the marine theme which presides over the Moll d'Espanya as a whole. This footbridge leads the visitor to the Maremagnum leisure space where visual concerns seem to transcend primary architectural functions, illustrating the 'insistence on the fictional character of architecture [. . .] diametrically opposed to the abstractness of modern architecture' that Heinrich Klotz sees as a defining feature of the postmodern built environment (1992: 243). Like any shopping mall, the Maremagnum contains a variety of stores promoting consumption. Shopping malls and luxury leisure centres are often referred to—as, for example, in Fredric Jameson's analysis of the Bonaventura Hotel in Los Angeles (1984: 80–4)—as quintessential postmodern spaces: enclosed, safe environments which guarantee pleasure through continuous consumption and insulation from the urban reality outside. However, the Maremagnum commercial complex does not entirely fit such definitions of postmodern hyperspaces, since it does not constitute a labyrinthine shopping fortress with exclusive and excluding interiors, but rather a passageway between the two open public spaces in front and behind. Thus in this case the shopping mall, so often cited as the paradigmatic example of postmodern self-enclosing architecture, connects rather than separates interior and exterior public spaces. Furthermore, the public areas surrounding the Maremagnum are devoted not only to consumer practices but also to traditional ones such as contemplating the sea, strolling, chatting, romancing, playing. The visitor is less likely to encounter crowds of tourists, particularly on weekdays, than groups of school children on a day-trip, pensioners, and people who work or live in the nearby facilities. These subjects imbue the urban spaces with social meaning through their everyday activities, as anonymous 'authors' of a spatial discourse that Michel de Certeau defines as:

the thicks and thins of an urban 'text' they write without being able to read it. These practitioners make use of spaces that cannot be seen; their know-ledge of them is as blind as that of lovers in each other's arms. The paths that correspond in this intertwining, unrecognized poems [sic] in which each body is an element signed by many others, elude legibility. It is as though the practices organizing a bustling city were characterized by their blindness. (1993: 153)

This blindness is, paradoxically, the other side of an intense encounter with the visual. Postmodern architectural strategies en-hancing the spectacular and allegorical elements of the urban land-scape are highly evident in this redeveloped environment. The entrance to the Maremagnum illustrates this with its overhanging glass roof: a gigantic mirror/screen where the framed visitors become at the same time fragmented subjects and objects of a visual spectacle (Fig. 11). The voyeuristic and narcissistic pleasures provided by this interactive architectural feature engage the visitor's gaze while pro-viding a panoramic yet fragmented image of the 'new' city.[1] Follow-ing similar visual strategies, the glass façades of other buildings such as the Cines Maremagnum (Fig. 12) comprise a collage of reflections of the city's 'new' image, dominated by its bars, sky, and sea (Bar-cel-ona); indeed, the docklands have been redesigned precisely to promote such an image.

According to Klotz, postmodern architecture is dominated by its referential rather than functional quality. Thus postmodern urban landscapes are places whose 'narrative contents':

lift architecture out of its primary subservience to function and [. . .] use it as a medium extending beyond functionality and serving to represent an

---

[1] Richard Sennett has defined the myth of Narcissus in his book *The Intimate Society* as having 'a double meaning: his self-absorption prevents knowledge about what he is and what he is not; this self-absorption also destroys the person who is so engaged. Narcissus, seeing himself mirrored on the water's surface, forgets that the water is other and outside himself and thus becomes blind to its dangers' (1978: 324).

Fig. 11. Front entrance to the Maremagnum shopping centre,
Barcelona, reflecting those standing and sitting below

Fig. 12. Maremagnum cinema, Barcelona,
reflecting the harbour of Port Vell

Fig. 13. Open public space, Port Vell, Barcelona. The shapes of the street-
lighting mimic submarine periscopes and boat masts

'imaginary world'—that is, as a means of fiction. The contents of postmodernism can refer to a great variety of things. They can indeed create
'a beautiful world of appearances' that distracts one from the bare factuality
of architecture as a protective cover and that deflects one's attention to the
completely different realms of environments as a narrative representation.
(Klotz 1992: 241)

This analysis is apposite to the red-brick paved area behind the
Maremagnum. Filling a raised section of this space, a series of con-
cave parabolas and little mounds of red bricks with shrubs on top
create a visual allegory of a desert-like landscape. Following this
'oasis' of red bricks and simulated palm trees, which lead up to the
white Imax building, a wooden board surface is lined with three rows
of metallic silver street lights, interspersed with benches. The street
lights, facing the pier, emphasize the marine theme by evoking the
shape of submarine periscopes or ship masts (Fig. 13). Paralleling
this 'forest' of street lights in the form of periscopes and masts, and
supported by two rows of these structures, is a roof of metal girders

reminiscent of the straw shelters found on tropical beaches. The green lawn linking the Moll d'Espanya with the Moll Bosch i Alsina continues the marine theme with a series of monoliths set along paved pathways and in the grass, their shape and leaning position suggesting boat sails.

But, despite this display of postmodern architectural imagery, Barcelona's docklands do not constitute a Baudrillardian post-modern landscape where 'reality' has been replaced by 'simulacra'. Indeed, throughout Barcelona's entire redevelopment there has been considerable stress on local cultures and historical contexts. The narrative or allegorical qualities of postmodern architecture need not stand in opposition to an emphasis on socio-historical context. As Nigel Coates indicates: 'Narrative architecture is not about telling stories, but about amplifying the situation [. . .]. Narrative architec-ture never obliterates the existing world, but exploits and overlays it. It is an architecture of reverberation between the known and the unknown' (1988: 103). The idea of public architecture as a trigger for the popular imagination is not new. Examples of an aesthetic concern with form are found everywhere in Barcelona's streets; for example, the now fully restored *noucentista* and *modernista* buildings, not to mention Gaudí's Parc Güell and Temple of the Sagrada Familia, the latter currently under completion at last. Postmodernism represents a return to this earlier concern with the decorative, ending the long sovereignty of Bauhaus-inspired modern architectural theory which, in its rational pursuit of purity and functionalism, discarded orna-ment and aesthetic considerations. Barcelona's redevelopment can be seen as postmodern on account of the architectural strategies employed to stimulate popular engagement with the urban environ-ment. Thus, avoiding the modern obsession with standardization, the architecture and overall design of the Moll d'Espanya, with their attention to non-functional detail, promote the city as a postmodern space where eclecticism rules and imagination matters, though ration-alism is not entirely abandoned. As Ian Chambers notes:

The argument, central to both the Marxist and Baudrillardian critique of the sign (fetishism, simulacrum), is that surfaces and appearances are simply the deceptive, seductive and mystifying manifestations of an underlying reality: the alienation of the human condition. But this reduction to a hidden value— the values of 'authenticity' supposedly masked by false appearances—denies the ontological reality of signs, appearances and everyday life. It denies that they, too, are sites of sense, of meaning. To appreciate this opening, this

particular possibility, means once again taking a sabbatical from the ideological critique that has traditionally directed our attention. (1993: 194)

POSTMODERN URBAN REDEVELOPMENT
AS GLOBAL PHENOMENON

The redevelopment of Barcelona's docklands is far from unique.
Indeed it mirrors a familiar pattern found in many so-called advanced
nations, where the renovation of city ports, waterfronts, and decaying urban areas has become a key feature associated with the postmodern vision of the city. The current vogue for redeveloping ports
and waterfronts has its origins in North American and Canadian
urban renewal projects of the 1970s. As Hoyle observes: 'Virtually
every North American city possessed of an urban waterfront on a
river, a lake or the sea, has taken some steps towards the rediscovery
and redevelopment of the interface zone; Seattle, Baltimore, Toronto
and Vancouver are among those that have done so in a spectacular
manner [. . .] but large numbers of others have done so in a more
modest fashion' (Hoyle, Pinder, and Husain 1988: 15). Since the
1980s this trend has also become a familiar urban strategy in European post-industrial cities. The dockland redevelopments of London,
Rotterdam, and Barcelona are part of this global phenomenon. As
the renovation of Barcelona's old centre, docklands, and waterfront
illustrates, these zones are often in desperate need of economic and
social revitalization if they are to become a dynamic part of the city.
Despite—or precisely because of—their precarious state, such areas
are often perceived as having a huge potential for imaginative projects and economic investment, as Trancik comments:

These sites offer enormous potential for reclamation as mixed-use areas,
especially since the exodus from the inner city seems to be reversing. The
obsolete shipping or rail yard frequently occupies a desirable waterfront site.
[. . .] For the developer, advantages in reusing such sites are obvious; however, the contribution that well-conceived spatial changes might make to the
urban fabric or the entire city offers social advantages that go far beyond
those of economic gain. (1986: 17)

Hoyle's analysis of the successive changes undergone by the port–
city interface over the ages shows how, in the modern period, cities
became increasingly detached from their ports, to the point that the

historical and cultural links between city and port are now threatened with extinction unless the decline can be halted and reversed. To date, the modern economic and technological forces that have accelerated this decline appear to be unstoppable. Given the precarious social and urban conditions governing such obsolete modern industrial sites, any attempt to revitalize these dockland and seafront areas must be welcomed. As Hoyle notes:

Port–city relations have now become a major issue in many parts of the world in economic and political terms. The retreat from the waterfront has become a recognised trend; some of its consequences have become unacceptable, but some of its elements have led to exciting innovations. One result of this situation is that there is now a widespread return to the waterfront—a redevelopment of the 'abandoned doorstep' for new uses associated especially with recreation rather than with international trade. (Hoyle, Pinder, and Husain 1988: 15)

From a theoretical perspective, these revitalization projects create the possibility of bringing such obsolete urban spaces back into the city's consciousness and geographical boundaries, encouraging a rediscovery of the city's topography. The revitalization of the seafront also provides popular access to open urban spaces which, though neglected, are an essential part of the city's culture and history. Here one must not forget the extent to which the emphasis on aesthetics and playfulness, typical of such redevelopment projects, conveniently masks an ongoing process of capitalist speculation with urban space. For the economic forces which are currently 'saving' post-industrial wastelands by converting them into postmodern spaces are the same forces which, not so long ago, built up the modern industrial city only to abandon it to decline when profits began to dwindle. As Tweedale writes: 'Urban redevelopment, typified by dockland redevelopment schemes, is the conventional response of many capitalist governments to the inner-city problem. [. . .] Addressing the social processes which have created the inner-city problem is not in the interests of capital, but the restructuring of the urban environments in specific forms clearly facilitates capital accumulation' (Hoyle, Pinder, and Husain 1988: 188–9). Tweedale notes that the revitalization of urban areas often involves massive public funding for the transformation of industrial wastelands into public housing and commercial developments, in the process eradicating long-established local communities. In other words, there is a thin line between the revitalization of run-down areas and the capitalist re-territorialization of those urban spaces through economic investment and speculation. For these redevelopment projects to fulfil their potential for transforming urban wastelands into open public spaces, they need to be accompanied by tight controls over the penetration of local socio-economic structures by market forces. Sadly, this is often not the case; in recent years there has been a significant decrease in planning authority control over the private building sector. The London Docklands redevelopment of the 1980s illustrates this tendency to privilege private initiative through the creation of development corporations. Similarly, the removal of planning restrictions works to the detriment of local planning authorities, who lose their previous jurisdiction over the redevelopment process. The two key examples where the local authorities have taken a relatively strong stand on urban redevelopment policy and have kept control over its implementation are those of the redevelopment of the ports of Rotterdam and Barcelona. In these two cases, market forces have been successfully harnessed to a clear planning policy based on historical, local, and social concerns. This is crucial if efforts to rectify the social and architectural balance between city and port are to succeed.

Throughout the recent redevelopment process, Barcelona became the privileged subject and object of official publicity campaigns, and a 'stage' for public spectacles advertising the new aestheticized image of the city. The resulting narcissistic relationship between Barcelona and its inhabitants is clearly part of an orchestrated official strategy for promoting a particular vision of the city through official events and mass publicity campaigns—for example, those launched by the City Council with the slogans 'Barcelona ficat guapa' [Barcelona, make yourself pretty], 'Historia d'amor entre una ciutat i l'olimpisme' [The love story of a city and the Olympics], or 'Barcelona la passió, i tu' [Barcelona, passion, and you], encouraging a personal and collective perception of the city as seductress or enticing object of desire.

Such official publicity campaigns, marketing an aestheticized image of Barcelona and promoting an intimate personal relationship with the city, do not in themselves provide grounds for a negative attitude towards Barcelona's redevelopment. Nor can the extensive redevelopment of the city's old quarters, docklands, and waterfront be dismissed as simply a postmodernist exercise in nostalgia or specularity, serving to mask late capitalism's reterritorialization of the city—though clearly it has involved a considerable amount of both. Even those who—like Harvey (1992) and Jameson (1984)—are critical of the postmodernist promotion of the city as an aestheticized, sanitized space tailor-made for an exclusive economic elite are bound to recognize the potential for generating social cohesion and civic participation. Publicity campaigns may not provide a long-term solution to social and economic inequalities, but they can encourage a progressive ideal of social coexistence: one involving respect and understanding for others. The mounting of public spectacles and the concern with aesthetic effect criticized by Harvey can function as a positive strategy for integrating the city's various social and cultural communities, who thereby internalize the rebuilding of the city as a common project for creating a genuinely collective civic space. A renovation project on the scale of that implemented in Barcelona necessarily generates public controversy and debate about different architectural and social visions of the city, which must in itself be seen as a good thing. Although it can be argued that the economic and social impact of urban developments triggered by spectacles such as the Olympics is short-term and limited, mass events of this kind can be used—as they have been in Barcelona—to procure the massive funding needed to upgrade the urban infrastructure, while also providing some of the social services and facilities long demanded by the city's inhabitants. The Games also helped to overcome years of political mistrust between the various local, regional, and national political institutions and organizations. Without the Olympics it is unlikely that projects such as the docklands redevelopment would ever have been fully implemented.

THE 'NEW' BARCELONA:
URBAN PROGRESS OR PLASTIC SURGERY?

Figuratively speaking, it can be said that Barcelona's redevelopment has transformed the ailing modern city into a gigantic postmodern mirror reflecting an idealized image of itself to local and global audiences alike. Indeed, most of the buildings and spaces built as part of the redevelopment process possess some form of reflexivity, enhancing the narcissistic engagement between the *flâneur* and a fragmented mirror-image of the city. Glass and other reflective materials are used extensively on the external surfaces of most of the city's ultramodern buildings, as in the massive reflecting screen designed by Antonio Poch for the entrance to the Maremagnum shopping centre. The postmodern *flâneur*—touring the visual spectacle of the city—moves from one carefully designed and strategically located architectural site to another as if in an art gallery, contemplating in the new buildings the images of the 'new' city's identity. Thus the buildings become a figurative exhibition of artworks projecting the city's uniqueness. The important point here is that the use of reflecting surfaces incorporates the spectator into this permanent exhibition, as an integral element of the cityscape reflected back at him or her. The spectator is thus positioned as subject and object simultaneously.

This kind of aestheticizing architectural strategy has been seen by critics hostile to postmodernism—Harvey, Jameson, Baudrillard, and in Barcelona's case Manuel Vázquez Montalbán (1992)—as a sanitization of of the city, transforming it into a narcissistic mirror at the expense of eliminating its socially 'undesirable' Other(s). Franco Mancuso, while praising the quality of many of the architectural projects implemented in 1990s Barcelona, expresses his concern that these:

have often been chosen for their ability to create an image rather than the fact that they can meet the enormous requirements posed by social demand. [. . .] These projects also satisfy actual requirements; it could not be otherwise in the case of parks, squares, theaters, stadiums, street and gardens. But on more than one occasion, they have abounded with spectacular effects and elements that seem to have been designed to astonish, impress, stand out and stick in the visual memory. (1989: 7)

This postmodern promotion of the city as spectacle can be detrimental to the concept of urban space as a civic arena for social coexistence. Harvey articulates this critical view of postmodern architecture and urban redevelopment, echoing Guy Debord's critique of capitalist culture in his seminal text *The Society of the Spectacle*: 'Urbanism is the mode of appropriation of the natural and human environment by capitalism, which, true to its logical development toward absolute domination, can (and now must) refashion the totality of space into *its own peculiar décor*' (Harvey 1992: 121). Writing about the urban redevelopment of Baltimore and the relocation of its City Fair to the former Inner Harbour, Harvey notes that this kind of postmodern redevelopment illustrates and requires '[a]n architecture of spectacle, with its sense of surface glitter and transitory participatory pleasure, of display and ephemerality, of *jouissance*' (1992: 90–1). Harvey suggests that this organized promotion of urban spectacle and self-indulgent display constitutes a subtle form of social control, since it encourages a sense of civic unity, pride, and loyalty to the city which, temporarily, masks class differences. Harvey's analysis provides a convincing, though deterministic, analysis of the contemporary redevelopment of the modern city as ultimately negative and dominated by the omnipotent forces of late capitalism.

While it is undeniable that the postmodern architecture presiding over Barcelona's urban renovation is characterized by an emphasis on referentiality and spectacularity, I would argue that this does not necessarily make it socially negative. On the contrary, the role of the narcissistic, self-reflective architectural features employed in the popular acceptance of the city's new image can be seen as a positive factor, providing a stronger sense of collective identity and enhancing its inhabitants' identification with their urban environment. Additionally, the city's redevelopment has improved not only its aesthetic appearance but also its urban infrastructure and social cohesion. This has benefited not only the bourgeoisie but also the working classes, the unemployed, children, and pensioners. The overwhelming popularity of the city's renovation cannot be attributed solely to the official publicity campaigns, no matter how successful these may have been. More important are those factors which affect people's daily lives such as transport, social facilities, and access to local public spaces.

For this reason, it is crucial to recognize that the success of Barcelona's redevelopment is closely linked to the fulfilment, albeit partial, of a number of popular demands for which neighbourhood pressure groups had campaigned since the late 1960s.[2] Barcelona's

---

[2] From 1965, when the local neighbourhood associations of Veïns del Poble Nou and Veïns de la Barceloneta began their public resistance to the 1953 Plá Comarcal (extended by the 1976 Plá General Metropolitá), the Barcelona Citizen Movement led the campaign for better urban infrastructures while protesting against rampant capitalist speculation. In 1972 the various local groups operating in Barcelona joined together under the umbrella of the Federació d'Associacions de Veïns de Barcelona (FAVB), continuing to play a key role in articulating a broad range of demands on the part of Barcelona's various local communities. As Manuel Castells indicates with reference to the Citizen Movement's socio-political influence on recent Spanish urban redevelopment (Madrid in this instance):

inhabitants were not passive spectators prior to the city's recent redevelopment; on the contrary, they have to a great extent shaped their environment by exerting pressure on urban developers and the civic authorities. This, more than the playful nature of postmodern architecture or the spectacles generated by the 1992 Olympics, explains what I observed during my fieldwork in Barcelona in March 1996: namely, the existence of a general consensus that the quality of life has improved noticeably as a result of the changes in the urban environment. This consensus is shared by a wide range of socio-political groups, including some who remain critical of certain aspects of the redevelopment. Indeed, certain areas of the city and sectors of its population are still waiting to benefit from the changes. Nevertheless, there is a general sense of pride in the city, which is a positive if provisional step towards enhancing spatial and social cohesion.

PUBLIC CONSENSUS: THE MIRROR AND ITS EXCLUSIONS

My reluctance to engage in a critique of Barcelona's redevelopment is based, as previously stated, on the net gains to city life. This does not mean that the redevelopment has been wholly positive. Indeed, it could be said that one of the most worrying aspects is precisely the high degree of popular consensus throughout the whole process. For this popular support, while validating the social and urban improvements that have taken place, also suggests the success of official efforts to get the city's inhabitants to identify with the positive aestheticized images of the city offered to them. Even if the strategic emphasis on transforming Barcelona into an aesthetically pleasing spectacle in principle seems commendable, doubts remain about its inhabitants' participation in future urban development. The consensus which has characterized the recent changes needs to be viewed

At the level of specific urban effects, the major causal argument is that all the themes—from shanty town redevelopment, to historic conservation, to the re-equipment of peripheral housing estates—had been promoted alone by the Citizen Movement. The Franquist administration not only had followed an entirely contrary policy, but the opposition parties, including PCE and the radical left, never took the urban programme seriously, only considering neighbourhood mobilization as a matter of political agitation the revolutionary outcome of which would far outweigh all its demands. So, chronologically speaking, all the topics and concepts that became the common wisdom of leftists and centre administrations, as well as of the media, in the second half of the decade originated with the Citizen Movement. (1983: 262) in the context of earlier resistance to the urban policies of the former Francoist City Council, and the fact that many of the demands generated by the earlier protest movement were at least partially met by the recent renovation process. There is a notable contrast between this earlier popular engagement and the current lack of public debate on future models for the city's development, which can be seen as marking a disturbing shift from the notion of the citizen as active critic to that of the citizen as passive spectator.

Furthermore, the promotion of the city as a narcissistic mirror reflecting back at its citizens an aestheticized, sanitized image of itself overlooks the existence and importance of those socially marginalized groups which cannot legally, economically, or socially afford to enter the city's official image. The new strategies of policing designed to rid central city shopping areas of 'undesirables' reduce the diversity of experiences which is a fundamental aspect of city life. The creation of a 'safer' environment necessarily results in increased social homogenization, permitting a narcissistic self-mirroring predicated on the reduction of contact with 'Others'. As Richard Sennett notes: 'The result of a narcissistic version of reality is that the expressive powers of adults are reduced. They cannot play with reality, because reality matters to them only when it in some way promises to mirror intimate needs' (1978: 326).

One of the most interesting recent examples of organized resistance to official urban policy is that constituted by the squatters' movement, the Okupas.[3] While their existence is directly linked to the growing housing shortage in Spain's major cities, coupled with rising rents and house prices, and unemployment among young people, their struggle to create an alternative personal yet collective cultural space in the heart of the city also represents an ideological position. As one squatter put it in 1996: 'Okupar es querer y necesitar espacios libres donde crecer, realizarse y crear. El derecho a la vivienda es sólo la excusa' [Squatting means wanting and needing free spaces that allow personal growth, self-realization, and creativity. The right to a home is just an excuse] (Miranda 1996: 42). The improvised

---

[3] According to the magazine *Ajoblanco* (Miranda 1996), there were in 1996 approximately 2,000 squatters in Spain, half of them based in Barcelona, the majority in the Gràcia district. The first squats by squatters' organizations took place in 1984 in Barcelona and 1985 in Madrid. In 1995 the various Barcelona squatters' groups constituted themselves as the Assemblea d'Okupes de Barcelona, to co-ordinate strategy, demands, and action.

'tactics' of the Okupas can be seen as individual actions defying the grand 'strategies' imposed by the city's institutional regulators. As de Certeau writes, such individual actions constitute a creative response to the city: 'an individual mode of reappropriation [. . .] multiform, resistant, tricky and stubborn procedures that elude discipline without being outside the field in which it is exercised, and which should lead us to a theory of everyday practices, of lived space, of the disquieting familiarity of the city' (1993: 157). Ironically, the Okupas of today mirror the popular urban protest movements of the 1970s, many of whose participants are today bureaucrats and intellectuals working for the City Council, including its town-planning departments. This same Council, despite the origins of many of its members in the popular anti-Francoist protest movement, on 28 October 1996 ordered the eviction by force of the squatters occupying the Princesa Sofía Cinema.[4] As one of the squatters involved explained:

El cine lucha por lo mismo que, supuestamente, lucharon ellos; quiere lo mismo que, supuestamente, quisieron ellos y actúa como, supuestamente, actuaron ellos. Pero el Cine es, para ellos, [ahora] una amenaza que perturba el normal funcionamiento de su ciudad y de sus mentes, las que lucharon por una falsa libertad que les llevó hasta un poder corrupto. (Miranda 1996: 44)
[The squat in the Cinema is fighting for the same things that they allegedly fought for; it wants the same things they allegedly wanted, and is acting in the same way they allegedly acted. But they perceive us as a threat to the proper functioning of their city and of their minds, which fought for a false freedom that has given them a corrupt power.]

Although the redesigning of Barcelona is frequently associated with the ideal of a postmodern urban environment, to which the idea of a pluralistic society is central, violent incidents such as the ejection of the squatters from the Princesa Sofía Cinema cast doubt on the City Council's commitment to the concept of the city as an open, creative public space. One has to ask whether the current local authorities have fully assimilated the lessons learnt from their years in the anti-

---

[4] The occupation of the Princesa Sofía Cinema—located in the Vía Laietana just a few metres from the offices of the City Council, the national police headquarters, and the local law courts—posed an instant symbolic challenge to institutional power and urban policy. Closed for over twenty years thanks to a speculative operation which has brought its owners and the City Council into legal confrontation, it was occupied for seven months in 1996 by a squatters' collective who transformed the derelict empty building into a flourishing alternative open cultural space.

Franco opposition: namely, that the construction of a civic society has its foundations in negotiation and compromise rather than violence and inflexibility. The monopoly control of the redesigning of the city exercised by the left from the early 1980s enabled Barcelona's local institutions to effect a hugely successful urban transformation; but it has also hindered the development of, and thus created an urgent need for, a new urbanistic vision able to offer a counter-model to those of officialdom. The Okupas' spontaneous tactics, while reaffirming a human need for new cultural spaces that allow growth and creativity, remind us that the future of the city does not lie in the beauty of its monuments and buildings but in its ability to accommodate and fulfil the needs and dreams of its inhabitants. The Okupas are a small, marginal collective and their vision of the city is, indeed, utopian; yet, as Manuel Castells points out:

Urban movements do, however, produce new historical meaning—in the twilight zone of pretending to build within the walls of a local community a new society they know to be unattainable. And they do so by nurturing the embryos of tomorrow's social movements within the local Utopias that urban movements have constructed in order never to surrender to barbarism. (1983: 331)

WORKS CITED

Baudrillard, J. (1983). 'The Ecstacy of Communication', in H. Foster (ed.), *The Anti-Aesthetic: Essays on Postmodern Culture*. Washington: Bay Press, 126–33.
Castells, M. (1983). *The City and the Grassroots: Cross-cultural Theory of Urban Social Movements*. Berkeley and Los Angeles: University of California Press.
Certeau, M. de (1993). 'Walking in the City', in S. During (ed.), *The Cultural Studies Reader*. London: Routledge, 151–60.
Chambers, I. (1993). 'Cities without Maps', in J. Bird, B. Curtis, T. Putnam, G. Robertson, and L. Tickner (eds.), *Mapping the Futures: Local Cultures, Global Change*. London: Routledge, 188–98.
Coates, N. (1988). 'Street Signs', in J. Thackara (ed.), *Design after Modernism: Beyond the Object*. New York: Thames & Hudson, 95–114.
Debord, G. (1994). *The Society of the Spectacle*. New York: Zone Books.
Featherstone, M. (1991). *Consumer Culture and Postmodernism*. London: Sage Publications.
Harvey, D. (1992). *The Condition of Postmodernity*. Oxford: Blackwell.

Hoyle, B. S., Pinder, D. A., and Husain, M. S. (eds.) (1988). *Revitalizing the Waterfront: International Dimensions of Dockland Redevelopment.* London: Belhaven Press, 3–20.

Jameson, F. (1984). 'Postmodernism, or The Cultural Logic of Late Capitalism', *New Left Review*, 146: 53–92.

Klotz, H. (1992). 'Postmodern Architecture', in C. Jenks (ed.), *The Postmodern Reader.* London: Academy Editions, 234–48.

Mancuso, F. (1989). 'Perspectives on the Catalan Experience', *Rassegna*, 37.1: 4–7.

Miranda, I. (1996). 'Okupas: ¿Qué pasó en el Princesa?', *Ajoblanco*, 91: 40–9.

Sennett, R. (1978). *The Fall of Public Man.* New York: Vintage Books.

Trancik, R. (1986). *Finding Lost Space: Theories of Urban Design.* New York: Van Nostrand Reinhold Company.

Vázquez Montalbán, M. (1992). *Barcelonas.* London: Verso.

18

Spanish Quality TV?
The *Periodistas* Notebook

PAUL JULIAN SMITH

TV

> I can still not be sure what I took from the whole flow. I believe
> I registered some incidents as happening in the wrong film,
> and some characters in the commercials as involved in the film
> episodes, in what came to seem – for all the occasional bizarre
> disparities – a single irresponsible flow of images and feelings.
>
> (Williams 1974*a*: 91–2; cited Corner 1999: 62)

Like Raymond Williams, recently arrived in Miami and dazzled
by the unaccustomed spectacle of US television, the literary or film
scholar might be forgiven for disorientation when venturing into TV
studies. Stephen Heath has also decried the 'extension, availability,
[and] proximity' of television, 'all of which is played out on its screen
from show to show in the endless flow' (Heath 1990: 297; Corner
1999: 69). Whereas a novel or film is clearly delimited in length,
available only from approved agents, and formally separate from the
times and spaces of everyday life, the twenty-four-hour, domesticated rhythm of television is inseparable from the modern experience
it has both reflected and created.

But if television is ubiquitous, then it need not be the 'bad
machine', endless and irresponsible. And nor do warnings of the
globalization of electronic media preclude the emergence of new
national programming. In this piece, then, I will argue against the
sometimes apocalyptic tendencies of some media theory (the philosophical pessimism of 'flow') and for a newly differentiated account
of genre, nationality, and industrial practice in relation to programme content. As we shall see, some programming sets itself

apart from the everyday and some production companies (even when controlled by multinational conglomerates and operating under the fiercest commercial competition) aim for quality local programming that will attract a select but profitable demographic.

In his excellent synoptic study *Critical Ideas in Television Studies*, John Corner has sought to mediate between social science approaches and the humanities approaches typified by Williams and Heath above. The latter, he believes, often lack both 'specific analysis of formal structures' and 'detailed engagement with broadcasting history' (1999: 69). Corner argues that television must be seen in an institutional context, as an 'ecology' (1999: 12) distinct from other mass media such as newspapers (1999: 15), not least for the way it consistently blurs the boundaries between the public and private spheres. Combining sociologists' concern for 'objectifiable aspects [such as] organization and functioning' with the humanist critics' openness to 'aesthetics, discourse, and value' (1999: 10), Corner treats the distinct, but linked, fields of production and reception, pleasure and knowledge, narrative and flow. We can take these fundamental categories in turn.

Production, argues Corner, is relatively neglected in an empirical context, given the difficulty of academic access to a sometimes suspicious media industry (1999: 70). Where policy documentation is available (likewise interviews with participants), it raises questions of evidential validity. As a 'moment of multiple intentions' (1999: 70), production takes on different usages in TV theory, relating diversely to historical contexts, institutional settings, production mentalities, and production practices (1999: 71). Questions of both the 'authorial scope' of producers and the 'autonomy' or even 'autism' of institutions (1999: 74) are raised most acutely by two forms of programming: news and drama. In both areas empirical enquiry has revealed surprising 'occupational complexity and contingency' and 'complexity of television "authorship"' (1999: 76–7), even when a select 'quality' programme is produced by a company with distinctive audience demographics, corporate history, and socio-aesthetic profile (1999: 78).

The sociologically tinged concept of production is, however, inseparable from the interest in reception that was spearheaded by the humanities, and most particularly cultural studies (Corner 1999: 80). For reception is also multiple and contingent, occurring at the intersection of social and psychological needs and producing unintended consequences (1999: 82). And while some scholars see reception as reproducing 'structured social inequalit[ies]' (1999: 84), others, of the 'uses and gratifications' school (1999: 85), stress not the pernicious effects of the medium on public communication but rather the 'cultural competence' of the viewer, most especially of drama (1999: 86). More particularly recent changes in 'multiple consumption opportunities' have seen a change in programme address: from the 'ideologies of the home to [. . .] individualized commodity taste' (1999: 90).

The newer focus on gratification and taste has arisen out of attempts to study the elusive topic of television pleasure, once more an emphasis of cultural studies. If television, unlike cinema, is universally required to provide both public information and entertainment, then critics read the pleasure it provides either negatively, as a form of 'cultural debasement' (1999: 93), or positively as a challenge to elite, high culture (1999: 94). TV pleasures are visual, parasocial, or dramatic. They may be based on new knowledge, comedy, or fantasy or (alternatively) on the familiar notions of distraction, diversion, and routine (1999: 99). The debate around 'quality' to which I return later is also riven by 'a tension between publicly protected cultural values and the popular pleasures of cultural markets' (1999: 107).

If pleasure is critically debated, knowledge is no less problematic. Corner rehearses 'three types of badness' often attributed to television: misselection (in which the TV 'gatekeeper' rules out inadmissible content); misrepresentation (in which the imagistic brevity and narrativization of TV form traduce the complexity of the real); and misknowing (in which the perceptual or cognitive aspects of the knowledge process itself are debased) (1999: 109–10). The move from print to electronic media is thus seen as a decline: from ideas to feeling, appearance, and mood; or from 'Is it true? Is it false?' to 'How does it look? How does it feel?' (1999: 113). Inversely, commentators have seen the extension of public knowledge through broadcasting as the 'democratization of everyday life' and the creation of a 'mediated democratic polity' (1999: 114) impossible through print.

Crucial to Corner here is the question of drama. The emotional engagement generated by fiction, and most particularly workplace dramas, 'informs social understanding' in such areas as occupation, family, health, and money (1999: 115). Narrative then (even in the infinite form of soap opera) can perhaps be read as a final antidote to flow theory. For although the incursion of narrative into TV journalism (where segments have long been known as 'stories') has been read as an 'erosion' (1999: 47) of the informational and expository values of the medium, both spoken and enacted narrative constitute a 'significant dimension of modern public knowledge' (1999: 59) The depth of virtual relationship enjoyed by viewers with the characters of series drama – 'the sense of coexistence between real and fictive worlds' (1999: 59) – thus forms a distinctive socio-aesthetic profile that is worthy of analysis and is not to be dismissed as the narcotic alienation of a 'dramatized society' (1999: 48, citing Williams 1974*b*).

QUALITY TV

> Quality makes money.
> (Grant Tinker, President MTM; cited Feuer, Kerr, and Vahimagi 1984: 26)

Corner highlights the conflict in debates on quality between institutions and aesthetics. On the one hand ' "quality" signals a concern with defining more clearly what [. . .] can be assessed as a good product and thereby used as a marker in both public and corporate audits of the industry' (1999: 106). This objectifiable dimension, derived from management theory and relating to such areas as corporate restructuring and industrial standards, slips however, into more subjective notions: 'questions of generic preference, class, gender and age-related variations in cultural taste, and different ways of relating to the popular' (1999: 106). As so often, it is in drama and entertainment that such issues are raised most acutely.

Other scholars further complexify this schema. Geoff Mulgan cites no fewer than seven types of quality, of which only the first two are dealt with by Corner: producer quality and professionalism (1990: 8); consumer quality and the market (1990: 10); quality and the medium: television's aesthetic (1990: 15); television as ritual and communion (1990: 19); television and the person (1990: 21); the televisual ecology (1990: 24); and, finally, quality as diversity (1990: 26). Most commentators, however, line up on one side of the divide between production and reception. John Thornton Caldwell sees the producers' need for what he variably calls 'lossleader', 'event status', and 'special' programming (1994: 162–3), which undercuts three cherished beliefs of media theorists: namely the supposed populism, mundaneness, and boundlessness of televisual flow (1994: 163). On the contrary, writes Caldwell, 'lossleader events programmes make every effort to underscore and illuminate their textual borders', making the 'bounds of distinction [. . .] a crucial part of the genre' (1994: 163). Kim Christian Schrøder, on the other hand, attempts to pin down the 'phantom' of cultural quality by offering a 'reception perspective on cultural value' (1992: 199). Following Bourdieu's lead on the role of distinction in conferring 'aesthetic status on objects that are banal or even "common" ', Schrøder rejects the elitism and paternalism implicit in both British and American television culture (1992: 199–200), arguing that 'quality' can exist only as 'quality for someone' (1992: 211). He further proposes that for certain audiences popular series drama does indeed trigger the ethical and aesthetic values traditionally attributed to art, while engaging a third dimension: an 'ecstatic' realm of release and loss of control (1992: 213).

Schrøder's is a position piece which does not engage closely with particular programmes, aiming rather to 'open a discussion' on populism and diversity (1992: 215). But he does challenge the specific corporate study responsible for introducing the quality debate into academic TV studies: Feuer, Kerr, and Vahimagi's *MTM: 'Quality Television'* (1984). 'This new addition to critical discussion is not occasioned by a general re-evaluation of the products of the cultural industry,' writes Schrøder, 'but by a handful of outstanding programmes (notably *Hill Street Blues*) from one unique production company (MTM) which function almost as the exception that proves the rule of commercial American television. By labelling MTM programmes "at once artistic and industrial" [. . .] the analysis clearly presupposes a frame of understanding in which the artistic is almost by nature at odds with the industrial' (1992: 201).

If we turn to Feuer, Kerr, and Vahimagi's study, however, we discover that this is by no means the case, for they consistently relate institution and aesthetics, industry and art. Thus the 'MTM style' is inseparable from factors that are both material and formal: shooting on film rather than video tape, employing actors schooled in new improvisational techniques, offering creative staff an unusual amount of freedom (1984: 32). A specialist 'indie prod', MTM was both exceptional (in fulfilling the distinctive criteria for televisual 'authorship') and typical (in being subject to the same commercial laws of ratings and cancellation as the rest of the industry) (1984: 33). In spite or because of these commercial constraints (which fostered a demand for both repetition of the old and innovation of the new), MTM marked off the boundaries between it and the mainstream producers in both content and form: highlighting sensitive topical issues (1984: 140), blurring the genres of comedy and drama (1984: 149), and changing the look and sound of prime time with hand-held camera and overlapping sound (1984: 148). *Hill Street Blues*, MTM's most celebrated workplace drama, thus emerged out of 'a complex intersection of forces in late 1970s American television [including] NBC's short lived but decisive strategy to sidestep Nielsen aggregates [i.e. brute numbers of viewers] by buying "high quality" consumers via "quality" programmes' (1984: 150).

MTM's industrial context is thus as complex and overdetermined as the artistic texture of its programming with its dense construction, dextrous orchestration of tone, panoramic points of view, and intricate, yet integrated, story-lines (1984: 151). *Hill Street* was as difficult to police for the jittery network, fearful of offending sponsors, as it was for media academics, anxious to pin down its ambiguous liberal politics in a time of reaction. What seems clear, however, is that the series offered select viewers new and challenging forms of pleasure and knowledge; and that the corporate study of MTM gives the lie to media academics who view 'quality' as the cynical underscoring of phantom bounds of distinction.

SPANISH TV

Except for the occasional strip show or pornographic film, the programming of all [Spanish] channels is very similar to American broadcast television (not to mention the dominance of U.S. products as a percentage of all telefilms, series, and feature films broadcast). [. . .] The quality varies as much as in any broadcast system, and like most national media industries everywhere, the various Spanish TV channels repulse and attract on a pretty even score across their audiences.

(Maxwell 1995: p. xxiv)

There would appear to be few territories less promising for quality television, however defined, and more hospitable to the philosophical pessimism of 'flow' than Spain. Anecdotally, literate Spaniards dismiss their television system as the 'teletonta' or 'telebasura'.

Domestic and foreign journalists reconfirm the stereotype, citing the 'incessant controversy' around the corruption and bias of state television (*El País* 1999: 35) and the crass appeal to sex in the ratings war unleashed by commercial networks such as Telecinco and Antena 3 (Hooper 1995: 317). One Spanish academic stresses the defencelessness of Spain in the global marketplace, lacking as it does a 'national champion to defend [its] colours' (Bustamante in Graham and Labanyi 1995: 361); one Briton laments the lack of 'an effective method of regulating programme output [and of] redefin[ing] the notion of public service in relation to the more complex multi-channel and multi-media situation' (Jordan in Graham and Labanyi 1995: 368).

The most distinguished scholar of Spanish television, Richard Maxwell, offers a near apocalyptic institutional history. Maxwell stresses the suddenness of change in Spain: 'In a little more than fifteen years, Spanish television made the transition from absolute state control to a regulated competitive system of national and regional networks of mixed private and public ownership' (1995: p. xxiv). Maxwell has not changed his position; this statement is repeated verbatim two years later, as is his claim that Spanish programming is very similar to that of the US networks (1997: 265). Maxwell's narrative is one of relentless decline: from 'the death of the Dictator and the twilight of national mass media' (1995: 3), through the 'crisis' associated with the rightist UCD (1995: 40), to the 'diminishing returns' of the Socialists' modernizing corporatism (1995: 72). He concludes: 'No longer fit for a nation, except on paper, national mass media have been absorbed into processes of privatization of communication around the world, and Spain has just been one more stomping ground of this global juggernaut' (1995: 153–4).

Less dramatically, Maxwell analyses here and later (1997: 261–2) the legislation specific to Spain which apparently contributed to such general effects: the Statute of [State] Radio and Television of 1980 that redefined the role of RTVE; the Third Channel Law of 1984 that regulated regional broadcasting; and the Private TV Law of 1988 that gave birth to Antena 3, Telecinco, and Canal Plus. Linking this local legislation to the global juggernaut are Maxwell's three 'salient issues': 'privatization, globalization (or transnationalization), and regionalization (or decentralization)' (1995: p. xxv). The Spanish media experience is 'illuminating', writes Maxwell, 'because of the clearly defined bonds and collisions among regional, national, and transnational media spaces' (1995: p. xxv).

Maxwell is not concerned with programme content; and it comes as some surprise to read in a footnote that he takes pleasure in Spanish television: 'The absence of hierarchical judgments or elitist frameworks [in this study] to inform readers of Spanish media talents is intentional. That I like Spanish TV is irrelevant. Its worth is a question of taste, tradition, closed markets, and cultural translation' (1995: 156 n. 9). What is curious here is how US media theorists are so fascinated by globalization that they fail to engage with the distinctively national content of programming.[1] Indeed, as we shall see, Spain may even speak back to US producers, modulating, however slightly, the route of the juggernaut through transnational space. Such subjective matters as 'questions of taste and tradition' (of reception and pleasure) clearly merit equal attention to that accorded objectively verifiable standards of production and knowledge. Certainly Spanish programmes deserve academic consideration comparable to that granted their equivalents in the UK and USA. Developments since Maxwell's pioneering studies suggest that, far from being dominated by North American programming, domestic production of comedy and drama has proved crucial to the survival of the multinationals in Spain; and a recent 'territory guide' in one of the media trade journals also gives a more nuanced perspective than the global view of academic theory.

Television Business International devoted a special issue to 'Spanish TV's New Challenges' in June 1997. On the eve of the launch of two competing digital platforms, *TBI* asks whether the heavily indebted broadcast sector is ready for yet more channels and when the new Partido Popular government will implement the EU directive's quotas on independent production (1997: 17). The state RTVE remains 'the sick man of Spanish TV' (1997: 18) with audience share falling from 43 per cent in 1991 to 26.9 per cent in 1996 (1997: 19), while free-to-air 'private net[work]s Antena 3 and Telecinco are neck-and-neck in audience share' (1997: 20). Pay TV Canal Plus is also 'one of the success stories of the 1990s' (1997: 24), in spite of tax increases imposed by a new government on a company closely linked to the previous Socialist regime (1997: 25). Likewise the 'local

---

[1] See D'Lugo (Maxwell 1997) for a similar reading of Spanish cinema caught between globalization and regionalization which does, however, pay close attention to content.

heroes' serving six independent regions are 'living through good times', with audience share growing in prime time to 19 per cent, the highest peak since the arrival of private television in 1990 (1997: 26). Finally domestic production has experienced a relative 'boom' with 'home produced fiction [. . .] well received on television, beating all the American product' (1997: 29).

Such commercial surveys not only contradict academic pessimism; they also provide almost the only data on programme content, noting such trends as the 'diversification into dramas and sitcoms, [which] creat[es] hits like [. . .] *Médico de familia* which pulls in shares of over 50 per cent on Telecinco' (1997: 29). The pleasures of such domestic narratives, clearly central to public entertainment and information in Spain, deserve a sympathetic and informed analysis in both their institutional and artistic aspects, an analysis that they have yet to receive.

TELECINCO

> Telecinco cree firmemente en la libre competencia que caracteriza un verdadero mercado y en la rentabilidad como única estrategia empresarial.
>
> [Telecinco firmly believes in the free competition that characterizes a true market and in profitability as the only business strategy.]
>
> (Telecinco 1999a ['Telecinco hoy: introducción'])[2]

If ever there was a candidate for television as 'bad machine' it would appear to be Telecinco. It was Telecinco that pushed the envelope for sex programming at the start of the 1990s with the notorious stripping game show *¡Uf, qué calor!* [*Phew, it's getting hot*]; and, with a shifting team of majority foreign stockholders that evaded Spanish legislation and include Berlusconi's Fininvest, it is exemplary of Maxwell's privatized, globalized juggernaut. However, detailed engagement with broadcasting history (not to mention formal analysis of programme content) points to a different and more complex

---

[2] I cite this unpaginated website by its section titles. The translations from the Spanish of all documentation from Telecinco are my own. My thanks to Álvaro Lucas at the Telecinco Press Office for kindly providing me with a full range of print and video materials; and to Madeline Conway for the loan of a video tape.

story, one in which, paradoxically perhaps, loss of ratings led to an increase in innovative, in-house production.

Brief reports in the trade press document the chequered history of Telecinco. In 1990 'Telecinco['s] launch [was] under threat' (Grabsky 1990: 6) with the future of the nascent company in jeopardy after a boardroom struggle between publishing group Anaya, who favoured news and cultural programming, and Berlusconi and ONCE (Spain's national organization of the blind) who preferred movies and mini-series. By 1994 when strip, game, and reality shows had lost their novelty value, *Cineinforme* reported (1994: 18) that Telecinco was 'a la búsqueda de una nueva identidad' [in search of a new identity], attempting to correct a loss of share through a new programming policy that emphasized original programming. By 1996 share had increased by two points to 21.5 per cent of national viewing, and Spanish publishing group Correo increased its stake (Scott 1996: 13). The year 1997 saw both reports that Berlusconi and his brother faced fraud charges over management of Gestevisión, a subsidiary of Telecinco, in 1991–3 (del Valle 1997: 10) and that 'Telecinco plans expansion into the Americas' (Green 1997: 8), capitalizing on in-house productions that were now 'the most popular in Spain'. Finally in 1998 the Supreme Court ruled that the granting of private TV licences by the Spanish government in 1989 (to Canal Plus and Gestevisión-Telecinco), which remained controversial, was indeed lawful (Pérez Gómez 1998: 8).

Once more it is *Television Business International* (1997) that gives the fullest account of Telecinco's 'turn around', based as it is on two aspects of managerial 'quality': corporate restructuring and industrial standards. After aggressive competition for audience share with rival private web Antena 3 had led to falling ratings and mush-rooming debt, Maurizio Carlotti was brought in from Italy by Fininvest as director general in 1994 (*TBI* 1997: 22). Attacking the 'financial chaos rampant in the Spanish television sector', Carlotti rapidly reduced debt and cut staff, announcing that Telecinco 'would no longer compete to be an audience leader'. Relieved of this burden and with a modest target share of 18–21 per cent, 'paradoxically', writes *TBI*, '[Telecinco has been] allowed to take the lead' with dis-tinctive new formats including satirical gossip shows, mixes of news and humour, and Letterman-style talk (1997: 23). Key, however, is fiction production, with Telecinco's own studios nicknamed 'the Fiction Factory' and substantial investment committed to feature films and expansion to the Americas (*TBI* 1997: 23). Such industrial and cosmetic changes (a new logo and design) are 'aimed especially at promoting a youthful, fashionable image to attract the more middle-class audience that Telecinco is increasingly directed toward'. Like NBC in the 1970s, then, Telecinco sought, temporarily at least, a select demographic (young, wealthy, and urban) in the belief that quality could make more money than the *telebasura* for which they were once notorious. And by looking at Telecinco's own policy documentation we can move, as Corner recommends, from historical contexts and institutional settings to production mentalities and practices. We will also be able to analyse one crucial aspect of managerial quality: 'delivery of schedules in line with stated company policy' (Corner 1999: 106).

Unsurprisingly Telecinco's own account coincides with the 'turn around' narrative of the trade press (Telecinco 1999*a*). The introduction to the first section of its website ('Telecinco hoy' [Telecinco Today]) claims the Spanish TV market has matured and Telecinco is known for both its profitability and its innovative programming. Professional management has led to leadership in its target audience ('entre 15 y 54 años, de clase media, media-alta y alta, residentes en poblaciones superiores a los 10.000 habitantes' [between 15 and 54, middle, upper middle, and upper class, in towns bigger than 10,000 inhabitants]). The website lays particular emphasis on news programming, based on innovative Digital Editing technology. While state TVE is still ahead for individual bulletins, Telecinco claims to lead in total hours of news ('Telecinco hoy: programación y audiencia').

The account of shareholders and management structure stresses (against popular conception) the 'national and international' make-up of the group: Italian Mediaset (holding company for Fininvest), German producer and distributor Kirch, Spanish multimedia Correo, and publisher Planeta ('Accionariado y organigrama'). The description of the Telecinco Group stresses its multimedia holdings: including advertising, news, music, multiplexes, and the Picasso Studios ('la mayor productora de ficción de España' [largest fiction producer in Spain]) and claiming economies of scale have now made Telecinco one of the most profitable channels in Europe.

Significantly Telecinco claims to combine public values with private markets. The 'independencia y credibilidad' [independence and credibility] of its news service is one of the 'pilares básicos' [pillars] of the group ('Informativos Telecinco'); the other is original production.

Telecinco promotes its prizewinning talk shows (with live programming a speciality), as it does its in-house drama: 'Las series de ficción de producción propia constituyen una de las señas de identidad de la cadena. Actualmente Telecinco, a través de su productora Estudios Picasso, cuenta con numerosos éxitos entre los que se encuentran *Médico de familia* [y] *Periodistas*' [Original production in series drama is one of the distinguishing features of the chain. Currently Telecinco, through its producer Estudios Picasso, has many hits including *Family Doctor* [and] *Journalists*] ('Programación'). Such series benefit from their own 'estilo propio' [particular style] and are 'encaminada[s] a satisfacer a todo tipo de público' [intended to satisfy all kinds of audience]. It is in the section on acquisitions and coproductions that the word 'calidad' [quality], implicit throughout, explicitly appears. 'Cult' US drama imports (*Murder One*, *Ally McBeal*) are also a key characteristic of the channel's programming. It is perhaps no accident that such quality, issue-driven content is directly followed by Telecinco's mission statement of social service: the channel is committed to the environment, to social solidarity, and to the audio-visual education of children, a concern for public values shown by its provision of a telephone information service and its increase in subtitled provision for the deaf, as recommended by the Ministry of Culture ('Al servicio de la sociedad').

It would be naive to take such self-presentation without a grain of salt, although the objective data on renewed profitability and innovative programming coincide with the external sources of the trade press. The value of this policy documentation, however, is as evidence for the interplay between institutional settings and production mentalities, between organization and aesthetics. Devoted to profitability and controlled by foreign interests, still Telecinco sees fit to risk the ratings for a moment and court viewers with quality domestic drama.

PERIODISTAS: SERIES CONCEPT

Telecinco lanza un nuevo periódico
Martes, 13 de enero 1998
A las 21,30 horas, nace 'Crónica Universal' en Telecinco, un periódico que tendrá periodicidad semanal y que cada noche del martes desarrollarán grandes figures de la interpretación.

Amparo Larrañaga, Belén Rueda y José Coronado dan vida, junto a un prestigioso reparto de otros 15 actores fijos, a los protagonistas de unos episodios muy elaborados que componen la serie 'Periodistas'. Comedia de carácter profesional con algunos ingredientes dramáticos, supone una importante evolución respecto a las anteriores series de televisión, al disponer de un mayor esfuerzo de producción.

(Telecinco 1998b: 1)

[Telecinco Launches New Newspaper
Tuesday, 13 January 1998
At 9.30 pm Telecinco gives birth to 'Chronicle of the World', a weekly newspaper featuring great actors every Tuesday night. Amparo Larrañaga, Belén Rueda, and José Coronado, together with a prestigious cast of 15 fixed characters, play the protagonists in the highly crafted episodes that go to make up the series *Periodistas*. A workplace comedy with dramatic elements, this series represents an important step forward compared to previous series, enjoying as it does significantly higher production values.]

The production mentality behind the *Periodistas* concept is revealed by the glossy Telecinco annual report for 1998 (Telecinco 1998a). Under its four watchwords of 'innovación, independencia, calidad, y rentabilidad' [innovation, independence, quality, and profitability] (1998a: 17), Telecinco promotes its 'primera factoría de la ficción' [first Fiction Factory], the Picasso Studios, which produces 400 hours a year with an average of ten projects being shot simultaneously (1998a: 24). 'Ficción de calidad' [Quality Fiction] boasts 'innovación en [. . .] sus estructuras narrativas' [new narrative structures] (1998a: 43) including an action series set in a police station, the first series shot wholly in a national park ('aboga por la defensa del medio ambiente' [lobbying for the defence of the environment]), an all-female drama, and, finally, the first sitcoms and suspense dramas to 'reproduc[ir] el sistema de producción norteamericano' [reproduce North American production systems] (1998a: 43). Within this slate, Telecinco's two crown jewels are *Médico de familia* (with the highest ratings of any programme since the introduction of private TV) and *Periodistas*, distinguished by its workplace setting and topical subject matter (1998a: 40).

Yet more revealing, however, are the publicity materials produced by Telecinco's press office and thus unseen by *Periodistas*' prospective audience. The first press kit came in newspaper form (Telecinco 1998*b*). (Print advertising for the new series also playfully blurred the boundary between news and drama, presenting the characters in mock news stories.) Claiming the series sought to give 'el rostro más humano de los periodistas' [the more human face of journalists], it featured the back story of no fewer than eighteen characters. The 'reparto de lujo' [luxury cast] (1998*b*: 2) is headed by Luis (José Coronado), a New York correspondent separated from his wife who returns to Spain as head of local news, and Laura (Amparo Larrañaga), a single woman dedicated to her career who is promoted to deputy editor, and thus becomes Luis's immediate boss. Interviews with Daniel Écija, director and executive producer, and Mikel Lejarza, Vice-President of Content at Telecinco, reveal an unstable combination of novelty and tradition in the concept. Écija states, 'No queremos pasarnos de la raya, sólo moverla un poco' [We want to push the envelope, not to burst it], while Lejarza claims, 'En Telecinco nos gusta innovar' [At Telecinco we like to innovate], but admits that a similar US series would have five times the budget (1998*b*: 3). Elsewhere claims are less modest: we are informed that this is the first series in Spain set in a journalistic milieu, and that it draws on 'clásicos fundadores' [classic [newsroom] pioneers] such as MTM's *Mary Tyler Moore Show* and *Lou Grant* (1998*b*: 4); or again, we are told that '*Periodistas* inaugura un Nuevo Género Televisivo' [*Periodistas* inaugurates a new TV genre], whose main characteristics are a risky shift to the professional arena, away from those 'historias de corte familiar' [domestic problems with which the audience can easily identify]. Other novel features include the ensemble cast (both veteran and novice), the high-quality scripts (team-written and co-ordinated), and the exterior sequences, permitted by a relatively high budget.

In a second 'issue' of the mock newspaper sent to journalists on 14 September 1998, the press office gave figures for the first season. Telecinco's gamble had paid off with an average share of 26.6 per cent and 4,700,000 audience (Telecinco 1998*c*: 1). It also scored the highest numbers in the most sought after demographic (given here as '25–44'), an audience who enjoyed its 'humor nuevo y joven, con un tono más ácido e irónico' [new young brand of humour, with a more acid and ironic tone]. Chiming here with the sophisticated, youthful, and often female target audience are the novel domestic set-ups: households comprising a divorcé and daughter, male friends, female friends, a separated woman and her child, an unmarried couple, and a single woman and her mother. Issues raised by the second season include the neglect of the elderly, nuclear pollution, and the destructive potential of religious sects (1998c: 1). A follow-up interview with executive Lejarza has him stressing that the first season's episodes on euthanasia, squatting, and domestic violence had 'anticipated' the news (1998c: 2). Moreover, introducing an 'efecto cine' [cinema effect] on television, *Periodistas* has enjoyed the 'mayor calidad de imagen' [best image quality] and become the 'serie de más calidad' [best-quality series drama] on television (1998c: 2).

Figures reveal the considerable investment in both financial and human resources required to achieve this goal: after twenty-one episodes the series had used 180 actors, employing 110 people in the production of each episode. And spurning the sofas and kitchens of domestic drama familiar on Spanish TV, it devoted at least two days per episode to location shooting in an often uncooperative Madrid. Forty-four per cent of the remaining scenes are shot in the press room and 11 per cent in the bar in which the characters socialize, with the home sets of the two principal characters accounting for just 4 and 5 per cent of scenes.

As ratings soared to a peak of over 6 million viewers on 20 April 1999 and the series was sold to Portugal and Italy, it seemed Telecinco's quest for profit through quality was assured. The hybrid comedy-drama of *Periodistas* trounced prime-time competitors, whether US feature films or domestic drama starring such prestigious film stars as Carmen Maura and Jorge Sanz.[3] Moreover, moving to Monday at 9.50 p.m. (Spanish prime time), *Periodistas* was flanked by two more of the successful generic hybrids for which Telecinco was well known: *El Informal* (news and humour) and *Crónicas Marcianas* (Letterman-style chat and comedy). The schedule was thus in line with stated policy objectives and delivered the required audience: *Periodistas* has been sponsored by a luxury watch brand and major advertisers include a high proportion of designer fragrance, cosmetic, and hair care products.

Market forces, however, do not exclude social responsibility. Indeed the series addresses precisely those areas cited in Telecinco's mission statement: the environment (e.g. food safety), solidarity with

---

[3] For much of its lifetime *Periodistas* has competed with TVE's domestic drama *A las once en casa* or its import *ER*.

minorities (prisoners, the homeless, the disabled), and children (child abuse). And with Telecinco's distinctive profile based as much on its news operation as on its original drama, the series fused these two 'pillars'. In a reflexive gesture typical of MTM's quality drama, it thus incorporated the debate over informational independence and authority into its characteristic plots. Indeed the fact that the drama anticipated the news (with an episode on euthanasia preceding a real-life drama on the same theme by just days) lent *Periodistas* added expository value, routinely denied news programmes criticized for being overly dependent on narrative. Executive Lejarza claims that television is not good or bad, only up to date or out of date (Telecinco 1998c: 2). The apparently uncanny topicality of *Periodistas* testifies to its closeness to Spanish audiences, a closeness that reflects their national tastes and traditions more pleasurably (and profitably) than rival and lower-rated transnational production: in a typical week (22–8 March 1999) *Periodistas* stood at second place in the charts (after a national football match), while Schwarzenegger's *The Last Action Hero* was at nine and Telecinco's prize import *Ally McBeal* at ten.[4]

The Telecinco website has featured a group photo of the cast of *Periodistas* inviting viewers to participate in an on-line activity: sending the picture and autograph greetings of your favourite star to a friend by e-mail. This is unusually explicit evidence for the parasocial function of TV stars as intermediaries between viewers, evidence that can also be gleaned from press coverage. The press clippings for March 1999 (some 200 pages in length) focus either on public manifestations of the quality of the series (the award of prestigious prizes to its actors, including one from the readers of respected film periodical *Fotogramas*) or on gossip about their private lives (paparazzi shots in magazines such as *Interviú* which blur the divide between real and fictional partners and pregnancies) (Telecinco 1999b). Such coverage reveals the erosion of informational values which Corner had suggested is typical of TV 'stories', whether news or drama. But it seems clear that *Periodistas* has succeeded in its attempt to blend social understanding and emotional engagement in a way that counts as 'quality' for an audience as diverse as movie buffs and gossip addicts. And focusing as it does on the news production process (making explicit the 'goalkeeper' function of the media), the series

---

[4]   Statistics from the standard independent source, SOFRES.

overtly poses the journalistic questions 'Is it true? Is it false?' typical of print culture, even as it asks the 'How does it feel?' and shows us the 'How does it look?' typical of the electronic media.

Is there, then, a 'Telecinco style', analogous to the 'MTM style'? While Telecinco is hardly an 'indie prod' and its executives prefer not to make comparisons with US product, *Periodistas* is, in fact, strikingly similar in form to the pioneering North American workplace dramas and sitcoms. The topicality, generic fusion, and technical innovation are comparable; the development and delayed resolution of deep and surface plot-lines, the 'rounding' of characters through unexpected facets, and the shifts in tone from comedy to pathos, all are familiar. More precisely the muted piano and wind theme tune cites *Hill Street Blues* as clearly as the morning meeting which begins each episode and re-establishes the ensemble cast for the viewer. But perhaps the clearest sign of *Periodistas*' novelty in Spain is an aspect that diverges from the US models. While North American titles are typically enigmatic or laconic (*Hill Street Blues*, *LA Law*, *ER*), the Spanish title is terse but unambiguous. Unfamiliar with the workplace format in domestic product, Spanish audiences were perhaps felt to need more explicit framing in order to prepare themselves for Telecinco's relatively risky venture.

PERIODISTAS: SPECIMEN EPISODE

Capítulo 28 (21–12–98) – 'Dos con leche y uno solo'
El abuelo Manolo y su amigo Matías (de *Médico de familia*) aparecen por la redacción de *Crónica Universal*. El motivo es que han encontrado un dedo en un bote de comida y deciden aprovechar de su relación de amistad con Herminio, el bedel del periódico, para denunciar el caso. Al principio, nadie les presta atención pero Luis insistirá para que José Antonio se ocupe del tema. Además, Laura se encuentra algo indispuesta. Mamen le aconseja que se someta a un chequeo médico, pero Laura ha sido precavida y ya se ha hecho unos análisis. Para sorpresa de todos, los resultados indican que está embarazada. Willy y Clara hacen un reportaje sobre cómo puede cambiar la vida de alguien a quien le toca la lotería. Para ilustrar el caso, deben entrevistar a una madura mujer que se hizo millonaria hace un año gracias a la lotería. Esta mujer tratará a insinuarse a Willy despertando en Clara extrañas reacciones. Blas no lleva nada bien la separación

de Mamen, y menos en estas entrañables fechas. Es tal su deso-
lación, que terminará emborrachándose en la fiesta de Navidad
del periódico. Mamen, por su parte, se siente culpable de haber
provocado tal situación. (Telecinco 1998*d*)

Episode 28 (21 December 1998): 'Dos con leche y uno solo'[5]
Grandfather Manolo and his friend Matías (from *Médico de
familia*) appear in the press room of *Crónica Universal*. The
reason for their visit is that they have found a finger in a tin of
food and decide to use their friendship with Herminio, the care-
taker at the newspaper, to get publicity for their mis-adventure.
At first no one takes them seriously but Luis then insists José
Antonio take up their case. Laura is feeling unwell. Mamen
advises her to get a check up, but Laura has been prudent and
has already had tests. To surprise all round, the results show she
is pregnant. Willy and Clara do a report on how winning the lottery can change your life. In order to illustrate the story, they
interview a middle-aged woman who became a millionaire a
year ago thanks to the lottery. This woman will try to win over
Willy's affections, awakening strange reactions in Clara. Blas is
not coping well with his separation from Mamen, especially in
this festive season. He is so upset that he winds up getting drunk
at the office Christmas party. Mamen, for her part, feels guilty at
having caused this situation.

This Christmas episode of *Periodistas* is perhaps atypical of the series
as a whole, lacking both topicality and the hard issues for which
the drama is known. However the guest appearance by members of
Telecinco's other hit *Médico de familia*, typical of special 'event' programming for the holidays, is not simply an example of gratuitous
cross-promotion but rather raises important questions of cultural
taste and audience profile central to *Periodistas*' production and
reception. More characteristically, the social issues that are raised are
immediately personalized: the plot-line of the finger found in the tin
of (archetypal) chickpeas is here treated humorously, shown as it is
from the point of view of the elderly characters familiar to audiences
from the other show. (In other episodes, nuclear contamination, say,
will be presented with proper seriousness.) And the journalistic 'story'
on the social effects of the lottery becomes regular character Willy's
attempted seduction by an attractive and independent middle-aged
winner who appears only in this episode. Typical, however, of the

---

[5] This untranslatable title is explained below.

screenwriters' avoidance of cliché is that the latter has not been adversely affected by her sudden wealth but rather has taken pleasure in and advantage of it, seeing young, sexy Willy (the programme's inveterate don Juan) as yet another promising acquisition.

The pre-credit sequence, set in Luis's kitchen at breakfast time, introduces this continuing theme of comic or ironic reversal of sex and age roles. With typical overlapping dialogue, Luis argues loudly with Blas (prizewinning Basque film actor Alex Ángulo) about how to use the toaster. Deftly and silently Luis's teenage daughter solves their problem. The tone is subtly modulated here. Blas is recently separated from wife Mamen, hence his presence in Luis's flat, typical of the casual and consensual households in a series which features not one married couple with children. And when Blas battles with the toaster, moaning 'No lo comprendo' [I don't understand it], he is clearly also referring to his marital problems, which will trace a narrative arc in the following hour.

This episode, which credits three directors and scriptwriters, features eleven locations and some twenty-seven segments, of which seven are shot as exteriors. The latter amount to only ten minutes in all (the same as the single establishing sequence in the newsroom) and are frequently unmotivated by the plot. When Laura and Mamen discuss Christmas preparations while strolling in a shopping mall, the effect is topical, given the time of year, but hardly dramatic. Such exteriors seem intended to reinforce the quality 'look' and reputation which Telecinco's press agency promoted so vigorously. Inversely a late sequence shot in the crowded pedestrian shopping areas south of Madrid's Gran Vía provides a moment of what Schrøder calls 'ecstatic' release from the everyday (1992: 213). Blas spots Mamen in the crowd and, as they embrace, reconciled, the camera first circles around them before soaring above the festive shoppers in a rare crane shot.

In interiors the main technical innovation is the steadycam. The sinuous unbroken takes (reminiscent of a less frenetic ER) are used to disorienting effect in the post-credit newsroom sequence where we follow the elderly visitors through the bustling, cluttered set, as they are fobbed off by each of the regular characters in turn. The public space of the open-plan newsroom, subdivided into the semi-private spaces of kitchen and bosses' offices, serves, like the other recurring location of the downstairs bar, to facilitate the interconnection of the various personal and professional relationships. Not only do Luis and Laura, Blas and Mamen, Willy and Clara (three couples display-ing distinct forms of conflict) share the same spaces; they are typically joined by camera movement (panning or tracking shots) which fluidly link one piece of dialogue to the next. In a very wordy episode, with none of the set-piece action pieces on which the series prides itself (an explosion in a service station, a car pitching into a reservoir), same-sex discussions, marking solidarity and friendship, alternate with opposite-sex arguments, reflecting both desire and distrust. Typically, however, when pregnant boss Laura gives deserted secre-tary Mamen a sisterly hug, the 'warm moment'[6] is ironically undercut by Mamen's wary reaction: career woman Laura has not previously been known for offering emotional support.

The mix of comedy and pathos is characteristically combined with deep-level plot-lines that remain unresolved and surface stories concluded by the end of the hour. The main example of the former is the sexual and professional tension between Luis and Laura, central to the concept as described in Telecinco's initial press kit, which cites the premiss of US comedy drama of the 1980s *Moonlighting* (Telecinco 1998*b*: 2). When, in the first half, Luis chooses to commit to Laura, she rejects his attempt to take over her life and considers abortion; when she decides to commit to him at the end, he rejects her in turn, having just learned that he has also impregnated the wife from whom he is separated. Surface stories include the comic subplot of the severed finger (whose origin is revealed at the end) and the seduction of the great seducer Willy (who finally rejects his would-be protector's tempting offer). As in all quality drama series, continuing narrative threads are used to lend regular characters unexpected traits and thus render them 'round': the sexy, superficial, and im-poverished Willy was hardly likely to reject a wealthy patron, as he does; Luis, a paragon of professional ethics, is, as his young daughter reminds him in a comic reversal, unforgivably careless in his private life; ambitious Laura, who has always resisted her mother's advice to marry and have kids, suddenly sees the attractions of maternity. In this female-led character comedy, plot, psychology, and tone are interdependent.

When Laura complains to Mamen that men are a different species from women, she ruefully qualifies this: men are the inferior species.

---

[6] See Feuer, Kerr, and Vahimagi (1984: 37) for MTM's characteristic use of this technique in character comedy. Unlike MTM's generic hybrids, *Periodistas* ends with an unambiguous comic 'tag' as the final credits play.

Flattering the female audience with a gallery of attractive and active urban women, *Periodistas* also courts youth. Laura's mother (the only older person in the regular cast) is impossible; the elderly visitors are patronized by the journalists (and audience) even as they complain of discrimination on the basis of age, the kind of issue taken seriously in other episodes. More importantly this episode appeals to a distinctive cultural context that contradicts Maxwell's assertion that a globalized Spanish TV is 'no longer fit for a nation' (1995: 153). The episode is dense with references to specifically Spanish practices associated with the festive season and variably integrated into the plot-lines: the lottery (whose singing children are imitated by the office clown), Mamen's purchase of too much *turrón* in the shopping mall (the sign of her personal problems), the grapes of New Year's Eve, and the gifts of *Reyes*. Arguably the most distinctively national element, however, is the language itself with its multiple registers and references. The episode title 'Dos con leche y uno solo' thus features an untranslatable pun. Apparently referring to 'Two white [coffees] and one black', the double pregnancy plot reveals it to mean: 'Two inseminated [women] and one solitary man'. Condemned to lose in translation the idiomatic ambiguity of US titles (as in the pallid Spanish version *Canción triste de Hill Street*), domestic drama here exploits a peculiarly Spanish tolerance for obscenity that would be inadmissible on the US networks.

Fit for the *estado de las autonomías*, *Periodistas* makes little of its Madrid location and takes care to include representatives in its choral cast of the historic nationalities and regions: Mamen is Galician, while trainee José Ramón and gossip columnist Ali are Andalusian. But *Periodistas* also acknowledges that an awareness of cosmopolitan culture is part of the Spanish urban lifestyle that the series both reflects and fosters. A visit to a sushi bar or a bookstore-cum-café are everyday occurrences in *Periodistas* not likely to be available to viewers in Albacete. Satirical colleagues compare Willy to Richard Gere in *American Gigolo* ('He started with silk shirts and ended up a Buddhist'); while sophisticated Ali compares the noisy antics of the *Médico de familia* household to US prime time soap of the 1980s *Falcon Crest*.

What Maxwell calls the 'bonds between regional, national, and transnational media spaces' (Maxwell 1995: p. xxv) are played out in such dialogue. But the festive incursion of Telecinco's most popular comedy into its most prestigious drama raises questions of cultural taste and competing definitions of quality repressed by a normal episode. Sitting on the domestic sofa and eating lentils in the family kitchen (precisely those locations that *Periodistas'* concept sought to avoid), José Ramón and Ali can barely conceal their distaste. Broadly acted, crudely stereotypical, and unapologetically domestic and every-day, *Médico de familia* represents another, older appeal to 'the popular' by the same channel and studio. Ideologically ambiguous (difficult to 'police'), *Periodistas* here both underscores the textual borders between its self and its other (between cosmopolitan sushi and parochial lentils) and incorporates that earlier cultural profile into its own broad framework. This incorporation is quite literal: in an atypically farcical moment José Ramón believes he has ingested the missing finger along with the lentils he has so greedily consumed in the family kitchen. Poised once more between repetition and inno-vation, *Periodistas* dare not desert a mass prime-time audience even as it addresses itself to the quality demographic.

WORKS CITED

Alvarado, M., and Buscombe, E. (1978). *Hazell: The Making of a TV Series*. London: British Film Institute.
Bustamante, E. (1995). 'The Mass Media: A Problematic Modernization', in H. Graham and J. Labanyi (eds.), *Spanish Cultural Studies: An Intro-duction*. Oxford: Oxford University Press, 356–61.
Caldwell, J. T. (1994). *Televisuality*. New Brunswick, NJ: Rutgers Univer-sity Press.
Cineinforme (1994). 'A la búsqueda de una nueva identidad', 648 (Apr.): 18.
Corner, J. (1999). *Critical Ideas in Television Studies*. Oxford: Clarendon Press.
Feuer, J., Kerr, P., and Vahimagi, T. (eds.) (1984). *MTM: 'Quality Televi-sion'*. London: British Film Institute.
Grabsky, P. (1990). 'Telecinco Launch under Threat', *Broadcast* (19 Jan.): 6.
Graham, H., and Labanyi, J. (eds.) (1995). *Spanish Cultural Studies: An Introduction*. Oxford: Oxford University Press.
Green, J. (1997) 'Telecinco Plans Expansion into the Americas', *TV World* (Dec.): 8.
Heath, S. (1990). 'Representing Television', in P. Mellencamp (ed.), *Logics of Television*. Bloomington: Indiana University Press, 267–302.
Hooper, J. (1995). *The New Spaniards*. London: Penguin.
Hopewell, J. (1999). 'Spanish and US TV Go Co-Prod', *Variety* (19–25 Apr.): 33, 38, 40.

Maxwell, R. (1995). *The Spectacle of Democracy: Spanish Television, Nationalism, and Political Transition*. Minneapolis: University of Minnesota Press.

—— (1997). 'Spatial Eruptions, Global Grids: Regionalist TV in Spain and Dialectics of Identity Politics, in M. Kinder (ed.), *Refiguring Spain: Cinema/Media/Representation*. Durham, NC: Duke University Press, 260–83.

Mulgan, G. (ed.) (1990). *Questions of Quality*. London: British Film Institute.

El País [staff reporters] (1999). 'La incesante polémica sobre la TV estatal' (3 July): 35.

Pérez Gómez, A. (1998). 'The Granting of Private TV Licences by the Spanish Government in 1989 Considered Lawful by Supreme Court', *Iris*, 4.1 (Jan.): 8.

Schrøder, K. C. (1992). 'Cultural Quality: Search for a Phantom?', in K. Schrøder and M. Skovmand (eds.), *Media Cultures*. London: Routledge, 199–219.

Scott, A. (1996). 'Stakes Rise at Telecinco', *Broadcast* (19 July): 13.

Telecinco (1998*a*). *Informe anual 1998*. Madrid: Telecinco.

—— (1998*b*). 'Dossier de prensa de la serie *Periodistas*' (12 Jan.).

—— (1998*c*). 'Dossier de prensa de la serie *Periodistas*' (11 Sept.).

—— (1998*d*). 'Sinopsis del capítulo [. . .] 28 (21–12–98)', plot synopsis accompanying specimen video cassette.

—— (1999*a*). Corporate website, consulted 19 July: www.telecinco.es/telecinco/10/10_frameset.html.

—— (1999*b*). 'Seguimiento/*Periodistas*/ Marzo 1999', press file.

—— (1999*c*). '*Periodistas* cierra su tercer temporada batiendo su propio récord de audiencia', press release (20 Apr.).

Television Business International (1997). 'Spanish TV's New Challenges', special issue (June).

Valle, D. del (1997). 'Berlusconi Faces Fraud Charges at Tele 5', *Cable and Satellite Europe*, 165 (Sept.): 10.

Williams, R. (1974*a*). *Television, Technology, and Cultural Form*. London: Fontana.

—— (1974*b*). 'Drama in a Dramatized Society', inaugural lecture, University of Cambridge. Reprinted in A. O'Connor (ed.) (1989), *Raymond Williams on Television*. London: Routledge, 3–13.

Index